C000180053

The **Nautical** Institute

# THE MARINER'S ROLE IN COLLECTING EVIDENCE
# — IN LIGHT OF ISM

### Third edition

## A PRACTICAL GUIDE

by
**Dr Phil Anderson BA (Hons)**
**DProf FNI MEWI AMAE Master Mariner**

Foreword by
**Sir Anthony Clarke**
**Master of The Rolls**

**Published by The Nautical Institute**
**202 Lambeth Road, London SE1 7LQ, England**
**Telephone: +44 (0)207 928 1351**
**Fax: +44 (0)207 401 2817**
**Publications email: pubs@nautinst.org**
**Website: http://www.nautinst.org**

First edition — The Master's Role in Collecting Evidence 1989

Second edition — The Mariner's Role in Collecting Evidence 1997

**THE MARINER'S ROLE IN COLLECTING EVIDENCE**
**— IN LIGHT OF ISM**

Third edition

Copyright © The Nautical Institute 2006

Typeset by J A Hepworth
1 Ropers Court, Lavenham, Suffolk CO10 9PU, England
email: javatony@uwclub.net

Printed in England by O'Sullivan Printing Corporation
Trident Way, International Trading Estate, Brent Road
Southall, Middlesex UB2 5LF, England

Front cover image courtesy The International Salvage Union

ISBN 1 870077 76 8

# CONTENTS

## Part B — INCIDENT CATEGORIES
### Producing, collecting and preserving evidence

### Chapter One — Cargo related incidents

# FOREWORD TO THE FIRST EDITION
## by G.R.A. Darling RD QC

This book satisfies a long-felt need for a clear and practical guide to masters and other officers responsible for collecting evidence to he used in making or defending maritime claims. The authors of the book, shipmasters, managers, P and I Club executives and lawyers, have used their unique blend of experience and expertise to provide the necessary guidelines together with easily accessible check lists and interesting illustrations and brief introductory notes on the different kinds of claims, which may have to he made or defended. The language is admirably clear and non-technical.

It is of the utmost importance at the time of every incident that evidence should be preserved and collated, while the facts are fresh in the minds of the witnesses. The master's role is vital — probably often as a main protagonist but also always as an authoritative 'on-the-spot' co-ordinator. Eventual success in making or defending claims will largely depend upon the vigour, with which the shipmaster performs these duties. This book will help shipmasters to act vigorously, intelligently and effectively in performing those duties. For that reason it will be an invaluable asset, which every shipmaster must have ready in his bookshelf on board. It will also be useful to those involved in preparation ashore for prosecuting, settling or defending claims.

I have no hesitation in commending it for universal use at sea and ashore.

Gerald Darling

*Gerald Darling*

ROYAL COURTS OF JUSTICE

STRAND, LONDON, WC2A 2LL

# FOREWORD I TO THE SECOND EDITION
## by the Honourable Mr. Justice Clarke

### Admiralty Judge, The Royal Courts of Justice, London

Some time ago I was asked to contribute a few thoughts to put at the beginning of the video which has been produced to complement this book. The following occurred to me:

*Courts depend upon evidence. Contemporary evidence is of the utmost importance. It is vital to make a note or report of any incident immediately, if possible while it is still in progress. Photographic or video evidence is of particular assistance to the judge or arbitrator in trying to establish the true facts.*

It seemed to me then that the video underlined those truths. So does this valuable book but on a more comprehensive scale.

Casualties and incidents of one kind or another are bound to occur from time to time in the navigation and operation of ships. When they do, legal disputes are not unlikely to arise — especially in these combative times. The principal aim of the sensible cargo-owner, charterer and shipowner is of course to settle them quickly and cheaply, but fairly. If a dispute cannot be settled it may have to be determined by arbitration or litigation.

Contrary to popular belief, judges and arbitrators cannot simply invent evidence. They rely upon the oral and written statements of witnesses, but more importantly they rely upon contemporary documents which come into existence at the time of the casualty or incident. Contemporary log entries and reports made immediately are regarded as more likely to be reliable than statements made much later after discussion with, say, a marine or engineer superintendent or a solicitor, who may have suggested a party line to the witness.

It can immediately be seen that the mariner's role is of vital importance. He is, after all, the man (or woman) on the spot. It follows that a book of this kind is of inestimable value. The more contemporary material that is available the more likely it is that a dispute can be settled on satisfactory terms. It should be remembered that, even if the shipowner is liable, it will often be much more sensible, less time consuming and less expensive to settle at an early stage rather than to spend many years incurring legal fees and ultimately settling for much more, including payment of the other side's legal costs.

I am very pleased to note that this book stresses not only the importance of log books, operation records and informal notes made at the time, but also the fact that of equal or greater importance is evidence which cannot lie, such as photographs, videos, course recorders, engine loggers and computer data.

Moreover, unlike this very generalised foreword, Phil Anderson's book sets out detailed advice relating to many different but foreseeable problems, including cargo claims, loss and damage giving rise to claims against underwriters, charterparty disputes such as speed and warranty claims, bunker disputes, unsafe port claims, pollution, general average, collisions, labour disputes and personal injury claims.

In my judgement (which I should warn the reader is not always held to be reliable by the Court of Appeal), every officer, superintendent, agent, consultant, lawyer, arbitrator and judge should have a copy. I am pleased to have been sent a draft and am hoping to receive the finished article.

Anthony Clarke

# FOREWORD II TO THE SECOND EDITION
## by Captain E.H. Beetham FRSA FNI

### President of The Nautical Institute

I hope you never have to use this book, but if you do you will find it most valuable for the practical advice it gives when things go wrong. The benefit however is in reading it first.

Shipping cargoes across the oceans of the world in all weathers, visiting strange ports, working with and relying on people you have never met before, inevitably involves loss and damage at some time.

Similarly, while I hope it never happens, there is always the risk of collision, the unforeseen circumstances which lead to a grounding or the over-heavy berthing which can lead to contact damage.

The industry expects that when claims are made they will be settled on the basis of the evidence presented. The need to provide this evidence is part of the mariner's professional role.

The Nautical Institute recognises this and, thanks to the pioneering work of the North East Branch, is now the leading authority on this subject. Fortuitously in Newcastle there are a group of vibrant members working on ships in different companies sailing under different flags, carrying a variety of dry and liquid cargoes.

In addition there are four P&I Clubs who have generously worked together to pool their collective wisdom and this had enabled a much deeper appreciation of the shipowners' interests to be articulated.

Finally there a number of law firms, whose clients come from opposing sides of a dispute who have been able to identify the underlying principles upon which claims are settled. It must be noted here that good evidence will often enable a claim to be settled by correspondence, which is infinitely preferable to a lengthy and costly court case based upon insubstantial opinion.

A book of this type has to be conceived and to put it together requires leadership. We find this leader in Mr. Philip Anderson FNI who perhaps not surprisingly is currently the Chairman of the North East Branch. Having worked as an expert witness and as a consultant for plaintiffs and defendants I can say that this one publication has saved shipowners more money than any other I know. The industry owes a debt of gratitude to Mr. Anderson and the team who produced this book.

The Mariner's Role in Collecting Evidence started out as The Master's Role in Collecting Evidence, but the name was changed when it was realised that everybody on board has a positive role to play in accident reporting and loss prevention. To identify just the master, who probably signs the final report, as the only person involved would be wrong. It is more likely that the watchkeeping officers are going to see the damaged cargo first or witness a personal injury. As such, everybody on board must he involved.

A book of this type needs to be updated to reflect changes in the law, new developments like the ISM Code and better practices, as they become part of the shipping culture. This new volume includes a number of substantial and helpful amendments.

A new initiative to help promote this important message is the production of a video. It is cleverly done, with animations illustrating the tendency to not bother and real life footage of incidents demonstrating how professionals should behave. The consequences of bad practices come out vividly in a court scene where an officer who lacked diligence is cross examined and humiliated.

Like all good training I am pleased to say there is a similar sequence where the same officer did everything properly and a real sense of professional pride is conveyed. This is an imaginative and effective video which will enhance awareness. When linked to this volume both a sense, purpose and the achievement of results can be realised. Details on how to obtain the video are contained on the back page.

Sea staff have the responsibility of ensuring that cargoes are loaded, carried and discharged in good order and on time.

There can be no doubt that this practical book should he available on all ships and owners would be well advised to encourage their officers to read it and use it when needed. A number of companies have incorporated this book in their standing orders and say evidence should be collected in accordance with ...'. That is a testimonial in its own right and recognition of the particular value of the work of those who have contributed to this publication.

Eric Beetham

THE RT HON SIR ANTHONY CLARKE

# FOREWORD TO THE THIRD EDITION
## by the Right Honourable Sir Anthony Clarke

### Master of the Rolls, The Royal Courts of Justice, London

I have been asked if I would write a third foreword to the third edition of Phil Anderson's excellent book. I am delighted to do so, although there is very little to add to what I said in the foreword to the last edition, which I see is to be the first foreword to this edition. As can be seen from that foreword, I was then the Admiralty Judge and had a good deal of experience of maritime disputes of one kind and another, which I obtained over many years at the Admiralty and Commercial Bar (both as arbitrator and counsel) and later as the Admiralty Judge. It seemed to me then and it seems to me now that "The Mariner's Role in Collecting Evidence" was of inestimable value.

I wrote the foreword shortly before joining the Court of Appeal, where I have been ever since, latterly as Master of the Rolls. Very few of the appeals I have participated in have been maritime cases and fewer still have involved disputes of fact which turn on the resolution of issues of primary fact. Sadly, cases of collision, mouldy cargo and the like now seem a distant memory. Nevertheless, I have had some connection with the ISM Code and am aware of its importance.

I cannot pretend that I have read every word of this new edition. I am however quite certain that it will make as valuable a contribution to maritime dispute resolution as the first two editions did. It seems extraordinary that it is now some fifteen years since the first edition was published. The essential truths in that edition remain valid today. In short the role of the mariner, especially the master, in preserving evidence and making careful contemporary records is as important now as it was then.

Like the last, this edition will be a vital aid to shipowners, charterers, underwriters, brokers and lawyers alike (to name but a few). It will also make disputes easier for arbitrators and judges to resolve. Dr. Anderson deserves our congratulations.

# ACKNOWLEDGEMENT
## to previous contributors

The first edition of 'The Master's Role in Collecting Evidence' was published in 1989. The work was generally revised and updated in 1997 and underwent a slight name change in the second edition — the 'Mariner's Role in Collecting Evidence'. This was the first major commercial publication produced by The Nautical Institute and quickly established itself not only as a best seller — but, more importantly, as an industry standard work of reference.

The first two editions of the book were written very much by committee — or rather expert working group. I had the great pleasure and honour to act as Chairman and General Editor of those working groups who created the unique volume. The full working group was quite large but that group was split up into a number of smaller groups each with its own specialisation. Within each group there would be at least one serving mariner, one lawyer or P&I claims executive, and other individuals with relevant expertise and knowledge ranging from maritime college lecturers, ship managers, surveyors, consultants, adjusters and many more. An enormous amount of knowledge was pooled and shared.

However, to write a book 'by committee' is logistically a very difficult and time-consuming task. I had recognised for a number of years that the book was in need of a major update and rewrite — to be brought in line with a new way of thinking with regard to the production of evidence through the management systems, procedures and records generated through the ISM Code. The prospect of undertaking a major rewrite by committee really wasn't an option. I therefore accepted an invitation from the Institute to undertake the writing of this third edition alone.

However, I was most fortunate to inherit the wisdom and contributions from the earlier members of the team. I would therefore like to extend a truly well deserved acknowledgement to those previous contributors and hope that they will find this present volume worthy of their previous efforts.

A royalty from the sale of the first and second editions of the book was donated into an Educational Charitable Trust which had been established by the North East Branch of the Nautical Institute. Over the years this trust fund provided help and support for many individuals and projects — although, in recent years — there had been few requests for help.

During my travels around the Institute Branches, whilst serving as President, I was touched by the generosity of the Sri Lankan Branch who had been providing support to a local school. Unfortunately, it had not been possible for the branch to maintain the level of support it would have wished. It has therefore been decided to donate the royalties from the sale of this edition to supporting that school. I hope this will find general agreement with the original contributors.

Dr. Phil Anderson

Grateful thanks are extended to all previous contributors

Capt. Ken Appleby
Capt. Paul Armitage
Mr. Keith Atkinson
Capt. Mark Baller
Capt. Don Bateson
Capt. Iain Beange
Mr. Richard Bracken
Mr. Jon Boaden
Mr. Pat Bond
Capt. Ian Bower
Capt. Peter Boyle
Mr. Jeremy Bray
Mr. Angus Campbell
Capt. Andy Cook
Capt. George Cuthbert
Ms. Liz Davey
Mr. David Dearsley
Capt. Mike Easton
Ms. Julie Fisher
Ms. Patricia Forrest
Ms. Angela Gamblin
Mr. Ken Govan
Capt. David Heaselden
Capt. Ed Higgins
Capt. Matt Humby
Capt. David Inwood
Mr. Peter Jackson
Capt. James Jamieson
Capt. Brian Jones
Capt. Bill Kirrane

Mr. George Latsoudis
Capt. Ian MacPherson
Capt. Stephen Mackin
Mr. Stuart McBride
Capt. Savraj Mehta
Mr. Jeremy Miles
Mr. Guy Mills
Ms. Reena Mohamedi
Capt. John Murray
Capt. Mark Newgent
Capt. John Owen
Capt. Mark Rawson
Mr. John Reece
Capt. Bob Ridge
Capt. David Robinson
Mr. Mark Robinson
Mr. Mike Salthouse
Capt. Stirling Scott
Capt. Peter Sim
Mr. Roger Stokes
Capt. Steve Targett
Capt. Bruce Taylor
Mr. Nick Tonge
Mr. Hugh Townson
Capt. Colin Trappe
Capt. Robert Tym
Ms. Belinda Ward
Capt. Alistair Watson
Mr. Paul Watson
Mr. John Wilkinson

**Footnote:**

All references to the masculine, throughout the book, equally apply to the feminine.

# HOW TO USE THIS BOOK

## PLEASE READ THIS PAGE BEFORE USING THIS BOOK

There are a number of important issues which should be understood, and kept in mind, when using this book:

• The Company Safety Management System (SMS) Procedures, as set out in the Safety Management Manuals (SMM), should be considered the definitive guide to follow in each Company — this present volume and the guidance it contains should be considered secondary, although hopefully complementary, to the company SMM.

• *The Mariner's Role in Collecting Evidence – In Light of ISM* is intended primarily as a reference source and guide. This book is divided into three main parts:

**A. General Guidelines** — this section should be studied in its entirety because it will provide the basic knowledge and understanding of the nature of evidence and why and how it should be collected. This foundation knowledge will be crucial in order to use Section B to maximum advantage.

**B. Incident Categories — Producing, Collecting and Preserving Evidence** — this section provides specific guidance and suggestions on evidence gathering for individual types of incidents. It is not intended that Section B should be read in its entirety — indeed if one was to do that it would be found to be quite repetitive in parts. The intention is that Section B will be consulted to provide the detailed guidance for a specific incident — e.g. cargo related, or a personal injury. Although it may well happen that one incident involves more than one category — therefore both / all relevant categories will need to be considered in Section B. Each category will include a general introduction, which should be studied, and then split into sub-categories — to be consulted as appropriate.

**C. Codes and Reports** — carefully selected relevant original text documents have been included for ease of reference and for further and more detailed guidance on reporting and evidence collection generally.

• In general, the perspective adopted throughout this book is based on English Law and the systems and procedures of the United Kingdom — although original IMO documents are referred to where possible. However, it is believed that the guidance provided will have use and relevance for most other legal regimes around the world.

• Whilst this book will provide useful guidance and suggestions regarding the collection of evidence it is important to realise that it would be impossible to anticipate every conceivable incident or permutation within an incident. It is therefore crucial to understand the basic principles involved — as derived from Part A of the book — think the incident through and apply professional skill and judgement in collecting evidence and preparing reports.

# THE NAUTICAL INSTITUTE

The Nautical Institute, which is publishing this book, was founded in 1972 with the aim of promoting high standards of knowledge, competence and qualifications amongst those in control of seagoing craft. The Institute has some 7,000 members and 40 branches throughout the world.

The Institute is a major publisher of professional guide books covering the nautical discipline and is represented on governmental and industry committees. Its internet forum seeks to provide feedback from seafarers into technical, legal and operational standards.

## *SEAWAYS*

*SEAWAYS* is the monthly journal of The Nautical Institute, sent out free of charge to all members by mail in the UK and airmail overseas. The journal is the principal organ for keeping the profession up to date and contains features and reports directed at the qualified mariner. The international nature of the Institute is reflected in branch reports from around the world and news and people items keep the profession in touch.

*SEAWAYS* also contains the much acclaimed Marine Accident Reporting Scheme (MARS) containing confidential near miss reports from members all over the world. The reports are regularly used for discussion on board in safety meetings and for instruction.

## The Nautical Campus

This is a global career management and learning resource site for all maritime professionals, with four major sections promoting continuous professional development and career mentoring for those in the maritime industry both at sea and ashore.

For further information see the Institute's website

www.nautinst.org

## Part A

# GENERAL GUIDANCE

### Introduction

THE FIRST 'FACT OF LIFE' IN COMMERCIAL SHIPPING is that ships are at sea to earn money — more than that — they must earn a profit for their owners or shareholders. However, they must do this safely and in compliance with a whole raft of rules, regulations and legislation — indeed a raft that seems to get ever bigger!

The second 'fact of life' is that shipping is a potentially hazardous occupation and things can, and often do, go wrong.

Accidents and other incidents will often have devastating effects on individuals, at a personal level, but will also, invariably, lead to claims against the ship operator. They may also be the subject of a Formal Inquiry, a Safety Investigation, a Police Investigation, a Coroners Investigation, a Coast Guard or port State Control Inspection and a whole lot of other potential inquiries and investigations. Whilst the ship operator may have various insurances to protect itself against such losses, at least partially, the reality is that the financial costs of these accidents and claims come out of the ship operator's pocket — whether by way of uninsured losses, deductibles or increased premiums. In addition to the financial losses there is also a very real risk of losing time whilst such inquiries and investigations take place which may involve detention of the ship or ship's staff. In shipping, as in any other industry, time is money and the delay of a ship for a day can represent an enormous potential loss of earning capacity and may even mean that it loses the next charter fixture because it did not make the cancelling date.

The effect on the balance sheet can be devastating and each accident, claim or other incident eats away at the potential to make a profit.

The third 'fact of life' in commercial shipping is that a safe ship is a profitable ship — certainly in the medium to long term.

It therefore makes sense to make the necessary investment to do what is necessary to make the ship safe. There are many aspects of that task but one very important issue to understand is that if an accident does happen then the ship operator needs to be able to demonstrate that it did all that it reasonably could to avoid the accident. In order to achieve that, it will need to produce the relevant evidence — much of which will be generated on board ship.

Legal disputes involving the vessel are amongst the many risks inherent in the business of owning and operating ships. Owners' success in these disputes may depend almost entirely on the availability of contemporaneous evidence from the vessel. In cases where the relevant information and documents are available, claims can usually be resolved quickly, avoiding lengthy legal wrangles and crippling legal costs. In the event that claims are brought before a court or tribunal, judges and arbitrators place great weight upon documentation and other contemporaneous evidence from a vessel. If good, clear, and methodical records are produced, the judges and arbitrators will infer that the vessel was operated in a "seamanlike" manner and are more likely to come to a decision in favour of the shipowner.

In response to an alarming increase in the number of accidents and incidents occurring during the 1980s and early 1990s and in an attempt to help the shipping industry better manage safety, the International Maritime Organization (IMO) developed a comprehensive set of guidelines which were to be applied to almost all commercial sea-going ships around the world. The International Management Code for the Safe Operation of Ships and for Pollution Prevention (International Safety Management) (ISM) Code became mandatory in two phases in 1998 and 2002 depending on the type of ship. A copy of the current version of the Code, Resolution A.741(18) as amended by MSC.104(73), is reproduced in full at Part C 1 towards the rear of this book.

It is not the intention here to discuss the ISM Code in detail — detailed expositions can be found in:

* *Guidelines on the application of the IMO International Safety Management (ISM) Code*, Third Edition, published by the International Chamber of Shipping (ICS) and the International Shipping Federation (ICS), 1996.

* *The ISM Code in practice*, by Arne Sagen, published by Tano Aschehoug, 1999, ISBN 82-518-3825-8.

* *ISM Code — a Practical Guide to the Legal and Insurance Implications*, Second Edition, by Dr. Phil Anderson, published by Lloyds of London Press / INFORMA, 2005, ISBN 1-84311-471-2.

* *A Seafarer's Guide to ISM*, Second Edition, by Peter Kidman and Dr. Phil Anderson, published by North of England P&I Association, 2005, ISBN 0-9546537-3-4.

* *Cracking the Code — The relevance of the ISM Code and its impact on shipping practices*, by Dr. Phil Anderson and others, published by The Nautical Institute, 2003, ISBN 1 8700 77 63 6.

* *Auditing the ISM — A Guide for ISM Auditors*, by Ajoy Chatterjee, Chief Surveyor with the Government of India, Directorate General of Shipping, India, published by The Institute of Marine Engineers (India), 2004, ISBN; 81-912330-0-9.

However, it is felt appropriate to discuss certain aspects as they may directly impact upon the subject of this book — the collection of evidence.

A simple way of comprehending the whole of the ISM Code is to understand the following mantra:

**Say what you do, Do what you say, Show that you do what you say**

The first part of the mantra is manifested in the Safety Management and other Procedures Manuals and other related guidance notes, checklist etc — as well as the various rules and regulations which must be complied with.

The second part of the mantra is the bringing alive of the Safety Management System (SMS) — putting into action the best practices contained within the written procedures. Within that activity of bringing the SMS alive should be the development of a safety culture.

However, it is not sufficient to have a system — even a working system — or even a system that is working very well — it is necessary to document and record what has been done.

Thus, the third part of the mantra requires a good contemporaneous record to be maintained of what has been done and when and where it was done.

In one sense there is nothing really new in the underlying obligations to comply with rules, regulations and legislation — what is perhaps new is the expectation that the ship operator must be able to demonstrate such compliance objectively. The full significance will have a major effect on the way in which claims and disputes will be handled and, ultimately, the exposure of ship operators to liabilities.

The temptation is for a potential claimant to try and undertake a 'fishing expedition' whereby they will interrogate the workings of a SMS to find weaknesses and will hope to continue digging until they have sufficient evidence to discredit the ship operator. Whilst this principle has still to be fully considered by the courts, it is suggested that the court will not allow a wholesale dig into the SMS but rather would restrict such activity to those areas of the SMS specifically relevant to the issues involved. If the ship operators are able to produce the good, contemporaneous evidence to deal with those directly related issues then they should be able to rest assured that they need do little more. However, if they are unable to demonstrate that they did all that they were supposed to be doing according to the relevant rules, regulations and their own procedures relevant to the particular issues, then they openly expose themselves to the claimants, and indeed the court, to look much wider at how the SMS had been set up and how various aspects were working in practice. The consequences could be devastating for the ship operator.

If the documentary records show that the ship operator failed to comply with certain rules and regulations then it may well have a problem. If claimants can show that the ship operator failed to comply with some of its own procedures within the SMS then it will have a bigger problem. But if the ship operator is not able to show anything, because there are no contemporary records, then it really will be in serious trouble since this, in itself, could constitute a major non-compliance with the ISM Code.

The ISM Code was intended to formalise the procedures for operating a ship at the level of industry best practice and of documenting what was done. ISM does not expect perfection — accidents will probably always happen — although the goal will be to reduce them to a minimum. It is important that ship operators ensure that they are able to demonstrate that they are doing all that they reasonably can to reduce and manage risks including learning lessons from any hazardous occurrences and near misses that may have occurred. If an accident does then occur they should be in a strong position to demonstrate that they have complied with their various obligations to:

- Exercise due diligence — for example to make the ship seaworthy.

- Exercise a duty of care — for example towards people on board their ship.

- Exercise a duty of utmost good faith — for example towards its insurer's.

A failure to fulfil any of these obligations could not only jeopardise possible legal defences but also affect the right to limit financial liability, in appropriate cases and possibly even insurance cover. Whilst many of these issues have still to be addressed by the Courts, in light of ISM, the author would suggest that an educated interpretation of the ISM Code and its underlying philosophy would lead naturally to the above conclusion.

The way in which the ISM Code has developed, in its short life since Phase One implementation, has led to considerable differences in the respective Safety Management Systems which have been set up in different ship operating companies. Underpinning some systems there are well over 20 large procedures manuals in which the Company has tried to set out every conceivable task that might be required to be undertaken by those on board ship along with an accompanying procedure. Other companies operate perfectly adequately with two concise volumes of well written procedures based on general principles. Clearly the ability to demonstrate compliance with all the procedures in the 20+ volumes will be considerably more difficult than the procedures in the two volume SMS.

The ISM Code is a 'Goal Setting' management tool. The main goals are to:

- Develop a documented system to help the Company comply with existing rules, regulations, legislation etc.

- Develop a 'safety culture'.

The ultimate goal being to make the ships safer and the seas cleaner.

The ISM Code allows certain latitude on how any individual Company meets their obligations and complies with the rules and regulations etc. So, whilst there may be different routes a Company can take — the ultimate goals are the same. The way in which any particular Company achieves its goals is set out in the procedures contained within its Safety Management and other procedures Manuals. Consequently, the mariner must ensure that he or she not only complies with all appropriate rules and regulations etc. but must fulfil those obligations in accordance with the procedures of the SMS. Objective evidence that such compliance did take place must also be produced. Clearly this has a direct bearing on how evidence is to be collected.

## Background

When *The Master's Role in Collecting Evidence* was first conceived in the mid 1980s it was breaking new ground. Whilst a very basic level of legal principles and liabilities was taught in the marine colleges, no-one had really addressed the issue of bringing the master, and other mariners, fully into the team in these aspects of the commercial operation of the ship. Obviously log books and many other contemporaneous records have been maintained on board ships for many centuries — although the full significance of the entries, or the failure to make entries, in those records may not have been fully appreciated by those on board. This situation may have arisen because the full consequences were more likely to arise after the particular voyage had been completed. In the event of a casualty, or other serious incident, the lawyers and consultants would converge upon the ship — do what they had to do — and then disappear again. Similarly, the way in which a report was written — the important differences between objective and subjective statements — may not always have been fully recognised.

When the author first came ashore and started to work with lawyers as a claims handler in a P&I Club he recalls becoming disappointed, and maybe even angry, at their apparent attitude towards the ability, or rather perceived inability, of masters and other mariners to collect the necessary evidence or to write useful reports which would help defend the ship owner's interest and thus reject claims. One's immediate response was to ask: "Well if there is a problem, if the masters do not understand what is required, then what have you done to rectify the situation?"

It was explained to the lawyers that masters of ships and other mariners on board tend to be intelligent and professional people trying to do a good job — if they are not producing what is required then it is probably down to some gap in the education and training process — ultimately a question of communication. Accordingly, it has to be the responsibility of all those involved to help bridge that gap. However, it was crucial that the lawyers and insurers understood that it would be of little use just issuing lists of information and evidence required — it was more important to give masters and mariners the respect they deserve as professionals and explain WHY the particular pieces of evidence, reports etc were required and explain how they would be used. Thus was born the idea of *The Master's Role in Collecting Evidence*.

*The Master's Role in Collecting Evidence* was an attempt to remedy this problem. The main objective of this work was to guide masters and officers to adopt a systematic approach in collecting together all the necessary and factual information which may be required to resolve particular claims and disputes which arise during the course of a voyage, and to explain why that evidence is relevant.

The initial problem which was encountered in putting together this work was how the technical and legal requirements of evidence could be expressed accurately and still be of practical use to ship's personnel in the front line. The solution was to solicit the active participation of people from all areas of the shipping community in producing the document.

In an attempt to ensure that the book was both technically and legally correct but also practical in its application a large, multi-disciplinary team of lawyers, insurers, seafarers, educators and other professionals from related sectors, was brought together to participate in the writing, preparation and production of the book. A considerable debt of gratitude is owed to that original editorial team. The book was supported by seven P&I Clubs who took bulk orders for distribution around their members' fleets. More than 70,000 copies of the book were sold and it became not only a best seller for The Nautical Institute but an industry standard work of reference.

The second edition of the book included a certain amount of 'tweaking' but perhaps the most significant change was the change in the title itself. It had been perceived that the initial title of 'Master's Role' was perhaps too 'exclusive' and thus the work was re-titled 'Mariner's Role' to make it more 'inclusive'. Another part of the evolutionary process was to include specific reference to the significance of the new ISM Code. However, the book remained very much along the lines of the original volume and was again produced by a multi-disciplinary team.

It is the view of the author that much has been learned during the intervening period and the importance of evidence collection is even more important today than it has ever been. The initial pioneering efforts of those original authors and participants is still to be applauded but he believes that the time has come to undertake a full review of the layout and content of the book in light of the requirements of the ISM Code and other areas of compliance with the 'systems' approach to management on board ship.

*The Mariner's Role in Collecting Evidence* has now been completely revised and expanded by the original Chairman and General Editor in order to take into account recent changes in the law and commercial practice and in particular the relevance of the ISM Code.

A further major departure has taken place from the approach taken in the first and second editions of the book. In the first and second editions the underlying emphasis was very clearly the idea of collecting and preserving evidence in anticipation of legal and insurance claims and disputes arising such that the evidence could be used by the ship operator, or its insurer, to deal with claims in the most expeditious way possible. This is still a very important factor in this third edition but the horizon has now been extended. In addition to commercial, legal and insurance claims and disputes, a ship operator and those on board ship are potentially faced with an increasing number of other situations where the collection and preservation of evidence will be crucial if problems and loss of time are to be avoided.

For example, during internal and external audits of the ISM and the ISPS systems — the auditors, whether they be from the flag State Administration, Recognised Organisation or the office ashore, will require sight of objective evidence to demonstrate compliance with the system. Similarly, port State Control Inspectors and Coast Guards will also expect to see similar objective evidence. If a casualty occurs on board, particularly if there has been a death, serious personal injury, environmental damage, collision or fire etc. then there may well be statutory requirements to report the incident to the flag State Administration who may then conduct an initial / formal investigation. This may result in certain parties being punished or a safety investigation to establish causation with the purpose of learning lessons and preventing similar incidents in the future. The flag State may also have a responsibility to report details of the incident to the IMO. The local port State authorities may also conduct an investigation if the incident occurred within their territorial waters. There may also be tanker / bulk carrier vetting inspections taking place, on behalf of potential charterers, P&I Club condition surveys, Classification Society surveys etc., etc. Again, all these investigations and inspections will require sight of objective evidence. If the evidence is readily available, is comprehensive and complete then the propensity for problems is reduced considerably and the profile of the ship and company will be enhanced — if the required evidence is not readily available then considerable time and effort will be involved trying subsequently to pull the evidence together and the opportunity for further problems for the ship, and the company, will be increased enormously.

Accordingly, the author has extended his focus beyond considering just what the Court or Arbitration Tribunal might require by way of evidence — to also try and take into account individuals and organisations with slightly different agendas. The author has therefore taken into account a range of other perspectives and has drawn upon a number of official sources for guidance as listed in the references at the end of this chapter.

The author has used his best endeavours to ensure that the work is both legally and commercially accurate and is in a form which will be readily understood by ship's personnel and will be capable of being used onboard any well-run vessel. He also believes that it will be an invaluable source of reference for those working ashore whether that be in a ship operators office, a P&I Club or other marine insurance claims handling facility, training establishment, surveyors and consultants, Government Inspectors and Recognised Organisations, port State Control Inspectors as well as lawyers and the courts.

**Layout of this book**

This work is not, and was never intended to be, a legal text book. However, the subjects discussed involve legal issues and, where relevant and appropriate, brief explanations of the legal concepts are provided.

Furthermore, the work does not attempt to cover every conceivable type of accident, incident or claim category that could arise, but does concentrate on the more frequently occurring incidents. However, if the master or ship's officer is familiar with the general approach put forward in this work, he should be in a position to work out for himself what evidence is likely to be required in most types of incidents.

It has been the intention of the author that this work will be of practical use on board any type of commercial vessel of any nationality. However, whilst attempts have been made to keep the advice and recommendations general, the legal concepts are based on English law and U.K. rules, regulations, guidance and statutes are used to provide suitable examples to help explain the basic principles.

The volume is divided into two main sections. The first section, Part A, provides a general introduction to the principles and concepts underpinning the idea of the mariner's role in collecting evidence — in light of ISM. It is strongly recommended that this section is studied in its entirety to establish the foundations and principles of collecting evidence. The second section, Part B, is divided into five chapters — each addressing a particular incident type category:

Chapter One — Cargo Related Incidents

Chapter Two — Ship Related Incidents

Chapter Three — People Related Incidents

Chapter Four — Environment Related Incidents

Chapter Five — Commercial / Operational Related Incidents

Each chapter is divided into a number of relevant sub-chapters. Each chapter and sub-chapter is intended to 'stand alone'. In this way the user can refer to the relevant chapter e.g. People Related Incidents, review the introductory paragraphs to that chapter and then review the specific sub-chapter which coincides with the issue under consideration. Users should then have a clear idea of the sort of evidence which is likely to be required and the type of information which should be included in the master's report.

The chapters and sub-chapters generally follow an established pattern:

1. Provide a general discussion and a brief conceptual background to the particular incident category under consideration;

2. Set out the nature of the potential exposure or problem for which evidence may be required;

3. Consider any ISM implications;

4. Consider the nature of the evidence which may be available or required — where relevant, checklists have been provided to assist the mariner in assembling the evidence;

5. Consider what information may be required in a report;

6. (Where appropriate and where possible) A case study to try and bring alive the relevant issues for that topic area.

There are also five annexes, in Part C, providing easy access to complimentary guidance literature from primary source material.

The author, as far as possible, has avoided making reference to specific court cases but relevant legislation, either by way of IMO Resolutions or Circulars or UK Statutes have been used where considered appropriate.

The suggestions regarding evidence which might be available and the appropriate check-lists should not be considered as exhaustive — although attempts have been made to make them as comprehensive as possible. These lists are merely guidelines. Particular circumstances will dictate which items are relevant. In all cases, the master and officers will have to consider what additional information will be required to present a complete record of a particular incident.

Where appropriate, a case study has also been included. The case studies are, where possible, based on actual court or arbitration hearings. Where suitable cases were not available the author has drawn on his wide experience to construct realistic scenarios. Case studies are most useful as they demonstrate the value placed on the evidence from the vessel which either helped the shipowner defend the action, or, in cases where the relevant evidence was lacking, contributed to the shipowner being held liable by the court or tribunal. They also bring to life the whole subject and relevance of collecting evidence.

## Guidelines

The contents of the book are intended to provide guidance only and should be used to develop general principles. The mariner should think about the particular incident which might have occurred and think for himself or herself what sort of evidence will be required and understand why that evidence will be required and how it is likely to be used. From that position they will gain maximum advantage of the particular section of the book and also achieve the professional satisfaction of incorporating this important aspect of their job into their daily activities.

The mariner's own SMS and / own Company standing instructions must take precedence and *The Mariner's Role in Collecting Evidence — In Light of ISM* should be used in conjunction with the requirements of the SMS to complement it and not as a substitute.

This work has not been written with the intention that the master and officers should somehow replace lawyers, investigators, surveyors, and other consultants in assembling evidence. However, it is in recognition that masters and ships officers have an important role to play in the collection of evidence.

First, they can be of great assistance to lawyers, surveyors, or other consultants instructed by ship owners and their insurers to go on board the vessel to investigate an incident. Similarly, having the relevant evidence readily available if an investigator from the flag State Administration or a local authority comes on board will create a very good and favourable impression. When an incident occurs, a significant period of time may elapse before the lawyer or surveyor is able to come on board the vessel. In that period of time, valuable information may be destroyed or lost inadvertently. The master and officers can ensure that they gather together all the relevant information and documents for the lawyer or surveyor to examine when they do finally arrive. In addition, they can interview witnesses immediately after the incident while memories are still fresh. The assistance of the master and officers will make the job of the lawyer or surveyor far easier, will save a considerable amount of time, and will go a long way to ensuring that as thorough an investigation as possible is carried out.

Second, there are many minor incidents and disputes which arise during the normal course of a vessel's trading. These may not develop into claims for a considerable period of time after the incident occurred. The costs involved in investigating such claims by engaging lawyers or other consultants can be disproportionate to the amount at stake. Although the claims may be relatively small, they tend to arise often and, cumulatively, they represent a substantial amount of money. Therefore, the information recorded by the master and officers on a regular and routine basis will be essential in defending these claims.

Finally, an increased awareness of the type of evidence required to defend a claim will also lead to an increased awareness of potential problems which could arise on a vessel, and therefore, could lead to greater care being taken by the master and officers in operating the vessel and in their day-to-day work.

**What is evidence?**

If you asked a lawyer this question you would, no doubt, receive a rather complicated and convoluted answer! For the purpose of this work, however, we can probably simplify a definition along the following lines:

> Evidence is something that furnishes, or tends to furnish, proof of something. A fact is said to be proved when the Court or Inquiry is satisfied with its truth[1].

In a criminal trial, evidence is the means by which the prosecution tries to prove its case and the defendant tries to cast doubt upon the prosecution's evidence. Similarly, in a civil case, it is through adducing evidence that the claimant attempts to prove his case and the defendant attempts to counter the claimants case. We will briefly consider the standards of evidence in the sections below when we consider how the evidence will be used in civil and criminal actions and inquiries.

We do not need to go into any more detail, at this level, on the nature of evidence — however, it is felt useful to consider references to different types of evidence you may encounter when reading reports etc. in order to get through the 'jargon':

• Direct or Real Evidence

Physical things, evidence in the form of the thing itself. A broken pipe, a failed flange, a broken anchor chain, etc. Often real evidence cannot be disputed and is very valuable in proving facts.

• Personal Evidence

What is told by the witness, the record of interview. The value of personal evidence depends upon the quality of the witness and the ability and skill of the investigator / interviewer.

---

[1] Taken from Chapter 9 of the IMO Model Course 3.11

- Documentary Evidence

  Evidence provided by a document such as certificates, logbooks, bell / movement books, letters, manuals, photographs, etc.

  A document is anything on which signs or symbols have been marked and includes tape recordings, computer tapes or discs.

  Care should be taken that the document is taken for what it really is. A safety certificate is a document attesting that a surveyor signed the certificate to say the equipment met the required standard. It does not mean that the surveyor actually examined the equipment or that the equipment remained to standard. Similarly, a log book is a record of what was written, rather than what actually happened.

  Original documents are of far greater value. Photocopies can be tampered with. Contemporaneous records (written at the time) are far more valuable than fair copies (as with the deck log and the mate's fair copy). Original documents are useful but not infallible. Photocopies may not be acceptable in certain circumstances.

- Prima Facie Evidence

  At first appearance — evidence which is sufficient to establish a fact in the absence of any evidence to the contrary. If two ships collide there is 'prima facie' evidence of a breach of the Collision Regulations. If a ship founders there is 'prima facie' evidence that the ship was unseaworthy.

- Circumstantial Evidence

  A fact from which an investigator or court may reasonably and logically infer the existence of a further fact relevant to the incident. It is indirect or presumptive evidence showing a strong connection between evidence and the incident. A trace of a ship's paint on a fishing boat is strong circumstantial evidence that the ship matched with that paint was in contact with the fishing vessel.

  Circumstances equally capable of another reasonable explanation is of limited value unless reinforced by other evidence.

  In investigations circumstantial evidence may, in itself, be of limited value, but may point the way for further inquiry.

- Hearsay Evidence

  Evidence through a third party — 'second hand' evidence.

  Under certain jurisdictions 'hearsay' evidence is not admissible in criminal or other judicial proceedings. In a technical inquiry such evidence may be important, but it should always be corroborated to the maximum extent possible. This is particularly true where grudges between parties may exist or where somebody may have a particular interest.

Accident reports, based on unsworn evidence and documents which were seen by the investigator but not produced, are hearsay and may not be admissible in formal / court proceedings.

- Expert Evidence

  Given by a person skilled and experienced in a specific professional or technical area, able to give evidence based on his/her knowledge from facts reported to him/her or discovered by him/her by tests, measurements or similar means.

  The reports of tests on a ship's equipment, or reports on paint analysis etc. is expert evidence. Expert evidence is only as good as the expert who gives it. In an adversarial court much time can be taken with testing an expert witness[2].

## Why should evidence be collected?

To understand the reasons for collecting evidence it is important to be quite clear about what evidence actually is. Evidence is proof — objective proof. It is information tending to establish facts. In theory, therefore, when a particular fact is disputed (e.g. the speed of the vessels when they collided) it is the evidence which will assist the judge, arbitration panel or investigator to determine which of the two cases to believe.

The availability of evidence and its presentation may also have an influence on the results of a trial, arbitration or inquiry due to the impression such evidence can give concerning the day-to-day operation of the vessel in question. This is where the documentation created as part of ISM systems will come into its own.

The information which forms the evidence need not be contained only in documents such as logbooks and witness statements, it might also be contained in videos, photographs, computer disks, physical objects (e.g. broken twist locks or corroded hatch covers) or in the analysis of an expert witness, such as a surveyor.

There are probably two main reasons why the exercise of collecting and preserving evidence is worthwhile:

1. The evidence will significantly impact on the result of a litigation, arbitration, investigation or inquiry

   Claims have to be proved on the balance of probabilities. Cases are proved by evidence, which must therefore be available. Some defences, such as under Article IV, Rule 2 of the Hague Visby Rules, require certain issues to be proved, such as the cause of the cargo loss and the exercise of due diligence by the carrier to make the vessel seaworthy before and at the commencement of the voyage in respect of the loss complained of. Disputed facts are 'won' by good evidence.

2. To obtain proper advice from the outset

   For such advice to be given, it is essential to determine exactly what has happened.

---

[2] Based upon Chapter 9.3 of the IMO Model Course 3.11

It will save costs in the long run if, in circumstances where a claim or defence is hopeless, the party is so advised as early as possible so that settlement can be pursued

The investigation which takes place following an incident has two goals — to discover exactly what took place and to collect and preserve all evidence which establishes what took place. However, in practice, finding out exactly what happened is much more difficult than would at first appear. This is particularly true of collision incidents, when it is not unknown to be presented with statements from which, if the facts described took place, it is impossible for the collision to have occurred. Generally this will be either because the perceptions of the witness involved are, often understandably in the circumstances, inaccurate, or the witness is seeking to give evidence as to what he would like to have happened rather than what did actually happen. Witnesses are often concerned about blame being directed at them and wish to present themselves in the best possible light. Regrettably, this does not assist the investigation. In such circumstances, it will require a thorough investigation of all records available to pick up clues as to what in fact took place. If possible it is better that this be done at the time of the initial investigation so that the relevant witness' can be encouraged to give accurate accounts in the Logbook, Note of Protest and any other documents subsequently prepared.

In addition to the above, the availability of clear and complete evidence supporting the facts surrounding the incident will make it easier to determine the strengths and weaknesses of the claim or defence, will facilitate discovery, and will help give the impression of a well run ship, not to mention a well thought-out case.

### Who should collect the evidence? — the lawyer's role

In larger cases, where loss of life or serious injury have occurred or where substantial amounts of money are likely to be involved, it will probably be prudent to consider the appointment of a lawyer at a very early stage. Lawyers should be experienced in conducting investigations following casualties, in collecting the relevant evidence and in taking witness statements. The lawyer should be aware of the legal issues which are likely to have a bearing on the result of claims arising out of the incident and should be able, therefore, to take statements and evidence accordingly. However, in addition to this, there may be at least two further reasons why it is sensible to involve a lawyer from the start. The first is in relation to legal costs. If the matter is to proceed to arbitration or litigation, it will be necessary to instruct a legal firm in due course in any event. It is generally more difficult and time-consuming to take over a case part way through than it is to be involved from the start. Secondly is the issue of legal privilege which is discussed in some detail below.

### Who should collect the evidence? — the mariner's role

Whilst the lawyers role is very important — the role of the master and ship's officers is also very important. In respect of the larger type incidents, the lawyers job can be made much easier and more efficient if the master and ship's officers have already done some preparatory work in advance of the lawyer arriving on board, particularly regarding the collecting together of contemporaneous evidence, certificates, documents and other records. The extent to which this may be done will be determined by the speed with which the lawyer can attend on board following an incident.

In incidents which might not involve significant sums of money, the master and ship's officers can provide most valuable assistance by ensuring that the relevant evidence is collected together. This will provide the ship operator, and its insurers, with the tools necessary to properly handle claims and disputes. This in turn will lead to a more efficient and effective operation.

What then is required of the mariner in collecting evidence and preparing reports in light of the ISM Code?

The evidence should be considered on at least two levels — firstly evidence to demonstrate compliance with the specific rules and regulations and, secondly, to demonstrate that the SMS was functioning as it should.

Looking at the first level of compliance; there will clearly be a certain amount of overlapping, and the relevance of each area will vary from incident to incident, but the evidence required will probably fall into one or more of the following categories:

- Compliance with national / international / local rules and regulations etc. e.g.

  - MARPOL

  - STCW

  - COLREGS

  - Code of Safe Working Practices for Merchant Seafarers

  - ISPS, etc.

- Compliance with contractual obligations, e.g.

  - To exercise due diligence to make the vessel seaworthy under a contract of carriage.

- A demonstration of the practice of good seamanship — or otherwise industry best practice.

- A demonstration of good management practices.

In many cases the test will be an objective one although there will be occasions when subjectivity enters the equation. Any failure to comply at this level is not, in itself, a non-compliance with the ISM Code — it is a non-compliance with the particular section of MARPOL, SOLAS or some contract etc. The next level of considering the evidence is at the ISM level. If a loss has occurred because of some failure to fulfil obligations under one of more of the above categories then the next question to ask is whether that failure to comply was because of some failure in the overriding management system — i.e. the SMS of the ISM Code.

It may be that there were procedures in place but those procedures had been ignored — this may have been because of an isolated lapse on the part of an individual or be indicative of an ineffective system which is not working. In the former case the ship operator may still be in a position to raise the necessary defences — provided it can demonstrate that this really was an isolated incident. However, if it turns out to be a system that is not working then the ship operator is likely to find itself in considerable difficulty — this is likely to constitute a major non-compliance with the ISM Code.

It maybe that the procedures were being followed but just did not cover the particular point adequately. If that is the case and provided the ship operator can demonstrate that it took immediate corrective action to ensure that the problem would be avoided in the future then they may minimise their exposure to liabilities — particularly punitive penalties. However, if the ship operator subsequently did nothing to prevent a recurrence then again it may find itself massively exposed and open to very serious penalties — including the prospect of losing its Document of Compliance (DOC) and / or SMC which would effectively stop them trading.

Accordingly, the mariner will need to be constantly thinking on these two levels when collecting evidence — the immediate level of compliance with the various rules and regulations etc., and also compliance with the SMS. This mode of thinking should permeate their day to day work activities on board.

### When should evidence be collected?

The simple answer is 'immediately' — or at least as soon as possible!

Much of the evidence which may be required is actually produced as an on-going process in the daily life of the ship e.g. writing up the log book, keeping records of chart corrections etc.

A possible pitfall in dealing with a major casualty is that a party may simply assume a defensive role and respond to claims as and when they arise. It may be some months or even years before claims are presented. However, following such delay, it will be virtually impossible to collect the full and credible evidence that may be required to defend such claims. It is much better to make a positive effort to collect evidence immediately after a casualty. The reasons for so doing include:

a)  The details are fresh in the minds of those involved.

b)  Contemporaneous evidence (i.e. evidence which is taken at the time it occurred) or near-contemporaneous evidence (i.e. taken soon after the event) is given more weight by a court than a witness statement taken months, or even years, after the incident.

c) In its immediate aftermath, the incident is the focus of attention of all those involved. After some time has passed, people become involved in other matters. A casualty then appears to be less important and it is difficult to redirect attention to a past event.

d) Important witnesses may leave, or even be sacked, as a result of the incident. Alternatively, they may change jobs, retire or die. It is wise, therefore, to take their evidence promptly.

e) The company may wish to promote a policy of 'putting the incident behind them and focusing on the future'. Lawyers may find that they are in conflict with this policy if they are taking statements three years after the incident occurred.

f) Whilst the incident is the focus of attention, parties are more likely to receive support from all quarters, including third parties. Experience shows that information and documents are more readily available from third parties in the immediate aftermath of an incident, while sympathy levels are high and the desire to help prevalent, than after the passage of time when third parties are more likely to take the view that they do not wish to become involved.

Whilst these comments about the importance of immediacy of investigation and evidence collection have been in respect of a major casualty — it is very important to understand that they apply equally to any incident — however big or small.

### What evidence should be available — in light of ISM?

As was stated earlier, it is not the intention here to provide a long treatise about the ISM Code — there are a number of publications available which do that quite adequately — see the references at the end of this chapter.

However, some brief explanation is necessary in order to fully understand the significance and relevance within the context of collecting evidence. A copy of the text of Resolution A.741(18) as amended by MSC.104(73) — The International Management Code for the Safe Operation of Ships and for Pollution Prevention (International Safety Management (ISM) Code) is reproduced as Part C 1 towards the rear of this book.

In many ways, and for many companies, there was not much which was really new with the ISM Code. They already managed safety quite well; they already had their company standing instructions, which had evolved over many years and which set out best practice as far as that company was concerned. The practice of good seamanship was in itself a 'risk management' tool — it was just never called that. For some companies it was just a matter of writing down, in a systematic way, their existing good practices — as procedures — maybe with a little fine-tuning here and there. For other companies there was a more radical approach necessary.

However, by 1st July 1998 or 1st July 2002 — depending on the ship type — just about all seagoing commercial ships had to comply and have their SMS in place and working. The operating company had to be issued with a Document of Compliance (DOC) and each ship had to be issued with a Safety Management Certificate (SMC) to confirm that they complied. What is actually required by the ISM Code is concisely set out in Section 1.4 of the Code:

*1.4      Functional requirements for a safety management system*

*Every company should develop, implement and maintain a safety management system which includes the following functional requirements: ·*

*.1        a safety and environmental-protection policy;*

*.2        instructions and procedures to ensure safe operation of ships and protection of the environment in compliance with relevant international and flag State legislation;*

*.3        defined levels of authority and lines of communication between, and amongst, shore and shipboard personnel;*

*.4        procedures for reporting accidents and non-conformities with the provisions of this Code;*

*.5        procedures to prepare for and respond to emergency situations; and*

*.6        procedures for internal audits and management reviews.*

The instructions and procedures required under the Safety Management System (SMS) are usually set down in Procedures Manuals. Section 11.3 of the Code explains:

*11.3 The documents used to describe and implement the safety management system may be referred to as the Safety Management Manual. Documentation should be kept in a form that the company considers most effective. Each ship should carry on board all documentation relevant to that ship.*

Initially many companies, often under the guidance of 'ISM Consultants', including certain Classification Societies, set up the SMS to try and cover every conceivable activity which might take place on board — and often included many activities which would never take place on board that particular ship. The thinking behind this approach seems to have been that the SMS would be all inclusive — it would provide the master and those on board with checklists and instructions on every conceivable task they may have to undertake — so no one could possibly find fault with it — could they? The result was a veritable library of 20 or more volumes of Procedures Manuals. When an auditor reviewed the practice against the written procedures he / she would inevitably find numerous non-conformities. There were far too many procedures and check lists in many cases. Indeed in one of the few cases which have been through the High Court in London where ISM issues have been considered[3], the judge commented about the documentation placed on board by the vessel's managers as being "…too voluminous to be digestible…" The judge found that it was of fundamental importance that the vessel should

---

3    Papera Traders Co. Ltd & Others v Hyundai Merchant Marine Co. Ltd & Another (The *Eurasian Dream*) (2002) 1 Lloyd's Rep.719 (Cresswell J)

be provided with a ship specific manual dealing with fire prevention and control. Instead, the vessel was provided with a large amount of irrelevant and / or obsolete documentation, much of which did not refer to the specific type of ship in question — i.e. a car carrier.

A number of companies have now realised their mistake and have substantially trimmed back their procedures manuals to a size which means that they can be 'digested' and actually used in practice. Other companies have still to come to terms with that issue.

It was intended that each Company would produce its own manuals to reflect the culture / ethos of that particular company such that the procedures set out how things were done in that Company. Some Companies did this but many others used the services of Consultants / Classification Societies who provided 'ready made' or 'off-the-shelf' systems or at least templates which the Company could then use to 'customise' the SMS to their own Company way. This appeared to be sufficient / adequate for some flag State Administrations to verify compliance with the Code and to issue DOCs and SMCs. Unfortunately some of these 'off-the-shelf' systems are very generic — such that they have procedures for crude oil washing on container ships and other similar inconsistencies!

When an incident occurs which leads to a claim, dispute or possibly investigation by the authorities — it is these procedures manuals which will be examined to identify what procedures those on board should have been following. They will then look for objective evidence to satisfy themselves that those procedures were indeed being followed. If that objective evidence is not available, or if it demonstrates a clear non-conformity with the written procedures then the ship operator is, potentially, at a disadvantage. Not only is it likely to cost the ship operator a lot in terms of time and money but could also expose the directors of the company, the Designated Person, the master and others to personal fines and possibly even imprisonment.

On the other hand if the objective evidence was available and demonstrated that the correct procedures were being followed but that a mistake or error occurred, for to err is human, then there is no reason to think that the Company, master etc will not be allowed the mistake — provided all involved were doing their best. This was illustrated in one of the other cases addressing ISM issues which passed through the Admiralty Court in London[4] where the Admiralty Judge allowed the owners an 'Error of Navigation' defence where the vessel had missed its alteration of course position and had run aground — even though there was a chief officer and pilot on the bridge.

The ISM Code will be the best friend a ship operator could ever wish for or the worst enemy he could ever imagine.

The significance is that the SMS, particularly the procedures manuals, will be scrutinised very closely. The more serious the incident / more money there is at stake the closer will be the scrutiny. We will now consider some relevant ISM issues from the perspective of the office and the ship respectively.

---

4    The *Torepo* (2002) EWCA Civ. 1132

## 1. In the office ashore

The operation of the SMS is a shared responsibility between those in the office and those on board the ship. However, the ultimate responsibility for ensuring that the SMS is properly set up and is operating satisfactorily is with the Company. The Company may or may not be the owner of the ship but, in any event, if the Company does not fulfil its obligations to properly set up and run the SMS then it can have very serious implications for the owner and its insurers.

Section 12 of the Code explains, briefly, how the Company should monitor the working of the SMS. If an accident / incident does happen, it can be anticipated that the internal audit reports, non-conformity reports, minutes of the management review meetings and other records of the Company verification, review and evaluation will be examined very carefully. Paper trail audits will also be followed on any item that may have been picked up that required some attention.

If these reviews have not been carried out, or if they have not been carried out adequately, then the consequences are likely to be very severe for the Company — in extreme cases this could be viewed as a major non-compliance with the ISM Code itself — in which case they may have their DOC withdrawn by the flag State Administration.

In some Companies, engineering superintendents are used to conduct the ISM internal audits on board when they visit the vessels. Usually the main reason for the visit to the vessel of the superintendent is related to machinery maintenance and the Internal Audit tends to be secondary. If the Internal Audits have not been conducted adequately, and this is likely to become apparent in the event of a detailed investigation, the ship operator will probably find itself in very serious difficulty. This may constitute a major non-conformity with the ISM Code and not only lead to withdrawal of the DOC / SMC but could render the vessel technically unseaworthy.

The role and activities of the Designated Person (D.P.) will also come under close examination — depending upon the nature of the incident. The internal procedures for the reporting by the D.P. to the 'highest levels of management' will probably be examined — such reporting will clearly need to be minuted / recorded.

The way in which the D.P. reviews and responds to reports of accidents, hazardous occurrences and non-conformities will also, probably, be examined with corrective action and follow up audits. Similarly, the way minutes of safety committee meetings are reviewed and responded to is likely to be of interest. These types of areas will be important to provide an indication of the level of commitment to the safety culture and the operation of the SMS by those in the office as well as onboard ship.

One aspect which is likely to attract frequent interest is the vetting and recruitment policy of the company. Under Section 6 of the Code the responsibilities and obligations with regard to resources and personnel are set out. Section 1.2.3.1 of the Code requires the SMS to ensure compliance with mandatory rules and regulations.

Clearly that will include the STCW Convention and Code which sets out the detail of the qualifications, experience and levels of skill which the individual seafarers should have. If an accident or incident has occurred on board ship it is quite likely that the finger will be pointed at an individual — someone to blame — frequently it will be the master but it may also be the officer of the watch or some other officer or crew member. A potential claimant or investigator will probably endeavour to try and allege not only that the individual was incompetent, or similar, but also that the ship operators had been negligent in recruiting the particular individual. In a recent case before the Singapore Court[5] - where a container ship ran aground on account of negligent navigation by a second mate — the judge found that the officer was incompetent and that the ship operators had failed to exercise due diligence to make the vessel, seaworthy in that they had failed to take reasonable care with their vetting and recruitment policy. The carrier was not allowed the 'Error of Navigation' defence under the Hague Rules.

The Company should have good and clear vetting and recruitment procedures in place and these should be capable of being audited for any particular individual. They should include not only checking the validity of the Certificates of Competency but also the relevant experience for the particular position on board and the type of ship to which the individual is being posted. In addition the Company must have procedures to check that the seafarers they are employing are medically fit. If the Company uses manning agents then they may very well need to demonstrate that they actively vet, probably by way of an internal audit, that the manning agents are consistently applying the Company's vetting and recruitment procedures. This activity should also be reviewed as part of the Company Management Review and properly minuted.

It is interesting to note that in the case of the *Torepo*, referred to above, the Admiralty Judge remained focused on the SMS as it applied to the bridge management and the navigation. He seemed satisfied with what he saw and did not allow the claimants lawyers to proceed upon a fishing expedition through the entire SMS looking for unrelated issues which might trip up the ship operator. However, in the other case referred to above — the *Eurasian Dream* — the judge was not at all happy with what he saw and he allowed a detailed interrogation into the whole way in which the SMS was set up and was being operated.

The important lesson to learn and understand here is that if the ship operator does have a reasonable SMS and is making genuine efforts to make it work then the ship operator should have little to fear from the courts or investigators. However, if they are only 'paying lip service' to ISM then they can expect to be caught out and suffer very severe consequences.

## 2. Onboard ship

The evidence coming from the ship should demonstrate that the procedures, as set out in the manuals, are being followed and applied in practice.

---

[5]    The *Patraikos 2* – [2002] 4 SLR 232

If there are irrelevant procedures in the manuals, or procedures which are incapable of being complied with, then these issues should be brought to the attention of the D.P. / shore management for possible corrective action. The SMS should be dynamic and in the process of continually being improved — capable of being changed as and when required and necessary.

There may be particular laws of the flag State Administration which will have to be taken into account when designing and implementing the SMS. For example, whilst section 1.2.2.2 says that the safety management objectives of the Company should establish safeguards against all identifiable risks, it does not actually go so far as to make it a formal requirement that the Company needs to have a risk management / risk assessment procedure. However, as far as U.K. flag ships are concerned they are obliged to have such a system fully implemented — this requirement comes under SI 1997 No. 2962 — The Merchant Shipping and Fishing Vessels (Health and Safety at Work) Regulations 1997 — Regulation 7. If an accident occurs and it becomes apparent that a risk assessment was not done, or there is no objective evidence available to confirm that a risk assessment was done, then not only is the ship likely to be detained but the individuals responsible, including managers / directors of the Company may find themselves exposed to substantial fines and even up to two years imprisonment. It is believed that similar requirements exist throughout the member countries of the European Union and elsewhere around the world.

If an accident or incident occurs then the relevant section of the SMS manuals will be examined to establish how the particular activity should have been performed. Objective evidence will then be sought to establish whether in fact the activity was being carried out in accordance with those procedures. If it was not or if there is no objective evidence to confirm compliance then the ship operator and those involved with the SMS implementation are, potentially, in some difficulty.

The ISM Code creates the expectation of audit trails. It is by following those audit trails that, ideally, the ship operator, and its staff, can demonstrate that they were doing what they / the manuals said they should have been doing. There can be very serious consequences however if the Company, or their staff, attempt to falsify the records by creating an audit trail with erroneous information. An example which came to light recently was the checking of the portable fire extinguishers on board a particular ship. The procedures required the third officer to visually check the condition of all portable fire extinguishers every two weeks. Records were maintained by the third officer in which it was confirmed, by ticking the appropriate box on the form, that all extinguishers were checked every two weeks. However, during a port State Control Inspection the PSCO observed a fire extinguisher which was in a dirty and damaged condition. It transpired that the third officer had not in fact inspected any of the extinguishers but, rather, had ticked all the boxes on the form in the comfort of his cabin. The consequences on that occasion was that the PSCO considered the whole of the SMS to be discredited and a full detailed inspection was carried out. A number of further non-conformities were found and the ship was delayed from sailing for three days whilst corrective action was taken. If such a situation came to light in court then it could have devastating effects for the ship operator since the judge would probably doubt the credibility of not only the SMS but on the whole of the evidence produced by the ship operator.

When an accident or incident occurs, as was mentioned above, the finger will inevitably be pointed at an individual who can be blamed. It may very well be necessary to produce objective evidence that the individual had received all the necessary and relevant training and familiarisation as anticipated in the various parts of Section 6 of the ISM Code — and indeed the STCW Convention and Code. It may be necessary to produce records of emergency drills and exercises carried out on board — this may also include minutes of de-briefing meetings following the exercise. Minutes of safety committee meetings may very well be examined to establish the level of apparent involvement and commitment to safety by those on board — a lot can be picked up from a quick glance at the minutes of safety committee meetings.

The reports of non-conformities, accidents and hazardous occurrences are also likely to be examined carefully. If there are no reports then it is likely that this will be viewed as being improbable and very suspicious by an investigator or the court. From other sources, e.g. other claims being handled by a P&I Club, it is relatively easy to identify incidents which should appear. If they are not there then the credibility of the SMS will again be open to challenge.

If problems, e.g. hazardous occurrences or non-conformities, have been identified, or if potential improvements to the SMS have been identified, and reported to the company and there has been no response received / corrective action taken, and if this has some bearing on the accident / incident being investigated, then the consequences may be very severe indeed.

It is a regular and frequent complaint from those on board ship that they do not have the time or resources to complete all the paperwork required by the ISM systems. Unfortunately, this will not be accepted by an investigator or the court as an excuse for not having the paperwork / evidence completed and available. Indeed the hours of work / hours of rest will be scrutinised very carefully if there is any slight possibility that fatigue may have been a causative factor. Not only will the STCW hours of work / rest records be examined but cross checks will be made to verify the accuracy of those records. If they are found to be inaccurate then an assumption may be made that a deliberate attempt has been made to mislead the investigator or the court which may have very serious consequences.

The author makes no apology for repeating this fundamental point — the SMS must ensure compliance with all three parts of the mantra:

- **Say what you do**

- **Do what you say that you do**

- **Prove that you have done what you say that you do**

And one final point — never try and falsify records or other documents. There is a very good chance that this will be discovered by the investigator or lawyer or indeed the court. Once discovered it will cast doubt on the credibility of any evidence produced by that party.

### What evidence should be available — proactive evidence production

Much of the evidence which will be relied upon to explain what happened and why it happened will, or should, already exist. Records which are kept of the daily activities on board ship whether that be the log books, maintenance records, hours of rest / work etc will be pieces of the jig-saw which can be pieced together to understand what might have gone wrong and why it went wrong.

With additional requirements of the ISM Code it will be expected that procedures are in place for particular activities to take place and for these activities to be recorded e.g. a permit to work system for entry into an enclosed space or for bridge and equipment to be tested prior to sailing and for a checklist to be completed to confirm that this had been done.

With the introduction of Voyage Data Recorders (VDRs) — and similar automatic data recording devices this collection of proactive evidence has taken a great leap forward.

### Operational records

Any well run vessel keeps many operational records, for example:

- Crew overtime sheets

- Maintenance reports

- Daily workbooks

- Life saving and fire fighting appliances (LSA & FFA) maintenance books

- Fire and safety drill books

- Requisition sheets for spare parts

- Oil record book

- Garbage disposal records

These operational records can be important as a supplement to the brief log book entries and can help to form a more complete picture of events onboard.

### Log books

A number of different types of log books will be kept on board every vessel. These will include the official log, the deck or mate's log, the engine room log, rough logs, as well as the radio log, and sick bay log. For the purposes of this book, the official log, the rough log, the deck or mate's log, and the engine room log are the most important.

Judges and arbitrators place great weight on these logs as a contemporaneous record of the vessel. Therefore, it is of paramount importance that all log books are maintained in an orderly manner and fully and accurately record all relevant factual information. Movement books, bell books, course recorder print-outs or any other type of rough logs are also important items of evidence and should be maintained in a neat and orderly manner.

> The master should ensure that the officers and crew are aware of the importance of a log book and take care in making entries. Entries in the log books should always be written neatly and legibly in ink. If a mistake is made, a single line should be drawn through the relevant passage. Words should never be erased, either by rubbing out, or by painting with erasing fluid. Erasures appear suspicious when log books are examined by the opposing party to a dispute, and, in any event, forensic techniques are available whereby words which have been erased can be read. Furthermore, a judge or arbitrator examining a log book which has many erasures and is untidy may draw adverse inferences about the way a vessel is generally operated.

### Automatically recorded data

There had been a call for many years for an event recorder which would assist accident investigators in determining the cause of an accident as is standard in the aviation industry. A performance standard was developed for a VDR whose purpose is to maintain a store, in a secure and retrievable form, of information concerning the position, movement, physical status, command and control of a vessel over a period leading up to and following an incident. SOLAS Chapter V — Regulation 20 — requires:

*Voyage data recorders*

1. *To assist in casualty investigations, ships, when engaged on international voyages, subject to the provisions of regulation 1.4, shall be fitted with a voyage data recorder (VDR) as follows:*

   .1 *passenger ships constructed on or after 1 July 2002;*

   .2 *ro-ro passenger ships constructed before 1 July 2002, not later than the first survey on or after 1 July 2002;*

   .3 *passenger ships, other than ro-ro passenger ships, constructed before 1 July 2002, not later than 1 January 2004; and*

   .4 *ships, other than passenger ships, of 3,000 gross tonnage and upwards constructed on or after 1 July 2002.*

2. *Administrations may exempt ships, other than ro-ro passenger ships, constructed before 1 July 2002 from being fitted with a VDR where it can be demonstrated that interfacing a VDR with the existing equipment on the ship is unreasonable and impracticable.*

Guidelines in IMO Resolution A.861(20) on VDRs require the interfacing and recording of the following data:

- Date and time

- Ship's position

- Speed

- Heading

- Bridge audio

- Communication audio

- Radar data

- Echo sounder

- Main alarms (these are quite extensive and vary from ship type to ship type)

- Rudder order and response

- Engine order and response

- Hull opening status

- Watertight and fire door status

- Accelerations and hull stresses

- Wind speed and direction

- Additional information[6]

Clearly there is the propensity to revolutionise the concept of evidence collection as VDRs become more widely used.

A range of ingenious electronic data collection tools are being designed for use on board which, the manufacturers claim, provide almost infallible evidence of what was done and when. They also have the potential to significantly reduce the amount of paperwork which tends to be generated with proactive data / evidence collection[7].

### Informal notes and diaries

Masters and officers often keep informal contemporaneous notes or in some cases diaries of events on board. These notes are of great evidential value. In particular, if a master or officer is called before a court or tribunal to give evidence, he may read passages from his notes in support of his oral evidence.

---

[6] A very useful and informative paper has been prepared by IACS on VDRs – 'Recommendations 85 – Recommendations on Voyage Data Recorder – Jan 2005' – www.iacs.org.uk

[7] See for example the website for D@tatrac - www.datrac.com

However, if any part of his notes are relied upon as evidence, the entire notes must be made available to all the parties to legal proceedings. Therefore, the master should ensure that his notes are of an objective and factual nature and should avoid giving his personal views which, in the event that his notes are made available to the other parties to legal proceedings, may embarrass the master and the ship operator and may even adversely affect the ship operator's case.

### Written procedures

In addition to the detailed comments set out above with regard to the sort of ISM documentation which should be available — there are certain items which should be available from the ship — although it may be necessary to obtain them from the Designated Person / Office ashore:

An important starting point in any investigation or evidence collection exercise is to establish what the correct procedures actually were. It will therefore be possible, and necessary, to consider to what extent those procedures were followed — or otherwise. These written procedures may be found in the Safety Management Manual, or similar, plus manufacturers instruction manuals, for example. The procedures will provide a very good indication of what sort of objective evidence will be required and should be available.

### External audits

Under the requirements of the ISM Code the Company office(s) will undergo a full verification audit every five years in respect of the original issue and reissue of its Document of Compliance (DOC) — there will also be annual verification audits — to ensure that the Company Safety Management System (SMS) is being adequately maintained. The verification audits will be conducted by the flag State Administration or a Recognised Organisation (R/O) acting on behalf of the Administration — frequently a Classification Society. The verification audit will be supported by quite a detailed report setting out the auditors findings — including any non-conformities and observations.

The ships will similarly be subject to a detailed verification every five years with a least one intermediate verification between the second and third anniversary in order to maintain its Safety Management Certificate (SMC). Again the Administration / R/O Auditor will issue a report setting out their findings. It is quite likely that these reports will be examined following an incident as a contemporaneous record of the way in which the Company was managing safety and complying with the requirements of the ISM Code.

Another category of external audit will be conducted by port State Control Inspectors — in this regard see the paragraph below on 'How will the evidence be used — in port State Control inspections?' The reports issued following those inspections are also likely to be examined following an incident — as a record of the way the Company had been managing safety.

### *Internal audits, master's review, Company management review*

Under Section 12 of the ISM Code there is a requirement upon the Company to '…carry out internal safety audits to verify whether safety and pollution-prevention activities comply with the safety management system…' and '…periodically evaluate the efficiency of and, when needed, review the safety management system…'

It is also required, under Section 5 that the master should also '…review the safety management system…'

It is not specified how frequently such internal audits, management reviews and masters reviews should take place but it appears to have been accepted across the industry that they must take place at least annually — although preferably more frequently. Each of the audits and reviews will generate its own detailed report and it is this report which will be one of the main sources of documentary evidence to demonstrate that the company was monitoring how the SMS was working and thus confirming that everyone was doing what they were supposed to be doing. It is these reports in particular which will be examined if it becomes necessary to consider questions of whether the shipowner had exercised the necessary degree of 'due diligence', or where questions of 'fault and privity' etc were an issue.

Considerable care and attention should therefore be put into conducting these audits and reviews and ensuring that they are fully and accurately documented and ensure that they follow the correct Company procedures.

### What evidence should be available? — reactive evidence production and collection

If an incident has happened then additional evidence will need to be created to record what has happened. There is an old saying that 'a picture is worth a thousand words' — this is very true and photographs, videos or even sketches and diagrams can be extremely valuable to show the scene of the event, the damage caused etc. Remember, the people who will be making decisions on the final outcome of the consequences of the incident will not have had the benefit of that first hand knowledge of having been at the incident site at the particular time. Photographs and the like can help to ensure that fair justice is done. Written reports, prepared whilst the facts are still available and fresh in people's minds, will also be of invaluable help when considering what happened, how, why and when.

### *1. Photographs and videos*

As the case history in chapter one demonstrates (see page 74), photographs and videos can provide essential evidence. In one instance, for example, owners were able to defeat a claim for cargo shortage by producing as evidence photographs that showed a cargo of grain, which had been discharged into road trucks, spilling out of the back gate of the trucks. Photographs and video can also show heavy weather conditions, inadequate fendering, how cargo was secured, or the general condition of the vessel. Similarly, sketches and drawings are of immense value in depicting certain incidents.

If possible, photographs, videos, or sketches should be used to support the master's written report. They should be clearly labelled to identify the ship or subject, indicate the date, time and place and be initialled by the master. Some cameras and video recorders will now automatically record the date and time.

### 2. Master's reports

A master of a vessel is likely to prepare a report whenever the vessel is involved in an incident which may give rise to legal proceedings. In the event that legal proceedings ensue, the report will be of clear evidential value to all the other parties to the legal proceedings. Any report by the master must be factual and objective. Suggestions on the type of information to include, for each category of incident, can be found in the relevant chapters in Part B of this book.

### How will the evidence be used — in criminal actions?

In many jurisdictions there is a clear distinction between the certainty of evidence required in criminal and civil cases. Where a person may be subject to punishment, particularly imprisonment (or worse) the burden of proof required is often that of '…beyond reasonable doubt…'

Many criminal cases, in the U.K., will be heard, in the first instance, in the local Magistrates Court. If the matter is particularly serious or contentious then it is likely to be referred on to a higher court where it will be heard by a judge and jury.

In the U.K. the usual prosecuting authority for violations of the ISM Code or other Merchant Shipping Acts would be the 'Enforcement Unit' of the Maritime and Coastguard Agency (MCA). In such circumstances the MCA would almost certainly have conducted their own investigation on board and / or would have received other very good evidence from reliable sources — e.g. a report from Dover Coastguard about an alleged violation of a vessel wrongly applying the Collision Regulations in a Traffic Separation Scheme. However, the defendant will be allowed to produce evidence in his or her defence. Clearly the quality of that evidence will need to be good if it is to challenge evidence produced by the MCA.

A very important issue relating to the evidence produced by a defendant is by way of mitigation of any penalty which may be imposed. For example, consider a case where an oil spill has occurred during a bunkering operation. The clean up and other consequential costs are settled on a strict liability basis — i.e. the polluter pays. The ship operator usually has insurance cover for these costs with a P&I Club, or similar. However, the master and / or other ships staff and / or the operating company may also be punished by way of a fine and, in some jurisdictions, imprisonment. The financial level of the fine will be very much at the discretion of the judge. It will, therefore, be most advantageous for the master / ship operator defendant to produce evidence which is going to show them in particularly good light. The better they achieve that objective, presumably, the lower the fine — and conversely.

The best evidence that could be produced, in such circumstances, is evidence showing a good safety management system which is working well. Where the correct procedures are routinely followed and such an incident has not occurred previously. In this regard reports of hazardous occurrences and near misses will be particularly helpful — but only if they are supported with evidence that they were analysed and proper corrective action taken and implemented. It can thus be demonstrated that this particular accident was just that — a most unfortunate 'one-off' accident — and was not symptomatic of a badly run ship. It would, therefore, be inappropriate for the court to severely punish the master / company but rather they should be encouraged in their genuine efforts but work even harder at their SMS and ensure that such an incident does not happen again.

On the other hand, a ship that cannot provide such evidence can expect a hefty fine and, in some jurisdictions, potentially long prison sentences — for example, those who deliberately by-pass an oily water separator should expect a serious punishment.

### How will the evidence be used — in civil actions?

In civil cases a less onerous level of proof is required, as compared with criminal cases, such that a test based upon '…the balance of probabilities…' is the standard required in many jurisdictions.

In 1999 a completely new set of rules and procedures for the civil courts, including the Commercial, Mercantile and Admiralty Courts, was introduced — the Civil Procedure Rules (CPRs). These are supported by comprehensive Practice Directions, new Court Forms and Pre-Action Protocols.

London solicitors Hill Taylor Dickinson produce an excellent set of small books on a range of maritime law related issues in the '…at a glance…' series. One such volume provides a very good and clear introduction to the English Civil Procedures Rules — The Woolf Reforms[8]. On page 3 they provide a most helpful summary of the major changes which have been brought about by the new rules:

1.  The overriding objective is that cases will be dealt with justly, taking into account value, importance and complexity.

2.  Disclosure of information and documentation is encouraged prior to proceedings being issued. Parties may face sanctions if they act unreasonably.

3.  The progress of litigation has been speeded up. Unmeritorious claims are weeded out at an early stage, but defendants still incur legal costs in so doing.

4.  Alternative Dispute Resolution (e.g. mediation) is actively encouraged.

---

[8]   Hill Taylor Dickinson – www.htd-law.com

5. A fast track system has been created for claims worth between £5,000 and £15,000. These claims are to proceed to trial within 30 weeks of being allocated to the fast track.

6. The number of documents to be disclosed is, in general, reduced and is proportionate to the size of the claim.

7. Expert reports are to be directed to the court rather than to the parties. The court will often order a single joint expert report, especially in fast track claims or in relatively non-contentious areas of the claim.

8. Claimants are able to make offers to settle which could have serious interest and costs consequences for the defendant.

These new rules have been successful to the extent that more cases are now settling either before proceedings are issued or before the case comes to trial. The level of costs incurred on relatively small claims is still quite high due to the fact that litigation has become "front-end loaded". Money has to be spent collecting evidence, for example taking statements and analysing ISM Code documents upon receipt of protocol documents rather than waiting until proceedings are issued. The next stage may well be to introduce a regime of fixed costs for all fast track cases.

Since almost all shipping related disputes are likely to involve claim amounts in excess of £15,000 they will follow the multi-track route. Even so the relevant evidence which will be required will have to be available at a relatively early stage and much of this will have to be disclosed to opponents early on and before the matter ever gets to court. The more refined and focused the evidence is the better chance there will be for a quick resolution of the claim or dispute without having to incur the high costs of a full court case.

**How will the evidence be used — in flag State accident investigations?**

In formal inquiries, and similar investigations examining marine casualties, the test adopted would usually be similar to that in the civil courts — i.e. '…on the balance of probability…' If the Administration intends to prosecute, for example in the U.K. under one of the Merchant Shipping Acts, they will probably do so in the Criminal Courts. In which case, the section on criminal actions above will be relevant.

However, if the purpose of the inquiry is to consider whether the company should have its DOC withdrawn, for example, or the master should have his Certificate of Competency suspended or cancelled, for example, then it is more likely to be an internal inquiry. Even so, the Company or the master will still be entitled to produce evidence in their own defence.

**How will the evidence be used — in safety investigations?**

In the U.K. the Marine Accident Investigation Branch (MAIB) is responsible for the investigation of all types of marine accidents, both to vessels and to those on board. The MAIB is an independent branch within the Department for Transport (DfT) and is separate from the Maritime and Coastguard Agency (MCA). The head of the MAIB, the Chief Inspector of Marine Accidents, reports directly to the Secretary of State on accident investigation. He and his professional staff, who are drawn from the nautical, fishing, marine engineering, and naval architecture disciplines, are appointed by the Secretary of State under the provisions of the Merchant Shipping Act 1995. An administrative staff deals with records, data analysis and publications, policy matters, and provides general support.

The MAIB's sole objective in investigating an accident under the regulations is the prevention of future accidents by establishing its causes and circumstances; it is not the purpose to apportion liability, nor, except so far as is necessary to achieve the objective, to apportion blame. The MAIB is not an enforcement or prosecuting agency.

The general procedures the MAIB follow in their safety investigations are set out in detail in MGN 289 (M+F).

The sort of information and evidence they will require is set out below, which has been extracted from MGN 289:

**Information needed in reports**

(1) **Initial reports of accidents** should include as much of the following as possible:

    (a)    name of vessel and IMO, official or fishing vessel number;

    (b)    name and address of owners;

    (c)    name of the master, skipper or person in charge;

    (d)    date and time of the accident;

    (e)    where from and where bound;

    (f)    latitude and longitude or geographical position in which the accident occurred;

    (g)    part of ship where accident occurred if on board;

    (h)    weather conditions;

    (i)    name and port of registry of any other ship involved;

    (j)    number of people killed or injured together with their names, addresses and gender;

    (k)    brief details of the accident, including sequence of events leading to the accident, extent of damage and whether accident caused pollution or hazard to navigation.

    (l)    If the vessel is fitted with a voyage data recorder, the make and model of the recorder.

(2) **Follow-up accident reports** and initial reports of serious injuries should include the above information as well as the conclusions of any on-board examination covering the cause, how a future similar incident might be avoided, and what action has been taken or recommended.

The MAIB's Incident Reporting Form (IRF) provides a convenient format for reports but plain narrative giving the above information may be used if the form is not available. As full an account as possible should be given whether or not the form is used; the list of items above is not intended to be limiting and any matter should be included which will help to make the circumstances clear or to show how similar incidents may be prevented. Sketches, plans and photographs of the damaged areas, taken both before and after the event, are often helpful and may be attached to the report.

(3) The reports in (2) should be signed by the master, skipper or the owner's representative, and by the ship's safety officer if one is carried.

(4) IRFs are available on the MAIB's website — www.maib.gov.uk

The Incident Report Form (IRF) is reproduced in Part C 5 towards the rear of this book.

If the evidence is readily available from the ship then the MAIB Inspector is likely to form a favourable impression and the subsequent report which is prepared will reflect that good impression.

### How will the evidence be used— in ISM verification / inspections?

Section 13, in Part B, of the ISM Code sets out the basic requirements for Certification and Periodical Verification. The full text of Resolution A.741(18) as amended by MSC.104(73) — The International Safety Management (ISM) Code is reproduced in Part C 1 towards the rear of this book.

The verification process will be undertaken by the Administration, by an organisation recognised by the Administration or, at the request of the Administration, by another contracting government to the Convention. It was considered useful, within the context of this book on collecting evidence, to examine the guidelines given by one administration to its own surveyors / auditors / inspectors as to the sort of things they should be looking for, and the questions they should be asking when undertaking an ISM verification. In this way we can be prepared and appreciate what sort of evidence we will need to have to hand to not only satisfy the surveyor but also to create a good and favourable impression.

The following notes are extracted from the U.K. Maritime and Coastguard Agency — 'The ISM Code — Instructions for the Guidance of Surveyors' — Chapter 4:

In order to comply with the requirements of the ISM Code every company should develop, implement and maintain a SMS. The SMS should embrace the objectives of the Code to ensure safety at sea, prevention of human injury or loss of life, and avoidance of damage to the environment, in particular, to the marine environment, and to property. Compliance with the requirements of the ISM Code should be verified by determining:

- that the SMS meets the requirements of the ISM Code.

- that the objectives laid down in paragraph 1.2.1 of the ISM Code are met.

- that personnel have received the appropriate training and familiarisation in the tasks for which they are responsible.

- that they are carrying out their work in accordance with the company's procedures.

- that tasks are being carried out with due regard for safety?

The method of carrying out the audit should be outlined and will include, but not be limited to, the following:

- interviews with key members of the management team as laid down in the audit plan.

- a detailed examination of the SMS; familiarity with and understanding of the safety and environmental policy, manuals, procedures and instructions, working practices, recruitment and training records, management reviews, internal audits, classification records, accident and non-conformity reports.

- discussions with members of staff at all levels.

- the raising of non-conformities and that they should be drawn to the attention of a company representative at the time that they are identified.

- the categories of non-conformities should be explained.

The objectives of the ISM Code are to ensure safety at sea, prevention of human injury or loss of life, and avoidance of damage to the environment, in particular, to the marine environment and to property. The achievement of these goals is heavily dependent on the human element i.e. the people who operate the system. The knowledge and experience of the officers and crew, their familiarity with the company's SMS, their training and records thereof should be checked by observation and interview. Where practicable, the auditor(s) should witness as many on board procedures as practicable and these may include, but are not limited to:

- pre-arrival and departure checks on the bridge and in the engine control room;

- securing the vessel for sea;

- voyage planning;

- navigational briefing;

- mooring stations fore and aft;

- bridge procedures in harbour;
- engine room operations;
- preparation of machinery for sea;
- machinery maintenance including system preparation;
- anchor stations;
- bunkering operations;
- pilot embarkation/disembarkation;
- passenger musters and handling;
- cargo operations/handling;
- watch handover;
- onboard training;
- new joiner (crew) instructions;
- emergency drills;
- safety committee meetings;
- routine inspections;
- navigation under pilotage; and
- watchkeeping at sea.

In the normal course of events a General Inspection will be conducted in parallel with the SMC audit so for this purpose an emergency drill must be witnessed.

The 'ISM Code — Instructions for the Guidance of Surveyors' can be downloaded from the MCA website at www.mcga.gov.uk

### How will the evidence be used — in port State control inspections?

A port State Control Officer (PSCO) is likely to form quite a quick initial impression by what he / she sees as he approaches and boards the ship. This 'first impression' is likely to affect his attitude and general approach to conducting the rest of his inspection. As part of this 'Initial Inspection' the PSCO will usually require sight of certain certificates and documents, ask a few questions of the master and other members of the crew and have a general walk around the vessel.

In a very useful and well produced guide to port State Control, published by North of England P&I Association[9], the author, Peter Kidman, provides a most helpful table (on pages 19/20) of areas a PSCO may look at during an initial inspection:

[9] *Port State Control – A Guide for Cargo Ships* – Second Edition 2003 – By Peter Kidman – INTERCARGO and North of England P&I Association ISBN 0 9542012 8 0

| First impressions (on boarding) | External condition of the<br>• hull<br>• freeboard marks<br>• accommodation ladder<br>• mooring arrangements |
|---|---|
| Certificate check (in the master's cabin) | General status of certificates / documentation – verify<br>• missing or expired<br>• not translated or posted up as required<br>• discrepancies<br>• outdated or unsigned endorsements<br>• uncertified copies of original certificates<br>• inconsistencies or omissions in record books<br>• certificates issued by non-recognised organisations<br>Safe manning – verify<br>• compliant manning levels<br>• minimum rest periods<br>Crew certification – verify<br>• presence of original and valid certificates<br>• English translation<br>• medical certificates<br>• minimum age compliance<br>ISM Code – verify<br>• crew members are familiar with the company 'safety and environmental policy'<br>• the 'safety management system' documentation is readily available<br>• status of interim certificates, if any<br>• the ship type is covered in the DOC<br>Ship security – verify<br>• presence of original and valid certificates<br>• correct procedures have been followed according to the ISPS Code, part A reg. 19.4 if the ship has an interim ISSC<br>• Master and / or crew are basically familiar with the essential shipboard security procedures |

| 'Walk around'<br><br>( to check on the<br>overall condition<br>of the ship) | PSCO would be likely to verify the general condition of exposed decks<br>• deck plating<br>• bulwark and stays<br>• guard rail<br>• hatch coamings and covers<br>• piping and vents<br>• presence of improper temporary repairs<br>• presence of recent welding / hot work<br>• presence of liquid seepages<br>Cargo handling gear<br>• cargo gear and additional equipment<br>• cargo securing devices<br>Navigation and radio communication equipment<br>• navigation equipment<br>• management of voyage charts / publications<br>• hand-over procedures for watch and control of ship<br>• bridge visibility<br>• record of steering gear tests / drills<br>• radio installation and equipment<br>• reserve radio and batteries<br>• record of operation and maintenance<br>• fire detection and alarm systems<br>Lifesaving appliance (LSA)<br>• lifeboats, rescue boats and life rafts<br>• launching arrangements<br>• personal lifesaving appliances<br>• record of periodic inspections and testing / drills<br>• management of emergency plans and instructions<br>Fire fighting arrangements (FFA)<br>• fire doors<br>• means of escape<br>• fire pumps<br>• fire main, hydrants and hoses |
|---|---|

| | |
|---|---|
| • | fire extinguishers<br>   • record of periodic inspections and testing / drills<br>   • management of fire control plan and instructions<br>Machinery spaces<br>   • main and auxiliary engines<br>   • piping, pumps and valves<br>   • electrical generators<br>   • cables, terminations and joint arrangements<br>   • lighting<br>   • cleanliness of spaces<br>   • emergency escape routes<br>Pollution prevention<br>   • oily-water separator and associated equipment<br>   • Shipboard Oil Pollution Emergency Plan (SOPEP) or Shipboard Marine Pollution Emergency Plan (SMPEP) arrangements<br>   • garbage arrangements<br>Living and working conditions<br>   • condition and sufficiency of food and potable water supply<br>   • arrangements and cleanliness of food stores, galley, pantries, refrigerated chambers and mess rooms<br>   • sanitary arrangements, including condition of doors, flooring and drainage<br>   • operation and maintenance of ventilation, lighting, heating and water supply<br>   • medical facilities, including medicines and equipment<br>   • record of accommodation inspections<br>   • availability of personal protective equipment |

If all the 'evidence' is readily available to satisfy the PSCO during their inspection then it is unlikely he / she will spend much time on board — they will move onto the next ship. However, if the necessary evidence was not available or the PSCO was otherwise not satisfied with what he / she found then he may decide that 'clear grounds' have been established for a more detailed inspection. At this point the PSCO will start digging deeper and the next step could very easily lead to a detention of the vessel or even a banning order. Once problems have been identified, and particularly if it became necessary to impose a detention order on the vessel then this would almost certainly be notified to other port State control bodies who would then be keeping an eye out for that vessel visiting their port and would also pay it a visit. The fact of the detention would also be available to insurers and potential charterers — in other words it will haunt the ship for some considerable time. Clearly, it is well worth the time and effort to ensure that all on board is 'ship shape' and the evidence is readily available to demonstrate that fact.

### The duty of discovery

Under certain systems of law, notably English Law, there is a strict duty on a party to disclose, by way of discovery, all documents relevant to the issues of the case (subject to questions of privilege, which are discussed below). If a party is unable to disclose documents pertinent to the issues at stake due to a failure to preserve such documents, this may prejudice the party at trial. Similarly, it may be extremely embarrassing if certain documents are not disclosed from the outset, but are found to exist by the opponents or by the tribunal.

### The doctrine of privilege

A master of a vessel is likely to prepare a report whenever the vessel is involved in an incident which may give rise to legal proceedings. In the event that legal proceedings ensue, the report will be of clear evidential value to all the other parties to the legal proceedings. This section deals with the question of whether a master's report must be produced to all parties to the proceedings or whether it may be exempt from such production as a "privileged" document.

English arbitration and court proceedings are conducted on the basis that each party to an action submits evidence in support of their case. The general rule is that the parties to the proceedings must disclose and produce all relevant documents. In this context "disclosed" means that the existence of the documents must be made known. "Produced" means that they must be made available for inspection. The one exception to the general rule is that documents which are privileged are exempt from production (although not disclosure). In some other jurisdictions, the rules in relation to production of all relevant documents are even more strict than in England.

A master's report is relevant to legal proceedings and may be used by the other parties to the proceedings as evidence unless it is privileged. The report may be privileged on the ground of legal professional privilege or on the ground that it is a self-incriminating document.

### Legal professional privilege

Legal professional privilege arises as a result of the need for a legal advisor to gather evidence and examine the issues relevant to a case without the fear of prejudicing a client's interest in the proceedings. All correspondence between a legal advisor and his client is privileged provided that it is written to or by the legal advisor for the purpose of giving legal advice or assistance. A master's report will be protected from production if it is prepared by a master subsequent to an incident likely to give rise to litigation proceedings, and if it is prepared for the purpose of obtaining legal advice and is addressed solely to the owners' legal advisors.

In recent times, it has become common practice for masters to submit accident reports endorsed with the following words:

*"confidential report for the information only of the company's legal advisors prepared for the purpose of obtaining professional advice in proceedings pending, threatened, or anticipated".*

Such an endorsement will not of itself protect the document from production as it is the purpose for which the report was produced which will determine whether or not it is privileged. However, it will assist in demonstrating that the requirements, by reason of which privilege may be claimed, are fulfilled. If the report is so endorsed, it should be submitted directly to the owners' legal advisors.

Despite the likelihood that the master's report may not be privileged on the ground that it is routinely prepared, a report prepared contemporaneously to an incident which may be the subject of legal proceedings is an invaluable document. Such a report would provide owners and their legal advisors with a complete account of the events surrounding the incident and allow them to prepare fully for legal proceedings. The evidential value of such a document, therefore, clearly outweighs the possible risks that the report will be used as evidence by the other parties to legal proceedings.

## Self-incriminating documents

A master's report may also be privileged from production on the ground that it would incriminate or expose the master or owners to criminal proceedings in the United Kingdom. Although a master's report will rarely be incriminating, the doctrine of self-incrimination may be significant in the context of criminal proceedings under the Merchant Shipping Acts. Privilege may only be claimed if the risk of incrimination is real.

## Taking statements

If there is likely to be a significant delay between an incident occurring and the investigation team or lawyer attending on board, it may be appropriate for the master to consider taking his own statements by way of interviewing any witnesses. This may also be an appropriate activity in the case of relatively small incidents where lawyers are unlikely to attend.

As with any other activity, there are skills to be acquired in interviewing techniques if a satisfactory result is to be achieved.

One of the biggest mistakes made by untrained interviewers is to suffer from 'confirmation-bias' i.e. seeking or only taking note of information that fits his / her preconceived theory — in other words hearing only what you want, or maybe expect, to hear. This may be particularly difficult to overcome for any master conducting such an interview if the master himself is also a potential witness of fact. Objectivity is crucial and if the master fears that his objectivity may be influenced then he may be prudent to delegate one of his other, impartial, officers to conduct the interviews. It should also be recognised that an officer, or crew member being interviewed may feel somewhat uncomfortable if his evidence suggests that some fault may lie with the actions, or inactions, of the master.

It is not feasible, in a volume such as this, to provide extensive instruction in interviewing techniques; however, there are ten useful 'commandments' which can be learnt and which should help an interviewer conduct a successful interview:

1. Stop talking

   You cannot listen if you are talking.

2. Put the witness at ease

   Help the witness feel that he / she is free to talk.

3. Show that you want to listen

   Look and act interested. Listen to understand what is being said rather than concentrating on your next question. This is difficult as the next question may desert you, but it may return and, by a full story, may be answered anyway.

4. Remove distractions

   Don't doodle, or give the impression you are not listening or that you would rather be elsewhere.

5. Empathise

   Try to put yourself in the other person's place.

6. Be patient

   Allow plenty of time, do not interrupt.

7. Hold your temper

   Any impatience or anger can pass the initiative to the interviewee.

8. Avoid argument and criticism

   Causes the witness to become defensive, possibly qualify answers or 'clam up'.

9. Try and make your question flow responsive to his / her priorities.

   Shows you are listening and that you understand. Try not to break continuity, you can always return to other issues later.

## 10. STOP TALKING

This is the first and last commandment[10].

Remember also that the statement should be factual i.e. it should record where the witness was, at what time, what he/ she saw or heard. It should not include subjective opinion on what the witness might have inferred or assumed might have happened. Of course it should be emphasised to the witness that his / her opinion is important and will be listened to at the appropriate time — but for the sake of the statement they must stick purely to the facts. Remember that such a statement is unlikely to be granted a privileged status and therefore may very well be reviewed by opponents as well as the court.

In appropriate cases it may be wise to include an interpreter to assist the witness — to ensure that they understand the questions correctly and to allow them the opportunity to provide full and accurate answers.

### Hazardous occurrences, near misses and non-conformities

Thus far we have concentrated our attention on the collecting of evidence in anticipation of actual accidents or incidents occurring — which may be the subject of a third party or insurance claim or an inquiry by an Administration or similar body.

However, a very important issue which, in light of the ISM Code, we must continue to return is the opportunity to prevent accidents and incidents occurring in the first place. It is for this reason that the issue of reporting, investigating and analysing not only accidents but also hazardous occurrences and non-conformities is given a prominent position in the ISM Code itself:

9. *Reports and analysis of non-conformities, accidents and hazardous occurrences*

9.1 *The safety management system should include procedures ensuring that non-conformities, accidents and hazardous situations are reported to the company, investigated and analysed with the objective of improving safety and pollution prevention.*

9.2 *The company should establish procedures for the implementation of corrective action.*

These non-conformities, hazardous occurrences, near misses all provide learning opportunities. They are alarm bells starting to sound to indicate that things are starting to go wrong with the system. If they are not attended to then they will develop and become 'accidents just waiting to happen' and, sooner or later, will develop into actual accidents. If they are attended to whilst they are hazardous occurrences or near misses then the probability of them developing into an actual accident will have been reduced considerably. In order to be able to properly investigate and analyse the problem, and thus prescribe the most appropriate corrective action, it will be necessary to examine the evidence.

[10]    Based upon 'The Ten Commandments of Interviewing' as set out in Chapter 6.1 of the IMO Model Course 3.11

## Dealing with the media

Following a major accident or incident, mariners should be aware that statements made by crew members to the media may be inadvertently used out of context and prejudice the legal position of the owners or simply result in bad publicity for the vessel. Therefore, following such incidents all enquiries from the media should be directed to company head office or the company's media spokesperson.

## Giving evidence

Giving evidence as a witness in a trial can be a daunting experience. The importance of being properly prepared for your day in court cannot be overstated. It is natural for witnesses not to perform well under the pressure of questioning. A lack of experience and preparation will inevitably go against a witness.

The following very useful tips on giving evidence were set out in a circular issued by the Australian Law Firm Phillips Fox and were extracted from a booklet on the subject by Phillips Fox Adelaide office partner David Purcell. They should help you make the most of your time in court and create a favourable impression on the judge and jury.

Your primary duty as a witness is to assist the court by telling the truth as you know it. When giving your evidence, follow the guidelines below:

### Honesty

The most important principle for witnesses is to be honest. Dishonesty in the witness box is often revealed by the witness's demeanour and is particularly evident in cross-examination. If you tell a 'little white lie' when giving evidence on a matter that may seem unimportant (because the honest answer is embarrassing or you believe it will create a bad or false impression) and the judge finds out about that lie, it will be very difficult for the judge to believe you on any other important matters.

### Plain speaking

Telling the truth in a simple straightforward way will improve your chances of being believed by the judge. Whenever possible answer questions with a 'Yes' or a 'No'.

### Concise and simple

Short and concise answers are the best for both the examination-in-chief and the cross-examination.

Treat each question on its own merit without thinking about previous questions or answers or the impression they might be creating. Do not try to predict where the line of questioning is heading. Focus on responding to the actual question rather than considering why it is being asked. The impression you are trying to create is one of honesty and sincerity. Attempts at jokes or light-heartedness are inadvisable in a court-room.

You should not volunteer any material other than in response to a particular question, or ask counsel if you can elaborate the full story or explain an answer further. However, you must still be allowed to give an accurate and complete answer and not be cut off by hostile questioning from the cross-examining counsel.

*Take your time*

Take your time over the question and give a considered answer. There is no rush when giving evidence. Make sure that you concentrate and fully understand each question before answering.

However, be careful not to take too much time, as an unreasonable delay between the question and the answer may suggest uncertainty. If you are in any way unsure or don't understand a question, say so. The question will then be restated or rephrased.

If you are asked to read a document make sure that you do read it carefully, even if the document is very familiar to you.

*Keep calm*

Although the judge expects a certain level of nervousness in most witnesses, a witness who is highly agitated can appear evasive or unsure or, at worst, unreliable or dishonest. The calmer you remain while giving evidence the more impressive you will be and the greater the impact of your evidence.

Cross-examining counsel will often attempt to unsettle a witness and / or induce them to lose their temper. Don't succumb to these tactics. Your evidence will have more impact if you respond calmly to an aggressive counsel.

If when answering a question you are required to be critical about another person or about what they have said or done, be careful to ensure that the tone of that evidence is unemotive and objective.

Resist any temptation to favour a particular party's side. Your role is to tell your story in a simple, honest and straightforward way, not to advocate for either party. The best impression you can create is one of objectivity and candour.

But if a question invites a strong answer and you have a strong view, give it. You should be forthright in your evidence where necessary, but refrain from becoming over-emotive.

*Making concessions*

Witnesses are often loath to agree with what is put to them by a cross-examining counsel, or to make what they regard as a concession. If your genuine view is that what has been put to you is correct, you must agree with counsel. The most believable witness is the one who gives 'warts and all' evidence.

*Do not ask questions*

While giving your evidence you are restricted to answering only the questions that you are asked. You may not ask questions of counsel or the judge, except to request that a question be repeated where you did not hear or understand it. You may also ask for time to consider a question or document.

Challenging counsel with a response such as 'How would you know?' is unimpressive. So is asking the judge 'Do I have to answer that?' If the question is technically objectionable, rely on counsel to object. If you do not know an answer to a question, say so. Do not guess the answer if you are in any way unsure. Give the best answer you can in the circumstances.

*Modifying answers*

If on reflection you believe that an earlier answer you gave was wrong, bring this to the judge's attention. Most judges will recognise that mistakes are made from time to time and getting to the truth is most important.

| **Checklist for Witnesses** | |
|---|---|
| Try to adhere to these points when giving evidence as a witness:<br><br>• Tell the truth.<br>• Concentrate on the barrister addressing you and on the judge.<br>• Direct your answers to the judge, not to the barrister asking the questions.<br>• Try to give your evidence at a speed that allows the judge to make a record of what you have said.<br>• If you do not hear or understand a question, politely ask for it to be repeated or clarified.<br>• Pause to consider the question if necessary.<br>• Answer the precise question asked. | • Keep your answers as brief, clear and concise as possible.<br>• Give your evidence honestly and courteously.<br>• Have confidence in your evidence.<br>• Speak loudly and clearly.<br>• Speak only when you are spoken to.<br>• If you realise you have made a mistake in your evidence, tell the judge as soon as possible.<br>• Never guess an answer. If you are not able to answer a question or you are unable to recall an event, say so.<br>• Do not get defensive or upset during your cross-examination. |
| (Philips Fox included the following footnote as a warning / disclaimer:<br><br>'This guide was prepared by partner David Purcell exclusively for the information of clients, contacts, partners and staff of Philips Fox. While it directs attention to and comments upon aspects of the law as at November 1997, it is not intended to provide legal advice in this area. Professional advice should be sought prior to acting upon the information conveyed in this guide.) | |

*Can you talk to counsel?*

In court recesses during your cross-examination, you must not discuss your evidence with the solicitor who has asked you to give evidence or their barrister.

*Addressing the judge*

You should address the judge as 'Your Honour'. You should address the barrister as 'Sir' or 'Madam'. When giving your evidence, remember that the judge may be trying to write down your evidence in longhand. Try to give your answers at a speed that allows the judge to follow them.

Always direct your answers to the judge and speak as loudly and clearly as possible. Keep your sentences short and to the point and don't be afraid of the judge or counsel. You are there to give your honest version of events — unless you are the defendant, you are not on trial!

## Conclusion

With good quality, well organised documentary evidence it should be possible to understand what happened and why. Within the spirit of the ISM Code this will provide an opportunity to implement corrective action and improve the system by trying to ensure that the accident or incident is not repeated. However, it is this same evidence which will be used to assess and determine liability or guilt. If the accident has occurred as a result of some unintended action then there will be much more to be gained from learning lessons and ensuring the same mistake is not repeated rather than punishing the Company or individuals. Unfortunately it doesn't always work out like that! However, the chances of minimising the consequences for the Company and the individual will be enhanced considerably if the evidence demonstrates that they were doing their very best to manage safety and protect the environment but in spite of that an accident or mistake occurred.

Remember the 'Three Fold Mantra':

• **Say what you do**

• **Do what you say that you do**

• **Show that you do what you say that you do**

Satisfying the first two parts of the mantra — even to a very high degree — will not be enough. It is crucial that you can prove it — and to do that you must produce and collect the relevant evidence.

## References

- UK Statutory Instrument 2005 No. 881 — The Merchant Shipping (Accident Reporting and Investigation) Regulations 2005.

- UK Marine Guidance Note MGN 289 (M+F) — Accident Reporting and Investigation — MAIB.

- MAIB — Incident Report Form (a copy of which appears as Part C 5).

- UK Maritime and Coastguard Agency — MCA — The ISM Code — Instructions for the Guidance of Surveyors.

- IMO Model Course 3.11 — 'Marine Accident and Incident Investigation — Training Manual' — (for flag State Administration personnel).

- IMO Resolution A.849(20) — Code for the Investigation of Marine Casualties and Incidents — A.20/Res.849 — 1 December 1997 (a copy of which appears as Part C 2).

- IMO Resolution A.884(21) — amendments to the Code for the Investigation of Marine Casualties and Incidents (Resolution A.849(20)) — a21/Res.884 — 4 February 2000 (a copy of which appears as Part C 3).

- ILO Convention 134 of 1970 — Concerning the Prevention of Occupational Accidents to Seafarers.

- ILO Convention 147 of 1978 — Concerning Minimum Standards in Merchant Ships.

- ILO Recommendation R 142 Prevention of Occupational Accidents (Seafarers) Recommendations, 1970.

- IMO SOLAS, 1974 as amended by the Protocol of 1978 — Chapter 1 Part C.

- IMO Resolution A.3222(IX): The Conduct of Investigations into casualties.

- IMO Resolution A.440(XI): Exchange of information for investigations into marine casualties.

- IMO Resolution A.442(XI): Personnel and material resource needs of Administrations for the investigation of casualties and contravention of conventions.

- IMO Resolution A.637(16): Co-operation in maritime casualty investigations.

- IMO MSC/Circ.224: Submission of damage cards and intact stability casualty records.

- IMO MSC/Circ.388 Fire casualty records.

- IMO MSC/Circ.433: Reports on investigations into serious casualties.

- IMO MSC/Circ.621: Guidelines for the investigation of accidents where fatigue may have been a contributing factor.

- IMO MSC/Circ.953: Reports on Marine Casualties and Incidents (Revised harmonised reporting procedures — Reports required under SOLAS regulation 1/21 and MARPOL 73/78 articles 8 and 12 (a copy of which appears as Part C 4).

- IMO — International Convention on Load Lines, 1966 — Art.23.

- IMO — International Convention for the Prevention of Pollution from Ships 1973, as amended by the Protocol of 1978 (MARPOL 73/78) — articles 8 and 12.

- IMO — International Convention on Standards of Training, Certification and Watchkeeping for Seafarers, 1978 — as amended 1995 — Regulation I/5.

- IMO — The Convention relating to Intervention on the High Seas in Cases of Oil Pollution Casualties 1969, as amended by the Protocol of 1973 — The Intervention Convention.

- IMO Resolution A.847(20) Guidelines to Assist Flag States — Annex para 7 — flag State Investigations.

- Paris MOU — Guidelines for port State Control Officers on the ISM Code.

- IACS — Procedural Requirements for ISM Code Certification.

- IACS — Procedure for Training and Qualification of ISM Code Auditors.

- U.S. Department of Homeland Security — United States Coast Guard — Navigation and Vessel Inspection Circular No. 04-05 — port State Control Guidelines for the Enforcement of Management for the Safe Operation of Ships (ISM Code).

- IMO — MSC/Circ.622/Rev.1 — Piracy and Armed Robbery against Ships — Recommendations to Governments for preventing and suppressing piracy and armed robbery against ships.

- IMO — MSC/Circ.623/Rev.3 — Piracy and Armed Robbery against Ships — Guidance to shipowners and ship operators, shipmasters and crews on preventing and suppressing acts of piracy and armed robbery against ships.

- U.K. Marine Guidance Note 241 — Measures to Counter Piracy, Armed Robbery and Acts of Violence against Merchant Shipping.

# Part B

# Incident Categories

# CARGO RELATED INCIDENTS

## General introduction

THE PRIMARY PURPOSE OF MOST COMMERCIAL SHIPS is to carry cargo from load port(s) to destination and to do this profitably. It must also be done safely and without incident such that the cargo arrives at destination in the same good order and condition as it was in at the time of loading.

Unfortunately things can, and do, happen which lead to claims and disputes relating to the cargo. In this first chapter we will explore the nature of cargo claims arising under bills of lading and consider what evidence will be needed from the vessel for the ship operator and / or its liability insurers to deal with such claims in the most efficient way possible — to demonstrate that they did exercise due diligence to make the vessel seaworthy and / or did properly care for the cargo whilst it was in their custody. It frequently happens that cargo interests dispute their obligation to make their contribution to General Average (G.A.) and / or Salvage – alleging that the event which led to the G.A. / Salvage incident occurred as a result of a failure on the part of the carrier to exercise due diligence to make the vessel seaworthy at the commencement of the voyage. These issues will also be considered. Under the terms of charterparties it may be far from clear, as between the shipowner and the charterer, who will ultimately be responsible for the cargo related claims.

At the end of the day the arguments will be won or lost on the strength of the evidence available. Whether that argument is won or lost can make the difference between the venture being a commercial success or a failure. If the later is the case then not only will the ship operator and its insurer suffer but many peoples livelihoods may also be at risk.

## Cargo damage, loss or shortage

The most fundamental principle underlying the carriage of goods by sea is that the carrier (a term which almost always includes the shipowner) is entrusted with another person's property to transport it from one place to another. Therefore, if the cargo is lost or damaged in transit, the carrier will have to account for that loss or damage. The contracts under which goods are carried by sea generally determine the obligations and responsibilities of the carrier. In respect of any one voyage, there may be several related contracts. Sometimes the terms of all the contracts are consistent but often they will conflict with each other. In order to properly defend a claim for cargo damage, loss or shortage, the carrier must be able to demonstrate that it has fulfilled its obligations under the governing contract(s) of carriage, that the vessel was in an efficient state and that the cargo was cared for properly.

## a. Conceptual background

To fully understand the conceptual background to cargo damage, loss and shortage claims, and consequently the evidence which will be required to deal with them, it will be worth spending a little time to understand some basic principles:

**Pt B1**

**C
A
R
G
O**

- The fixture
- The ship
  - (i)   A seaworthy ship
  - (ii)  The exercise of due diligence
- The cargo
- The bill of lading
- The voyage
- The claim

Each of these issues will be addressed in turn.

### The fixture

A charterparty and bill of lading often represent two separate contracts in relation to the same voyage. Both of the contracts may be relevant and the master and the shipowner may have to show what they have done to comply with the terms of the contracts. Therefore, it is essential that the master is familiar with the terms of all of the contracts applying to a particular voyage and with local practices and regulations which affect the performance of these contracts. The master will be able to obtain information about the contracts from owners and charterers and obtain information about local custom from owners' local agents and P&I correspondents. It is also important that the master is aware of the instructions issued by the charterers and keeps a careful record of all instructions issued in respect of the voyage.

International conventions, especially the Hague Rules/Hague-Visby Rules and Hamburg Rules, attempt to arrive at a common approach to some of the basic issues in relation to the carriage of goods. Many contracts of carriage incorporate either the Hague Rules or the Hague-Visby Rules (the differences between the two being of little practical importance to good cargo practice) and the obligations and responsibilities imposed on the carrier by these rules provide the framework for this chapter.

### The ship

If cargo is lost or damaged, there is a presumption that the carrier has not taken care to ensure the ship is in a thoroughly efficient state. The Hague and Hague-Visby Rules impose an obligation to exercise due diligence to make the ship seaworthy.

### (i) A seaworthy ship

A seaworthy cargo ship is one which can take its cargo to sea without risk of danger and damage to either the ship or the cargo arising out of the ordinary marine environment or the failure of the ship. The concept of seaworthiness extends beyond the integrity of the vessel's hull and machinery. The vessel must be properly equipped and manned with a competent crew who are well trained in all shipboard procedures. The vessel must be in good condition and must have everything it requires in order to perform properly.

### (ii) The exercise of due diligence

The Hague and Hague-Visby Rules require the carrier to exercise due diligence to make the ship seaworthy before it puts to sea. Exercising due diligence means taking good care.

If problems arise on board during the course of a voyage, the test for determining whether or not the carrier has taken good care to make the ship seaworthy is as follows:

- Should the defect have come to light by the careful checking of the ship before the voyage began?

- If so, would a careful owner have repaired that defect before sending the ship, with her cargo on board, to sea?

In order to ensure that good care has been taken, there is no substitute for the proper and regular checking of all aspects of the ship and its manning, of all work, maintenance, and repairs carried out on board. Moreover, all procedures and standing instructions which are in force on board should be reviewed in order to ensure that these are adequate and well suited for the ship putting to sea and safely carrying her cargo. All checks and regular maintenance work should be carried out as often as necessary to avoid failure in the vessel, its personnel or its procedures. The reader is referred to Part A, the General Guidance, and in particular the sections dealing with the ISM Code, the implementation of which will necessarily involve a thorough review of shipboard procedures. More specific comments on the ISM implications are also set out below.

The master and the crew should not rely on the findings of the outside examiners such as classification society or underwriters' surveyors. These surveyors have different interests and do not usually work to the same guidelines, standards or requirements. All of the checks and regular maintenance work carried out by the crew should be properly recorded and documented. If something does go wrong and cargo is lost or damaged, then the presumption will be that the carrier has not taken good care to make the vessel seaworthy. In order to refute this presumption, the carrier must have evidence in the form of log books, work schedules, work books, work specifications, accounts, standing instructions, reports and contemporaneous correspondence to show that good care has been taken to make the vessel seaworthy.

## The cargo

In addition to the obligation to take good care to make the ship seaworthy, the Rules also impose an obligation on the carrier to take good care to look after the cargo from the time it is entrusted to him until the time that it is delivered to the receiver (see Hague Rules, Article III, rule 2). If the cargo, at the time of delivery, is lost or damaged, the carrier will be called upon to explain how the loss or damage occurred.

The period of time during which the carrier must take good care of the cargo can only be determined by looking at many different factors. The relevant contracts (for example, the charterparty and bill of lading) will usually determine the period of time during which the carrier remains responsible for the cargo. However, local laws may override or refuse to recognise contractual provisions which conflict with local regulations or practice.

The obligation on the carrier is to do everything necessary to deliver the cargo to the receiver in **as good condition** as when it was entrusted to the carrier. The carrier, therefore, must ensure that all cargo handling operations, including the loading, stowing, carrying, and discharging, are done properly and carefully. Moreover, the carrier must ensure that the cargo is properly cared for and kept so that the condition of the cargo is maintained. The master should be fully aware of any special attention that the cargo may require. Information and instructions with regard to the treatment of cargo should be sought in writing from the shipper. If the master has any reservations about this information, he should request the assistance of the shipowner or their local agents who may appoint an independent surveyor or expert. The master should ensure that all the crew members are also aware of their individual responsibilities concerning the cargo operations, in particular, with regard to the supervision and control of stevedores and the stowage and securing of the cargo.

The carrier may be held responsible for any problems which arise out of any of the cargo handling operations which it has contracted to undertake or arrange. In addition, the carrier will be held responsible for any cargo handling operations for which, under the local laws, it is primarily responsible, whether or not it has contractually undertaken to do these operations. Therefore, it is essential that the master is aware of the local laws, custom and practices as well as the provisions in the relevant contracts which relate to cargo handling operations. The owners' local agents or local P&I correspondents should be able to advise of local laws which dictate that particular cargo operations fall within the carrier's responsibility.

If a particular cargo handling operation, which is the carrier's responsibility, is not carried out properly, the carrier will be unable to avoid liability if loss or damage occurs to the cargo even if the master inserts into the statement of facts an endorsement stating that the carrier is not responsible. Such endorsements may be of evidential value for indemnity proceedings and the master may note on the statement of facts or in correspondence any irregularities relating to the cargo handling operations.

The standard of care required of the carrier is independent of the usual custom or practice. The carrier's obligation is to look after the cargo properly and carefully and it will be of no defence to a claim for damage to say that the cargo was carried in accordance with usual practice.

In order to avoid liability if cargo is lost or damaged, the carrier will have to demonstrate that its obligation of caring for the cargo (during loading and discharging operations as well as during the voyage) has been fully and properly discharged. Therefore, the master must ensure that all cargo handling operations are accurately recorded and fully documented so that the carrier will be able to bring forward the evidence necessary to defend a claim. Contemporary evidence relating to loading and discharging operations may be vital in successfully defeating a cargo claim. For example, the evidence may demonstrate that cargo was never loaded or that it was damaged at a time or by someone for whom the shipowner is not responsible. Even if the shipowner has to, in the first instance, pay the claim, the contemporary evidence may assist him in claiming an indemnity from a third party who is responsible for the damage.

## The bill of lading

From the viewpoint of both the carrier and the shipper, documents which demonstrate the amount and the condition of cargo carried on the ship are essential. The bill of lading is the most important of such documents. The Hague and Hague-Visby Rules provide for the bill of lading to be a record of the **quantity of cargo and its apparent order and condition** at the time the cargo is entrusted to carrier's care and responsibility (see Hague Rules, Article III, rule 3).

> Without ever having seen the cargo, prospective buyers often decide to purchase goods on the basis of the description in the bill of lading. If bills of lading are issued which inaccurately describe the cargo, the consequences may be extremely costly for the carrier. Therefore, it is essential that all the information on the face of the bill of lading is checked carefully.

The carrier is under an obligation to verify the amount of cargo and to verify its condition and identifying marks at the time the cargo comes into his custody and care. The master should ensure that all the proper arrangements are made for this purpose and should seek clarification from the shipowner if they have not been made.

The carrier will be unable to avoid liabilities which arise as a result of a failure to check the cargo unless a check is not reasonably possible. Furthermore, endorsements on the bill of lading, such as "shipper's figures", "figures as per shore tally", "quantity and condition unknown", or "said to be...", will seldom absolve the carrier of blame if he was able, but has failed to check the particulars of the cargo to his own satisfaction.

The master should not state anything in the bill of lading which he believes to be inaccurate. If the bill of lading does contain inaccurate information, the master should correct it with an appropriate clause before signing it. If the shippers and/or the charterers insist that bills of lading are issued which do not accurately reflect the quantity or condition of the cargo or the date it was loaded, it is essential that the master obtain clear instructions and advice from the shipowner and his P&I Club lawyers.

In addition to the bill of lading, there are many other documents which record the quantity and condition of the cargo. The mate's receipt, cargo manifest, stowage plans, tallies, and draft surveys, as well as notebooks, correspondence, and reports are all of great evidential value. The carrier will rely on such documents to demonstrate the condition and quantity of the cargo at the time it was entrusted to him and defend any claim for loss or damage.

### The voyage

The carrier, having provided a seaworthy vessel which is fit to go to sea with her cargo on board and having received the cargo into its care, must perform the voyage dictated by the contract of carriage. Under the Hague and Hague-Visby Rules, the carrier is obliged, in the absence of any agreement to the contrary, to carry the cargo directly to its destination (see Hague Rules, Article IV, rule 4). Therefore, the route of the voyage is crucial to the proper fulfilment of the contract of carriage. Any unjustifiable deviation from the agreed, direct, or customary route will constitute a breach of the contract of carriage and may jeopardise the shipowner's P&I insurance cover. A **deviation** is justifiable in only three situations.

Firstly, if there is a real or immediate danger, the carrier may deviate for the purpose of protecting and preserving the cargo. In certain circumstances, if the well being of the cargo so demands, it may be the carrier's duty to deviate. Secondly, the carrier may deviate for the purpose of saving human life. However, he may not unnecessarily delay the vessel at the scene of a casualty.

Finally, the contract of carriage may permit a deviation from the contractual voyage if it contains a "liberty to deviate" clause. It is not safe to rely on such clauses as they are interpreted in a most narrow and restrictive manner. The Hague and Hague-Visby Rules, which will usually be incorporated into the contract of carriage, excuse deviations for the purpose of saving life and/or property, or for any other reasonable purpose. It is virtually impossible to define what is meant by **reasonable**. However, the question of whether a deviation is reasonable will be considered not only from the point of view of the carrier but from the point of view of the cargo owners as well.

The carrier is also under an obligation to ensure that the vessel proceeds promptly to her destination. The duration of the voyage is crucial to the proper fulfilment of the contract of carriage, and any unnecessary delay will be treated in the same way as a deviation from the contractual voyage.

In the event the vessel deviates from the agreed, direct, or customary route, or in the event of delay in the prosecution of the voyage, the master should notify the shipowner immediately. In addition he should ensure that the precise and detailed reasons for the deviation or delay are fully and accurately recorded, and documents such as the log book, ship to shore communications, course recorders, and charts must be made available to owners.

## The claim

The main objective of the Hague and Hague-Visby Rules is to ensure that the cargo is delivered **in like good order and condition** which means that the condition of the cargo should not have deteriorated whilst it was in the care and custody of the carrier. However, the Rules recognise the possibility that, for reasons beyond the control of the carrier, it may fail to meet that obligation.

In such cases, the Rules may protect the carrier from liability for claims arising out of his failure to deliver the cargo "in like good order and condition" (see Hague Rules, Article IV, rules 1-2). However, before it can rely on these exceptions the carrier must fulfil all of its obligations under the Rules. The carrier, in seeking to defend a claim for cargo loss or damage, must first demonstrate that it has exercised due diligence to make the ship seaworthy and that it has properly kept and cared for the cargo. If the carrier fails to show that it has fulfilled these obligations, it will not be able to rely on the exceptions.

The reader should note three important points relating to the Rules. Firstly, the exceptions will only come to the aid of the carrier if it has done everything possible to look after the cargo and prevent loss or damage occurring. Secondly, the scope of the exceptions are continually diminishing; the carrier is expected to learn not only from its own mistakes but also from those of other carriers within the shipping community. Thirdly, as with the deviation provisions, the exceptions are interpreted in a narrow and restrictive sense and the carrier can never rely on them confidently.

The obligations imposed on the carrier by the Rules have been devised to keep loss and damage to a minimum. Thus, it is likely that where cargo loss and damage has arisen, the carrier will be found to have been in breach of the Rules. This does not mean that the carrier will be found liable for every cargo claim brought against it. However, the carrier will be in a far better position to defend claims and to produce the evidence required to refute them if it has implemented, in the first instance, the very systems and procedures on board the vessel which minimise the risks of claims arising.

## b. Potential exposure / problem

It can be understood, from the above, that the carrier (usually the ship owner – although the charterer could be considered the carrier in certain jurisdictions and in certain circumstances) is exposed to potential cargo claims for alleged damage, loss or shortage of the cargo. This exposure to liabilities arises under the terms of the contract of carriage – which will usually include the Hague, or Hague-Visby Rules in one guise or another (e.g. in the form of a Carriage of Goods by Sea Act [COGSA] or similar. The claim may be pursued by the cargo owner or the cargo insurer under subrogated rights.

In addition to the actual claims for cargo damage, loss or shortage there may also be a number of related losses – many of which may be uninsured. There may be costs involved in separating, segregating, reprocessing or disposing of damaged cargo. The costs of such operations may be recoverable from insurance but the lost time to the vessel will not. The ship may be arrested or otherwise detained whilst the extent of the loss is quantified and / or security is put up by way of a guarantee. This loss of time to the vessel is unlikely to be covered by insurance. It maybe that some cargo, e.g. damaged foodstuff, is rejected and left on board — this could pose a very serious problem if there is another cargo ready to load.

A shipowner would usually be insured for cargo liability claims with a P&I Club. However, they are likely to have a significant cargo deductible which will come straight out of the Shipowner's pocket and any claims made against the Club will affect the amount of money that the shipowner will have to pay into the Club by way of Premiums / Calls in future years.

### c. ISM implications

It may well be asked, what have cargo damage claims to do with safety management and the ISM Code? Surely, this category of incident is purely 'commercial'?

Of the three cases which have been before the courts where ISM related issues have been considered — i.e. The *Eurasian Dream*, The *Torepo* and the *Patraikos II* — all three incidents were disputes under contracts of carriage evidenced by bills of lading and specifically the obligations under Article III Rules 1 and 2 of the Hague Visby Rules. The judge in the *Eurasian Dream* case said that:

"…Seaworthiness must be judged by the standards and practices of the industry at the relevant time, at least so long as those standards are practical and reasonable…"

The standards and practices of the industry in this respect are now the ISM Code. The test of whether the necessary due diligence has been exercised will be evident from the procedures of the SMS and the evidence produced to demonstrate that those procedures were followed.

The following, non-exhaustive, list attempts to address some of the more obvious potential implications and, consequently, suggest areas of the SMS which will come under close scrutiny:

Section 1.2    Objectives

The objectives of the ISM Code, as set out in Section 1.2 does not only apply to protection of people and the environment but also includes '…the …avoidance of damage to … property…' – which would include cargo.

Section 5    Master's responsibility and authority

Section 6    Resources and personnel

In Sections 5 and 6 of the Code there is a lot of emphasis put upon the obligation of the company to provide the proper people — including the master and crew — who are properly qualified, trained and in all respects suitable to carry out their particular job on board that particular ship. In the *Eurasian Dream* case, the master was qualified and did have considerable experience on bulk carriers — however, he had no experience on car carriers and this lack of experience was one of a number of factors which led the judge to conclude that the ship was unseaworthy. The master and other officers were also inadequately trained and familiarised with the particular ship, specifically its fire fighting equipment, and this was another factor in the unseaworthiness equation.

Section 7    Development of plans for shipboard operations

Cargo operations would almost certainly constitute a 'key shipboard operation' as anticipated by Section 7 of the ISM Code. Clearly the type of ship will determine what procedures and plans would be included in the SMS. Clearly if there is a cargo operations manual, or a cargo securing manual, etc then the text of these do not need to be reproduced in the safety management manual – it would usually be sufficient to make a statement that cargo will be secured in accordance with the 'Cargo Securing Manual' – Ref…….. Although any such manuals should be subject to normal document control.

Section 8    Emergency preparedness

To what extent cargo operations would fall subject to the requirements of Section 8 – Emergency Preparedness – would depend upon the nature of the cargo. Certainly, with oil or gas cargoes there may well be specific emergency procedures whereas with containers there may not. However, there will no doubt be cross references into emergency procedures – particularly fire fighting and personal injuries.

Section 9    Reports and analysis of non-conformities, accidents and hazardous occurrences

Records of the activities anticipated by Section 9 may well be examined to confirm that learning opportunities were being taken as part of the SMS. Similarly minutes of on board safety committee meetings may be examined to determine the level of involvement and commitment to safety management on board

Section 10    Maintenance of the ship and equipment

To what extent this may be relevant will obviously be determined by reference to the cause of the cargo damage. If the failure of a piece of equipment was involved then the procedures and records will be examined very carefully. In the case of the *Eurasian Dream* there were numerous items of fire fighting equipment which were found to be deficient and these issues also contributed towards the judge finding the ship to be unseaworthy.

Section 11    Documentation

If it appears that there have been problems with compliance with the SMS then it is likely that a closer look will be made at the documented procedures themselves. If these are voluminous, irrelevant or otherwise inadequate then the company is likely to come under severe criticism.

Section 12    Company verification, review and evaluation

There is a very clear obligation on the company to ensure that the SMS is working properly on board its vessels. If a serious incident has arisen, as in this case with a collision, then it can be anticipated that the active monitoring by the company will be looked at very closely by way of audit trails.

Section 13    Certification and verification

As a matter of course the validity of the SMC and DOC will be checked

### d. Nature of evidence required

*Documentary evidence*

In a claim for cargo loss or damage, the documents listed below should be assembled whenever possible and numbered in consecutive order. They should then be referred to in the master's report which is discussed in the next section. It is recognised that in certain instances these documents will be more easily available from the shipowner's office, but if they are available on the vessel and attached to the report they will be of great assistance in limiting the amount of commentary which has to be included in the report. The documents are as follows:

*Cargo related incidents — documentary evidence*

| | |
|---|---|
| 1. | A convenient plan of the vessel which includes a description of the distribution of hatches and holds, the position of the vessel's equipment, the distribution of double bottom tanks, wing tanks and peak tanks and capacities; |
| 2. | Vessel's tonnage certificate; |
| 3. | Class certificates including recommendations, reservations, and conditions of class at the time of the loss or incident; |
| 4. | Crew list; |
| 5. | Reports of the master or deck or engineer officers on regular inspection and |

|     | maintenance of the vessel and her equipment; |
| --- | --- |
| 6. | Standing orders for regular inspection and maintenance of vessel prior to sailing; |
| 7. | Inspection, repair, and maintenance schedules; |
| 8. | Inspection, repair, and maintenance logs; |
| 9. | Repair and maintenance accounts; |
| 10. | Records of steel thickness; |
| 11. | Shipboard management system, owner's verification records, internal and external audit records; |
| 12. | Corrections and maintenance records for nautical publications; |
| 13. | Technical manuals and operators' manuals; |
| 14. | Repair records from outside contractors; |
| 15. | Condition reports; |
| 16. | Crew documents, qualifications certificates of competency, manning certificates; |
| 17. | Certificate of fitness (chemical and gas carriers); |
| 18. | Cargo system and auxiliary system test and calibration records; |
| 19. | Performance/specification/manufacturer's date of cargo handling equipment/systems; |
| 20. | Vessel's deadweight/freeboard calculations; |
| 21. | Vessel's calculation of bending moments in various stages of employment; |
| 22. | Stability calculations; |
| 23. | Mate's receipts; |
| 24. | Bills of lading; |
| 25. | Charterparty(-ies); |
| 26. | Draft surveys with all accompanying calculations; |
| 27. | Letters of protest; |
| 28. | Deck log abstracts for the period of loaded voyage including loading and discharging operations and the period or voyage before loading if, during this time, heavy weather was encountered or hold cleaning was carried out; |
| 29. | Ventilation records if not included in the deck log; |
| 30. | Temperature records if not included in the deck log; |

| 31. | Bilge sounding records if not included in the deck log; |
|-----|---------------------------------------------------------|
| 32. | Engine logs for the same period; |
| 33. | Statement of facts at load and discharge port; |
| 34. | Time sheets at load and discharge port; |
| 35. | Notice of readiness at load and discharge port; |
| 36. | Tally sheets at load and discharge port; |
| 37. | Cargo manifest; |
| 38. | Cargo preparation procedures and records; |
| 39. | Inspection records, surveyor's reports, draft survey calculations prior to loading; |
| 40. | Cargo handling equipment test records; |
| 41. | Cargo isolation/segregation procedures and diagrams; |
| 42. | Cargo log book entries; |
| 43. | Cargo calculation records before and after loading; |
| 44. | Cargo security methods and plan; |
| 45. | Reports of laboratory analyses of cargo samples; |
| 46. | Hatch closing/sealing procedures; |
| 47. | Stowage plan (for each port if cargo loaded at several load ports); |
| 48. | Course recorder printout; |
| 49. | Echo sounder rolls, engine telegraph recorder; |
| 50. | Empty Hold Certificate; |
| 51. | Integrated bridge system printouts; |
| 52. | Cargo/ballast/fuel records; |
| 53. | Routine position reports; |
| 54. | Working chart (with the original markings) if the course or incidents of the voyage were unusual; |
| 55. | Correspondence with charterers, shippers, agents, stevedores, supercargo, or any person or organisation involved in cargo handling operations including pre-arrival notice of readiness, part clearance/health clearance, documentation; |
| 56. | Copies of all cables or radio messages received by the vessel in particular, demonstrating the weather encountered, contact with other vessels, and Ocean Routeing (or similar) messages; |

| | |
|---|---|
| 57. | Photographs demonstrating the condition of the vessel, weather encountered, methods of loading and discharging of the cargo, and stowage of cargo - These will greatly enhance owners' case in the event of disputes. In addition, a note should accompany the photographs identifying when they were taken, by whom, and what they purport to depict. The negatives should be carefully preserved; |
| 58. | Videos — There is an increasing possibility that vessels will carry video equipment, and these can and should be used to identify obvious deficiencies in loading or discharging techniques, methods of stowage, or heavy weather encountered; |
| 59. | Computer printouts — If the vessel has on board a computer capable of doing stability, draft, and trim calculations, the printouts or recorded disks should be preserved. |

### e. Report

Although the master's report should set out the information in the same order that it is listed below, the master should ensure that he assembles the contemporaneous evidence first. The master's report should include the following information:

**1. Details of the master:**

Master's name

Home address

Home telephone number

Age and date of birth

Qualifications

Date of master's certificate and where obtained

Date of first seagoing experience

Date when first assumed command of a vessel

Date when first sailed on present vessel.

**2. Details of the vessel:**

Vessel's name

Port of registry

Flag

Type of vessel, for example, 'tween decker, bulk carrier, obo, or other

LOA

Beam

Summer draught

Gross registered tonnage

Net registered tonnage

Summer DWT

Classification society status

Number of holds, number of hatches, and type of hatch covers

Layout of double bottom, ballast, and peak tanks (prepare diagram if necessary)

Engine model and type

Position of bilge sounding pipes (prepare diagram if necessary)

Position of DBT sounding and overflow pipes (prepare diagram if necessary)

Note whether the vessel has any of the following navigational equipment:

- AIS
- Gyro/magnetic compass
- Repeaters on wings
- Radar (note the range and type of radar)
- Decca/loran
- RDF
- Satellite navigation equipment
- Echo sounder
- Course recorder
- Radio equipment including VHF
- Anemometer
- Other equipment

Vessel's complement.

3. **Details of preliminary voyage to load port:**

Previous cargo carried

Weather encountered

Ballast distribution

Condition of holds prior to loading (if relevant, include the work done by crew to clean holds)

Whether or not the bilge pump suction ability was checked on passage or before loading

Whether or not ballast tanks were pressed up on passage before loading.

4. **Details of loading operation:**

Name of load port

Details of pre-arrival notice requirements

When and where the Notice of Readiness was tendered

Details of free pratique formalities

Draft restrictions

Date(s) of arrival

Name of loading berth(s)

Time(s) of berthing

Name of owners' representative, if attending

Name(s) of surveyor(s) if attending and the parties which they represent

Cargo type or types

Whether or not specific instructions were given as to the nature of cargo and method of loading and if so by whom

Details of reporting procedures

Method of loading (ship's equipment, shore equipment, grabs, elevator, or other).

5. **Loading sequence:**

Dates and times when cargo loaded

Quantity loaded

Stoppages

Whether or not a tally was taken of the cargo and if so by whom (ship's agents, charterers' agents, shippers' agents, or deck officer)

Problems involved in loading operations and whether any protests were issued

Details of shippers' documentation procedures

Details of any cargo information obtained or provided.

Whether or not an inspection of the cargo stowage areas had been carried out prior to loading

Whether cargo handling equipment was tested/inspected prior to arrival

Whether necessary isolation procedures or fuel, ballast or other cargo was checked and found effective.

6. **Details of lashing, stowage and trimming:**

Whether or not specific instructions were given, and if so by whom

Whether or not shore labour or equipment was used and if so which companies were involved, and by whom was the shore labour appointed

Whether or not dunnage was used and if so by whom was it provided and what was its nature

Who carried out trimming operations

Who carried out lashing operations

Describe the number and dimension of lashing wires used and points (if necessary prepare a diagram)

Details of draft survey (if any) before commencement and on completion of loading

Whether or not the mate's receipt was claused

Who issued the bills of lading and whether or not they were claused and consistent with the mate's receipt (if not, why not)

Details of the closing of hatches, when were they closed, checked (and by whom) and whether or not any problems were encountered.

7. **Details of loaded voyage** (the following information should be included if it is not apparent from the deck log abstracts or deck log)**:**

Date of sailing, destination, speed, and course intended

Periods of heavy weather encountered including method of assessment of wind speed, for example, wave observation or anemometer

Changes in course or speed and reasons for the alterations

Wave and sea state on Beaufort scale

Damage suffered by deck fittings and equipment (if any)

Loss of deck fittings and equipment (if any)

Frequency of weather reports received and their accuracy

Whether or not ocean routeing or similar service was used

Whether or not the ship was in radio contact with other vessels and if so their names

Ballast distribution on sailing and any changes made or occurring during voyage

Whether or not hatches were opened and if so why and when

Periods during which cargo was ventilated and in which holds

Whether or not readings listed below were taken and if so with what frequency:

- Cargo temperatures
- Bilge soundings
- Seawater temperatures
- Air temperatures

Whether or not regular checks had been carried out on the securing of the cargo

Whether or not regular checks had been carried out confirming isolation of the cargo from fuel, ballast and other cargo

Whether or not regular checks had been carried out on the water tightness of hatch covers.

8. **Details of discharging operation:**

Name of and time of arrival at discharge port

Draft survey on arrival

Name and time of berthing at discharge berth

Details of the shore/terminal reception area

Name of attending surveyor

Name of attending supercargo

Name of ship's agent

Whether or not specific instructions were given regarding method of discharge and if so by whom

Type of equipment used and whether it was ship's equipment or shore equipment

Dates and times when cargo discharged

Quantity discharged

Whether or not a tally of the cargo was taken and if so by whom (ship's agents, charterers' agents, shippers' agents, or deck officer)

Whether or not particular problems were encountered during the discharging operation

Whether or not shore labour was involved and if so what company and by whom was the shore labour appointed.

9. **Details of loss, shortage, or damage:**

When was the first report of loss, shortage, or damage made and by whom and to whom was it sent

Did a joint inspection take place and if so name parties involved, their representatives and note the date of the inspection

Where was cargo discharged and stored

Whether or not any attempt was made to segregate damaged cargo from good cargo and if so

- How was this done

- Was the method used agreed by the ship and if not was a protest made

- What is an estimate of the period of delay to the vessel whilst the cargo was being segregated

- Was cargo abandoned on deck and if so how much approximately

Weather conditions encountered during discharge

If damage arose as a result of insufficiency of packing, how was the packing deficient and did the equipment used by the stevedores, type of dunnage used, method of stowing or lashing, or general handling of the cargo contribute to the damage.

## f. Case study

### Background to the incident

A bulk carrier of about 70,000 DWT was operating under a time charter for one trip from the West coast of the United States to India, and loaded almost a full cargo of bulk wheat.

During the initial stages of the voyage, the vessel encountered severe weather conditions as a result of which there was an ingress of water through the hatch covers which seriously damaged the cargo. Further damage was caused at the discharge port when sound and wet cargo were mixed. A total of nearly 8,000 mt of cargo was affected, and a claim in excess of one and a half million US dollars was brought against the vessel.

The charterers, who were initially liable for the damage, claimed an indemnity from the owners, and the dispute was submitted to arbitration. The owners sought to rely on the Hague Rules' perils of the sea defence. However, the charterers alleged that the owners had failed to exercise due diligence to make the patent hatch covers seaworthy.

## Consideration of relevant evidence

In support of their arguments that the weather encountered by the vessel had been severe the owners submitted the vessel's log books as well as a video taken by the master during the voyage. The log book entries showed that from an early stage in the voyage, the vessel encountered winds of force 6 to 7 from the South East with accompanying rough seas, increasing in strength over the following two days to force 8. The vessel then encountered force 9 winds from the West South West with heavy seas causing the vessel to pitch and roll and ship seas. In the next two days the worst weather was recorded with westerly winds of force 9 to 11 and huge waves. At this stage the vessel had to heave to for about 24 hours and eventually headed south to get away from the violent weather. During this period the vessel suffered damage and well-secured drums of lubricant at the stern were carried away. The winds slowly abated to below force 7 during the following two to three day period.

The evidence contained in the log books was supported by a twenty minute video film taken by the master during the voyage. The arbitrators found that the film did not demonstrate that the weather had been as ferocious as recorded in the log book, but conceded that it was not possible to film during the worst of the weather and that the film would not show the full magnitude of the high seas and swell. The arbitrators were also impressed by the oral evidence from the master of the vessel who they found an honest and reliable witness, corroborating evidence from another vessel in the area during the same time as the subject vessel, the extent of damage suffered by the vessel and the carrying away of the drums of lubricant.

Before the owners could invoke the perils of the sea defence they had to demonstrate that they had exercised due diligence to make the vessel seaworthy before the voyage commenced. The owners submitted evidence of the maintenance of the vessel prior to the voyage as well as contemporaneous evidence demonstrating the condition of the hatch covers.

The vessel had been in dry-dock one month prior to the voyage and had undergone general repairs including repairs to the hatch coamings. At this time hatchways and closing appliances were inspected by class surveyors and were found to be in good condition. A letter from the classification society stated that hose testing of the hatch covers was carried out with satisfactory results and that the surveyor was satisfied with the water tightness of the hatch covers. The master had stated during his testimony before the arbitrators that the surveyor had not only watched the hose testing on the hatch covers, but also went down into each hatch after the test in order to ensure that there were no leakages. A ballast voyage was then undertaken between the dry-dock port and the first load port on the chartered voyage.

The owners also submitted contemporaneous evidence. The reports of three independent surveyors, who examined the hatch covers at the discharge port, confirmed their good order and condition. In addition, the surveyors' reports showed that there was salt water damage to all the hatches. If there had been salt water damage to only some of the hatches, the arbitrators may have drawn adverse inferences about the seaworthiness of these hatches. Finally, the video film taken by the master demonstrated that the vessel on the whole looked well maintained and the hatch covers, in particular, appeared to be in good condition.

### *Outcome*

The arbitrators held that if the owners had exercised due diligence to make the vessel seaworthy they could successfully rely on the perils of the sea defence because the vessel had encountered severe weather even though the weather was not entirely unexpected or unusual. The arbitrators stated that if this was not correct the defence would never apply to areas like the North Atlantic or North Pacific where severe weather is often encountered in the winter.

The arbitrators found that the evidence suggested that the owners had exercised due diligence to make the vessel seaworthy before the vessel sailed from the first load port. They also commented that they had no reason to believe that the hatch covers were not properly secured on the completion of loading.

The arbitrators further stated that in certain circumstances well maintained hatch covers will flex in periods of severe weather and permit the ingress of sea water. Therefore, provided owners had exercised due diligence to make the vessel seaworthy, they could avoid liability by relying on the perils of the sea defence.

Although it is very difficult to rely on a heavy weather defence, the arbitrators in the present case were impressed by the well kept log book and the video film.

Although not every vessel will have a video camera on board, a series of still photographs could also be of great evidential value in demonstrating bad weather and the condition of the vessel.

## General Average

The principles of general average have evolved from ancient times as a means of compensating parties with a common interest in a maritime venture, if property has to be sacrificed or expenditure incurred, to save the venture as a whole. From its simple origin as an agreement between merchants, general average has matured into a complex branch of shipping law governed by precise rules and conventions.

### a. Conceptual background

### *What is general average?*

The main principles of general average are contained in the York-Antwerp Rules, 1994. The Rules define a general average act as follows:

*"There is a general average act when, and only when, any extraordinary sacrifice or expenditure is intentionally and reasonably made or incurred for the common safety for the purpose of preserving from peril the property involved in a common maritime adventure."*

In the context of marine insurance, the word "average" means a partial loss. General average must be distinguished from "particular average" which means an insured loss. For example, if fire is discovered on board a laden vessel, the following items make up the general average loss:

- Cost of damage caused by water or any other methods used to extinguish the fire

- Cost of repair if ship's structure has to be altered to gain access to fire

- Value of any cargo damaged or jettisoned during efforts to control fire

- Cost of using the ship's equipment and the wages of the crew during the general average incident.

In another example, if a vessel runs aground in a dangerous position, the following items would make up the general average loss:

- Cost of tugs to refloat the vessel, including the value of any salvage award

- Cost of running ship's engines and other equipment to assist refloating

- Cost of discharging cargo into lighters and the cost of reloading

- Cost of pollution removal if cargo has been jettisoned and the value of the lost cargo

- Stores consumed and wages paid to crew during the general average incident.

It is important to note that items of particular average are not calculated as part of the general average loss. In the grounding situation, for example, damage caused to vessel as a consequence of the grounding would not be a part of the general average loss, but would form a hull and machinery claim.

### Who are the interested parties and how is general average assessed?

The general average incident will necessarily involve some part of the cargo or ship being sacrificed or extra expenditure being incurred to save the entire venture. The interested parties to the maritime venture, normally the shipowner, the cargo owner, and the charterer, will compensate the party who has suffered the general average loss by making contributions in proportion to the value of their relative interests in the venture as a whole.

The **shipowner's** interest in the venture is determined by the current value of the vessel at the termination of the venture. Time charter hire is normally excluded from owner's total interest but may be included depending on the terms of the charter. In voyage charters, the amount of bunkers onboard would be included in the shipowners valuation.

The **time charterer's** interest in the venture is determined by the value of bunkers remaining onboard at the time of the incident, plus the freight at risk on the voyage.

The **cargo owner's** interest is determined by the sound market value of the cargo on the last day of discharge.

The assessment of each party's contribution is called an "average adjustment". In recent times, the principles by which an adjustment is made are generally governed by the York-Antwerp Rules, 1994. The rules ensure that all average adjustments conform to an international standard. The adjustment is made by an **average adjuster**. The average adjuster is appointed by the shipowner to collect all the facts surrounding the incident and to collect guarantees from various parties before cargo is discharged. The adjuster will have all the facts and figures at his disposal, and thus, in addition to calculating the contributions due from each party, he will be frequently requested to adjust any resulting hull claim.

### *When is general average declared?*

The declaration is normally made by the shipowner, but in certain countries any one of the interested parties may initiate an adjustment. A declaration must be made before the delivery of the cargo. Shipowners usually will allow delivery of the cargo when the other interested parties to the venture provide suitable security sufficient to cover their contribution.

### b. Potential exposure / problem

The most likely problem with which the ship operator is going to be confronted is a non-payment by cargo interests of their contribution towards the General Average losses or expenditure. Clearly, the ship operator should have ensured that suitable G.A. guarantees had been obtained prior to handing over the cargo – this should overcome the problem of a pure 'bad debt'. However, what frequently happens in practice is that cargo interests allege that the event which led to the G.A. incident was caused by some unseaworthiness of the vessel before or at the commencement of the voyage and that the carrier / ship operator had failed to exercise due diligence to make the vessel seaworthy. If the cargo interests can sustain this allegation then they will not be obliged to contribute to the G.A.

It is therefore important to ensure that the circumstances leading up to the G.A. incident are thoroughly investigated with such a possible allegation of unseaworthiness in mind — this will usually be beyond the interest of the G.A. adjuster / surveyor.

### c. ISM implications

As was explained in the section on 'cargo damage, loss or shortage' above, the standards and practices of the industry, post 1 July 1998 / 1 July 2002, are now the ISM Code. The test of whether the necessary due diligence has been exercised will be evident from the procedures of the SMS and the evidence produced to demonstrate that those procedures were followed. This general concept will also apply to allegations being made by cargo interest who might be challenging their obligation to contribute to G.A.

The following, non-exhaustive, list attempts to address some of the more obvious potential implications and, consequently, suggest areas of the SMS which will come under close scrutiny:

Section 1.2    Objectives

The objectives of the ISM Code, as set out in Section 1.2 does not only apply to protection of people and the environment but also includes '…the …avoidance of damage to … property…' – which would include cargo.

Section 5    Master's responsibility and authority

Section 6    Resources and personnel

In Sections 5 and 6 of the Code there is a lot of emphasis put upon the obligation of the company to provide the proper people – including the master and crew – who are properly qualified, trained and in all respects suitable to carry out there particular job on board that particular ship. In the *Eurasian Dream* case, the master was qualified and did have considerable experience on bulk carriers – however, he had no experience on car carriers and this lack of experience was one of a number of factors which led the judge to conclude that the ship was unseaworthy. The master and other officers were also inadequately trained and familiarised with the particular ship, specifically its fire fighting equipment, and this was another factor in the unseaworthiness equation.

Section 7    Development of plans for shipboard operations

Clearly it will depend upon what has happened which has led to the G.A. situation to determine the relevance of Section 7. However, the usual types of incidents would include machinery failure, fire, and similar events which would tend to be covered as a 'key shipboard operation'. The type of ship will determine what procedures and plans would be included in the SMS.

Section 8    Emergency preparedness

To what extent the G.A. incident would fall subject to the requirements of Section 8 – Emergency Preparedness – would depend upon the nature of the event. However, by its very nature it is likely to involve an emergency type situation and hence Section 8 will be of relevance.

Section 9    Reports and analysis of non-conformities, accidents and hazardous
             occurrences

Records of the activities anticipated by Section 9 may well be examined to confirm that learning opportunities were being taken as part of the SMS. Similarly minutes of on board safety committee meetings may be examined to determine the level of involvement and commitment to safety management on board

Section 10    Maintenance of the ship and equipment

To what extent this may be relevant will obviously be determined by reference to the cause leading to the G.A. incident. If the failure of a piece of equipment was involved then the procedures and records will be examined very carefully. In the case of the *Eurasian Dream* there were numerous items of fire fighting equipment which were found to be deficient and these issues also contributed towards the judge finding the ship to be unseaworthy.

Section 11    Documentation

If there appear to have been problems with compliance with the SMS then it is likely that a closer look will be made at the documented procedures themselves. If these are voluminous, irrelevant or otherwise inadequate then the Company is likely to come under severe criticism.

Section 12    Company verification, review and evaluation

There is a very clear obligation on the Company to ensure that the SMS is working properly on board its vessels. If a serious incident has arisen, as in this case with a collision, then it can be anticipated that the active monitoring by the company will be looked at very closely by way of audit trails.

Certification and verification

As a matter of course the validity of the SMC and DOC will be checked


**d. Nature of evidence required**

Following a general average incident, ship agents and surveyors play a significant role. A ship agent, in addition to the normal duties of port and husbandry agency, will assist the master in the aftermath of a general average incident to make a declaration which complies with the local law and custom of the port. Once the average adjuster has confirmed that security has been obtained from all the interested parties, the agent will be instructed by the ship operator to permit delivery of the cargo. If cargo has been discharged to lighten the vessel, or cargo has been transhipped to a final destination, the agent will be responsible for keeping full and complete records of all movements and expenditure attributable to the general average.

After any incident, a large number of surveyors representing various interests will descend on the vessel. Some of these surveyors will not be involved directly in the general average process, for example, those acting on behalf of hull underwriters, the classification society, or state officials. However, if it has become necessary to sacrifice or discharge a part of the cargo before arrival at the final destination stated on the bill of lading, the ship operator will appoint surveyors to report on the condition and quantity of cargo. Such surveyors, usually called general average surveyors, will act in the interests of all the parties involved (and may also represent hull and machinery interests). If possible, the account representing expenditure incurred should be examined and approved by the general average surveyor before settlement.

On the other hand, surveyors appointed by cargo interests only represent the interests of their client. They may criticise the action taken by the master or allege that the vessel was unseaworthy — as discussed above. Therefore, if an incident occurs which may give rise to a general average act and, if time permits (for example, in a grounding incident), the master should consult ship operators and cargo interests to discuss the best possible course of action. Prior consultation may resolve disagreements and help to avoid later disputes.

In most cases of general average, the main evidence for the adjustment is obtained from the various survey reports. The master should ensure that a clear and accurate account of events is given to surveyors. The survey reports will be supported by witness statements and the vessel's records. When draft surveys and other calculations are being performed, it is advisable for the master to ensure that a responsible officer is on hand to guide and assist the surveyor.

Examples of documentation used to prepare the adjustment are as follows:

- Casualty reports prepared by the master.

- Survey reports prepared by attending surveyors.

- Log extracts and other available records from the vessel.

- Copies of communications/instructions relating to the incident.

- Statements, which are prepared by owner's solicitors, taken from personnel involved in the incident.

- Details of all expenses incurred as a consequence of the general average act fully supported by invoices (including onward charges for cargo if transhipped).

- Salvage award.

- Copies of all port papers covering the period during which the incident occurred.

- Full cargo manifest and valuation information for cargo.

- Vessel's valuation adjusted for any damage repairs allowable in general average.

- Statement of fuels and stores consumed and labour used during the general average act.

- All documentation covering the security provided by all interested parties.

## e. Report

### The master's role

The master must be prepared to assume the widest possible role in solving all the problems created by an incident if there is an urgent need to do so and assistance is not readily available. Apart from good seamanship and reasonable judgement, the master must ensure that the history of the incident is recorded accurately and fully. The record should include details of all actions taken by the various parties involved and include their names and organisations. If possible, the master should ensure that a photographic record of the events is made. The master's evidence will be crucial as it is usual for a year or more to elapse between the incident and issue of the "Statement of General Average".

If salvage services are involved, the master should ensure that a full record is made of the salvor's actions and the equipment used. This evidence, together with an assessment of the dangers involved, will determine the level of the salvage award (further information on salvage may be found in the next section below).

## f. Case study

### Background to the incident

A 30,000 deadweight tons bulk carrier was time chartered into a service carrying to carry bulk grain from North America to Europe. The time charterers sub-chartered the vessel on a time charter basis to carry steel and containers Westbound across the Atlantic.

Under the sub-charter the vessel loaded in one Northern European port:

- steel coils in holds 1,2,3 and 5

- in hold number 4 a mix of twenty-eight 20 foot and 40 foot containers were loaded in a stack in the hatch square.

On passing Lands End, at the extreme Western tip of England, at 2000 hrs. the vessel started to encounter a Westerly swell coming in from the Atlantic. The vessel started to roll and pitch. At 2130 hrs there was a loud crashing sound. The master was called to the bridge. The third mate and chief officer were sent to investigate. In number 4 hold they found that the stack of containers had fallen over to starboard. Two large pieces of machinery parts from some containers were moving violently between the collapsed stack and crashing into the ships side.

Upon reporting the situation to the master, fearing for the safety of ship and cargo, the decision was taken to divert to the port of Cork, on the South coast of Ireland, as a port of refuge. A note of protest was lodged and General Average declared upon arrival Cork.

Because of lack of suitable facilities in Cork, the collapsed stack and loose machinery parts were secured and the vessel proceeded to Liverpool where suitable cranes and labour was available to remove the collapsed containers and their contents.

G.A. adjusters were appointed and G.A. security was obtained from cargo interests. The offloading and remedial steps to get the containerised cargo reconditioned and put back on board took three weeks. General Average expenditure amounted to a figure close to U.S. $400,000. Particular Average damage to the cargo was quantified at more than U.S. $1,500,000.

A number of the individual cargo owners presented their damage and loss claims to the shipowner, as carrier under the bills of lading, and also challenged their obligation to contribute to the General Average expenditure.

### Consideration of relevant evidence

Expert surveyors were appointed in Liverpool to oversee the removal of the collapsed stow of containers, the reconditioning of the cargo and the reloading where possible. They re-coded and quantified the extent of damage to individual containers and their contents. The surveyors also conducted an investigation to try and establish why the stack had collapsed. Their written reports were backed up with numerous photographs.

Maritime solicitors were instructed to interview the master, and other ship staff, and to generally work alongside the surveyors to investigate the reason why the stack collapsed.

The surveyors established that the containers had been loaded into a stack with almost no securing. There was no securing of any description to the tank top of the hold. There were no twist locks or bridging pieces to lock the containers together. The only securing were four chains at each end of the stack, each with a breaking strain of 20 tonnes. The chains connected the top most corner of the upper most container to the bottom corner casting of the lower most container at the extreme ends of the stack. The total stack weight was in the region of 500 tonnes.

From interviews with the master and chief officer (C/O) it transpired that:

- Both the master and C/O were very experienced bulk carrier people.

- Neither the master or C/O had ever carried containers before.

- Neither the master or C/O had ever been involved in a serious incident previously.

- They were both concerned about the adequacy of the lashings and securing of the container stack at the load-port.

- A sub-charterers supercargo insisted that he had been loading containers into bulk carriers in this manner for 12 years and had never encountered a problem.

- The super-cargo's claim was apparently confirmed by the stevedore foreman.

- Although unhappy with the situation the master conceded to the apparent superior knowledge of the super-cargo and sailed.

### Outcome

From an analysis of all the evidence it was agreed by the P&I Clubs involved, and their respective members, that:

- The vessel was probably unseaworthy at the commencement of the voyage on account of the inadequate stowage and securing of the containers in hold number 4.

- The seaworthiness of the vessel was probably compromised on account of the lack of experience of the master and C/O with the carriage of containers.

- The sub-charterers were complicit in the inadequate stowage and securing of the containers through the actions of their super-cargo and appointed stevedores.

- The head charterers had to accept some responsibility towards the shipowners under the terms of the head charterparty on account of the activities of their sub-charterers.

An agreement was therefore reached to settle the cargo claims on the best possible terms out of court and also to concede any G.A. contributions that were being withheld by cargo interests.

Both the master and the chief officer were so badly affected by the incident that neither of them returned to their seagoing career.

## Salvage

"Salvage" is payment made or due to a salvor for saving a ship and/or its cargo from loss, damage, wreck, capture, or rescue of property from fire.

A salvor is any vessel or person who renders salvage services to a vessel, and may include pilots, foyboatmen and others who provide equipment to render the services. The salvor must be a volunteer; consequently port authorities or the crew of the salved vessel may all be excluded from claiming salvage as they are under a public or private duty to assist the vessel.

There are three basic criteria which must be met for services to be regarded as salvage:

- Firstly, the object of the salvage should be in danger, although not necessarily imminent danger.

- Secondly, the services rendered by salvors must be beneficial to the salved property.

- Thirdly, the services must be successful (although there is an exception to this in respect of claims under Article 14 of the Salvage Convention which relate to circumstances where there is a threat of damage to the environment).

## a. Conceptual background

### The salvage contract

Salvage services do not need to be rendered under contract provided that they meet the three criteria above. Most salvage services are conducted on Lloyd's Open Form (LOF) which is a no cure no pay agreement.

LOF is designed to expedite the saving of property in danger as there is no possibility of debate about the amounts payable to salvors at the time of danger. If subsequently the parties cannot agree to the reward due under the LOF, the matter is placed before an arbitrator chosen by the Committee of Lloyds.

The arbitrator after consideration of all the available evidence makes a salvage award which he believes fair and just to all parties concerned. In cases of salvage not governed by contract, the amount of the award will usually be decided by a court. Payment of the salvage award is made to the salvors. The parties with an interest in the property salved make contributions to the award in proportion to the salvaged value of their interest.

If salvage services are required and if time allows, it is important that the master informs his owners as soon as a casualty occurs to prevent the salvage services becoming more urgent and consequently more expensive. The London Salvage Convention 1989 gives the master authority to conclude a salvage contract on behalf of the owners of the vessel and on behalf of those who have property on board, namely the cargo owners and possibly charterers.

However, the convention does not apply in some countries and the master may not have this authority. Therefore, where time and circumstances permit, the ship operator or the master should obtain the authority of the cargo owners and charterers before agreeing to the terms on which the salvage services will be rendered. Where it proves impossible to contact them or where there is insufficient time because of the circumstances or urgency of the situation, the master himself may negotiate the terms of the salvage agreement with the salvors, subject to the owner's standing instructions. From a practical point of view the master will not normally know, in the heat of the moment, whether the convention applies to his circumstances or not. The safest course of action, therefore, is to assume that it does not apply and to try to seek cargo owners and charterer's agreement before agreement to salvage services unless the matter is urgent and the time taken to obtain that agreement would greatly increase the risk to the ship and cargo. The master should not hesitate to do what is necessary in the circumstances to save life and preserve ship and cargo.

Finally, it is important to note that most salvage agreements, including the LOF, require full co-operation between the crew of the salved vessel and the salvors. Although there may be substantial tension between the two parties, the master should ensure that his crew fully assist and co-operate with the salvors.

LOF 90, LOF 95 and the 1989 Salvage Convention also contain provisions for the payment of an award of special compensation to salvors in circumstances where there was a threat of damage to the environment. This can occur where the amount which would normally be awarded as salvage is less than the salvors' expenses of the whole salvage operation plus a reasonable margin. This is usually because the ship and cargo have little or no value at the time of completion of the operation. Awards for special compensation are paid only by the shipowner (or his P&I Club) and not by owners of other property on board.

In cases where there is a risk of damage to the environment, however remote, a comprehensive record of all salvors' activities (not just those related to pollution) should be kept. This record should include full details of all equipment and men used on a daily basis, and will enable shipowners' solicitors to check salvors' evidence of their expenses.

### b. Potential exposure / problem

As with any other G.A. type incident, described above, the most likely problem with which the ship operator is going to be confronted is a non-payment by cargo interests of their contribution towards the salvage. Clearly, the ship operator should have ensured that suitable Salvage / G.A. guarantees had been obtained prior to handing over the cargo — this should overcome the problem of a pure 'bad debt'. However, what frequently happens in practice is that cargo interests allege that the event which led to the salvage services being required was caused by some unseaworthiness of the vessel before or at the commencement of the voyage and that the carrier / ship operator had failed to exercise due diligence to make the vessel seaworthy. If the cargo interests can sustain this allegation then they will not be obliged to contribute to the salvage costs. It is therefore important to ensure that the circumstances leading up to the salvage incident are thoroughly investigated with such a possible allegation of unseaworthiness in mind.

### c. ISM implications

As was explained in the section on 'cargo damage, loss or shortage' above, the standards and practices of the industry, post 1 July 1998 / 1 July 2002, are now the ISM Code. The test of whether the necessary due diligence has been exercised will be evident from the procedures of the SMS and the evidence produced to demonstrate that those procedures were followed. This general concept will also apply to allegations being made by cargo interest who might be challenging their obligation to contribute towards the cost of salvage.

The following, non-exhaustive, list attempts to address some of the more obvious potential implications and, consequently, suggest areas of the SMS which will come under close scrutiny:

Section 1.2    Objectives

The objectives of the ISM Code, as set out in Section 1.2 does not only apply to protection of people and the environment but also includes '...the ...avoidance of damage to ... property...' – which would include ship and cargo.

Section 5    Master's responsibility and authority

Section 6    Resources and personnel

In Sections 5 and 6 of the Code there is a lot of emphasis put upon the obligation of the company to provide the proper people – including the master and crew – who are properly qualified, trained and in all respects suitable to carry out there particular job on board that particular ship. In the *Eurasian Dream* case, the master was qualified and did have considerable experience on bulk carriers – however, he had no experience on car carriers and this lack of experience was one of a number of factors which led the judge to conclude that the ship was unseaworthy. The master and other officers were also inadequately trained and familiarised with the particular ship, specifically its fire fighting equipment, and this was another factor in the unseaworthiness equation.

Section 7    Development of plans for shipboard operations

Clearly it will depend upon what has happened which has led to salvage services being required to determine the relevance of Section 7. However, the usual types of incidents would include machinery failure, fire, and similar events which would tend to be covered as a 'key shipboard operation'. The type of ship will determine what procedures and plans would be included in the SMS.

Section 8    Emergency preparedness

To what extent the salvage incident would fall subject to the requirements of Section 8 — Emergency Preparedness — would depend upon the nature of the event. However, by its very nature it is likely to involve an emergency type situation and hence Section 8 will be of relevance.

Section 9    Reports and analysis of non-conformities, accidents and hazardous occurrences

Records of the activities anticipated by Section 9 may well be examined to confirm that learning opportunities were being taken as part of the SMS. Similarly minutes of on board safety committee meetings may be examined to determine the level of involvement and commitment to safety management on board

Section 10    Maintenance of the ship and equipment

To what extent this may be relevant will obviously be determined by reference to the cause leading to the salvage incident. If the failure of a piece of equipment was involved then the procedures and records will be examined very carefully. In the case of the *Eurasian Dream* there were numerous items of fire fighting equipment which was found to be deficient and these issues also contributed towards the judge finding the ship to be unseaworthy.

Section 11    Documentation

If there appear to have been problems with compliance with the SMS then it is likely that a closer look will be made at the documented procedures themselves. If these are voluminous, irrelevant or otherwise inadequate then the Company is likely to come under severe criticism.

Section 12    Company verification, review and evaluation

There is a very clear obligation on the Company to ensure that the SMS is working properly on board its vessels. If a serious incident has arisen, as in this case with a collision, then it can be anticipated that the active monitoring by the company will be looked at very closely by way of audit trails.

Certification and verification

As a matter of course the validity of the SMC and DOC will be checked

### d. Nature of evidence required

It is important to note that the type of evidence listed in this section will be relevant whether the master finds his vessel in a position to render salvage services or whether the vessel is the recipient of such services. The evidence required from the vessel will depend on the circumstances in which salvage services are rendered and particular situations are discussed below. However, there are certain crucial items of evidence which will be required in all claims involving salvage, and therefore, if a casualty occurs, the master should follow the procedures listed below:

*Procedures*
- Ensure that an accurate record is kept of any conversations relating to a salvage agreement. If at all possible, where an agreement is reached by radio, an independent third party should be asked to take notes for future reference

- Ensure that a precise record is kept of the time of the commencement of salvage services, the times of any communication relating to salvage agreements, and time of arrival of salvage vessels

- Delegate a record keeper or clerk whose task it is to fully and accurately record events in writing, by photographs, or any available method; including any discussion with salvors as to methods proposed

- Ensure that deck, engine and radio log books are accurate and current, and in particular the deck logs contain regular records of the vessel's position.

In addition to the above items, in the following situations where salvage services may be required, the record keeper should keep a note of the items listed below. Some of them may be relevant to other sections of this book, which should be consulted for more detail, and the list below should not be viewed as a quick reference guide.

## Main engine breakdown

- The vessel's position, recorded at frequent intervals

- The extent of damage and the prospects of repairing the engine unassisted, and the crew's ability to complete such repairs

- The prospects of repair at sea or in a port of refuge

- The wind force and direction and tidal or other currents together with all weather forecasts

- If the vessel has to be towed, details of the tow, the distance towed, any difficulties on the tow, and the weather conditions during the tow including video film or photographs, and

- The identity of any alternative salvors.

## Grounding

- The nature of the bottom, the manner in which the vessel went aground, and soundings taken around the vessel at regular intervals

- The vessel's position and her heading when she grounded

- The prospects of refloating the vessel unassisted

- Whether or not the vessel is being driven further aground

- Whether or not the vessel's auxiliaries and main engine are available for use

- Details of the pre-stranding draft of the vessel and the draft when she went aground with particular reference to tidal conditions

- Any indication that the vessel is moving whilst aground

- Whether or not the vessel is hogging or sagging

- Details of any cargo damage

- The extent of damage to the vessel, if any

- Details of any personal injuries

- Weather conditions including the wind direction

- Weights on board the vessel and where carried, together with copies of all calculations of the ship stability

- Condition and contents of tanks at regular intervals

- Details of any pollution

- Details of other tugs or other vessels assisting to refloat the vessel and the length of time they were engaged in pulling the vessel, and

- Details of lightering operations, including the number of gangs used, the names of lightering vessels, the vessel's draft on commencement and completion of lightering, and the amount of cargo discharged. Details and causes of cargo lost/damaged during transshipment

- In addition the master should retain a copy of divers' reports on the condition of the vessel's bottom.


## Collision
- The condition of the vessel and the extent of damage

- If there was an ingress of sea water, the areas of the vessel which were flooded, the attempts made to seal openings, whether or not the doors were water tight

- Details of any personal injuries

- Calculation of the ship stability

- Details of any cargo damage

- Whether or not the vessel's pumps, generators and auxiliary machinery remain operable

- Whether or not there is a danger of the vessel sinking, and

- The equipment used by salvors

- In addition, the master should retain a copy of any reports made by surveyors or naval architects

- Details of any pollution.


## Fire
- Where on the vessel the fire started and the extent of damage

- What combustible material is there on board the vessel which the fire may reach

- Details of any cargo damage

- Attempts made by the crew to extinguish the fire including details of the use of foam, $CO_2$, or portable pumps (including calculation of the ship's stability which is carried out to determine which fire fighting options are available)

- Details of any personal injuries

- If available, readings of explosimeters, and

- Whether or not there is a danger of explosion and whether or not the tanks are gas free or inerted

- If tugs and other fire fighting craft involved, their names, positions, and details of their fire fighting operations

- The position of monitors and hoses, and

- The time taken to extinguish the fire.

If the fire is serious, a fire expert will probably be appointed by owners as soon as possible to determine the cause of the fire and possibly advise on fire fighting methods. The master should ensure that the area where the fire started is disturbed as little as possible.

### War

- Details of the current war situation in the area

- Whether or not the attack on the vessel is part of a campaign

- Details of the last attack on a merchant vessel, and

- The chances of a second strike

- Details of any personal injuries

- Details of any cargo damage

- The master should ensure that the Salvage Association is informed of any attacks and the extent of the damage

- Details of any pollution.

### e. Report

Masters often prepare a factual account of an incident shortly afterwards. This is usually in the form of a report to the owners or an aide memoire to assist in the preparing of the statements. This is clearly a useful practice but such a factual account should be in addition to detailed records set out above and not in place of them.

### f. Case study

This case study is based upon an incident which occurred on board the product tanker *Torepo* which became the subject of a dispute between the shipowners and cargo interests in which the ship had run aground and had to be salvaged. Cargo owners / their subrogated insurers were challenging their obligation to contribute towards the salvage costs. It was necessary to look in some detail at evidence which would demonstrate the extent to which the navigation and bridge management procedures were being operated effectively. In this case, which was heard by the Admiralty Judge Mr Justice Steel in the Admiralty Court in London in July 2002.

### Background to the incident
*Brief facts:*

- *Torepo* was a product tanker
- On a loaded voyage from Argentina to Ecuador via Patagonian Channel
- Vessel grounded
- Vessel had to be salvaged
- There were no serious personal injuries
- There was no pollution or loss of cargo
- The cargo owners attempted to recover their contribution to the salvage.

### The basis of the claim

- The cargo owners / subrogated underwriters were claiming for a recovery of their contribution towards the salvage expenses incurred in the refloating operation.

- The basic argument was that there had been a breach of the contract of carriage in that the ship was unseaworthy, and the ship operators had failed to exercised due diligence to make the vessel seaworthy.

- Specifically they argued that there were many factors which contributed towards that unseaworthiness, including:

  - No proper bridge team management,

  - No proper system for instructing crew in navigating in confined waters,

  - No proper passage plan for that part of the voyage during which the incident occurred,

  - The vessel was not equipped with adequate charts

  - The echo sounder was defective.

If the cargo claimants were successful with their arguments they would be entitled to recover their contribution to the general average and salvage expenses.

The case was heard before the Admiralty Judge — the Honourable Mr. Justice Steel — a very experienced lawyer and judge in shipping related matters. It is interesting to note that, in his judgement, the judge was clearly very critical of the way in which the claimants had set out their claim and their allegations. On the whole they were unspecific and unsubstantiated.

The judge was also very critical of the expert witness that the claimants had produced to comment specifically on the navigation systems and practices on board *Torepo*. Basically the judge considered the navigation expert to 'lack realism'. This is actually a very interesting, important and enlightened observation on the part of the judge. The expert witness put forward a case for almost absolute perfection — Justice Steel — made it clear that neither he, nor the court, nor ISM expects perfection — but best practice will be expected. It again comes back to the old problem of reasonableness and what might be reasonable within the context of this particular case.

Before we venture off to evaluate the evidence, let us look a little at the background to this incident which happened in July 1997.

*Torepo* was a product tanker of about 25,000 tons deadweight and was more than 20 years old. She was, apparently, in relative terms — bearing in mind her age — a well maintained and well run ship. This was confirmed by 50 or more vetting inspections by oil majors which the ship had been subjected to during the three years prior to this incident.

On this particular occasion the vessel was close to Buenos Aires in the Argentine and was to load a full cargo of gasoline for Ecuador. It was recognised by the master on board, and his navigator — the second mate, that there were at least three routes which the ship could take. They could go North and through the Panama Canal — this would certainly provide the best weather option at that time of year (mid winter in the Southern Hemisphere). They could go South which would provide at least two options: they could sail far South and go round Cape Horn — this would almost certainly involve bad weather. The third option was to cut across the tip of Chile and go through the Patagonian Channel. Up until the time of sailing the charterers would not make a decision as to which route they wanted the vessel to take. The second mate prepared the passage plans for each of the three possibilities. However, he realised that they did not have on board all the appropriate navigation charts — in particular the British Admiralty charts that were being used on board did not adequately cover the Patagonian Channel. The charts required were local Chilean Charts. The master attempted to order the charts from the local chart agent in Buenos Aires — but without success. The ship managers tried to obtain them in Europe and the master tried through the local British Admiralty chart agent in Montevideo, Uruguay. However, all these efforts were in vain — it transpired that these charts were only available inside Chile.

*Torepo* loaded the cargo and set sail — heading South. Eventually the charterers confirmed that the vessel was indeed to proceed through the Patagonian Channel. Local agents were appointed and the master ordered local pilots and also asked that the pilots bring with them copies of the relevant charts.

### The incident

At 0600 hours, on the day of the incident, the vessel was proceeding on her passage through the Patagonian Channel. Everything was proceeding smoothly. The master was in his cabin resting — he had left night orders to the effect that he should be called if the Officer of the Watch was in doubt about anything or otherwise needed the master. The master was intending to return to the bridge at about 0800 hours when the ship would be transiting a particularly difficult part of the Channel. On the bridge was the chief officer, one of the two local pilots (the second pilot was also resting), a helmsman and the cadet officer / lookout. During the course of a few short minutes a whole series of mistakes were to happen.

A major alteration of course was being approached. The pilot went to mark the ship's position on the chart and to transfer the position onto the next chart. As he did that he realised that the latitude and longitude positions did not coincide with the position of adjacent land and islands — in fact there was a difference of one mile. There is nothing particularly unusual about this sort of thing happening — often the surveys on which original charts had been drawn took place many years before and precise positions may have been difficult. However, this was sufficient to distract the pilot's attention for a few minutes. The chief officer realised that the alteration position was being approached but, presumably, by this time had developed a certain amount of confidence in the pilot and had assumed, wrongly, that the pilot must have been delaying the commencement of the turn on account of some local current or similar. The cadet / lookout saw a light open (become visible) but did not report this. In fact this was the light that should have indicated to the pilot when he should turn. By the time the pilot realised that he had over-shot the alteration position the vessel was closing quite rapidly on an island dead ahead. If an attempt was made to alter course at that stage then there would be a serious risk of ripping the side out of the ship which could result in loss of life or personal injuries, an explosion / fire, pollution, loss of cargo and possibly loss of the ship. Instead the correct course of action was taken, apparently without panic; as much speed as possible was taken off the vessel and she was driven straight onto the island. The greatest strength in the ship is in her bows where there are stiffening frames plus a collision bulkhead.

The vessel ran aground at a speed of about six knots. No one was injured, there was no explosion or fire, there was no pollution and no loss of cargo. There was damage to the ship structure at the forward end and a salvage tug had to be engaged which was able to safely pull the vessel off the island with no further loss or damage.

### Consideration of relevant evidence

#### • The witnesses

The main witness of fact was the master of the *Torepo*. The master had served with the company for six years and had sailed previously on Torepo as chief officer. The voyage in question was the master's first trip in command. It would be quite normal in such circumstances for the master to try his very best to make sure that everything ran smoothly during the voyage. He would expect people, both in the office ashore and on board ship, to be watching him very closely and he would want to demonstrate that the decision to promote him to master was a correct decision.

The judge found the master to be "…an intelligent and capable man who responded to cross examination in a straightforward manner…" The master had clearly made a favourable impression on the judge who tended to believe him.

### • Competence of master and crew

As was explained above, the master had sailed with the company for a number of years prior to the incident – and consequently he was familiar with the way the company ran their ships. He had sailed as chief officer on board Torepo and therefore knew the ship very well before he took command. The cadet who was acting as lookout had three years experience at sea.

One week before the incident a vetting survey had taken place on behalf of an oil major. In addition to other things, the inspector noted: '…competence of personnel is no problem…'

### • Vessel's equipment

The only item of equipment which the claimants drew attention to and alleged was not working was the echo sounder. They did not produce any evidence to substantiate that allegation. On the other hand the ship operator was able to produce documents to show that the equipment had been overhauled in dry dock only a week before the incident occurred. A certificate had been issued by the Classification Society confirming that there were no outstanding items and a detailed report of the dry docking had been prepared by a technical manager from the ship operator's office.

### • Procedures and systems

The oil major vetting inspector who had attended the vessel the week before noted in his report: '…the standard of record keeping was very good with everything readily available… operational procedures on board were good…'

The master wrote up standing orders and night orders and generally ensured that the company policy was being followed. The officers of the watch seemed to be aware of the company policy and also read and signed the standing orders and night orders.

A 'Navigational Procedures Manual' was in use on board along with the 'Bridge Procedures Guide' published by the International Chamber of Shipping.

Proper passage plans had been prepared to cover the possible alternative routes that the vessel might take. When the vessel sailed from Buenos Aires she did not have the correct charts on board for the Patagonian Channel — however, these were brought on board by the local pilots who had been engaged to advise the master during that passage. The passage plan and general exchange of information between master, pilots and officers of the watch did take place. Prior to the incident the chief officer had been monitoring the progress on passage including plotting the vessel's position on the chart at regular intervals and using 'Parallel Indexing Techniques' on the radar to check distances off the nearest land.

## Outcome

In his conclusions the judge stated: "...the claimants have failed to establish that the casualty was occasioned by causative unseaworthiness ...their claim accordingly fails..."

The witnesses and the documentary evidence were sufficient to satisfy the judge that, although relatively old, this was a well run ship with a Company and crew who were trying hard to implement and follow good practices i.e. trying hard to make their SMS work. In fact this incident occurred ahead of the Phase I ISM compliance deadline and therefore the preparations were still being made to have a fully verified ISM system in place. The author is in little doubt, having studied the judgement, that the judge did have ISM principles very much in mind when evaluating the evidence and considering what might be the correct level of operational practice.

What had happened in this case was a series of mistakes, human errors, which all occurred at the same time in the same place. They were errors in the navigation / management of the vessel. There was no evidence to indicate that similar errors or mistakes were a regular feature on board this ship — rather what happened was a most unfortunate, sequence of mistakes. Whilst these are the author's words and not those of the judge it is clear that whilst human beings are employed on board ships they will, occasionally, make mistakes — to err is human! Neither the courts nor the ISM Code expect perfection — mistakes will be made. We must use these mistakes as learning opportunities to make sure similar things do not happen in the future. Provided everything else indicates that those involved are trying hard to implement proper safe systems then they should not be punished because of an isolated mistake.

Of course it may not always be possible to exonerate someone who has made a mistake — particularly in cases of 'strict liability' — for example a pollution incident. However, even in such cases, if a ship operator is able to produce witnesses and documentary evidence that, ordinarily, they have very good pollution prevention procedures in place and these are very carefully followed — such that the present incident really was a 'one off' then the fine that may be imposed is likely to be at the lower end of the scale.

## Cargo responsibility clauses — charterparty disputes

There are many different types and forms of charterparties in use: Demise Charters, Time Charters and Voyage Charters. There are different charterparties for different ship types and different cargo types. Clearly it will not be possible to cover all types of charterparties within a book such as this. However, what would be a useful exercise here is to consider generally the nature of disputes which frequently arise under the 'Cargo Responsibility Clauses' of common time and voyage charters.

### a. Conceptual background

It is, first of all, important to recognise and understand, that there are likely to be at least two 'contracts of carriage' involved in any particular shipment of cargo. There is likely to be the contract of carriage evidenced by the Bill of Lading. That contract will be between the owner of the cargo and the carrier. Under most bills of lading, and under English Law, the carrier will almost certainly be the shipowner — although there may be exceptions and other jurisdictions do view the situation differently. The obligations on the carrier will usually be defined by, for example, Article III Rules One and Two of the Hague or Hague Visby Rules:

1. *The carrier shall be bound before and at the beginning of the voyage to exercise due diligence to –*

   a) *Make the ship seaworthy.*

   b) *Properly man, equip and supply the ship.*

   c) *Make the holds, refrigerating and cool chambers, and all other parts of the ship in which goods are carried, fit and safe for their reception, carriage and preservation.*

2. *Subject to the provisions of Article IV, the carrier shall properly and carefully load, handle, stow, carry, keep, care for, and discharge the goods carried.*

Consequently, the obligation to properly load and stow the cargo is upon the 'carrier' – i.e. the shipowner. If the cargo has not been properly loaded and stowed and becomes damaged then the cargo owner will, in all probability, seek compensation and his claim for compensation will be against the shipowner under the terms of the Bill of Lading.

However, under the terms of the governing Charterparty, it may well be that it is the charterer who has agreed to take on the responsibility to load and stow the cargo etc. This responsibility will usually be set out in a clause of the Charterparty which we will refer to as the 'Cargo Responsibility Clause'. Let us consider two such clauses, one under a Voyage Charter and one under a Time Charter, as examples, to understand what is involved:

BIMCO Uniform General Charter as Revised 1922, 1976 and 1994 (GENCON) – Voyage Charter

*Clause 2. Owners' Responsibility Clause*

*The Owners are to be responsible for loss or damage to the goods or for delay in delivery of the goods only in the case the loss, damage or delay has been caused by personal want of due diligence on the part of Owners or their Manager to make the vessel in all respects seaworthy and to secure that she is properly manned, equipped and supplied, or by the personal act or default of the Owners or their Manager.*

*And the Owners are not responsible for loss, damage or delay arising from any other cause whatsoever, even from the neglect or default of the master or crew or some other person employed by the Owners on board or ashore for whose acts they would, but for this Clause, be responsible, or from unseaworthiness of the Vessel on loading or commencement of the voyage or at anytime whatsoever.*

Clause 2 needs to be read in conjunction with Clause 5:

*Clause 5. Loading / Discharging*
*(a) Costs / Risks*
*The cargo shall be brought into the holds, loaded, stowed and / or trimmed, tallied, lashed and / or secured and taken from the holds and discharged by the Charterers, free of any risk, liability and expense whatsoever to the Owners.*

*The Charterers shall provide and lay all dunnage material as required for the proper stowage and protection of the cargo on board, the Owners allowing the use of all dunnage available on board. The Charterers shall be responsible for and pay the cost of removing their dunnage after discharge of the cargo under this Charter Party and time to count until dunnage has been removed.*

On the face of things, under the unamended 1994 Gencon, it will be the charterers who will actually be involved in the loading and stowing of the cargo.

Consider the situation under a typical Time Charter:

The New York Produce Exchange 1993 (NYPE 1993)

*Clause 8. Performance of Voyages*
*(a) The master shall perform the voyages with due despatch, and shall render all customary assistance with the Vessel's crew. The master shall be conversant with the English language and (although appointed by the Owners) shall be under the orders and directions of the Charterers as regards employment and agency; and the Charterers shall perform all cargo handling, including but not limited to loading, stowing, trimming, lashing, securing, dunnaging, unlashing, discharging, and tallying, at their risk and expense, under the supervision of the master.*

Again, on first sight, it would appear that, under an unamended NYPE Charter the charterers are the ones who will be loading and stowing the cargo. However, much judicial discussion has focussed on what was intended by the final few words of this part of Clause 8 – i.e. that the operation had to be done '...*under the supervision of the master...*'

A judgement in the English High Court[1] clarified the position and basically said that even though the charterers are undertaking these functions there is still a responsibility on the master to 'supervise' to the extent that he should ensure that the

---

[1]    Court Line v. Canadian Transport Company Ltd., [1940] A.C. 934

charterers are not loading and stowing the cargo in such a way that it may render the vessel unseaworthy – e.g. with regard to stability and ensuring that the cargo is adequately secured. The courts have consistently reconfirmed the situation that the seaworthiness responsibility is non-delegable as far as the shipowner is concerned.

In the Court Line case the judge pointed out that if it had been the intention of the parties to shift a greater degree of the responsibility for the loading and stowing etc. onto the master / Shipowner then there had already been set up a standard practice (which continues today) of inserting the words '... and responsibility...' after the word '...supervision...' in Clause 8 – such that it would now read:

*Clause 8. Performance of Voyages*
*(a) The master shall ... and the Charterers shall perform all cargo handling, including but not limited to loading, stowing, trimming, lashing, securing, dunnaging, unlashing, discharging, and tallying, at their risk and expense, under the supervision **and responsibility** of the master.*

This amendment to Clause 8 has not shifted all the responsibility onto the master / Shipowner, since the Charterers are still the ones undertaking the operation, but it is now a 'joint operation'.

A practical solution to deciding who would be responsible for which cargo claims arising under an NYPE C/P was agreed upon by participating P&I Clubs and became known as 'The Interclub Agreement' (ICA) – the current version dates from 1996. This is a mechanical formula which is applied depending upon whether Clause 8 is amended with 'and responsibility' or not – plus a number of other provisos.

The relevant section of the NYPE ICA 1996 reads as follows:

*(8) Cargo Claims shall be apportioned as follows:*
   *a)   Claims in fact arising out of unseaworthiness and / or error or fault in navigation or management of the vessel:*
        *100% Owners*
     *save where the Owner proves that the unseaworthiness was caused by the loading, stowage, lashing, discharging or other handling of the cargo, in which case the claim shall be apportioned under sub-clause (b).*
   *b)   Claims in fact arising out of the loading, stowage, lashing, discharge, storage or other handling of cargo:*
        *100% Charterers*
     *unless the words 'and responsibility' are added in Clause 8 or there is a similar amendment making the master responsible for cargo handling in which case:*
        *50% Charterers*
        *50% Owners*
     *save where the Charterer proves that the failure properly to load, stow, lash, discharge or handle the cargo was caused by the unseaworthiness of the vessel in which case:*
        *100% Owners*

c)   Subject to (a) and (b) above, claims for shortage or overcarriage:
            50% Charterers
            50% Owners
        unless there is clear and irrefutable evidence that the claim arose out of pilferage
        or act of neglect by one or the other (including their servants or sub-contractors)
        in which case that party shall then bear 100% of the claim.

d)   All other claims whatsoever (including claims for delay to cargo):
            50% Charterers
            50% Owners
        unless there is clear and irrefutable evidence that the claim arose out of the act
        or neglect of the one or the other (including their servants or sub-contractors) in
        which case that party shall then bear 100% if the claim.

It would be quite usual for the shipowner, as carrier under the Bill of Lading, to handle cargo claims in the first instance and then to seek an indemnity against the charterer under the terms of the Charterparty – specifically with reference to the Cargo Responsibility Clause.

## b. Potential exposure / problem

The nature of the problem which generally arises is who, as between the master / ship operator and the charterer, was responsible for loading, stowing and discharging the ship under the terms of the governing Charterparty. The party who had that responsibility would usually be the party who also had the liability for any consequences of not doing the job properly.

However, this is not always straight forward for even if, on the face of things, it was the charterer who had the responsibility for loading and stowing etc. — it will always be the responsibility of the master / ship operators to ensure that the ship is seaworthy at the commencement of the voyage and will thus have a responsibility to ensure that charterers do not load / stow the cargo in such a way as to endanger the vessel or otherwise render it unseaworthy e.g. on account of stability, or inadequate securing etc.

The master must be careful not to exceed his responsibility – by doing so he could run the risk of shifting responsibility, and thus ultimate liability, away from charterers onto the shipowners.

Clearly he must intervene if he sees charterers or their stevedores doing something which is likely to affect the seaworthiness of the vessel. However, he is not obliged to tell them how they should do it – indeed if he did that and they followed his advice and cargo was subsequently damaged then the responsibility / liability would probably rest with the master / shipowners.

Similarly, if charterers are stowing the cargo in such a way that it may damage other cargo, but not endanger the ship then the master may draw the attention of charterers to the errors of their ways but he should leave it up to them to find an alternative solution.

Clearly, this may put the master in conflict with his obligations towards the cargo owner under the contract of carriage evidenced by the B/L.

If the master does find himself confronted with this type of situation he should contact his company immediately for instructions and guidance. It may be appropriate to consider calling in the local P&I Correspondent and / or engaging an independent surveyor who can lend support to the master or otherwise assist in finding an amicable solution.

> Clearly the best solution will be not to allow the dispute to arise in the first place. This can be best achieved by all involved working together as a single team. A pre-loading meeting can ensure that everyone is clear about who will be doing what and that all parties are basically happy with what is being proposed with regard to the loading and stowing of the cargo. If there are any differences of opinion they can be addressed at that stage.

## c. ISM implications

As was explained in the section on 'cargo damage, loss or shortage' above, the standards and practices of the industry, post 1 July 1998 / 1 July 2002, with regard to seaworthiness and the exercise of due diligence are now manifested in terms of the ISM Code. The test of whether the necessary due diligence has been exercised will be evident from the procedures of the SMS and the evidence produced to demonstrate that those procedures were followed. This general concept will also apply to allegations being made by charterers who might be challenging their obligation to indemnify owners for settled cargo claims under the terms of the C/P.

The following, non-exhaustive, list attempts to address some of the more obvious potential implications and, consequently, suggest areas of the SMS which will come under close scrutiny:

Section 1.2    Objectives

The objectives of the ISM Code, as set out in Section 1.2 does not only apply to protection of people and the environment but also includes '…the …avoidance of damage to … property…' – which would include ship and cargo.

Section 5    Master's responsibility and authority

Section 6    Resources and personnel

In Sections 5 and 6 of the Code there is a lot of emphasis put upon the obligation of the company to provide the proper people – including the master and crew – who are properly qualified, trained and in all respects suitable to carry out there particular job on board that particular ship. In the *Eurasian Dream* case, the master was qualified and did have considerable experience on bulk carriers – however, he had no experience on car carriers and this lack of experience was one of a number of factors which led the Judge to conclude that the ship was unseaworthy. The master and other officers were also inadequately trained and familiarised with the particular ship, specifically its fire fighting equipment, and this was another factor in the unseaworthiness equation.

Section 7      Development of plans for shipboard operations

Clearly it will depend upon what has happened which has led to the cargo damage and the dispute under the Cargo Responsibility Clause. However, the usual types of incidents would include making the ship seaworthy and cargo worthy which should be included a 'key shipboard operation'. The type of ship will determine what procedures and plans would be included in the SMS.

Section 9      Reports and analysis of non-conformities, accidents and hazardous occurrences

Records of the activities anticipated by Section 9 may well be examined to confirm that learning opportunities were being taken as part of the SMS. Similarly minutes of on board safety committee meetings may be examined to determine the level of involvement and commitment to safety management on board

Section 10     Maintenance of the ship and equipment

To what extent this may be relevant will obviously be determined by reference to the cause leading to the cargo damage and the dispute under the C/P. If the failure of a piece of equipment was involved then the procedures and records will be examined very carefully. In the case of the *Eurasian Dream* there were numerous items of fire fighting equipment which was found to be deficient and these issues also contributed towards the judge finding the ship to be unseaworthy.

Section 11     Documentation

If there appear to have been problems with compliance with the SMS then it is likely that a closer look will be made at the documented procedures themselves. If these are voluminous, irrelevant or otherwise inadequate then the Company is likely to come under severe criticism.

Section 12     Company verification, review and evaluation

There is a very clear obligation on the Company to ensure that the SMS is working properly on board its vessels. If a serious incident has arisen, as in this case with a collision, then it can be anticipated that the active monitoring by the company will be looked at very closely by way of audit trails.

Certification and verification

As a matter of course the validity of the SMC and DOC will be checked.

**d. Nature of evidence required**

The nature of the evidence which might come under scrutiny in such cases will relate to the respective activities of the charterers and their servants e.g. the supercargo, stevedores, agents etc and the shipowner's servants – particularly the master. This will be in addition to the evidence which may be needed to deal with the cargo claim which had been presented by the cargo owner / subrogated cargo underwriter – in this regard see the section on 'Cargo damage, loss or shortage' at the beginning of this general chapter.

The additional evidence which might be required could include:

- Minutes of a pre-loading meeting between master, charterers representative and stevedores to discuss the loading and stowage of the cargo,

- Copies of the head charterparty and any sub-charterparties,

- Copies of any written, emailed, faxed etc instructions from the ship operator and / or the charterer regarding the terms of the C/P and specifically the loading and stowing operation as well as the masters responsibility,

- Copies of business cards, or other source of details, of people he dealt with during the loading operation,

- Photographs / video tape recording of stevedores badly handling or pilfering the cargo,

- Copies of Letters of Protest to charterers / their agents / stevedores concerning pilferage, bad handling, bad stowage, smoking etc

- Copies of any other correspondence with charterers, their agents or stevedores including notes of any discussions or telephone conversations,

- Copies of any correspondence with the ship operators office, including notes of any telephone conversations,

- Minutes of any meetings in which the master may have objected to a particular method of stowage (preferably such discussions should be backed up by a note in writing)

- Report or comments / observations from an independent surveyor — if appointed

Where minutes have been produced, letters of protest written etc. — the master should endeavour to have the charterers, or their representative, sign / initial a copy to confirm receipt.

**e. Report**

The master should include in his report a description of the loading process detailing any problems he may have encountered with the charterers / stevedores etc., what happened, when it happened, where it happened etc. and the attempts he made at finding a solution.

## f. Case study

### Background to the incident

A 35,000 dwt bulk carrier was time chartered under an unamended NYPE 1993 Charterparty form. She was due to load a full cargo of steel slabs and pipes. A charterers supercargo was to be in attendance throughout the loading operation.

The charterers intended to load the slabs in according to the 'California Block Stowage' method and the pipes at the sides of the holds. During the loading of the slabs the master objected to the method of stowage and what he considered to be the insufficiency of the lashing. The supercargo insisted that this was the method of stowage which was to be adopted and told the master that he should not interfere. The master subsequently drew up his own stowage plan and set out in detail how the cargo was to be loaded and secured — which was very different from the charterers original plan.

The charterers needed to turn the ship around quickly and therefore they agreed, under protest, to follow the masters instructions with regard to the stowage and securing.

During the voyage the vessel encountered heavy weather. Some of the steel slabs shifted in stow and caused considerable damage to the steel pipes.

The cargo owners of the damaged steel pipes brought a claim against the shipowner, as carrier under the B/L. The shipowners attempted an indemnity claim against the time charterers under the terms of the unamended NYPE C/P.

The dispute under the charterparty was referred to arbitration.

### Consideration of relevant evidence

Neither the charterers supercargo nor the master had maintained any contemporaneous notes of the discussions they had had during the loading operation. The charterers produced their original stowage plan and the master produced his stowage plan.

It was accepted by the master that he had over-ruled the supercargo and insisted that the steel cargo was to be loaded, stowed and secured according to his requirements. The master explained in his report to the ship operating company that the charterers proposal of a California Block Stow was unsafe.

The charterers produced an expert who claimed that the California Block Stowage was a normal method used in the shipment of steel slabs.

### Outcome

The arbitrators were not all convinced that the California Block Stow is a good method of carrying steel slabs in a bulk carrier lower wing tanks but they considered that that was not the issue they were having to consider. Their task was to consider whether the master had exceeded his responsibility under Clause 8 of the NYPE form.

The arbitrators concluded that he had and, as a consequence, had assumed the responsibility and liability, on behalf of his shipowners, of the loading and stowing operation. The charterers were not obliged to indemnify the shipowner for the claim they had settled with the cargo interests for damage to the steel pipes.

If the master did have doubts about the suitability of the proposed California Block Stow he should have called in additional help – from the ship operators office and possibly local P&I Club Correspondent and / or specialist steel surveyor. If appropriate the charterers could have been told that they would not be allowed to load the slabs using the California Block Stowage method and told that they must come up with an alternative method which the master would review and declare whether he considered that to be a safe and adequate method.

One reason for calling in additional help / advice at an early stage is that time charterers may attempt to put the vessel off hire under such circumstances which would clearly escalate the problem and the dispute.

## Part B — Chapter 2

# SHIP RELATED INCIDENTS

### General introduction

THIS CHAPTER WILL CONSIDER A RANGE OF INCIDENTS involving accidents to or by the ships themselves. Such incidents will often involve significant sums of money and are likely to involve both Hull and Machinery Underwriters as well as P&I Liability Insurers. To that extent the ship operator will need to have sufficient evidence to present its claim against the insurer. The ship operator may also require evidence to defend itself against third party claims being brought against the company or may require evidence to pursue a claim against a third party — or both.

Whilst the potential incidents will each be dealt with separately, clearly there will be a very good chance that a number of other incidents flow directly from the initial casualty. For example, in the case of a collision, it may well be that there are people injured, maybe a fire, a spill of fuel oil from a damaged bunker tank, cargo damage and maybe a subsequent salvage operation. It is therefore important to think laterally and use these guidance notes intelligently.

Since incidents within this general category tend to involve significant sums of money and other potential loss it is very likely that surveyors and lawyers will be instructed to investigate and collect evidence.

It is also possible, following such an incident as is being considered in this chapter, and if it was sufficiently serious, that the flag State Administration may conduct an initial or even a formal inquiry into the incident. This may result in prosecutions and fines being imposed against the master or other individuals on board or against the Company. The master or other officers may also have their Certificates of Competency suspended or withdrawn — although only the Administration issuing the Certificate would usually have the right to suspend or cancel a Certificate of Competency. A similar inquiry may be initiated by a port State Authority, or Port Authority, Harbour Master, Police etc. if the incident occurred within their territorial limits and jurisdiction.

### *Particulars of ship*

For incidents involving collisions, contacts and damage to property, non-contact damage, groundings and strandings:

| According to Resolution A.849(2) |
| --- |
| Name, IMO number, nationality, port of registry, call sign |
| Name and address of owners and operators, if applicable, also, if an overseas ship, of agents |

| |
|---|
| Type of ship |
| Name and address of charterer, and type of charter |
| Deadweight, net and gross tonnages, and principal dimensions |
| Means of propulsion; particulars of engines |
| When, where and by whom built |
| Any relevant structural peculiarities |
| Amount of fuel carried, and position of fuel tanks |
| Radio (type, make) |
| Radar (number, type, make) |
| Gyro compass (make, model) |
| Automatic pilot (make, model) |
| Electronic positioning equipment (make, model) (GPS, Decca, etc.) |
| Life saving equipment (dates of survey/expiry) |

### Documents required

For incidents involving collisions, contacts and damage to property, non-contact damage, groundings and strandings

| |
|---|
| **According to Resolution A.849(2) \*** |
| Ship's register |
| Current statutory certificates |
| ISM Code certification |
| Classification society or survey authority certificates |
| Official log book |
| Crew list |
| Crew qualifications (see also 1.4 of these guidelines) |
| Deck log book |
| Port log, log abstract and cargo log book |
| Engine movement book |
| Engine-room log book |
| Data logger print-out |
| Course recorder chart |

| |
|---|
| Echo sounder chart |
| Oil record book |
| Soundings book |
| Night order book |
| Master's/Chief Engineer's Standing Orders |
| Company Standing Orders/Operations Manual |
| Company Safety Manual |
| Compass error book or records |
| Radar log book |
| Planned maintenance schedules |
| Repair requisition records |
| Articles of Agreement |
| Bar records — daily purchases — voyage receipts, etc. |
| Records of drug and alcohol tests |
| Passenger list |
| Radio log |
| Ship reporting records |
| Voyage plan |
| Charts and record of chart corrections |
| Equipment/machinery manufacturer's operational/maintenance manuals |
| Any other documentation relevant to the inquiry |

*(Note: Any documents that may have relevance to the investigation should be produced. Where possible original documents should be retained, otherwise authenticated and dated photocopies should be taken in accordance with 9.1.2 of the Code. A number of these documents will contain details sought under 1.1 of these guidelines.)*

In addition to the above information, the master should ensure that:

- All witnesses to the incident write an account of the collision and the events leading up to the collision

- The practice of marking charts is continued while vessel is under pilotage and chart positions are left precisely as plotted

- Recording telegraph printer output and other printer output from the engine room are retained as part of the movement book

- Accuracy of clocks on bridge and in engine room, as well as automatic recorders are verified

- Course recorder marked in ink to indicate collision

- Operator of reflective plotter makes a note of marks

- A full photographic record of events is made

- Scraps of paper on which course calculations may have been made are retained.

### Collisions

The word 'collision' usually means, within the context of marine insurance and maritime law, the physical contact between two, or more, ships (although there have been exception when ships have been towed). In Annex 2 of MSC/Circ.953 a collision is defined as '…striking or being struck by another ship (regardless of whether under way, anchored or moored)…' A 'collision' does not include a physical contact between one ship and, for example, a navigation buoy — that is a 'contact' or, as the Americans call it, an allision — such incidents will be dealt with below under 'Contacts and damage to property'. A collision would not, usually, include a situation where one ship caused damage to another where there was no physical contact, for example where the wash from a ship moving past at speed in a canal or river caused a moored vessel to surge and, as a consequence, suffered damage. That would be a non-contact damage incident and will be dealt with below.

The type of evidence required is, of course, going to be very similar in all three scenarios — the reason for separating them however is because they represent different insurable risks and are likely to involve different insurers.

### a. Conceptual background

In the lead up to a collision taking place there is very likely going to be a series of incidents and increasingly intense activity developing on the bridge of both ships. It will be necessary to try and reconstruct what exactly happened on the bridge of each ship, who did what and when – it will also be necessary to try and find an answer to the more difficult question of why? Clearly, if the International Regulations for Preventing Collisions (COLREGS) were being followed then collisions simply should not occur.

Following a collision there will be many matters to attend to and the situation will require very careful management. Tasks will need to be prioritised and clearly safety of lives, the ship and the environment will be at the top of that list. However, it is crucial that a contemporaneous record is maintained of what is happening — if possible backed up with photographs and videos. The delegation of such tasks should not have been left until an incident occurs.

It is likely that in the aftermath of a collision, lawyers and surveyors acting for owners and their insurers will come aboard the vessel and play an active role in gathering evidence necessary to bring or defend claims for damage. However, they will rely heavily on the master and the crew to provide much of the evidence.

It is quite likely that lawyers acting for the other vessel in the collision may try and secure an arrest on your vessel and attempt to board to interview members of the crew. Requests may be made to participate in a joint survey.

The Classification Society and other surveyors will probably be attending on board. It is also likely that local authorities will put an investigator on board if the collision occurred within their jurisdiction, this may be the capacity as port State Control or coastguard, such as the MCA, and / or a safety orientated investigation such as might be undertaken by the MAIB. flag State Administration may also dispatch an investigator.

### b. Potential exposure / problem

A number of potential issues need to be identified:

i) Damage to own ship — primarily a H&M insurance matter but also a potential indemnity claim against the other ship.

ii) Potential claim from the other ship — under standard U.K. insurances this would usually be split according to a 'Running Down Clause' — $\frac{1}{4}$ P&I and $\frac{3}{4}$ H&M — however, some non-UK H&M Policies cover $\frac{4}{4}$ths.

iii) Limitation of liability — questions of 'seaworthiness' the test will depend whether jurisdiction has been founded in a 1957 or 1976 regime.

iv) Possible prosecution of master, other ship staff and possibly office staff by coastal state.

v) Possibly prosecution by a flag State.

### c. ISM implications

The ISM implications will clearly depend very much upon the primary and any underlying causes which led to the collision. The following, non-exhaustive, list attempts to address some of the more obvious potential implications and, consequently, suggest areas of the SMS which will come under close scrutiny:

Section 1.2.3 .1 (compliance with mandatory rules and regulations)

Obviously the COLREGS would fall under this Section – but also such regulations as the STCW Convention and Code. Hours of rest / work of the individual(s) involved would be examined as well as the management system which was in place to ensure that Section A-VIII/1 of STCW Code was being complied with.

Section 6      Resources and personnel

In the vast majority of collisions one or more individuals did, or did not, do something which ultimately contributed to the collision — often referred to as 'human error'. It may have been the master and / or the Officer of the Watch (OOW). Under Section 6 there is a very clear obligation upon the Company to engage only qualified, skilled and suitably experienced personnel. It can therefore be anticipated that a potential claimant or investigator will look very carefully not only at the qualifications and alleged experience of the individual but may also require to examine the Company selection and recruiting procedures and to follow an audit trail to demonstrate that these procedures were indeed followed when recruiting the particular individual who is the focus of attention.

It may also be necessary to produce evidence that suitable and adequate familiarisation and training was provided to the individual – e.g. in the operation of the radar etc. Relevant sections of STCW would also need to be considered.

Bridge team and crew resource management may also be an issue to be investigated. Passage /voyage planning and master / pilot relationship are other areas which may be relevant.

Section 7      Development of plans for shipboard operations

Clearly the navigation of the vessel (which would include collision avoidance) would be included as one of the 'key shipboard operations' anticipated by Section 7. As such it should be expected that there are clear company procedures set out in a Procedures Manual. Those procedures will be examined very carefully, not only in light of the collision incident itself but also during other periods of the ships life. This would be done by following audit trails.

Section 8      Emergency preparedness

A collision would, most certainly, fall within the category of 'potential emergency situations' anticipated in Section 8. The response of the master and those on board, following the collision event, will be examined against the written procedures. No doubt records of simulated drills involving collisions type incidents will also be examined.

Section 9      Reports and analysis of non-conformities, accidents and hazardous occurrences

Records of the activities anticipated by Section 9 may well be examined to confirm that learning opportunities were being taken as part of the SMS. Similarly minutes of on board safety committee meetings may be examined to determine the level of involvement and commitment to safety management on board.

Section 10      Maintenance of the ship and equipment

To what extent this may be relevant will obviously be determined by reference to the cause of the collision. If the failure of a piece of equipment was involved then the procedures and records will be examined very carefully.

## Section 11    Documentation

If there appear to have been problems with compliance with the SMS then it is likely that a closer look will be made at the documented procedures themselves. If these are voluminous, irrelevant or otherwise inadequate then the company is likely to come under severe criticism.

## Section 12    Company verification, review and evaluation

There is a very clear obligation on the Company to ensure that the SMS is working properly on board its vessels. If a serious incident has arisen, as in this case with a collision, then it can be anticipated that the active monitoring by the Company will be looked at very closely by way of audit trails.

### Certification and verification

As a matter of course the validity of the SMC and DOC will be checked.

## d. Nature of evidence required

### Evidence prior to a collision

Evidence recording the daily routine of the vessel will be crucial in determining how and why a collision occurred. This type of evidence will include copies of the vessel's rough log books. It is imperative, therefore, that all sections of the log book are completed fully and accurately at all times (refer to the introduction of this book). Sounding records are also likely to be important. Working charts and movement books are two items of evidence which have particular relevance in collision investigations.

### Working charts

The master should ensure that chart positions are left precisely as plotted and that positions which do not match others are not erased. As a large number of collisions occur under pilotage or in congested waters, the master should also ensure that the general practice of marking the ship's position on charts during the passage is continued while the vessel is under pilotage. Particular care should be taken to plot the vessel's location on the chart, for example, by indicating the distances abeam off buoys.

### Movement books

The master should ensure that movement books are kept in ink and that any alterations are made in ink, signed, and dated by the person making the alterations. The material deleted should be scored out with a single line leaving the writing underneath legible. The use of correction fluid should not be permitted. The master should also ensure that times are recorded as accurately as possible. Finally, he should ensure that printer outputs from telegraph recorders and the engine room are retained as part of the movement book.

## Evidence after a collision

### *General*

If possible, the master and the crew should collect, record, and preserve as much detail of the collision as they can immediately after an incident. Although a comprehensive list of the items of evidence required from the vessel is provided at the end of this chapter, the type of evidence discussed below is of particular importance. The master should ensure that a note of the following is made:

- The vessel's position at the time of the incident

  Every effort should be made to fix and confirm the position from more than one source.

- The exact time of the collision

  The accuracy of the clocks on the bridge and in the engine room as well as the accuracy of automatic recorders such as course recorders, telegraph loggers, and data loggers should be verified. The personal watches of the members of the crew who witnessed the incident should be checked. If a reflective plotter was in use prior to a collision, the crew member operating the plotter should ensure that he has made a note (not on the screen) of any marks he made on the screen with the time they were made.

- The heading of the vessel at the time of the collision

  It is important that the course recorder is marked in ink to indicate the time when the vessel collided, although care should be taken not to spoil the trace. If a course recorder is not available, the heading of the vessel should be determined by some other method which also should be recorded.

- An estimate of the angle of blow by or to the other vessel

- An estimate the speed of each of the vessels at the time of the collision

  The estimates can be verified at a later date by other data such as photographs and logs.

- Any alterations of course and speed prior to a collision

If possible, this note should be verified by a second person or equipment recording. In addition, the master should ensure that all crew members on the bridge as well as other members of the crew who witnessed the incident, record their account of events which occurred prior to and after the incident. The master should also ensure that any independent witnesses to the incident are identified. He should record the names of all the vessels in the vicinity and attempt to obtain the names and addresses of the operators and duty officers of these vessels by VHF.

Finally, the master should ensure that any scraps of paper which have been disposed of in the waste paper basket on the bridge are retained as these may contain the key as to why and how a collision occurred.

### Vessel under pilotage or in congested waters

As stated above, many collisions take place when a vessel is under pilotage or in congested waters. In such cases, the actions of the person controlling the vessel immediately before the vessel was involved in a collision, are particularly relevant in determining the cause of the collision. The master, in addition to gathering the evidence discussed in the preceding sections, should ensure that the watch keeper, helmsman, the look-out, and any other persons on the bridge at the time of the collision make a complete record of events. The pilot also should be requested to make a written account of the events before he leaves the vessel. A note should be made of the pilot's name, address and telephone number.

The master should record speed log readings and make a note of the state of the tide at the time of the collision. An estimate of tidal current is unlikely to be accurate. However, a note of the time of observed slack water will be useful when calculations are being made from tide tables. The master should note that S.A.L. logs may be inaccurate in freshwater.

### Vessel moored

It is generally the view that unless there is evidence that the moored or anchored vessel contributed in some way to the collision, the vessel underway is liable for the damage.

Regardless of whether the master is on the colliding vessel, he should ensure the following information is obtained:

- Whether or not the vessel or an adjacent vessel was testing her main engines in such a way as to contribute to the incident

- Whether or not the moorings on the moored vessel were defective, slack or ineffective in any way

- An estimate of the tidal direction and strength

- The identity of witnesses on shore, and

- Photographs of damage to own vessel, and if possible, of the damage to the other vessel.

As many of the incidents which take place when the vessel is moored are minor incidents, the insurers of both vessels may not require a joint survey, but will rely heavily on the master's evidence. It is important, therefore, that the master's report of the incident gives a detailed record of the damage.

### Involvement of lawyers

As stated above, lawyers are likely to play a significant role in gathering evidence in the aftermath of a collision. While the investigating lawyers are likely to be appointed by the vessel's insurers and will not be directly representing the interests of the master and crew, these interests do to a certain degree coincide with those of the insurers. Therefore, the lawyers may advise the master and the crew of their legal position and if the circumstances merit it, recommend that the crew or their union appoint their own lawyers.

Finally, there is an understanding between lawyers that if they represent owners of another vessel, they will not question crew members of the opponent's vessel. Therefore, the master should ensure that crew members identify any persons to whom they make statements. When a joint survey is arranged, the surveyor appointed on behalf of the other vessel is attending to inspect the physical damage to your vessel. He is not usually authorised to inspect the navigational equipment, log books or interview the crew.

**See General Introduction to this chapter for a list of documents that may be required in such an incident.**

### e. Report

If lawyers, representing the ship operator / insurers, are to visit the vessel then much of the detail listed in the following lists will be obtained by the lawyers during interviews with relevant individuals and will be included in their own reports and / or in witness statements. Similarly, an investigator representing a Flag or Coastal State Administration, or similar, will also expect to collect this information.

Accordingly, it would be extremely useful, and will save much time, if the master could ensure that the relevant information is available in advance of the lawyers / investigator attending on board.

In the case of a U.K. Registered Ship, or a non-UK ship in UK waters, a report will need to be made to the MAIB — see MAIB Incident Report Form at Part C 5 at the back of this book. Other jurisdictions may have similar requirements.

A report and analysis, along with any necessary corrective action should also be undertaken to comply with Section 9 of the ISM Code.

Lawyers attending on behalf of the ship operator / insurer can provide advice and guidance to the master on completing this additional reports.

**Particulars of the incident**

| In accordance with Resolution A.849(20) | Additional suggestions |
|---|---|
| | Details of vessel<br>- Name<br>- Nationality<br>- Port of registry<br>- Vessel's general description<br>- Radio equipment onboard<br>- Vessel's complement (details of rank and qualifications<br>- Watchkeeping arrangements<br>- Navigational equipment on board |
| Type of incident | |
| Date, time and place of incident | Date of collision<br>Approximate area of collision<br>Time zone |
| Details of incident and of the events leading up to it and following it | True courses steered during four hours before collision (time, position, altered course to)<br>Last fix before sighting the other vessel<br>First observation of other vessel:<br>- By what means<br>- Time<br>- Distance and bearing<br>- Lights and shapes observed<br>- Aspect<br>- Apparent course<br>True course of own ship at time of first observation<br>Position of own ship at time of first observation (state how obtained)<br>Speed of own ship at time of first observation<br>Action taken by own vessel at time of first observation |

Pt B2

S
H
I
P

| Details of incident (cont.) | Subsequent observations |
|---|---|
| |   - Times |
| |   - Distance and bearing |
| | First visual sighting of other vessel |
| |   - Time |
| |   - Distance and bearing |
| |   - Lights observed and shapes |
| |   - Aspect |
| |   - Apparent course |
| |   - Bearing and distance of other vessel when echo was first observed by radar |
| |   - What other lights and shapes (if any) were subsequently seen before the collision |
| | Steps taken to plot other vessel (eg reflection plot, formal plot) |
| | Record of actions of both vessels including times up to the time of collision (including engine movement) |
| | Sound signals made and when made |
| | Sound signals heard and when heard |
| | Details of any communications between vessels before collision (eg aldis, VHF) |
| | Time of collision |
| | Position of collision (state how obtained) |
| | Angle of contact between vessels (if possible take photographs or make a drawing) |
| | Which parts of each vessel first came into contact |
| | Heading of own vessel at time of collision |
| | Speed of own vessel at time of collision |
| | Heading of other vessel at time of collision |
| | Speed of other vessel at time of collision |
| | Description of movements of both vessels after collision |
| Details of the performance of relevant equipment with special regard to any malfunction | Radars in use and what range scales they were set on |
| | Position fixing system(s) in use and intervals between fixes |

Pt B2

S
H
I
P

| Persons on bridge | Personnel on bridge at or immediately before collision and their duties |
|---|---|
|  | If vessel under pilotage, name, address and telephone numbers of pilot — see also the evidence listed in the section 'Vessel under Pilotage or in Congested Waters' |
| Persons in engine room |  |
| Wheerabouts of the master and chief engineer |  |
| Steering mode (auto or manual) |  |
| Extracts from all relevant ship and, if applicable, shore documents including details of entries in official, bridge, scrap/rough and engine-room log books, data log printout, computer printouts, course and engine speed recorder, radar log, etc. |  |
| Details of communications made between vessel and radio stations, SAR centres and control centres, etc. with transcript of tape recordings wheer available | Details of communications after collision |
|  | Name and port of registry of other ship |
|  | Names of other vessels in vicinity when collision occurred |
|  | Communications with other vessels in vicinity |
| Details of any injuries/ fatalities |  |
| Voyage data recorder information (if fitted) for analysis |  |
|  | If the vessel is moored at the time of collision, see the evidence listed in the section 'Vessel Moored' |

## Particulars of the voyage

| In accordance with Resolution A.849(20) | Additional suggestions |
|---|---|
| Port at which voyage commenced and port at which it was to have ended, with dates | Details of voyage of own vessel:<br><br>- From where to where was the vessel going<br><br>- Time of sailing<br><br>- Draughts (drafts) on sailing (forward, mid and aft)<br><br>- Intended course to next port |
| Details of cargo | |
| Last port and date of departure | |
| Draughts (forward, aft and midships) and any list | Draught (draft) of own vessel at time of collision |
| Port bound for at time of occurrence | |
| Any incident during the voyage that may have a material bearing on the incident, or unusual occurrence, whether or not it appears to be relevant to the incident | |
| Plan view of ship's layout including cargo spaces, slop tanks, bunker/fuel lube oil tanks (diagrams from IOPP Certificate) | |
| Details of cargo, bunkers, fresh water and ballast and consumption (ie nature and tonnage) | Cargo on board at time of collision (ie nature and tonnage) |

## Particulars of sea state, weather and tide

| In accordance with Resolution A.849(20) | Additional suggestions |
|---|---|
| Direction and force of wind | Weather conditions at time of collision:<br>- Direction and force of wind |
| Direction and state of sea and swell | - Direction and height of sea<br>- Direction and height of swell |

| Atmospheric conditions and visibility | - Visibility |
|---|---|
| State and height of tide | |
| Direction and strength of tidal and other currents, bearing in mind local conditions | State of tide and currents |
| | - Last weather forecast |

## Particulars of personnel involved in incident

| In accordance with Resolution A.849(20) | Additional suggestions |
|---|---|
| Full name | |
| Age | |
| Details of injury | |
| Description of accident | |
| Person supervising activity | |
| First aid or other action on board | |
| Capacity on board | |
| Certificate of Competency/Licence:<br>  grade;<br>  date of issue;<br>  issuing country/authority;<br>  other Certificates of Competency held | |
| Time spent on vessel concerned | |
| Experience on similar vessels | |
| Experience on other types of vessels | |
| Experience in current capacity | |
| Experience in other ranks | |
| Number of hours spent on duty on that day and previous days | |
| Number of hours sleep in the 96 hours prior to the incident | |
| Any other factors, onboard or personal, that may have affected sleep | |
| Whether smoker, and if so, quantity | |
| Normal alcohol habit | |
| Alcohol consumption immediately prior to incident or in the previous 24 hours | |
| Whether under prescribed medication | |

| | |
|---|---|
| Any ingested non-prescribed drugs | |
| Records of drug and alcohol tests | |

## Assistance after the incident

| In accordance with Resolution A.849(20) | Additional suggestions |
|---|---|
| If assistance was summoned, what form and by what means | |
| If assistance was offered or given, by whom and of what nature, and whether it was effective and competent | |
| If assistance was offered and refused, the reason for refusal | |

Resolution A.849(20) also draws attention to additional information which may be required in the case of a collision:

| In accordance with Resolution A.849(20) |
|---|
| **General** |
| Local or other special rules for navigation |
| Obstructions, if any, to manoeuvring, e.g. by a third vessel, shallow or narrow waters, beacon, buoy, etc. |
| Circumstances affecting visibility and audibility, e.g. state of the sun, dazzle of shore lights, strength of wind, ship-board noise and whether any door or window could obstruct look-out and/or audibility |
| Geographical plot |
| Possibilities of interaction |
| Name, IMO number, nationality and other details of other vessel |
| **For each ship:** |
| Time, position, course and speed (and method by which established), when presence of other ship first became known |
| Details of all subsequent alterations of course and speed up to collision by own ship |
| Bearing, distance and heading of other ship, if sighted visually, time of sighting, and subsequent alterations |
| Bearing and distance of other ship, if observed by radar, timing of observations and subsequent alterations of bearing |

| |
|---|
| If other ship was plotted and by what method (auto-plot, reflection plotter, etc.), and copy of plot, if available |
| Check performance of equipment |

- Course recorder
- Lights/day signals carried and operated in ship, and those seen in other ship
- Sound signals, including fog signals, made by ship and when, and those heard from other ship and when

| |
|---|
| If a listening watch was kept on VHF radio channel 16, or other frequency, and any messages sent, received or overheard |
| Number of radars carried on ship, number operational at time of casualty, together with ranges used on each radar |
| Whether steering by hand or automatic |
| Check that steering was operating correctly |
| Details of look-out |
| The parts of each ship which first came into contact and the angle between ships at that time |
| Nature and extent of damage |
| Compliance with statutory requirement to give name and nationality to other ship and to stand by after collision |

In appropriate cases, investigators and lawyers may require a completed IMO Damage Card, or similar and intact stability reporting – please see Annex 5 of IMO MSC/Circ.953 / MEPC/Circ.372.

### f. Case study

"A", the vessel involved in this incident, was a small sludge carrier. She collided with "B", another vessel, in thick fog in the vicinity of a large United Kingdom pilot station (the reader should refer to the attached plots which were produced from evidence provided by the vessels involved in the incident).

At 0920 hours, "A" adjusted her course to 273 degrees true on an outward leg of a run to dump sludge. Between 0930 hours and 0935 hours, an echo was observed on radar 10 degrees on starboard bow distance 2.7 miles just west of BR Lanby Buoy. "A" and the echo both appeared to be heading for LF1 light float at the entrance of the main channel. The echo's bearing appeared constant during the next few minutes, and the master made a number of small alterations of course to starboard amounting in total to 40 degrees. "B" was first sighted 2.3 points on port bow at which time "A" was heading about 313 degrees true. "B" appeared to be heading at right angles to "A" at a distance of about 3 cables. "A" collided with "B" at about 0945 hours in a position estimated to be 8 cables ESE of BR Lanby.

At 0916 hours "B" was following a course of 112° BR Lanby 097 degrees true distance 4.5 miles reduced to half speed. At 0925, her course was altered to 095 degrees true to counteract set. At about 0940, an echo was observed 5 degrees on port bow distance 3 miles. A few minutes later, after speaking to the pilot on the VHF, the master ordered her course to be adjusted to 102 degrees true to bring LF1 light float right ahead with speed reduced to slow check. The radar echo distance of 2 miles was brought right ahead.

A crew member reported that the echo first moved from right ahead to 40 degrees on starboard bow closing to a distance of 4 cables. Soon after, "A" was seen 50 degrees on starboard bow distance 3 cables. The wheel of "B" was put hard a starboard, and the engines stopped and put full astern.

The collision occurred at 0943 hours according to a clock on "B" as recorded by the chief officer. The master of "B" recorded the collision as taking place at 0944/0945 hours. The master also estimated that at this time the BR Lanby buoy was at 50 degrees true distance 7 cables.

Although there were independent observers in the vicinity who were engaged in damage control exercises, the data provided by them did not appear to relate to this incident but to two other vessels passing close to one another. The evidence from "A" and "B" did not correlate, and the investigators of the collision had difficulty in ascertaining the cause of the incident.

### Detail of collision area

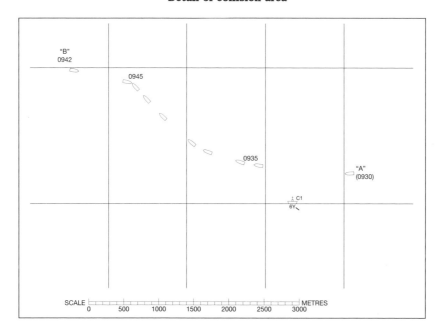

The owners and insurers of "A" were placed at a considerable disadvantage as "A" could not produce certain items of crucial evidence, which included a working chart, a plot of "B" as it approached ("B" also had not plotted "A" as it approached), and a movement book. In addition, there were no automatic recording devices such as course recorders or data loggers, onboard the vessel. As a result of the lack of evidence, "A" was found to be primarily at fault in causing the loss, and her owners were responsible for the damage suffered to "B".

## Contacts and damage to property

Damage caused by a vessel to third party property, such as any harbour, dock, pier, quay, jetty, land or anything whatsoever fixed or movable (more commonly referred to as 'fixed or floating objects' or 'FFO'), can often give rise to large claims which owners have great difficulty defending. In many countries, owners will be strictly liable which means that the vessel will be responsible for any accidental damage, although the vessel and crew were in no way at fault. The damage may be caused by a vessel coming into direct contact with, for example, a dock, pier, jetty, buoy, or crane, or the damage may be caused by the vessel's wash. In most instances, claims for the damage caused by the vessel will be covered by the vessel's P&I insurance – although under a number on non-UK terms such cover is under the H&M Policy.

Damage to property incidents appear to be considered by flag State and Coastal State Administrations as being of a similar category as collisions. Under paragraph 4.3 of Resolution A.849(20) – it would be considered a 'Serious Casualty' unless it also resulted in loss of life or severe pollution when it would be considered a 'Very Serious Casualty' – under paragraph 4.2.

### a. Conceptual background

Damage to fixed and floating objects usually occur when a vessel is entering or leaving a port. If damage occurs when a vessel is entering a port, the master should report the incident as soon as possible to owners. If possible, the master also should contact the local P&I representatives and request them to attend and assist.

If damage occurs when the vessel is leaving a port, the master should resist any temptation to ignore the incident in the hope that the damage will be minimal and there were no witnesses. Owners should be notified as soon as possible in order that enquiries may be made to ascertain the extent of the damage.

Occasions arise where a vessel has to moor to a fixed or floating object which has already suffered damage on one or more previous occasions and the damage remains extant. In such cases the master should draw the attention of the Port Authorities to this, and note the details of the damage in the log, and support this with sketches and photographic evidence. It is not unknown for damage to be claimed against more than one vessel for the same alleged damage. These allegations are usually made when the vessel was leaving the berth.

## b. Potential exposure / problem

A number of potential issues need to be identified:

i) Potential claim from the third party owner, or insurer, of the property damaged. This may include not only repair / restitution costs but also consequential losses arising as a result of the owner not having use of the property damaged until it was repaired. Consequential loss claims can be enormous.

ii) Limitation of liability — questions of 'seaworthiness' the test will depend whether jurisdiction has been founded in a 1957 or 1976 regime.

iii) There will be a possibility that the incident will be investigated under Resolution A.849(20) or UK S.I. 2005 No. 881. There may also be local laws, possibly harbour regulations, requiring such reporting.

## c. ISM implications

The ISM implications will clearly depend very much upon the primary and any underlying causes which led to the contact — but such incidents are likely to involve aspects of the navigation of the vessel. Accordingly, aspects of the ISM Code will be relevant. The following, non-exhaustive, list attempts to address some of the more obvious potential implications and, consequently, suggest areas of the SMS which will come under close scrutiny:

Section 1.2.3.1    (compliance with mandatory rules and regulations)

Regulations such as the STCW Convention and Code may need to be considered. Levels of competency may very well appear as having been causative of the incident. Also, hours of rest / work of the individual(s) involved would be examined as well as the management system which was in place to ensure that Section A-VIII/1 of STCW Code was being complied with.

Section 6    Resources and personnel

In the majority of contact incidents one or more individuals did, or did not, do something which ultimately contributed to the contact incident — often referred to as 'human error'. It may have been the master and / or the Officer of the Watch (OOW) or pilot. Under Section 6 there is a very clear obligation upon the Company to engage only qualified, skilled and suitably experienced personnel. It can therefore be anticipated that a potential claimant or investigator will look very carefully not only at the qualifications and alleged experience of the individual but may also require to examine the Company selection and recruiting procedures and to follow an audit trail to demonstrate that these procedures were indeed followed when recruiting the particular individual who is the focus of attention. Bridge team and crew resource management may also be an issue to be investigated. Passage / voyage planning and master / pilot relationship are other areas which may be relevant.

It may also be necessary to produce evidence that suitable and adequate familiarisation and training was provided to the individual – e.g. in the operation of the radar etc. Relevant sections of STCW would also need to be considered.

## Section 7    Development of plans for shipboard operations

Clearly the navigation of the vessel (which would include navigating in and out of port where most of the contact incidents occur) would be included as one of the 'key shipboard operations' anticipated by Section 7. As such it should be expected that there are clear Company procedures set out in a Procedures Manual. Those procedures will be examined very carefully, not only in light of the contact incident itself but also during other periods of the ships life. This would be done by following audit trails.

## Section 8    Emergency preparedness

A contact incident may very well fall within the category of 'potential emergency situations' anticipated in Section 8. The response of the master and those on board, following such an incident will be examined against the written procedures. No doubt records of simulated drills involving contact type incidents will also be examined.

## Section 9    Reports and analysis of non-conformities, accidents and hazardous occurrences

Records of the activities anticipated by Section 9 may well be examined to confirm that learning opportunities were being taken as part of the SMS. Similarly minutes of on board safety committee meetings may be examined to determine the level of involvement and commitment to safety management on board

## Section 10    Maintenance of the ship and equipment

To what extent this may be relevant will obviously be determined by reference to the cause of the contact incident. If the failure of a piece of equipment was involved then the procedures and records will be examined very carefully.

## Section 11    Documentation

If there appear to have been problems with compliance with the SMS then it is likely that a closer look will be made at the documented procedures themselves. If these are voluminous, irrelevant or otherwise inadequate then the Company is likely to come under severe criticism.

## Section 12    Company verification, review and evaluation

There is a very clear obligation on the Company to ensure that the SMS is working properly on board its vessels. If a serious incident has arisen, as may well be the case with a contact incident, then it can be anticipated that the active monitoring by the Company will be looked at very closely by way of audit trails.

### Certification and verification

As a matter of course the validity of the SMC and DOC will be checked.

## d. Nature of evidence required

In cases of substantial damage, owners and their insurers will appoint expert surveyors and in some cases civil engineers, to assess the extent of any damage and repairs. In order to assist the surveyors, who may not arrive at the scene immediately, it is essential that the master assembles as much contemporaneous evidence as possible. The manner in which port watches were routinely maintained would inevitably have a bearing on the value of such evidence.

However, the master should note that it is not only major incidents which require vigilance. Minor contacts with fixed and floating objects can lead to substantial claims by local authorities. Unless the owners and their insurers are able to produce contemporaneous evidence from the vessel they will have considerable difficulty refuting the allegations and minimising the extent of any claim.

**See General Introduction to this chapter for a list of documents that may be required in such an incident.**

## e. Report

The master should ensure that the report of the incident which he prepares includes the following information:

| |
|---|
| The date, time, and location, of the incident - |
| The information should be as precise as possible, for example, if the vessel comes into contact with a pier, the master should note the number of the pier |
| The conditions prevailing at the time - |
| The master should note whether it was day or night, the weather conditions, visibility, sea state, the incidence of swell, and the state of tides and currents |
| Details of the vessel's manoeuvres - |
| The master should note whether the vessel was entering or leaving a port or locks, berthing, assisted by tugs, or whether there was a pilot on board the vessel |
| Names and addresses of all crew members, pilots, tug crews, shore workers, or any other persons who witnessed the incident - |
| If time allows, the master should attempt to obtain from the witnesses their account of the incident |
| Details of the damaged object - |
| The master should note whether the damaged object was old or new, whether it was well used, whether it was well illuminated and marked, whether there were any signs of damage or defects to the object other than that caused by the vessel. If possible, the master should ensure that photographs, video recordings or sketches of the damage are taken. |

An incident involving a fixed or floating object may also give rise to an unsafe port claim against charterers of the vessel. Therefore, the master should refer to the discussion of unsafe ports and berths in chapter five for the type of evidence required from the vessel.

If an investigator is to attend, or if the incident is serious enough for a lawyer to attend to take statements, then the following information should be made available:

## Collision with fixed or floating objects

| Particulars of the incident<br>In accordance with Resolution A.849(20) |
| --- |
| Type of incident |
| Date, time and place of incident |
| Details of incident and of the events leading up to it and following it |
| Details of the performance of relevant equipment with special regard to any malfunction |
| Persons on bridge |
| Persons in engine-room |
| Whereabouts of the master and chief engineer |
| Mode of steering (auto or manual) |
| Extracts from all relevant ship and, if applicable, shore documents including details of entries in official, bridge, scrap/rough and engine-room log books, data log printout, computer printouts, course and engine speed recorder, radar log, etc. |
| Details of communications made between vessel and radio stations, SAR centres and control centres, etc., with transcript of tape recordings where available |
| Details of any injuries/fatalities |
| Voyage data recorder information (if fitted) for analysis |

| Particulars of the voyage<br>In accordance with Resolution A.849(20) |
| --- |
| Port at which voyage commenced and port at which it was to have ended, with dates |
| Details of cargo |
| Last port and date of departure |
| Draughts (forward, aft and midships) and any list |
| Port bound for at time of occurrence |
| Any incident during the voyage that may have a material bearing on the incident, or unusual occurrence, whether or not it appears to be relevant to the incident |
| Plan view of ship's layout including cargo spaces, slop tanks, bunker/fuel lube oil tanks (diagrams from IOPP Certificate) |
| Details of cargo, bunkers, fresh water and ballast and consumption |

| Particulars of sea state, weather and tide |
|---|
| **In accordance with Resolution A.849(20)** |
| Direction and force of wind |
| Direction and state of sea and swell |
| Atmospheric conditions and visibility |
| State and height of tide |
| Direction and strength of tidal and other currents, bearing in mind local conditions |

| Particulars of personnel involved in incident |
|---|
| **In accordance with Resolution A.849(20)** |
| Full name |
| Age |
| Details of injury |
| Description of accident |
| Person supervising activity |
| First aid or other action on board |
| Capacity on board |
| Certificate of Competency/Licence: grade; date of issue; issuing country/authority; other Certificates of Competency held |
| Time spent on vessel concerned |
| Experience on similar vessels |
| Experience on other types of vessels |
| Experience in current capacity |
| Experience in other ranks |
| Number of hours spent on duty on that day and the previous days |
| Number of hours sleep in the 96 hours prior to the incident |
| Any other factors, on board or personal, that may have affected sleep |
| Whether smoker, and if so, quantity |
| Normal alcohol habit |
| Alcohol consumption immediately prior to incident or in the previous 24 hours |

| Whether under prescribed medication |
|---|
| Any ingested non-prescribed drugs |
| Records of drug and alcohol tests |

| **Assistance after the incident** |
|---|
| In accordance with Resolution A.849(20) |
| If assistance was summoned, what form and by what means |
| If assistance was offered or given, by whom and of what nature, and whether it was effective and competent |
| If assistance was offered and refused, the reason for refusal |

## f. Case study

### Case history — 1

The subject vessel came into contact with a disused jetty in Wilhelmshaven, and the port authorities brought a claim for damages against the owners. The attending surveyors found that the jetty was not marked and, more importantly, not illuminated. The port authorities denied these allegations. However, the master, shortly after the incident, had collected evidence from the crew that the jetty was not lit and made particular reference to this point in his report. This contemporaneous evidence which supported the surveyors' findings, persuaded the port authorities to substantially reduce their claim for damages.

### Case history — 2

A loaded tanker whilst approaching its berth allegedly made heavy contact with one of the fenders. The fender, of a compound rubber shock absorbing type, showed evidence of not only the new damage but of pre-existing damage and recent temporary repairs. Doppler radar was fitted to the berth and was said to have been in use at the time that the vessel arrived. The claimants failed to provide a recording of the doppler radar in support of their argument.

A P&I surveyor was invited to attend the casualty before the vessels departure and collated details regarding the displacement of the vessel, the mooring operation, use of tugs, speed and angle of approach to the berth. Accurate log books maintained on the bridge and engine room provided valuable corroborative evidence to indicate that the contact could not have occurred in the manner described by the terminal. This further enabled the owners and their P&I Club to demonstrate that the alleged damages could not have been solely attributed to the incident. Owners contribution to the claim was properly limited to that amount which would have restored the fender to its condition immediately prior to the arrival of the vessel.

## Non-contact damage

It will be recalled that a collision involves physical contact between two ships. It is possible however, and it frequently occurs, that one ship causes damage to another without coming into physical contact.

### a. Conceptual background

The most usual scenario falling within this category of incident would tend to involve one ship travelling along the course of a river or canal, perhaps at excessive speed, where the wash being produced causes another ship which may be moored to a riverside berth to range along the berth and, as a consequence, suffer damage. In extreme cases the moorings may break. There will also be the propensity for personal injuries to result, pollution is also a possibility as well as damage to the berth itself or the shore installation.

Clearly if the moored ship does suffer damage as a result of the passing ship's negligence then it is very likely to have a legal claim against the passing ship.

In these types of incidents it is often the case that the passing ship was not actually aware that it had caused any damage. The first the ship may know about the incident is when an officer of the court appears on board with an arrest order. It is also possible that the ship suffering damage did not obtain details of the passing ship. However, by noting the time of the incident it would usually be quite easy to trace the offending vessel.

Another example of 'non-contact' damage incidents is where one ship hampers another ship in her manoeuvres and which results in the other ship colliding with another ship or contacting some object. If the third party can demonstrate the negligence of the ship causing the hindrance then there is likely to be a valid claim.

This particular category of incident does not appear to be specifically referred to in Resolution A.849(20) but, applying a 'ejusdem generis' ('of the same kind') rule then it would be logical to include this category rather than exclude it. Here it will be treated here as though it were a 'Serious Casualty'.

This category of incident would usually fall under P&I cover although this may not be the case if the H&M insurance is on non-UK terms, when the risk may be covered under the H&M policy.

### b. Potential exposure / problem

A number of potential issues need to be identified:

i) Potential claims from the third party owner, or insurer, of the ship or other property damaged.

ii) Limitation of liability – questions of 'seaworthiness' the test will depend whether jurisdiction has been founded in a 1957 or 1976 regime.

iii) There will be a possibility that the incident will be investigated under Resolution A.849(20) or UK S.I. 2005 No. 881. There may also be local laws, possibly harbour regulations, requiring such reporting.

### c. ISM implications

The ISM implications will clearly depend very much upon the primary and any underlying causes which led to the non-contact — but such incidents are likely to involve aspects of the navigation of the vessel. Accordingly, aspects of the ISM Code will be relevant. The following, non-exhaustive, list attempts to address some of the more obvious potential implications and, consequently, suggest areas of the SMS which will come under close scrutiny:

Section 1.2.3.1    (compliance with mandatory rules and regulations)

Regulations such as the STCW Convention and Code may need to be considered. Levels of competency may very well appear as having been causative of the incident. Also, hours of rest / work of the individual(s) involved would be examined as well as the management system which was in place to ensure that Section A-VIII/1 of STCW Code was being complied with.

Section 6     Resources and personnel

In the majority of non-contact incidents one or more individuals did, or did not, do something which ultimately contributed to the incident — often referred to as 'human error'. It may have been the master and / or the Officer of the Watch (OOW) or pilot. Under Section 6 there is a very clear obligation upon the Company to engage only qualified, skilled and suitably experienced personnel. It can therefore be anticipated that a potential claimant or investigator will look very carefully not only at the qualifications and alleged experience of the individual but may also require to examine the Company selection and recruiting procedures and to follow an audit trail to demonstrate that these procedures were indeed followed when recruiting the particular individual who is the focus of attention. Bridge team and crew resource management may also be an issue to be investigated. Passage /voyage planning and master / pilot relationship are other areas which may be relevant.

It may also be necessary to produce evidence that suitable and adequate familiarisation and training was provided to the individual – e.g. in the operation of the radar etc. Relevant sections of STCW would also need to be considered.

Section 7     Development of plans for shipboard operations

Clearly the navigation of the vessel (which would include navigating in confined waters, rivers and canals etc. — where most of the non-contact incidents occur) would be included as one of the 'key shipboard operations' anticipated by Section 7. As such it should be expected that there are clear Company procedures set out in a Procedures Manual. Those procedures will be examined very carefully, not only in light of the contact incident itself but also during other periods of the ships life. This would be done by following audit trails.

Section 8     Emergency preparedness

A non-contact incident may very well fall within the category of 'potential emergency situations' anticipated in Section 8 — possibly the response would be as if the incident was a collision. The response of the master and those on board, following such an incident will be examined against the written procedures. No doubt records of simulated drills involving contact type incidents will also be examined.

Section 9     Reports and analysis of non-conformities, accidents and hazardous occurrences

Records of the activities anticipated by Section 9 may well be examined to confirm that learning opportunities were being taken as part of the SMS. Similarly minutes of on board safety committee meetings may be examined to determine the level of involvement and commitment to safety management on board

Section 10     Maintenance of the ship and equipment

To what extent this may be relevant will obviously be determined by reference to the cause of the non-contact incident. If the failure of a piece of equipment was involved then the procedures and records will be examined very carefully.

Section 11     Documentation

If there appear to have been problems with compliance with the SMS then it is likely that a closer look will be made at the documented procedures themselves. If these are voluminous, irrelevant or otherwise inadequate then the Company is likely to come under severe criticism.

Section 12     Company verification, review and evaluation

There is a very clear obligation on the Company to ensure that the SMS is working properly on board its vessels. If a serious incident has arisen, as may well be the case with a non-contact incident with a collision, then it can be anticipated that the active monitoring by the Company will be looked at very closely by way of audit trails.

Certification and verification

As a matter of course the validity of the SMC and DOC will be checked.

## d. Nature of evidence required

It is generally the view that unless there is evidence that the moored vessel contributed in some way to the incident, the vessel underway is liable for the damage.

Regardless of whether the master is on the passing or hindering vessel, he should ensure the following information is obtained:

- Whether or not the vessel or an adjacent vessel was testing her main engines in such a way as to contribute to the incident

- Whether or not the moorings on the moored vessel were defective, slack or ineffective in any way

- An estimate of the tidal direction and strength

- The identity of witnesses on shore, and

- Photographs of damage to the other vessel.

As many of the incidents which take place when the vessel is moored are minor incidents, the insurers of both vessels may not require a joint survey, but will rely heavily on the master's evidence. It is important, therefore, that the master's report of the incident gives a detailed record of the damage.

**See General Introduction to this chapter for a list of documents that may be required in such an incident.**

### e. Report

The master should ensure that the report of the incident which he prepares includes the following information:

| |
|---|
| The date, time, and location, of the incident - |
| The information should be as precise as possible, for example, if the vessel passed such and such a berth, at a particular time. The bell book and deck log should record the engine movements and passing particular points e.g. navigation buoys such that a calculation of the ship speed can be made. |
| The conditions prevailing at the time - |
| The master should note whether it was day or night, the weather conditions, visibility, sea state, the incidence of swell, and the state of tides and currents |
| Details of the vessel's manoeuvres - |
| The master should note whether the vessel was entering or leaving a port or locks, berthing, assisted by tugs, or whether there was a pilot on board the vessel |
| Names and addresses of all crew members, pilots, tug crews, shore workers, or any other persons who witnessed the incident - |
| If time allows, the master should attempt to obtain from the witnesses their account of the incident |
| Details of the damaged object - |
| The master should note the name and details of the other ship(s) involved. |
| If possible, the master should ensure that photographs, video recordings or sketches of the damage are taken. |

If an investigator is to attend, or if the incident is serious enough for a lawyer to attend to take statements, then the following information should be made available:

| Particulars of the incident |
|---|
| **In accordance with Resolution A.849(20)** |
| Type of incident |
| Date, time and place of incident |
| Details of incident and of the events leading up to it and following it |
| Details of the performance of relevant equipment with special regard to any malfunction |
| Persons on bridge |
| Persons in engine-room |
| Whereabouts of the master and chief engineer |
| Mode of steering (auto or manual) |
| Extracts from all relevant ship and, if applicable, shore documents including details of entries in official, bridge, scrap/rough and engine-room log books, data log printout, computer printouts, course and engine speed recorder, radar log, etc. |
| Details of communications made between vessel and radio stations, SAR centres and control centres, etc., with transcript of tape recordings where available |
| Details of any injuries/fatalities |
| Voyage data recorder information (if fitted) for analysis |

| Particulars of the voyage |
|---|
| In accordance with Resolution A.849(20) |
| Port at which voyage commenced and port at which it was to have ended, with dates |
| Details of cargo |
| Last port and date of departure |
| Draughts (forward, aft and midships) and any list |
| Port bound for at time of occurrence |
| Any incident during the voyage that may have a material bearing on the incident, or unusual occurrence, whether or not it appears to be relevant to the incident |
| Plan view of ship's layout including cargo spaces, slop tanks, bunker/fuel lube oil tanks (diagrams from IOPP Certificate) |
| Details of cargo, bunkers, fresh water and ballast and consumption |

| Particulars of sea state, weather and tide |
|---|
| **In accordance with Resolution A.849(20)** |
| Direction and force of wind |
| Direction and state of sea and swell |
| Atmospheric conditions and visibility |
| State and height of tide |
| Direction and strength of tidal and other currents, bearing in mind local conditions |

| Particulars of personnel involved in incident |
|---|
| **In accordance with Resolution A.849(20)** |
| Full name |
| Age |
| Details of injury |
| Description of accident |
| Person supervising activity |
| First aid or other action on board |
| Capacity on board |
| Certificate of Competency/Licence: |
| grade; |
| date of issue; |
| issuing country/authority; |
| other Certificates of Competency held |
| Time spent on vessel concerned |
| Experience on similar vessels |
| Experience on other types of vessels |
| Experience in current capacity |
| Experience in other ranks |
| Number of hours spent on duty on that day and the previous days |
| Number of hours sleep in the 96 hours prior to the incident |
| Any other factors, on board or personal, that may have affected sleep |
| Whether smoker, and if so, quantity |
| Normal alcohol habit |
| Alcohol consumption immediately prior to incident or in the previous 24 hours |

| Whether under prescribed medication |
|---|
| Any ingested non-prescribed drugs |
| Records of drug and alcohol tests |

| **Assistance after the incident** |
|---|
| **In accordance with Resolution A.849(20)** |
| If assistance was summoned, what form and by what means |
| If assistance was offered or given, by whom and of what nature, and whether it was effective and competent |
| If assistance was offered and refused, the reason for refusal |

## f. Case study

### Background to the incident

Whilst proceeding inbound through a river approach to a major European port a 32,000 dwt container vessel passed a small chemical tanker which was alongside a riverside berth discharging her cargo.

The container vessel was proceeding at manoeuvring full ahead up until a position approximately one quarter of a mile from the moored tanker when the pilot ordered the engine to be slowed to half ahead. The tide was ebbing at about $1\frac{1}{2}$ knots. It was daylight and the visibility was good.

As the container vessel started to get closer to the tanker the third mate, who was the officer of the watch on the bridge, reported to the pilot that the mooring lines on the tanker seemed to be hanging loose. On verifying this through binoculars the pilot ordered the engine to be put to dead slow ahead. The estimated speed on passing the tanker was 5 knots through the water at a distance of about 150 metres.

The third mate and master of the container vessel continued to observe the tanker after it had been passed and saw the tanker serge along the berth, metallic noises were heard and a lot of activity could be seen on board.

The pilot was advised who called up the VTS station and reported the incident to them. An entry was made in the deck log book which was countersigned by the pilot.

The following morning a lawyer presented himself on board with an arrest order against the ship. He claimed to be acting for the tanker who was alleging that the container vessel was proceeding at excessive speed, without taking due care and attention and, as a consequence, the wake of the vessel caused the tanker to serge along the quayside, breaking two mooring ropes, causing serious damage to the ships gangway, fracturing a discharging pipeline and causing a spillage of the chemical cargo. The local P&I Correspondent was contacted who appointed a surveyor to attend the tanker to investigate. A lawyer was also instructed and a P&I Club letter of undertaking was provided for $700,000 to secure the release of the container vessel from arrest.

### Relevant evidence

The following item of evidence were secured from the container vessel:

- The original navigation chart with positions and times of passing buoys and other identifiable objects;
- Deck log book;
- Bridge movement book;
- Automatic engine / telegraph recorder print out;
- Statement from the master;
- Statement from the third mate.

The P&I Correspondent and the surveyor were able to obtain the following additional evidence:

- Statement from the pilot;
- Audio recording from the VTS station of the conversation with the pilot when he reported the incident – which included the time;
- Video recording of the VTS radar picture of the transit of the container vessel along the river which also showed relative speed and heading;
- A statement from a colleague of the appointed surveyor who was a cargo surveyor and who had attended on board the tanker about one hour before the incident and who recalled that the mooring lines were not tight at that time.
- The surveyors own report confirmed that the gangway was in a damaged condition and that two broken mooring ropes were shown to him. The ropes were old and not in good condition generally. It did appear that there had been damage to a cargo discharge pipeline. Apparently a small quantity, estimated at between 500 and 1000 litres of cargo spilt onto the deck of the ship and a small quantity did run overboard into the river. The cargo was described as a low hazard acid. Local river police had been advised but there was no trace of any pollutant when they attended to investigate. The tanker crew cleaned up the spill from their own deck.

### Outcome

A documented claim was subsequently presented by the tanker owners to the container vessel operators. The claim was for an amount of US$85,000. Following negotiations and based mainly on the strength of the evidence presented by the container vessel operators – an amicable out of court settlement was reached at US$7,500. The club letter of undertaking was returned for cancellation.

If it had not been for the keen observation of the third mate on the container vessel and the action taken at the time, including the collection of evidence, the final outcome may have been very different.

### Grounding, stranding and foundering

There are three similar categories of incidents covered in this section. It is believed that the three categories are similar enough, in their nature, to be considered together in so far as the role of investigating and collecting evidence is concerned.

However, it may be useful to provide some brief definitions which will allow us to distinguish between them:

*'Grounding' – Deliberate contact by a ship with the bottom while the ship is moored or anchored as a result of the water level dropping*

*'Stranding' – Contact by a ship with the bottom which prevents her from moving. Stranding is normally an involuntary act but it also occurs when a ship is intentionally run ashore to avoid a greater peril.*

It proved remarkably difficult to find a definition of 'Foundering' in any of the specialised Shipping or Maritime Law Dictionaries. This is a very old term which is still used by the IMO as well as the British Government and Insurers and appears to mean the sinking of a vessel — possibly following the striking of an object.

### a. Conceptual background

In the case of a grounding or a stranding, and maybe even a foundering, the question will arise as to whether the vessel can be salvaged or whether it has become an actual or constructive total loss. However, from the perspective of this book we are more interested in the collection of evidence to explain and understand why and how the ship ended up in that particular situation. Salvage and General Average incidents have been addressed separately in this volume.

The losses involved, as far as loss or damage to the ship is concerned, will fall to be covered under the H&M Policy. There may of course be personal injuries / fatalities involved, pollution and cargo loss or damage. For the sake of this section however, we will consider the matter as another navigational incident.

### b. Potential exposure / problem

A number of potential issues need to be identified:

i)   Potential claim against H&M Underwriters.

ii) Potential claim from coastal state for damage and / or wreck removal — the vessel may be a hazard to navigation and / or pollution risk.

iii) Limitation of liability — questions of 'seaworthiness' the test will depend whether jurisdiction has been founded in a 1957 or 1976 regime.

iv) There will be a possibility that the incident will be investigated under Resolution A.849(20) or UK S.I. 2005 No. 881. There may also be local laws, possibly harbour regulations, requiring such reporting.

### c. ISM implications

The ISM implications will clearly depend very much upon the primary and any underlying causes which led to the grounding, stranding or foundering — but such incidents are likely to involve aspects of the navigation of the vessel. Accordingly, aspects of the ISM Code will be relevant. The following, non-exhaustive, list attempts to address some of the more obvious potential implications and, consequently, suggest areas of the SMS which will come under close scrutiny:

Section 1.2.3.1    (compliance with mandatory rules and regulations)

Regulations such as the STCW Convention and Code may need to be considered. Levels of competency may very well appear as having been causative of the incident. Also, hours of rest / work of the individual(s) involved would be examined as well as the management system which was in place to ensure that Section A-VIII/1 of STCW Code was being complied with.

Section 6     Resources and personnel

In the majority of grounding, stranding or foundering incidents one or more individuals did, or did not, do something which ultimately contributed to the incident - often referred to a 'human error'. It may have been the master and / or the Officer of the Watch (OOW) or pilot. Under Section 6 there is a very clear obligation upon the company to engage only qualified, skilled and suitably experienced personnel. It can therefore be anticipated that a potential claimant or investigator will look very carefully not only at the qualifications and alleged experience of the individual but may also require to examine the Company selection and recruiting procedures and to follow an audit trail to demonstrate that these procedures were indeed followed when recruiting the particular individual who is the focus of attention. Bridge team and crew resource management may also be an issue to be investigated. Passage /voyage planning and master / pilot relationship are other areas which may be relevant.

It may also be necessary to produce evidence that suitable and adequate familiarisation and training was provided to the individual – e.g. in the operation of the radar etc. Relevant sections of STCW would also need to be considered.

Section 7    Development of plans for shipboard operations

Clearly the navigation of the vessel (which would include navigating in confined waters, rivers and canals etc. — where most of the grounding, stranding or foundering incidents occur) would be included as one of the 'key shipboard operations' anticipated by Section 7. As such it should be expected that there are clear Company procedures set out in a Procedures Manual. Those procedures will be examined very carefully, not only in light of the grounding, stranding or foundering incident itself but also during other periods of the ships life. This would be done by following audit trails.

Section 8    Emergency preparedness

A grounding, stranding or foundering incident may very well fall within the category of 'potential emergency situations' anticipated in Section 8 – possibly the response would be as if the incident was a collision. The response of the master and those on board, following such an incident will be examined against the written procedures. No doubt records of simulated drills involving contact type incidents will also be examined.

Section 9    Reports and analysis of non-conformities, accidents and hazardous occurrences

Records of the activities anticipated by Section 9 may well be examined to confirm that learning opportunities were being taken as part of the SMS. Similarly minutes of on board safety committee meetings may be examined to determine the level of involvement and commitment to safety management on board

Section 10    Maintenance of the ship and equipment

To what extent this may be relevant will obviously be determined by reference to the cause of the grounding, stranding or foundering incident. If the failure of a piece of equipment was involved then the procedures and records will be examined very carefully.

Section 11    Documentation

If there appear to have been problems with compliance with the SMS then it is likely that a closer look will be made at the documented procedures themselves. If these are voluminous, irrelevant or otherwise inadequate then the Company is likely to come under severe criticism.

Section 12    Company verification, review and evaluation

There is a very clear obligation on the Company to ensure that the SMS is working properly on board its vessels. If a serious incident has arisen, as may well be the case with a grounding, stranding or foundering incident with a collision, then it can be anticipated that the active monitoring by the Company will be looked at very closely by way of audit trails.

Certification and verification

As a matter of course the validity of the SMC and DOC will be checked.

## d. Nature of evidence required

The nature of the evidence required will be determined by the circumstances which led up to the incident. This is most likely to focus on the navigation of the vessel. However, the vessel could have ended up in the particular predicament because of a whole range of possibilities, for example:

- Navigational error — unintentionally stranded into shallow water
- Ran aground to avoid colliding with another vessel
- Deliberately ran aground to avoid sinking
- Ran aground because of a piracy or terrorist attack
- Forced aground through stress of weather, etc

The evidence that will be required will need to demonstrate what happened and why it happened.

**See General Introduction to this chapter for a list of documents that may be required in such an incident.**

## e. Report

The master should ensure that the report of the incident which he prepares includes the following information:

| The date, time, and location, of the incident - |
| --- |
| The information should be as precise as possible. The bell book and deck log should record the engine movements and actions taken. |
| The conditions prevailing at the time - |
| The master should note whether it was day or night, the weather conditions, visibility, sea state, the incidence of swell, and the state of tides and currents |
| Details of the vessel's manoeuvres - |
| The master should note whether the vessel was entering or leaving a port or locks, berthing, assisted by tugs, or whether there was a pilot on board the vessel |
| Names and addresses of all crew members, pilots, tug crews, shore workers, or any other persons who witnessed the incident - |
| If time allows, the master should attempt to obtain from the witnesses their account of the incident |
| Details of the damaged object - |
| The master should note the name and details of the other ship(s) involved. If possible, the master should ensure that photographs, video recordings or sketches of the damage are taken. |

Depending upon the circumstances such an incident could very well fall into the classification of 'very serious casualty' and if that is the case then a full investigation by the flag State would almost certain. Similarly, an investigation by the coastal state is a very high probability. If an investigator is to attend, or if the incident is serious enough for a lawyer to attend to take statements, then the following information should be made available:

| **Particulars of the incident** |
|---|
| **In accordance with Resolution A.849(20)** |
| Type of incident |
| Date, time and place of incident |
| Details of incident and of the events leading up to it and following it |
| Details of the performance of relevant equipment with special regard to any malfunction |
| Persons on bridge |
| Persons in engine-room |
| Whereabouts of the master and chief engineer |
| Mode of steering (auto or manual) |
| Extracts from all relevant ship and, if applicable, shore documents including details of entries in official, bridge, scrap/rough and engine-room log books, data log printout, computer printouts, course and engine speed recorder, radar log, etc. |
| Details of communications made between vessel and radio stations, SAR centres and control centres, etc., with transcript of tape recordings where available |
| Details of any injuries/fatalities |
| Voyage data recorder information (if fitted) for analysis |

| **Particulars of the voyage** |
|---|
| **In accordance with Resolution A.849(20)** |
| Port at which voyage commenced and port at which it was to have ended, with dates |
| Details of cargo |
| Last port and date of departure |
| Draughts (forward, aft and midships) and any list |
| Port bound for at time of occurrence |
| Any incident during the voyage that may have a material bearing on the incident, or unusual occurrence, whether or not it appears to be relevant to the incident |
| Plan view of ship's layout including cargo spaces, slop tanks, bunker/fuel lube oil tanks (diagrams from IOPP Certificate) |
| Details of cargo, bunkers, fresh water and ballast and consumption |

Pt B2

S
H
I
P

## Particulars of sea state, weather and tide
## In accordance with Resolution A.849(20)

| |
|---|
| Direction and force of wind |
| Direction and state of sea and swell |
| Atmospheric conditions and visibility |
| State and height of tide |
| Direction and strength of tidal and other currents, bearing in mind local conditions |

## Particulars of personnel involved in incident
## In accordance with Resolution A.849(20)

| |
|---|
| Full name |
| Age |
| Details of injury |
| Description of accident |
| Person supervising activity |
| First aid or other action on board |
| Capacity on board |
| Certificate of Competency/Licence: <br> grade; <br> date of issue; <br> issuing country/authority; |
| other Certificates of Competency held |
| Time spent on vessel concerned |
| Experience on similar vessels |
| Experience on other types of vessels |
| Experience in current capacity |
| Experience in other ranks |
| Number of hours spent on duty on that day and the previous days |
| Number of hours sleep in the 96 hours prior to the incident |
| Any other factors, on board or personal, that may have affected sleep |
| Whether smoker, and if so, quantity |
| Normal alcohol habit |
| Alcohol consumption immediately prior to incident or in the previous 24 hours |

| |
|---|
| Whether under prescribed medication |
| Any ingested non-prescribed drugs |
| Records of drug and alcohol tests |

| |
|---|
| **Assistance after the incident** |
| **In accordance with Resolution A.849(20)** |
| If assistance was summoned, what form and by what means |
| If assistance was offered or given, by whom and of what nature, and whether it was effective and competent |
| If assistance was offered and refused, the reason for refusal |

Resolution A.849(20) also draws attention to additional information which may be required in the case of a grounding:

| |
|---|
| **In accordance with Resolution A.849(20)** |
| Details of voyage plan, or evidence of voyage planning |
| Last accurate position and how obtained |
| Subsequent opportunities for fixing position or position lines, by celestial or terrestrial observations, GPS, radio, radar or otherwise, or by lines of soundings and, if not taken, why not |
| Chart datum comparison to WGS datum |
| Subsequent weather and tidal or other currents experienced |
| Effect on compass of any magnetic cargo, electrical disturbance or local attraction |
| Radar/s in use, respective ranges used, and evidence of radar performance monitoring and logging |
| Charts, sailing directions and relevant notices to mariners held, if corrected to date, and if any warnings they contain had been observed |
| Depth sounding taken, when and by what means |
| Tank soundings taken, when and by what means |
| Draught of ship before grounding and how determined |
| Position of grounding and how determined |
| Cause and nature of any engine or steering failure before the grounding |
| Readiness of anchors, their use and effectiveness |
| Nature and extent of damage |
| Action taken, and movements of ship, after grounding |
| (Note: information as in cases of foundering may also be required) |

Resolution A.849(2) also draws attention to additional information which may be required in the case of a foundering:

| In accordance with Resolution A.849(20) |
| --- |
| Draught and freeboard on leaving last port and changes consequent upon consumption of stores and fuel |
| Freeboard appropriate to zone and date |
| Loading procedures, hull stresses |
| Particulars of any alterations to hull or equipment, since survey, and by whom such alterations sanctioned |
| Condition of ship, possible effects on seaworthiness |
| Stability data and when determined |
| Factors affecting stability, e.g. structural alterations, nature, weight, distribution and shift of any cargo and ballast, free surface in tanks or of loose water in ship |
| Subdivision by watertight bulkheads |
| Position of, and watertight integrity of, hatches, scuttles, ports and other openings |
| Number and capacity of pumps and their effectiveness; the position of suctions |
| Cause and nature of water first entering ship |
| Other circumstances leading up to foundering |
| Measures taken to prevent foundering |
| Position where ship foundered and how established |
| Life-saving appliances provided and used, and any difficulties experienced in their use |

In appropriate cases, investigators and lawyers may require a completed IMO Damage card, or similar and intact stability reporting – please see Annex 5 of IMO MSC/Circ.953 / MEPC/Circ.372 in Part C 4 towards the back of this book.

### f. Case study

#### Background to the incident

A 12,500 gt general cargo ship was proceeding fully loaded through the Aegean Sea toward the Suez Canal. Full sea speed was 15 knots. A passage plan had been prepared and approved, the master's standing orders had been read and signed by all deck officers and the master had written up his night order book on the evening in question which had also been signed by the third officer and the second officer. In his night orders the master had reminded his navigating officers to: "Maintain the courses and follow the passage plan and to call him if in doubt or if required".

During the midnight to 0400 hrs watch the vessel was to pass between two groups of islands with a channel some 8 miles wide. At about 0200 hrs the second officer – who was the officer of the watch and who was accompanied by a look out – became aware of a significant number of lights on the starboard bow. His radar was detecting a number of small echoes at a distance of 7 miles. By 0210 hrs the lights were starting to become clearer and the second officer determined that they were small sailing vessels and appeared to be crossing very slowly from starboard to port. He thought they were probably a flotilla of yachts or maybe a yacht race sailing between the two islands. At 0215 hrs the second officer altered course 30 degrees to starboard which put all of the sailing vessels on his port bow. He continued to monitor the sailing vessels and was satisfied that they were passing clear.

At 0235 hrs he was just about to start bring the vessel back around to her original course line when he heard the echo sounder alarm. On checking the echo sounder it was showing ten metres below the keel and reducing. The ship started to vibrate and shudder. He immediately put the lookout onto hand steering and ordered hard to port at the same time putting the engines on dead slow and then stop. At this time the vessel was felt to be bumping along the bottom. The master arrived on the bridge, having been awakened by the vibrations — he noticed that the speed according to the GPS was zero. The vessel had run aground on an off-lying shoal.

General Emergency stations were called and the chief officer led a party to sound around the tanks and bilges on deck and the chief engineer to check the engine room. It was confirmed that the hull appeared to be intact.

Upon investigation it transpired that the second officer had put a position on the navigation chart at 0200 hrs but had neither put a position on the chart nor consulted the chart during the period he was altering course to pass the sailing vessels – up to the grounding shortly after 0235 hrs. He confirmed that he was monitoring his distance off the island on his starboard side using the radar and didn't intend getting any closer than 1½ miles. However, he had not appreciated or rather he had forgotten about the off-lying shoal area. Indeed it was the same second officer who had prepared the passage plan and had actually highlighted the shoal area in order to draw the attention of the officer of the watch to its existence.

A salvage tug and lightering barges were engaged. A little over 2000 tons of cargo were offloaded onto barges before the ship refloated and was safely pulled clear of the shoal area. Following an inspection it was confirmed that there was no serious damage to the ships hull, propeller, rudder or machinery.

The salvage / general average expenses to lighten and refloat the vessel came to US$2,000,000 of which cargo interests contribution was to be US$1,200,000.

Cargo interests refused to make their contribution alleging that there had been a breach of the contract of carriage by the ship owner / carrier. Specifically cargo interests alleged that the ship was not seaworthy and the carrier had failed to exercise due diligence at the commencement of the voyage to make the vessel seaworthy in that they did not have an adequate safety management system in place in respect of the navigation of the vessel and that the master and second officer were both negligent and incompetent.

### Relevant evidence

Evidence obtained from the ship included:

- The original working chart;
- The deck log book;
- Movement book,
- Engine log;
- Course recorder,
- Passage plan;
- Chart correction log
- Extracts from the SMM – procedures covering:
  - 'Bridge watch-keeping and bridge team management'
  - 'Navigation in coastal waters'
  - 'Passage planning'
  - 'Calling the master'
  - 'Duties of the master'
  - 'Duties of the Second Officer'
- Master's Standing Orders (signed by all deck officers)
- Master's Night Orders
- Hours of work / rest records of second officer
- Certificate of Competency (STCW) of second officer
- Certificate of Competency (STCW) of master
- Familiarisation, training and appraisal records of the second officer
- masters report of the incident
- Safety Management Certificate

In addition, the following evidence was subsequently collected:

- Formal statement from the master

- Formal statement from the second officer

- Formal statement from the lookout

- Formal statement from the chief officer focusing on his assessment of the second officer's experience and competence

- Records of internal audits

- Records of external audits

- Full personnel records of the master — including recruitment procedure, training, certificates held, previous sailing experience and appraisals

- Full personnel records of the second officer — including recruitment procedure, training, certificates held, previous sailing experience and appraisals

- Document of Compliance

### *Outcome*

The allegations being made by claimants identified three main aspects which would need to be dealt with and responded to:

1. The adequacy of the SMM procedures relating to the navigation of the vessel

2. The ability and conduct of the master

3. The ability and conduct of the second officer

It would then be necessary to consider whether the ship operators had done all they could or should have done with regard to:

1. Ensuring that the SMM procedures were being followed by those on board

2. Ensuring that their own procedures were being followed when recruiting staff, specifically the master and the second officer and that adequate familiarisation and training had been given, where appropriate.

Upon investigation it was established that the relevant procedures relating to navigation and bridge management were well written and, if followed, would ensure that the navigation of the vessel would have been conducted in a safe and efficient manner. The masters standing orders complemented the Company's own procedures.

The master was a very experienced captain who had sailed with the company for oven ten years, eight of which were in command. He was highly respected within the company both by the shore management as well as ship staff with whom he sailed. There were no similar previous experiences of major incidents on board any of the ships he had sailed. He had checked and approved the passage plan for the subject voyage and managed the bridge team in strict accordance with the company procedures and his own standing orders. The master had sailed for a total of about three years with the second officer and held him in very high regard. There was nothing which happened in the lead up to the grounding which would indicate any non-compliance with company procedures, or failure to apply good practice, by the master.

The second officer had been sailing for five years. He had served his cadetship with this same company and had sailed with them for two trips as third officer before being promoted to second officer. This was his second trip as second officer. He held a STCW Certificate of Competency to sail as second mate unlimited. On completion of the subject voyage he intended studying and sitting for his COC as first mate unlimited. He was well thought of by the company and the masters and senior officers with whom he sailed. As the ship's navigating officer he was the one who had prepared the passage plan.

The Company produced three detailed internal audit reports which had been conducted during the previous two years. These demonstrated clearly that the Company were verifying, by way of sample audit, that the correct procedures were being followed on board. Non conformities were being picked up and closed out.

Evidence adduced showed that the Company went to great lengths to ensure that they recruited good, well trained and experienced masters and officers and had an excellent retention record. They were also able to demonstrate that they actively promoted and monitored ongoing training for their staff. Formal appraisals of all staff were undertaken every voyage and at least every six months. These were reviewed by the personnel / crew manager who would deal with any issues. Both the master and second officer were long term members of the company staff.

In his statement the second officer could not explain why he did not put a position on the chart or otherwise consult the chart when he altered course to avoid the sailing vessels. He confirmed that he knew very well that this would be in breach of the company procedures and the masters standing orders. He believed he had plenty of sea room — he was not at all worried about the situation with the sailing vessels and saw no need to call the master. There was no suggestion of overwork or fatigue.

There was no past history of this second officer conducting his watch contrary to Company procedures or of behaving in anything other than a thoroughly capable and competent navigating officer. Maybe overconfidence was starting to creep in — it is difficult to say. But for whatever reason the second officer forgot about a navigational hazard, he failed to follow the correct procedures and, as a consequence, ran the ship aground. He was negligent but not incompetent.

Upon a review of the evidence presented, cargo claimants conceded that if the case was to go before the courts then the carrier probably would be entitled to rely upon an error of navigation / management of the vessel type defence. They therefore paid their contribution to the general average / salvage expenses.

[See also the brief account of the *Torepo* incident provided as the case study under the General Average and Salvage section of chapter one, page 83 — where similar issues were considered in a case which did actually become the subject of judicial consideration]

## Hull and machinery — damage or failure of ship and / or its own equipment

Although there are no legal requirements to compel a shipowner to insure its vessel (provided the vessel is free of mortgage commitments), most owners trading today have various forms of insurance cover. Normally, a shipowner may recover any loss which it suffers if:

- The damage is due to an insured peril

- The owner can provide sufficient evidence of the cause and extent of the damage suffered

- The vessel was in a seaworthy condition at the time of the incident which caused the loss and was engaged in a lawful trade, and

- The value of the loss exceeds any deductible/excess that may apply to the policy.

### a. Conceptual background

The legal requirement to demonstrate that the vessel was seaworthy effectively means that an owner has to be able to prove that, for the particular trade in which the vessel is involved, her hull, machinery and equipment are properly maintained, and that there are on board, sufficient stores, provisions, bunkers etc.

Accordingly, any damage to, failure of, or loss of these items which could affect the vessel's seaworthiness or the efficient state of the vessel must be reported to owners as soon as it occurs. This rule applies to any defect in the vessel which can be reasonably detected by the due diligence of the officers on board in the performance of their duties.

Owners are also under an obligation to maintain a safe working environment at all times on board the vessel. A relatively minor defect in a particular piece of equipment may affect the safety of the working environment. For example, a piece of machinery may have a safety feature which either becomes inoperative or detached (eg a defective foot operated emergency stop or a missing safety guard), and it then can become normal for the crew to operate it in this dangerous condition. The master and the safety officer, therefore, must be constantly vigilant against such minor defects and must also ensure that the officers and crew use the safety equipment provided.

If the ship's equipment becomes damaged, owners will generally be able to recover any loss if the requirements listed above are fulfilled. However, the master is under a duty to underwriters to act as if the vessel is uninsured. Amongst other things, this means that, following damage, the owners' duty to underwriters requires the master, officers and crew to take such further measures as may be reasonable for the purpose of preventing or minimising losses covered by the hull policy. The owners will be able to recover from underwriters the costs of such measures as "sue and labour" expenses. He must also provide a full and complete record of the incident.

### To whom evidence should be given

The master and officers should always check, if necessary with owners, the credentials of anyone asking for evidence or attending for survey before giving evidence themselves or allowing crew to do so. Occasionally surveyors and lawyers representing interests opposed to owners will attempt to obtain evidence either by not disclosing, or even concealing the identity of those for whom they are working.

### Risks covered

The extent of cover provided by marine insurance policies varies enormously. The master should verify his owner's cover for each vessel. The lists provided below give an indication of the type of risks covered by hull and machinery and protecting and indemnity ("P&I") policies.

*Hull and Machinery* (this list is compiled from the standard "ITC" clauses relating to damage to ship which were last revised on 01.11.95)

- Perils of the sea, rivers, lakes, or other navigable waters

- Fire, explosion

- Violent theft by persons outside the vessel

- Jettison

- Piracy

- Contact with land conveyance, dock or harbour equipment or installation

- Earthquake, volcanic eruption, or lightning

- Accidents in loading, discharging or shifting cargo or fuel

- Bursting of boilers, breakage of shafts, or any latent defect in the machinery or hull

- Negligence of the master, officers, crew or pilots

- Negligence of repairers or charterers

- Barratry of master, officers or crew

- Contact with aircraft, helicopters or similar objects, or objects falling therefrom.

- Pollution hazards (which includes damage to ship caused by preventive measures)

- Three-fourths collision liability (payment to third party).

*P&I Cover* (relating to damage to or failure of ship's equipment)

- Damage to third party's equipment and property

- One-fourth collision liability

- Oil pollution

## Role of parties involved

### *Salvage Association — acting on behalf of hull underwriters*

When damage to a vessel occurs which may give rise to a claim, owners have a duty to advise underwriters promptly. The underwriters will contact damage surveyors, usually the Salvage Association, who will in turn arrange for a surveyor to attend the vessel. The surveyor's job is to establish the facts surrounding the damage. The Salvage Association is an independent organisation which has representatives all over the world. In recent years, it has become common for hull underwriters to instruct the Salvage Association (or other independent surveyors) at an earlier stage to carry out comprehensive inspections of a vessel ("a condition survey") as a pre-condition of underwriters agreeing to provide insurance for that vessel.

### *P&I Surveyor — acting on behalf of owners*

When damage occurs to the property of a third party — for example, if a pipe fails during bunkering and oil is spilled in to the harbour — owners' P&I Club will protect their interests in the ensuing investigation and clean up operation. When damage occurs, the owners or master should alert the local P&I representative, who will instruct a surveyor to attend and assist. He will submit his report to the owners, and, if necessary, will also arrange security with the club.

### *Classification Society Surveyor — acting on behalf of class*

The role of a classification society in the merchant shipping community of today is to:

- Develop rules and standards for the design and construction of vessels

- Conduct surveys during the construction of vessels in order to verify that all rules and standards are complied with and to conduct regular surveys during a vessel's service in order to monitor the standard of maintenance

- Assign class when rules and standards are upheld.

When damage to any part of the ship occurs which could affect the vessel's seaworthiness, a surveyor representing the vessel's classification society will attend. All marine insurance policies impose an obligation on owners to maintain the vessel in class. If class is suspended as a result of a failure to comply with survey requirements or as a result of unrepaired damage, insurance cover is terminated automatically from that time. However, if the damage is an insured risk, termination of cover will only occur if the vessel sails from her next port of call without the prior approval of the classification society.

## b. Potential exposure / problem

### Stevedore damage

If stevedores cause damage to the ship's equipment, the master must take care to comply with the terms of the charterparty relating to stevedores. Stevedores often are appointed by charterers, shippers or receivers. However, charterparties may contain terms which provide that charterers are not responsible for any damage caused by stevedores. Such clauses often provide:

- That the master must notify stevedores of damages, normally by a written notice, within a very short time, usually 24 hours; the intention being that stevedores should have the opportunity to commission and pay for repairs before the vessel sails.

- And that failing such notification, charterers, shippers, receivers and stevedores are to have no liability to owners.

Charterers, shippers, receivers and stevedores may not always escape liability as a result of such clauses. However, it is important that, insofar as possible the master complies with any such clauses. Owner's position will always be assisted if the master can obtain the stevedores' confirmatory signature to a description of the damage. Moreover, if all the documentation covering the incident has not been completed at the time of the incident, recovery may not be possible.

The master should also ensure that all unrepaired stevedore damage is noted and photographed in detail in any off-hire survey and that charterers are invited to inspect damage repairs being carried out in dry-dock. If the damage is minor and does not effect the vessel's seaworthiness or efficient state, repairs may be deferred to the next dry-dock. Detailed reports by the master and chief engineer of stevedore (and other types) of damage are invaluable not only as evidence for legal purposes, but also to owners in preparing comprehensive specifications before placing repair contracts and thus avoiding costs and delay which result when "extras" are found to be necessary in the course of repairs.

### c. ISM implications

The ISM implications will clearly depend very much upon the primary and any underlying causes which led to the particular incident — but such incidents are likely to involve aspects of maintenance and operation of the vessel. Accordingly, aspects of the ISM Code will be relevant. The following, non-exhaustive, list attempts to address some of the more obvious potential implications and, consequently, suggest areas of the SMS which will come under close scrutiny:

Section 1.2.3.1     (compliance with mandatory rules and regulations) and 1.2.3.2 — (applicable codes and guidelines etc.)

Requirements such as those of the Classification Societies and manufacturers may need to be considered.

Section 6     Resources and personnel

In many H&M type incidents the problem may be traced back to a maintenance or inspection problem – it is therefore possible that the individuals responsible for such maintenance and inspection will come under scrutiny. Under Section 6 there is a very clear obligation upon the Company to engage only qualified, skilled and suitably experienced personnel. It can therefore be anticipated that a potential claimant or investigator will look very carefully not only at the qualifications and alleged experience of the individual but may also require to examine the Company selection and recruiting procedures and to follow an audit trail to demonstrate that these procedures were indeed followed when recruiting the particular individual who is the focus of attention.

Section 7     Development of plans for shipboard operations

Clearly the operation and maintenance of the ship and its machinery would be included amongst the 'key shipboard operations' anticipated by Section 7. As such it should be expected that there are clear Company procedures set out in a Procedures Manual. Those procedures will be examined very carefully, not only in light of the contact incident itself but also during other periods of the ships life. This would be done by following audit trails.

Section 8     Emergency preparedness

Clearly it will depend upon the actual problem which was the subject of the incident to determine to what extent if form part of an Emergency Preparedness procedure.

Section 9     Reports and analysis of non-conformities, accidents and hazardous occurrences

Records of the activities anticipated by Section 9 may well be examined to confirm that learning opportunities were being taken as part of the SMS. Similarly minutes of on board safety committee meetings may be examined to determine the level of involvement and commitment to safety management on board.

Section 10    Maintenance of the ship and equipment

This is likely to be the most relevant and significant part of the ISM Code applying to this type of incident. There should be clear and easy to follow audit trails to trace what might have gone wrong. There should also be records of non-conformities to be examined. If the failure of a piece of equipment was involved then the procedures and records will be examined very carefully.

Section 11    Documentation

If there appear to have been problems with compliance with the SMS then it is likely that a closer look will be made at the documented procedures themselves. If these are voluminous, irrelevant or otherwise inadequate then the Company is likely to come under severe criticism.

Section 12    Company verification, review and evaluation

There is a very clear obligation on the Company to ensure that the SMS is working properly on board its vessels. If a serious incident has arisen, as may well be the case with a contact incident with a collision, then it can be anticipated that the active monitoring by the Company will be looked at very closely by way of audit trails.

Certification and verification

As a matter of course the validity of the SMC and DOC will be checked.

## d. Nature of evidence required

### *Evidence required from the vessel*

Although the list provided below is not exhaustive, it gives an indication of the type of evidence required by the various parties involved in the event of equipment failure.

| *Evidence related to cause of damage* |
| --- |
| Damage report prepared by the master or chief engineer |
| Photographs of the damaged equipment in place and after removal |
| Parts of the damaged equipment and other relevant items which should be retained for inspection including consumables, such as old seals and broken bolts, analysis of which is often critical in determining cause of damage |
| Log books and maintenance records relating to damaged equipment |
| Any other records relating to the damaged equipment showing running hours, or evidence of previous inspections or surveys |
| Reports from other personnel involved in the incident. |

| *Evidence required if damage causes stoppage or delay* (in addition to above) |
| --- |
| Deck and engine log books covering the period of the incident |

| |
|---|
| Statement of fuel remaining on board at the beginning and end of the stoppage |
| Details of any deviation caused by the incident |
| If deviation to a port of refuge is required:<br>• reports or confirmation of class by classification society surveyor<br>• statement of facts from port agent<br>• details of all shore assistance provided that is attributable to damage |
| Names of all the surveyors who have attended the vessel with full details of the organisations they represent |
| Copies of fax, telex and radio messages sent or received, particularly those directed to time charterers dealing with deviation and off-hire times. |

| |
|---|
| *Evidence required when damage or failure impairs vessel's efficiency* |
| Details of additional time and fuel used as a consequence of the inefficiency |
| Details of the extra labour and equipment used and a record of times when they were used |
| Copies of all correspondence from the port agent, charterer or other third party holding vessel liable for delays. |

### e. Report

In addition, the master should:

• Ensure that statements and time sheets are accurate before signing them

• Ensure that written permission is obtained from the port authority if, as a result of delay caused by the vessel's inefficiency, the vessel has remained alongside a berth after completion of cargo operations. Many disputes have occurred when ships have remained alongside on the strength of the verbal assurance from jetty foreman, and consequently, owners have been faced with high penalty charges for remaining on the berth. The port agency will have details of charges involved.

### f. Case study

The subject vessel was a chemical tanker, on passage from Swansea to Gothenburg and Fredericia. She was loaded with 990 MT of enthanol and isopropanol. She sailed from Swansea on 12 December, 1981.

On 13 December, the vessel met severe heavy weather with winds up to force 10. During the morning of 14 December, the wind increased to force 11. The vessel passed through the Dover Straits, and at 0648 hours, the Sandettie NE buoy was seen close on the starboard bow. The vessel's helm was put immediately hard over to port, but this failed to have any effect on her set. At 0650 hours, a bump was felt on her starboard quarter followed by an explosion and abnormal noises from the engine room.

It was assumed that the propeller had touched the chain of the buoy. The 2nd engineer, on duty in the engine room, promptly advised that the main engine gear box was vibrating and that smoke was issuing from the stern gland. He requested that the engine be stopped.

On stopping the main engine, an inspection was made of the main engine gear box, and it was observed that the gearbox casing had been completely fractured just above the holding down bolts. It was also noted that the propeller was being turned by water movement. In addition an inspection was made of the stern tube seals. These appeared to be intact as there was no evidence of leakage into the engine room.

A mayday call was sent by radio at 0655 hours requesting immediate tug assistance. The call was answered by the Dover and French coastguards, and another vessel in the vicinity agreed to stand by until a suitable tug arrived.

Attempts were made by the ship's engineers to secure the shafting, but these were unsuccessful due to heavy seas turning the propeller. A constant watch was kept on the vessel's position. Due to the strong WSW wind causing the vessel to drift towards Fairy Bank and the anticipated change in the current direction, the master decided to anchor. At 0750 hours the port anchor was let go with the Fairy Bank buoy bearing 105 degrees, at a distance of two miles.

The vessel made radio contact with a tug steaming from Dunkirk at 1100 hours. The master of the tug requested agreement of the service being rendered under Lloyd's Open Form of salvage agreement. This was accepted by the master, and the tug came alongside at 1105 hours, at which time the standby vessel was released.

The master explained to the tug master that prior to commencement of tow, the vessel's propeller shaft would need to be secured to avert the possibility of the propeller turning (due to movement through the water), and causing failure of the stern tube seals. To assist this operation, the tug master was requested to hold the vessel's head to windward. Connection of the tow was completed at 1227 hours, and by 1235 hours, the tug had hauled the vessel's head to windward. The ship's engineers then secured the propeller shaft and gear box using timber, wires and bottle screws.

This work was completed by 1740 hours when the port anchor was weighed, and towage towards Dunkirk commenced. The vessel arrived in berth at Dunkirk at 2400 hours, following which the tug master boarded, and the redelivery certificate was signed by the master.

The following morning, the master attended the offices of the tug owners and signed Lloyd's Open form of salvage agreement. Security was lodged by the owners with Lloyd's (£220,390 for the ship and freight and £29,610 for cargo).

On 15 December, a surveyor, appointed on behalf of hull underwriters, accompanied by another surveyor, acting on behalf of the classification society, and owners' superintendent, made an examination of the damage to the M.E. gear box. A diver was employed to inspect the vessel's bottom and stern area. The diver's report showed that two blades of the four bladed propeller were damaged, one of them damaged severely.

It now became apparent that the vessel's cargo would need to be discharged before the vessel could be repaired. As Dunkirk had no facilities for storage of the alcohol, it would become necessary to tow the vessel to a suitable port. Enquiries revealed that there were alcohol storage tanks available in Antwerp. A contract was arranged with the owners of the salvage tug for towage to Antwerp.

The classification surveyor agreed to permit towage, provided that the propeller shaft and gear box were secured in order to prevent the propeller turning during towage. The work was completed on 16 December, and the vessel left Dunkirk at 1145 hours under tow of the attending tug.

The tow was handed over to Antwerp tugs at the entrance to the river Scheldt, and the tow continued to Antwerp where the vessel berthed alongside the shore tank installations at 1118 hours on 17 December. Discharge of the cargo into the shore tanks was commenced at 1625 hours, and completed by 0305 hours on the 18 December. At this stage, gas freeing of the vessel's cargo tanks began.

At Dunkirk, a specification for repair of damage was drawn up, and two repair contractors in Antwerp and Hamburg were requested to submit repair quotations. On the basis of these quotations, the repair contract was awarded to an Antwerp yard.

The vessel dry-docked following completion of gas freeing on 18 December. She was attended by the hull underwriters' surveyor and owners' superintendent. On examination it was found that the intermediate gear box casing, lower gear box casing, and the forward bearing housing were fractured. In addition, the gear teeth on both the pinion and main gear wheels were chipped and hammered, the flexible coupling was damaged, the intermediate shaft bearing brasses were fractured and distorted, three propeller blades were damaged to varying degrees, the tailshaft was bent, and finally, the tail shaft coupling bolts were damaged.

In view of the extensive damage, the gear box needed to be replaced. Enquiries revealed that a suitable gear box was not immediately available. The manufacturers of the original gear box agreed to deliver a new gear box by the end of March, 1982. The damaged gear box and coupling were removed from the vessel on the 23 December and delivered to the gear box manufacturers in order that some of the undamaged parts could be used in the new gear box.

The vessel remained in dry-dock until 29 January during which time all repairs apart from the work connected with the gear box and flexible coupling were undertaken. She was then placed alongside a lay-by berth awaiting arrival of the new gear box. In view of the anticipated delay to the vessel, arrangements were made to charter a substitute vessel for delivery of the cargo to its destination. Loading of the cargo into the substitute vessel was carried out on 8 January. The cargo was delivered at Gothenburg on 11 January and at Fredericia on 12 January. The new gear box and repaired flexible coupling were delivered to the yard on 27 March and fitted into the engine room. Installation of the gear box and realignment of the main engine were completed on 8 April. Following satisfactory engine trials and class approval, the vessel left Antwerp at 1648 hours the same day.

Under the terms of the Lloyd's Open Form of salvage agreement, negotiations were subsequently opened between various lawyers representing the ship and freight, cargo, and the tug owners. The parties agreed to a salvage settlement of £100,000 plus the costs of the salvors' lawyers of £2,918.57. This amount of £102,918.57 was apportioned between ship and freight and cargo on the basis of the value adopted during negotiations, and the relative amounts were settled by the respective parties.

### Main items of evidence used in claim

(Lloyd's standard form of salvage agreement was signed by the master on the owner's behalf on 15 December in Dunkirk).

*Provided by the ship*

- Deck log book

- Engine log book

- Master's report to the company

- Master's statement taken by the solicitor representing owners

- Chief engineer's statement taken by solicitor representing owners.

*Provided by other sources*

- Diver's report at Dunkirk

- Salvage Association's reports from surveyors at Dunkirk and Antwerp

- Class surveyor's report and certificate of seaworthiness for voyage to Antwerp

- Survey report covering transfer of cargo from ship to shore tanks in Antwerp

- Accounts and time sheets for all stages of investigation and repair

- Valuation certificate for vessel and cargo based on value at time of casualty

- General average adjustment.

## Fire / explosion

The fire / explosion category of incidents has been placed in chapter Two — Ship Related Incidents because many of the fires and explosions which occur on board ship tend to involve machinery spaces or the living accommodation. However, many others are directly related to the cargo being carried. Others may be related to a piracy, terrorist or other attack against the ship with weapons or bombs. Accordingly, the guidelines below will help identify general issues to consider but each incident will need to be considered on its own merits in order to decide what sort of evidence will be most relevant.

### a. Conceptual background

Fires and explosions can be amongst the most serious problems a ship may have to face. Unless the ship is in port or close to the shore – it is unlikely that help can be obtained from professional fire fighters. Consequently the ships crew will have to use the equipment and resources available to them to deal with the situation as best they can.

Good safe working practices would dictate that appropriate risk assessment exercises were undertaken in advance of any hazardous work being carried out and that appropriate 'Permit to Work' procedures had been followed. Such procedures are mandatory for UK registered ships under the Merchant Shipping and Fishing Vessels (Health and Safety at Work) Regulations 1997 and similar legislation will probably apply to many other jurisdictions. In any event it is likely that such procedures are contained within a good SMS. The investigator / lawyer will be looking for the cause of the fire / explosion and, consequently, the evidence collected will need to confirm that reasonably good preventative measures were indeed in place and were taken.

### b. Potential exposure / problem

To a large extent this will depend upon the nature of the fire / explosion and the damage caused – which may of course involve personal injuries and even fatalities. The following list includes other possibilities:

*   Potential claim against H&M Underwriters – for damage caused to own ship.

*   Potential claim from cargo owners / insurers if fire / explosion damaged their cargo. Defences may be available to the carrier — but the ship operator will have an increased evidential burden to overcome, post ISM, to demonstrate that in all other respects they exercised the necessary due diligence before and at the commencement of the voyage to make the vessel seaworthy

*   Limitation of liability — questions of 'seaworthiness' the test will depend whether jurisdiction has been founded in a 1957 or 1976 regime.

- There will be a very good possibility that the incident will be investigated under Resolution A.849(20) or UK S.I. 2005 No. 881. A Fire Casualty Record may be required as per Annex 6 of MSC/Circ.953 / MEPC/Circ.372. There may also be local laws, possibly harbour regulations, requiring such reporting.

## c. ISM implications

The ISM implications will clearly depend very much upon the primary and any underlying causes which led to the contact — but such incidents are almost certainly going to involve a range of issues within the Safety Management System. The following, non-exhaustive, list attempts to address some of the more obvious potential implications and, consequently, suggests areas of the SMS which will come under close scrutiny:

Section 1.2.3.1     (compliance with mandatory rules and regulations)

Regulations such as the STCW Convention and Code may need to be considered. Levels of competency may very well appear as having been causative of the incident — particularly fire fighting training.

Section 6     Resources and personnel

The actions and activities of those involved in dealing with the fire / explosion will be looked at very carefully — both by an investigator and the lawyers. It can therefore be anticipated that a potential claimant or investigator will look very carefully not only at the qualifications and alleged experience of the individual but may also require to examine the Company selection and recruiting procedures and to follow an audit trail to demonstrate that those procedures were indeed followed when recruiting the particular individual who is the focus of attention. It may also be necessary to produce evidence that suitable and adequate familiarisation and training was provided to the individual — e.g. in the location and operation of fire fighting equipment — including the fixed fire fighting installation e.g. $CO_2$.

Section 7     Development of plans for shipboard operations

Clearly the relevance of this section will depend upon where the fire / explosion occurred — but whether it was in the cargo compartment, engine room, living accommodation etc. — it can be anticipated that procedures should be in place to cover the particular situation. The Company response to its obligations under Sections 1.2.2.1 and 1.2.2.2 — i.e. providing safe working practices and establishing safeguards against all identifiable risks will also be influential factors which will come under close scrutiny. As such it should be expected that there are clear Company procedures set out in a Procedures Manual. Those procedures will be examined very carefully, not only in light of the fire / explosion incident itself but also during other periods of the ships life. This would be done by following audit trails.

Section 8     Emergency preparedness

A fire / explosion will certainly fall within the category of 'potential emergency situations' anticipated in Section 8. The response of the master and those on board, following such an incident will be examined against the written procedures. No doubt records of simulated drills involving fire and explosion type incidents will also be examined.

Section 9      Reports and analysis of non-conformities, accidents and hazardous occurrences

Records of the activities anticipated by Section 9 may well be examined to confirm that learning opportunities were being taken as part of the SMS. Similarly minutes of on board safety committee meetings may be examined to determine the level of involvement and commitment to safety management on board.

Section 10      Maintenance of the ship and equipment

To what extent this may be relevant will obviously be determined by reference to the cause of the fire / explosion incident. However, the inspection and of fire fighting appliances will almost certainly come under close scrutiny particularly if the failure of a piece of fire fighting equipment allegedly occurred.

Section 11      Documentation

If there appear to have been problems with compliance with the SMS then it is likely that a closer look will be made at the documented procedures themselves. If these are voluminous, irrelevant or otherwise inadequate then the Company is likely to come under severe criticism.

Section 12      Company verification, review and evaluation

There is a very clear obligation on the Company to ensure that the SMS is working properly on board its vessels. If a serious incident has arisen, as may well be the case with a fire or explosion incident, then it can be anticipated that the active monitoring by the Company will be looked at very closely by way of audit trails.

Certification and verification

As a matter of course the validity of the SMC and DOC will be checked

## d. Nature of evidence required

The investigator and the lawyer will both be looking for the cause of the fire / explosion — although for slightly different reasons. In the case of a serious fire / explosion it is quite likely that a fire expert, who will often be a forensic scientist, will be instructed to conduct an investigation. Accordingly, many of the items listed in the 'Documents Required' list in the General Introduction to this chapter will be relevant. In addition the following may also be relevant:

| |
|---|
| Record of any 'hot work' being carried out along with copies of risk assessments and 'Permits to work' |
| Record of fire fighting appliances used |

| |
|---|
| Record of inspections and maintenance of fire fighting equipment |
| Record of fire drills / exercises |
| Any warning letters / note of protests made to stevedores etc. regarding smoking |
| Photographs / videos of images relating to the fire / explosion and damaged equipment / cargo. |

### e. Report

A useful set of guidance notes, of issues to include in a report, are set out in IMO Res. A.849(20) and the list below:

Pt B2

S
H
I
P

| **In accordance with Resolution A.849(20) - Fire/Explosion** |
|---|
| How was the ship alerted to the fire? |
| How was the individual alerted to the fire? |
| Where did it start? |
| How did it start (if known)? |
| What was the immediate action taken? |
| Condition of fire-fighting equipment, supported by dates of survey/ examination |
| Extinguishers available: <br> • Type available in the vicinity; <br> • Types available on the ship; <br> • Types used |
| Hoses available/used |
| Pumps available/used |
| Was water immediately available? |
| Were air vents closed off to the space? |
| What was the nature of the material on fire and surrounding the fire? |
| Fire retardant specification of bulkheads surrounding the fire |
| Restrictions caused by (a) smoke, (b) heat, (c) fumes |
| Freedom of access |
| Access availability for fire fighting equipment |
| Preparedness of crew - Frequency, duration, content and locations of fire musters and drills |
| Response by land-based fire-fighting brigades |

If the incident is serious and an Investigator attends on behalf of the Flag, or coastal, State Administration, it may be necessary to complete an IMO Fire Casualty

Record. Details of the relevant procedure and form can be found in Annex 6 of MSC/Circ.953 / MEPC/Circ.372.

## f. Case study

A 3500 TEU container vessel suffered an explosion and fire in a container stowed below deck in number six cargo hold. The fire subsequently spread to other, adjacent, containers before being extinguished using the $CO_2$ hold smothering system.

A subsequent examination revealed that the offending container had contained a dangerous chemical which was prone to self heating and spontaneous combustion. The container had not been marked / labelled with appropriate International Maritime Dangerous Goods (IMDG) labelling to indicate that it contained Class 4 goods. Similarly the manifest and description provided by the shipper suggested that the contents of the container were harmless chemicals.

A professional fire investigator had to be engaged to establish the actual cause of the explosion and fire but the evidence collected from the vessel was crucial in preparing a recovery action against the cargo shippers and the charterers. The evidence included:

- A detailed report of the incident and the prompt action of the onboard emergency response team to fight and contain the fire.

- Cargo documentation — including bill of lading, general cargo manifest, dangerous goods manifest, stowage plan.

- Photographs of the fire damaged containers.

A recovery was made against the charterers, under the terms of the particular charterparty in operation at the time for damage caused to the ship and to other cargo in adjacent containers. Details of the offending shippers were circulated to other carriers operating container liner services in that geographical area.

# PEOPLE RELATED INCIDENTS

## General introduction

SHIP OPERATORS OWE A DUTY TO ENSURE THE SAFETY of persons on board the vessel. This duty extends beyond the physical limits of the vessel to areas where the safety of persons off the vessel is affected by the vessel's operation and the tasks carried out by the crew, eg. mooring operations, discharge with ship's crane and similar situations. As regards the people whose safety is to be ensured, this is not limited to crew members, but extends to passengers, shore personnel and even unauthorised persons on board such as stowaways (see the section below on third party claims).

People related incidents represent a very significant slice of the total claims, by number and by value, which are handled by P&I Clubs, accounting for roughly 40% of all claims.

## Personal injuries

If ship operators fail in their duty to ensure safety, the injured person will normally be entitled (depending on the jurisdiction), to compensation for suffering the injury, together with any loss of earnings, loss of pension rights or additional expenses, resulting from the accident.

In certain jurisdictions, in particular the USA, awards for personal injury are extremely high. It is important therefore that the master and ship operators are vigilant in monitoring the safety of the vessel and working procedures. If they become aware of any potential risks to safety, action should be taken as soon as possible to remove the risk. The master should also ensure that every incident which results in injury to crew or a third party, is recorded at the time, and by following the procedure detailed below.

Most ship operators provide an accident form which should be completed in the event of an injury. An example of such a form for use in any personal injury incident, is provided on pages 160/161. There is also a copy of the MAIB Incident Report Form included as Part C 5 towards the rear of this book.

It is quite probable, however, that a Company specific form exists which is linked in with the SMS and it is that form which should be used in practice.

The flag State Administration or local authority may require details of the accident to be officially reported, eg. in the United Kingdom the Marine Accident Investigation Branch form must be completed for "major" or "serious" injuries, in the following cases only:

i)   UK flagged vessels

ii) Any vessel in a UK port, and

iii) Passenger vessels carrying people to or from a UK port.

Details of the requirements of the UK regulations and the MAIB are set out in Statutory Instrument 2005 No. 881 — The Merchant Shipping (Accident Reporting and Investigation) Regulations 2005. They are simplified and further explained in Marine Guidance Note MGN 289 (M+F). There is a requirement to report a 'Major Injury' which means:

a) any fracture, other than to a finger, thumb or toe;

b) any loss of a limb or part of a limb;

c) dislocation of the shoulder, hip, knee or spine;

d) loss of sight, whether temporary or permanent;

e) penetrating injury to the eye; or

f) any other injury –

    i.    leading to hypothermia or to unconsciousness, or

    ii.    requiring resuscitation, or

    iii.    requiring admittance to a hospital or other medical facility as an inpatient for more than 24 hours.

The report to the MAIB should include the following information:

| |
|---|
| Name of ship, IMO and official number |
| Name and address of owner |
| Name and address of master |
| Date and time of accident |
| Where from and where bound |
| Latitude and longitude or geographical position in which the accident occurred |
| Part of ship where accident occurred |
| Weather conditions |
| Name and port of registry of any other ship involved |
| Number of people killed or injured, together with their names, addresses and gender |
| Brief details of the accident, including, where known the sequence of events leading to the accident, extent of damage and whether the accident caused pollution or a hazard to navigation |
| If the vessel is fitted with a voyage data recorder, the make and model of the recorder |

Attention is also drawn to the additional reporting requirements Section 6(4) and (5) of SI 2005 No. 881 as well as non-requirement under Section 6(6).

# ACCIDENT REPORT DETAILS CREW/PERSONAL INJURY

## CONFIDENTIAL REPORT PREPARED FOR THE INFORMATION OF OWNERS' SOLICITORS AND OWNERS' P&I CLUB FOR USE IN ANY LITIGATION

**(To be filled in by the master in every case where an accident occurs)**

1.  Vessel ............................................. Type .............................. GRT .....................

2.  Owners' name and address

    ...............................................................................................................

3.  Name of person injured

    ...............................................................................................................

4.  Seafarer, stevedore, shore employee, please identify

    ...............................................................................................................

5.  Address of person injured

    ...............................................................................................................

6.  Date of birth

    ...............................................................................................................

7.  Nationality

    ...............................................................................................................

8.  Rating

    ...............................................................................................................

9.  Date of accident ................................................................. Time ......................

    Place ...............................................................................................

10. Date when injured crewman ceased work

    ...............................................................................................................

11. Port of discharge ............................................................. Date .....................

    ...............................................................................................................

12. Brief description of facts surrounding accident and nature of injuries showing how the injured person was employed at the time (attach copy of Log Entry and Report by Officer under whose supervision man was employed at the material time. If accident due to breakage of gear, broken parts must be carefully preserved)

    ...............................................................................................................

    ...............................................................................................................

    ...............................................................................................................

    ...............................................................................................................

13. Has the Reporting Officer visited the scene of the incident, if so at what time?

...........................................................................................................................

14. Date and time notice of accident received and by whom

...........................................................................................................................

15. Particulars of medical treatment on board and/or shore, by whom given

...........................................................................................................................

16. State whether Doctor's Report submitted

...........................................................................................................................

17. Has the injury incapacitated the seaman from work, totally or partially?

...........................................................................................................................

18. Was the injured person at his usual place of work when the accident happened? If not, was he doing something he was authorised or permitted to do for the purpose of his work?

...........................................................................................................................

...........................................................................................................................

19. Was he under the influence of alcohol or drugs?

...........................................................................................................................

20. Were any third party's involved in the incident?

...........................................................................................................................

If so, give name, address of employing company and occupation of same and details of involvement

...........................................................................................................................

...........................................................................................................................

21. Was the accident caused by collision? If so, give name and owners of colliding vessel.

...........................................................................................................................

22. What was the state of the light when and where the accident occurred? If artificial lighting, give details

...........................................................................................................................

23. ANY FURTHER INFORMATION

Signed: Master ...................................................................Date:

Further guidance may be obtained from the ship operators P&I Club / or the ship operators office on reporting requirements.

### Personal injuries — Crew

If a member of the crew is injured, the master should ensure that a record of the accident is made as soon as practical.

If the injury is serious, the master should telephone ashore for medical advice. In the event of a life threatening injury, if possible (depending on the vessel's position), the master should consider medical help to be flown on board, or diverting to the nearest port. If time allows, owners should be informed of any diversion before it takes place and certainly afterwards. Particularly if the vessel has cargo on board – although a deviation to save life will be considered a 'reasonable' and 'justifiable' deviation. For less serious cases, medical assistance will be rendered on board by the crew unless the vessel is in port. The master should ensure that a note is kept of the type of treatment administered to the injured person on board, any treatment administered to him ashore, by whom the treatment was administered, and the exact time the treatment was given. A record should also be kept of any medical advice sought and what advice was given.

### a. Conceptual background

The ship operators' duty to ensure the crews' safety can be conveniently sub-divided into the following:

- To ensure a safe place of work and provide appropriate personal protective equipment.

- To ensure the employment of competent crew and otherwise comply with the requirements of the STCW Convention and Code.

- To ensure the provision and maintenance of adequate tools, appliances and other equipment on board the vessel.

- To ensure the provision of proper training, supervision and a safe system of carrying out the various tasks on board. Post ISM this would be contained within the Safety Management System.

The ship operator's duty is effectively to carry out their operations without subjecting the crew to unnecessary risks to their safety. Where there is a foreseeable risk which the ship operators could reasonably have taken steps to avoid, it will be considered an unnecessary risk. The risk to safety may be obvious, such as a faulty piece of machinery or oil spilt on the deck. It may, however, be less obvious, e.g. young cadet inadequately trained.

More so, as far as U.K. flagged ships are concerned, they must comply with the requirements of Statutory Instrument 1997 No. 2962 — The Merchant Shipping

(Health and Safety at Work) Regulations 1997 which imposes a wide range of duties and obligations upon the ship operating Company as well as employees including the provision of suitable instructions, the requirement to undertake risk assessments, the appointment of safety officers and much more. Failure to comply with the regulations can result in significant fines and / or lengthy prison sentences – including Company directors.

There is also a requirement under Statutory Instrument 1998 No. 1838 — The Merchant Shipping (Code of Safe Working Practices for Merchant Seamen) Regulations 1998 to carry certain minimum number of copies of the MCA book of that name.

Similar requirements may exist for other flag State Administrations.

The ship operators' duty extends beyond putting something right which is defective or broken, and may include improvements to working practices or the working environment which could reduce the risk of an accident. The following factors can be relevant, depending on the jurisdiction, in deciding whether there was a foreseeable risk:

- Whether there have been any similar accidents previously on this vessel or in the same fleet.

- Whether the crew have previously reported a potentially dangerous situation.

- Whether the safety committee on board have made any recommendations.

- Whether there are any applicable safety guidelines, e.g. published by the IMO or the flag state.

- What the practices are in the industry.

- Whether reports of similar accidents on board other vessels have been published.

It follows from the above that the master and ship operators in trying to avoid accidents on board and personal injury claims, should be aware of any safety risks which these factors point to and take steps where possible to avoid those risks. The ISM Code requires a safety management system, which must include procedures to ensure that accidents and hazardous situations are reported to the Company, investigated and analysed in order to improve safety.

## b. Potential exposure / problem

If crew members are injured during the course of their employment, the compensation provisions will usually be set out within the terms of their employment — i.e. their employment contract / articles of agreement or within an agreement drawn up by the seafarers national government and / trade union. In some countries the local law may prevail — particularly where an element of negligence on the part of the employer can be demonstrated. There may be issues of contributory negligence on the part of the injured crew member to take into account. The flag State Administration may also have legislation in place relating to employment provisions and compensation regimes.

It is therefore crucial that terms of engagement and employment of crew members are carefully considered and the legal liabilities are fully taken into account when the contracts are drawn up.

## c. ISM implications

The introduction of the ISM Code should, hopefully reduce the number of personal injuries to crew members. However, if accidents do happen then the working Safety Management System should help considerably in assessing and dealing with personal injury claims from crew members. Basically, if the ship operator has only paid 'lip service' to its ISM system then the crew member should have little difficulty demonstrating the failures of the SMS and succeed with a claim for maximum compensation – in appropriate cases the Company and possibly individuals, including directors of the Company, the master, Designated Person and others could find themselves facing fines and even imprisonment. On the other hand, if the ship operator has done all that it reasonably could to implement a good working SMS but the particular individual crew member injured was not prepared to accept his / her own personal responsibility for their own safety and / or refused to follow the SMS procedures, then the Company should be able to produce sufficient evidence by way of mitigation and or to demonstrate a high level of contributory negligence on the part of the injured crew member.

A copy of the text of Resolution A.741(18) as amended by MSC.104(73), the International Management Code for the Safe Operation of Ships and for Pollution Prevention (International Safety Management (ISM) Code, appears in Part C 1 towards the rear of this book.

Just about the whole of the ISM Code is likely to have some relevance to personal injury cases. However, we will focus on some of the more obvious / relevant sections:

Section 1.2 sets out the objectives of the Code

1.2.1 The objectives of the Code are to ensure safety at sea, prevention of human injury or loss of life, and avoidance of damage to the environment, in particular to the marine environment and to property.

Clearly the prevention of human injury is amongst the primary objectives of the Code.

1.2.2 Safety management objectives of the Company should, inter alia

.1 provide for safe practices in ship operation and a safe working environment;

.2    establish safeguards against all identified risks; and

.3    continuously improve safety management skills of personnel ashore and aboard ships, including preparing for emergencies related both to safety and environmental protection.

At least the principles of the Company Safe Working Practices will be set out within the Safety Management Manual, or similar, and may be cross referenced to other primary or secondary source material. For example, as far as U.K. registered ships are concerned, Statutory Instrument 1997 No. 2962 deals with 'The Merchant Shipping and Fishing Vessels (Health and Safety at Work) Regulations 1997, the Maritime and Coastguard Agency 'Code of Safe Working Practices for Merchant Seamen' and / or 'Personal Injury Prevention – A guide to Good Practice'[1] – clearly there may be other relevant publications which may be referred to.

1.2.3 The safety management system should ensure:

.1    compliance with mandatory rules and regulations; and

.2    that applicable codes, guidelines and standards recommended by the Organization, Administrations, classification societies and maritime industry organizations are taken into account.

Statutory Instrument 1997 No. 2962 deals with 'The Merchant Shipping and Fishing Vessels (Health and Safety at Work) Regulations 1997, would clearly fall within the category anticipated by 1.2.3.1.

The Maritime and Coastguard Agency 'Code of Safe Working Practices for Merchant Seamen' and / or 'Personal Injury Prevention – A guide to Good Practice' would no doubt fall under the category identified in 1.2.3.2.

If an accident does happen involving a personal injury to a crew member then the evidence will need to be considered against the background of the SMS, compliance with the requirements of the STCW Convention and Code, S.I. 1997 No. 2962 (as far as UK ships are concerned) and the Code of Safe Working Practices as representing 'industry best practices'.

Sections 2,3,4 and 5

A review will, no-doubt, be made of the Company Safety and Environmental Policy as set out to conform with Section 2 of the ISM Code. Specifically whether the operation of the SMS in practice lived up to the claims made in the S&E Policy. A review would be made of the Company responsibilities and authority (Section 3), the role and activities of the Designated Person (Section 4) and the master's responsibility and authority (Section 5) to establish whether appropriate steps had been taken to address the requirements and whether those steps were indeed being applied in practice.

---

[1]    *Personal Injury Prevention — A Guide to Good Practice*, by Richard Bracken, published by Anchorage Press and the North of England P&I Association, 1998, ISBN 0 9531785 1 X

There is considerable responsibility put upon the Company under Section 6 to not only ensure that it recruits the proper people but also ensure that the seafarers it employs are adequately trained and familiarised such that they can undertake their tasks on board in a safe and efficient manner. Depending upon the particular injury, audit trails will be followed to check whether, or to what extent, the Company complied with the various requirements of Section 6.

Section 7    Development of plans for shipboard operations

Clearly the relevance of this section will depend upon the nature of the task which the crew member was undertaking, or was involved in, when the injury occurred. However, it is very likely that it would involve a 'key shipboard operation'. Consequently the relevant procedures in the Safety Management Manual would be examined carefully and an audit trail would be undertaken to verify whether the correct procedures had been followed on that particular occasion. If not, the investigation would have to turn to establish why not. A whole range of issues may have to be investigated from hours of rest / work, whether the correct personal protective equipment was used, whether proper risk assessments had been carried out etc.

Section 8    Emergency preparedness

The relevance of this section will clearly depend upon the circumstances in which the injury was sustained.

Section 9    Reports and analysis of non-conformities, accidents and hazardous occurrences

Records of the activities anticipated by Section 9 may well be examined to confirm that learning opportunities were being taken as part of the SMS. Similarly minutes of on board safety committee meetings may be examined to determine the level of involvement and commitment to safety management on board.

Section 10    Maintenance of the ship and equipment

To what extent this may be relevant will obviously be determined by reference to the cause of the accident. If the failure of a piece of equipment was involved then the procedures and records will be examined very carefully.

Section 11    Documentation

If there appear to have been problems with compliance with the SMS then it is likely that a closer look will be made at the documented procedures themselves. If these are voluminous, irrelevant or otherwise inadequate then the Company is likely to come under severe criticism.

Section 12    Company verification, review and evaluation

There is a very clear obligation on the Company to ensure that the SMS is working properly on board its vessels. If a serious incident has arisen then it can be anticipated that the active monitoring by the Company will be looked at very closely by way of audit trails.

Certification and verification

As a matter of course the validity of the SMC and DOC will be checked.

## d. Nature of evidence required

### *Investigating an accident*

If the master learns of an accident he should carry out the following investigations to try and establish as far as possible what happened. The investigation should be carried out as soon as practical after the accident

- Examine the scene of the accident. If possible, photographs should be taken, and signed on the reverse by the photographer with the time and date the photos were taken — with some modern cameras this facility can be set automatically. Video film may also be extremely useful. It is also useful to have a note of the conditions where the accident occurred, eg. for a slipping injury, whether the deck was wet/dry, clean, unobstructed and whether it was daylight and what were the weather conditions — wind, sea state, rain, etc. If available use a lux meter to determine the lighting levels at the site of the accident. A sketch plan may also be useful.

- Check any relevant parts of the vessel's equipment or protective clothing to see if it was in good condition or was otherwise damaged. Any relevant piece of equipment must be retained. If for instance an accident occurs as a result of a broken wire or rope, samples should be kept for future analysis. Pieces of equipment or samples should, if possible, be placed in sealed bags, dated, signed for and witnessed. A note should be made as to whether the insured person was wearing any required safety equipment / PPE, and wearing it correctly.

- Interview the injured party, and any witnesses to the accident itself or to any relevant surrounding circumstances. It is important for the person being interviewed to be at ease. Requests for information should be of a non-threatening nature. The injured person and/or witnesses may be defensive, feeling that the claim or allegation of fault could ultimately be directed against them. Advise the person you are interviewing that the purpose of the interview is to help determine the cause of the incident and to prevent further accidents of this type. If the injured person was not wearing the correct safety equipment then this should be recorded in the witness statement. A brief record of the interview should be kept and attached to the master's report. In more serious cases where lawyers are attending, the master should still investigate the accident, but leave written statements to them.

- The master should always remember that he or his ship operator ought to contact the P&I Club correspondents or the Club direct, for advice on the investigation of any accident and the recording of evidence. Accidents which appear minor on the face of it, may lead to large claims a few years later — depending on the jurisdiction. It is important to realise that it may be a year or two before a claim is made. Therefore it is crucial to obtain the evidence immediately after the accident and that this evidence is retained by the ship operator.

### *Weight of evidence*

In the event the accident leads to a claim, some types of evidence carry more weight than others, because their proximity to the accident makes them difficult to dispute. The most useful evidence will normally be from a witness who actually saw the accident, or from photographs showing the condition of the vessel or equipment. However, background evidence may also have its place. The following categories of evidence (strongest first), may assist:

• First hand evidence from eye witnesses who saw the accident happen.

• Photographs, video evidence, pieces of equipment showing the scene of the accident and condition of equipment. It is important that these forms of evidence are taken as close in time to the accident as possible, and that nothing is moved or altered.

• Witnesses who come on the scene shortly after the accident may also be valuable if they have additional information which backs up the eye witness, or in the event that no-one saw the accident happen.

• Evidence as to the surrounding circumstances may also be important, eg. whether the injured party was drunk, what type of orders he had been given and whether he was supervised.

• Speculation by witnesses as to the cause of an accident where this is not clear from the facts, may be prejudicial. A witness statement should record what was seen or heard. The witness should not give an opinion on the cause of the accident which he is not qualified to give. Equally, witnesses who just repeat what others have said happened (and not what they saw) is not useful. The exception being where the master is unable to interview the source of the information, or the source of that information has changed his story.

After any injury the ship operator / their insurers may request the attendance of lawyers and / or surveyor on board to interview the crew and inspect the scene of the accident. There may also be attendance from a flag State Administration Investigator or Recognised Organisation (R/O). Maybe the port State Control or other local authority, such as the police, may board to conduct an investigation. It is important, therefore, for the master, immediately after the accident, to collect the basic factual information, names of the witnesses, photographs and details of the scene of the accident, as it may be some time before the lawyers/surveyors are able to attend. In the event of death or very serious injury, the master may find the local police or accident investigation body also attending to interview him and the crew. As with the accident report form, the master should keep his answers as factual as possible and avoid speculating on the possible cause of the accident.

In the event that the injury was caused by a failure of a part of the ship's equipment, the master should ensure that the damaged part is retained for future inspection. In certain jurisdictions, if owners are unable to produce the allegedly defective piece of equipment, there will be a presumption that the equipment was damaged and owners will be put in a position of considerable disadvantage. If the item of ship's equipment is seriously damaged, the master should request owners to call in a surveyor to inspect the damaged part.

### e. Report

The master's report should be headed as with the report form, "Confidential report prepared for the information of owners' solicitors and owners' P&I Club for use in litigation". Any basic report should include the following information in addition to a completed incident report form:

- Details of the circumstances surrounding the incident, eg. when and where the accident took place and the task which was being performed.

- The conditions at the time of the accident and whether or not they contributed to the accident, eg. wet/dry, dark/light, deck clean, weather and sea state.

- Whether or not the injured party in any way contributed to the accident and whether any third party was involved.

- The names and contact details of the witnesses to the accident, including crew members and non-crew members. Briefly, what the witnesses saw and where they were positioned, unless the accident is serious and solicitors will be attending to take formal statements.

- What the injured party said happened at the time. The nature of his injuries and whether he had any obvious pre-existing injury or bad health.

- Whether there was a system on board for carrying out the particular job e.g. as part of the SMS, or any standing orders, and whether these were complied with. Whether there were any applicable safety procedures and whether these were complied with? Whether the work was supervised, if so, by whom?

- Did the injured person comply with the requirements on the permit to work form, e.g. using a safety harness for working aloft.

- What training and / or familiarisation had been given to the injured person which might have relevance to the accident.

- The report should as far as possible be a factual record and not extend to guess work or personal opinions on what might have caused the problem. Remember all reports may be the subject of legal proceedings at a later date, often many years after a particular incident.

An investigation may also be commissioned by the flag State Administration or the local Authorities — in the U.K. the MCA and / or MAIB. If the injury would be classed as a 'major injury' according to U.K. Statutory Instrument 2005 No. 881 — The Merchant Shipping (Accident Reporting and Investigation) Regulations 2005 and / or MGN 289 (M+F) — the a report would have to be submitted to the MAIB.

More details appear in the introductory section of this chapter.

Appendix 2 to IMO Resolution A.884(21) deals with 'Areas of Human Factors Inquiry' — and appears in Part C 3 towards the rear of this book. This provides some excellent, additional guidance, on the sort of questions which will need to be addressed and the issues which will need to be considered when investigating a personal injury type incident.

### f. Case study

#### Background to the incident

A ro-ro/lo-lo ferry was alongside overnight prior to loading. The chief officer gave instructions that the main deck and lower hold were to be washed in accordance with the appropriate work order. When the main deck wash down was completed, the three main deck ramps were lowered in preparation for washing the hold. An AB then went to the main deck platform, which was wet, to disconnect the hose and transfer it to the hold position. Whilst out of sight, the AB fell backwards onto a ramp five metres below.

#### Consideration of relevant evidence

There was no risk assessment undertaken prior to commencing the wash down. The wash down water was supplied from a connection that could only be accessed via an unprotected 1.2 metre wide platform adjacent to the main deck ramp and ship's side. A personnel barrier was located at each end of the platform. When the ramp was in the 'down' position, there was a 5 metre drop from the platform.

The AB who had gone to disconnect the hose and transfer it to the hold position did not follow the correct procedure. The normal process was to shut the valve, relieving the pressure at the hose end; this then allowed the hose to be disconnected. However, it appears that the pressure was not relieved. While attempting to disconnect the hose, the isolating valve fractured and the A.B. fell backwards.

#### Outcome

He survived the fall, but suffered two broken wrists and a broken leg.

The fleet was reminded of the importance of conducting a risk assessment and generally implementing safe working practices and following correct procedures.

(This case study was based upon Case 16 as appeared in the MAIB 'Safety Digest' – Lessons from Marine Accident Reports 1/2005)

## Personal injuries — Passengers

### a. Conceptual background

The ship operators' duty to ensure passenger safety, involves similar considerations to that of the crew, e.g. a duty to maintain a safe living environment, and adequately trained crew and equipment (see crew section). The ship operator basically has a duty of care towards the passengers and must do all that it reasonably can to make those areas where the passengers might have access – both in-doors and on deck – safe. Many passengers are unfamiliar with ships and the sea and therefore require a level of protection. Some passengers may be quite old, others quite young, some maybe disabled some may decide to have too much to drink.

Of course it is preferable for adequate steps to be taken to prevent personal injuries to passengers in the first place however, passenger injuries, especially on board cruise ships are fairly common, and care must be taken to ensure that as much factual detail as possible is recorded regarding the sequence of events when an accident occurs.

There are some 'passengers' who appear to have established a pre-occupation with faking an injury to try and claim compensation. The only way to combat such criminal activity is to be systematic and methodical in recording and investigating accidents.

### b. Potential exposure / problem

If a passenger is injured whilst on board ship he / she may well consider pursuing a claim for compensation against the ship operator. It is quite likely that reference to a compensation scheme is incorporated into the Passenger Ticket – e.g. the Athens Convention. In some jurisdictions the levels of compensation can be very high.

Whether or not an individual decides to pursue a claim against the ship operator may be determined by the way in which they are treated at the time of the incident. If the ship staff show concern and care for the individual then it is quite unlikely that the matter will be taken further. However, on the other hand, if the injured party is treated in a dismissive way, or not at all, then the reaction will probably be to try and punish the ship by pursuing a claim for financial damages.

### c. ISM implications

The objectives of the ISM Code are not limited to safe working practices — they apply to the prevention of human injury and loss of life generally — along with a whole lot of other things.

Section 7    Embarkation, disembarkation, caring for passengers whilst on board

These should all be subject to procedural guidelines — which should of course be followed.

Section 9    Reports and analysis of non-conformities, accidents and hazardous occurrences

Records of the activities anticipated by Section 9 may well be examined to confirm that learning opportunities were being taken as part of the SMS. Similarly minutes of on board safety committee meetings may be examined to determine the level of involvement and commitment to safety management on board.

Section 10    Maintenance of the ship and equipment

To what extent this may be relevant will obviously be determined by reference to the cause of the accident. If the failure of a piece of equipment was involved then the procedures and records will be examined very carefully.

Section 11    Documentation

If there appear to have been problems with compliance with the SMS then it is likely that a closer look will be made at the documented procedures themselves. If these are voluminous, irrelevant or otherwise inadequate then the Company is likely to come under severe criticism.

Section 12    Company verification, review and evaluation

There is a very clear obligation on the Company to ensure that the SMS is working properly on board its vessels.

Certification and verification

As a matter of course the validity of the SMC and DOC will be checked.


**d. Nature of evidence required**

*Investigating a passenger related accident*

If the master learns of an accident he should carry out the following investigations to try and establish as far as possible what happened. The investigation should be carried out as soon as practical after the accident

- Examine the scene of the accident. If possible, photographs should be taken, and signed on the reverse by the photographer with the time and date the photos were taken with some modern cameras this facility can be set automatically. Video film may also be extremely useful. It is also useful to have a note of the conditions where the accident occurred, eg. for a slipping injury, whether the deck was wet/dry, clean, unobstructed and whether it was daylight and what were the weather conditions - wind, sea state, rain, etc. If available use a lux meter to determine the lighting levels at the site of the accident. A sketch plan may also be useful

- Check any relevant parts of the vessel's equipment to see if it was in good condition or was otherwise damaged.

  Any relevant piece of equipment must be retained. If for instance an accident occurs as a result of a broken chair or stairs, samples should be kept for future analysis. Pieces of equipment or samples should, if possible, be placed in sealed bags, dated, signed for and witnessed.

- Interview the injured party, and any witnesses to the accident itself or to any relevant surrounding circumstances.

  It is important for the person being interviewed to be at ease. Requests for information should be of a non-threatening nature. The injured person and/or witnesses may be defensive, feeling that the claim or allegation of fault could ultimately be directed against them. Advise the person you are interviewing that the purpose of the interview is to help determine the cause of the incident and to prevent further accidents of this type. A brief record of the interview should be kept and attached to the master's report. In more serious cases where lawyers are attending, the master should still investigate the accident, but leave written statements to them.

- The master should always remember that he or his ship operators ought to contact the P&I Club correspondents or the Club direct, for advice on the investigation of any accident and the recording of evidence. Accidents which appear minor on the face of it, may lead to large claims a few years later — depending upon the jurisdiction. It is important to realise that it may be a year or two before a claim is made. Therefore it is crucial to obtain the evidence immediately after the accident and that this evidence is retained by the ship operator.

### *Weight of evidence*

In the event the accident leads to a claim, some types of evidence carry more weight than others, because their proximity to the accident makes them difficult to dispute. The most useful evidence will normally be from a witness who actually saw the accident, or from photographs showing the condition of the vessel or equipment. However, background evidence may also have its place. The following categories of evidence (strongest first), may assist:

- First hand evidence from eye witnesses who saw the accident happen.

- Photographs, video evidence, pieces of equipment showing the scene of the accident and condition of equipment. It is important that these forms of evidence are taken as close in time to the accident as possible, and that nothing is moved or altered.

- Witnesses who come on the scene shortly after the accident may also be valuable if they have additional information which backs up the eye witness, or in the event that no-one saw the accident happen.

- Evidence as to the surrounding circumstances may also be important, eg. whether the injured party was drunk, what type of orders he had been given and whether he was supervised.

- Speculation by witnesses as to the cause of an accident where this is not clear from the facts, may be prejudicial. A witness statement should record what was seen or heard. The witness should not give an opinion on the cause of the accident which he is not qualified to give. Equally, witnesses who just repeat what others have said happened (and not what they saw) is not useful. The exception being where the master is unable to interview the source of the information, or the source of that information has changed his story.

After any injury the ship operator / their insurers may request the attendance of lawyers and / or surveyor on board to interview the crew and inspect the scene of the accident. There may also be attendance from a flag State Administration Investigator or Recognised Organisation (R/O). Maybe the port State Control or other local authority, such as the police, may board to conduct an investigation. It is important, therefore, for the master, immediately after the accident, to collect the basic factual information, names of the witnesses, photographs and details of the scene of the accident, as it may be some time before the lawyers/surveyors are able to attend. In the event of death or very serious injury, the master may find the local police or accident investigation body also attending to interview him and the crew. As with the accident report form, the master should keep his answers as factual as possible and avoid speculating on the possible cause of the accident.

In the event that the injury was caused by a failure of a part of the ship's equipment, the master should ensure that the damaged part is retained for future inspection. In certain jurisdictions, if owners are unable to produce the allegedly defective piece of equipment, there is a presumption that the equipment was damaged and owners will be put in a position of considerable disadvantage. If the item of ship's equipment is seriously damaged, the master should request owners to call in a surveyor to inspect the damaged part.

### e. Report

It is most likely that the Company will have a standard accident report form as part of the SMS documentation. This should be completed by the master or the safety officer as soon as possible after an accident following an investigation into the circumstances. This should include the passenger's full name and address, as well as a space provided for the comments of the individual or any witnesses to the event.

The master's report should be headed as with the report form, "Confidential report prepared for the information of owners' solicitors and owners' P&I Club for use in litigation". Any basic report should include the following information in addition to a completed incident report form:

- Details of the circumstances surrounding the incident, eg. when and where the accident took place and what the passenger was doing at the time.

- The conditions at the time of the accident and whether or not they contributed to the accident, eg. wet/dry, dark/light, deck clean, weather and sea state.

- Whether or not the injured party in any way contributed to the accident and whether any third party was involved.

- The names and contact details of the witnesses to the accident, including other passengers and crew members. Briefly, what the witnesses saw and where they were positioned, unless the accident is serious and solicitors will be attending to take formal statements.

- What the injured party said happened at the time. The nature of his injuries and whether he had any obvious pre-existing injury or bad health.

- Whether the accident may be linked with a system on board for carrying out the particular job e.g. as part of the SMS, or any standing orders, and, if so, whether these were complied with. Whether there were any warning signs and whether these were complied with?

- The report should as far as possible be a factual record and not extend to speculation or personal opinions on what might have caused the accident. Remember all reports may be the subject of legal proceedings at a later date, often many years after a particular incident.

In the case of a passenger reporting an injury to ship's personnel, his/her version of events should be recorded and their interpretation of how the accident was caused. At this point the master should be careful not to concur with any statement provided or give his opinion on what has been said. Details of where the accident occurred on board should be included in the report being as precise as possible, and if deemed appropriate, photographs to be taken of the site and of any ship's equipment involved. Any medication or treatment administered to the passenger should be recorded, including when the medicine was given. Complaints of shipowners' negligence due to lack of medicine, professional assistance at the time of the illness/injury may be alleged at a later date.

### f. Case study

**Background to the incident**

A ro-ro passenger vessel was engaged on a regular service across the Channel between England and France.

On the night in question the wind was increasing to force 6 / 7 from the South West and a large beam swell was being experienced. The vessel did have stabilisers but was still rolling and pitching moderately. Many of the passengers, and some of the crew, were suffering from sea-sickness and had difficulty walking about the vessel. An announcement had been made to encourage passengers to find a seat and to remain seated.

A self service café was open on board. A youth purchased a sparkling drink, with ice-cubes, but then lost his balance and spilt the drink onto a linoleum type floor surface of the cafe.

An elderly gentleman, who was making his way to the café cash desk, slipped on the spilt drink / ice and fell heavily. A duty officer was called to the scene and rendered first aid to the elderly gentleman.

### Consideration of relevant evidence

The café attendant and two eye witnesses were interviewed.

It became apparent that the café attendant had been on her own looking after the till in the café — she subsequently confessed that she 'did not feel at all well' with the motion of the ship. She had seen the youth spill the drink and had called the duty officer to arrange for someone to come and clean up and put up a warning sign. Before that could be arranged the elderly gentleman had slipped and fallen.

Two eye witnesses stated that they had seen the elderly gentleman struggling to make his way to the café and had tried to encourage him to sit down. They saw him slip and fall.

The duty officer took relevant details from the elderly gentleman following the administering of first aid.

### Outcome

The elderly gentleman was bruised and shaken but not seriously injured. However, he was encouraged to have a doctor check him over.

The training of the duty officer was such that during the administering of the first aid he showed care and concern towards the passenger. It was probably this caring attitude which helped defused a potentially aggressive situation developing. There was nothing further heard from the elderly gentleman.

Following an anlysis of the accident on board it was recognised that management of the situation which lead to the accident, and what followed immediately afterwards could be improved. The café attendant should have ensured that someone else was made aware of her partial incapacity as far as her sea-sickness was concerned. It was recognised that the café attendant should not have been left alone, particularly in adverse weather, and it was questioned whether there may be occasions when the café should be shut down completely in very rough weather.

## Personal injuries — Third parties

### a. Conceptual background

#### *Stevedores*

The ship operator has a legal responsibility to exercise a 'duty of care' and is obligated to provide a safe vessel and equipment at all times. Particular care should be given when a vessel enters a port and when she lies alongside her berth. It is on these occasions that stevedores and other shore personnel, who may not be familiar with that particular vessel, will be boarding. Stevedore injuries may be caused due to their unfamiliarity with the ship's workings and fittings, therefore all crew should ensure that safe working procedures are followed strictly by the stevedores. During loading and discharge operations, the crew should ensure that all equipment, eg. ship's cranes or derricks, are used correctly. Also, that the deck is free of potential hazards, eg. loose electrical cables, spilt oil.

Quite often the first evidence of an injury being sustained by a stevedore, will be several months or years later when a legal claim is presented to the ship operators. At that stage they will be in an extremely disadvantaged position to gather together the kind of evidence required to prepare a defence. The ship operators will be in a much better position if at least some details of the accident were recorded by those on board at the time.

In the event of a stevedore injury occurring, the procedures as described above for passenger injuries should be followed, the master completing and accident report form at the first opportunity. If the injured stevedore does make any comments at the time about the accident or nature of the injury, these should be carefully recorded. It is of particular importance when a stevedore is injured that statements are taken from eye witnesses. This is because other stevedores who may have witnessed what happened, may not be contactable for their version of events in the future. Any statements should be attached to the accident report form, which makes it clear the information is confidential.

#### *Other third parties*

In a similar way, a ship operator also owes that same duty of care to provide a safe environment on board towards a whole range of other third parties who may have reason to be on board e.g. pilots, surveyors, agents, immigration officers, crew relatives and even those who should not be on board e.g. stowaways. Again reporting procedures should be followed as soon as possible after it has become known that an injury has occurred. Full personal and contact details of the injured party should to included. The third party's reason for being on board and exact time and place of the incident should also be included. In the case of stowaways, it is unlikely that injuries will be common place yet in such event it may be difficult to obtain details of the incident from the stowaway due to language barriers. However, a report prepared by the stowaway in his native language, if only to limit the extent of allegations, may assist in the event of a claim being presented.

If medical assistance is necessary, all medication administered and first aid treatment provided should be recorded in detail to avoid further allegation of negligence. If appropriate, an ambulance should be called and the injured party advised to have a medical check-over.

With any injury reported, the master should try and avoid giving his opinion regarding the cause of the accident and confine himself to recording the facts of the investigation, to avoid implying ship operators liability.

## b. Potential exposure / problem

The injured third party will, usually, have to prove that his / her injuries were sustained as a result of some act of negligence or some default on the part of the ship operator. However, once they overcome that burden — which may be relatively easy in some jurisdictions — it will then be for the ship operator to demonstrate that they did all that they reasonably could to make their ship safe.

## c. ISM implications

The objectives of the ISM Code are not limited to safe working practices of the crew — they apply to the prevention of human injury and loss of life generally — along with a whole lot of other things.

Section 7     Procedures for Key Shipboard Operations.

Depending upon the circumstances and nature of the injury — consideration should be given to relevant SMS procedures and whether any failure to comply with the procedures could have contributed to the accident.

Section 9     Reports and analysis of non-conformities, accidents and hazardous occurrences

Records of the activities anticipated by Section 9 may well be examined to confirm that learning opportunities were being taken as part of the SMS. Similarly minutes of on board safety committee meetings may be examined to determine the level of involvement and commitment to safety management on board.

Section 10     Maintenance of the ship and equipment

To what extent this may be relevant will obviously be determined by reference to the cause of the accident. If the failure of a piece of equipment was involved then the procedures and records will be examined very carefully.

Section 11     Documentation

If there appear to have been problems with compliance with the SMS then it is likely that a closer look will be made at the documented procedures themselves. If these are voluminous, irrelevant or otherwise inadequate then the Company is likely to come under severe criticism.

Section 12    Company verification, review and evaluation

There is a very clear obligation on the Company to ensure that the SMS is working properly on board its vessels.

Certification and verification

As a matter of course the validity of the SMC and DOC will be checked.


## d. Nature of evidence required

### Investigating an accident to a third party

If the master learns of an accident he should carry out the following investigations to try and establish as far as possible what happened. The investigation should be carried out as soon as practical after the accident

- Examine the scene of the accident. If possible, photographs should be taken, and signed on the reverse by the photographer with the time and date the photos were taken — with some modern cameras this facility can be set automatically. Video film may also be extremely useful. It is also useful to have a note of the conditions where the accident occurred, eg. for a slipping injury, whether the deck was wet/dry, clean, unobstructed and whether it was daylight and what were the weather conditions — wind, sea state, rain, etc. If available use a lux meter to determine the lighting levels at the site of the accident. A sketch plan may also be useful

- Check any relevant parts of the vessel's equipment or protective clothing to see if it was in good condition or was otherwise damaged.

  Any relevant piece of equipment must be retained. If for instance an accident occurs as a result of a broken cargo wire or access ladder, samples should be kept for future analysis. Pieces of equipment or samples should, if possible, be placed in sealed bags, dated, signed for and witnessed. A note should be made as to whether the insured person was wearing any required safety equipment / PPE, and wearing it correctly.

- Interview the injured party, and any witnesses to the accident itself or to any relevant surrounding circumstances.

  It is important for the person being interviewed to be at ease. Requests for information should be of a non-threatening nature. The injured person and/or witnesses may be defensive, feeling that the claim or allegation of fault could ultimately be directed against them. Advise the person you are interviewing that the purpose of the interview is to help determine the cause of the incident and to prevent further accidents of this type. If the injured person was not wearing the correct safety equipment then this should be recorded in the witness statement. A brief record of the interview should be kept and attached to the master's report. In more serious cases where lawyers are attending, the master should still investigate the accident, but leave written statements to them.

- The master should always remember that he or his ship operators ought to contact the P&I Club correspondents or the Club direct, for advice on the investigation of any accident and the recording of evidence. Accidents which appear minor on the face of it, may lead to large claims a few years later depending on the jurisdiction. It is important to realise that it may be a year or two before a claim is made. Therefore it is crucial to obtain the evidence immediately after the accident and that this evidence is retained by the owner.

### Weight of evidence

In the event the accident leads to a claim, some types of evidence carry more weight than others, because their proximity to the accident makes them difficult to dispute. The most useful evidence will normally be from a witness who actually saw the accident, or from photographs showing the condition of the vessel or equipment. However, background evidence may also have its place. The following categories of evidence (strongest first), may assist:

- First hand evidence from eye witnesses who saw the accident happen

- Photographs, video evidence, pieces of equipment showing the scene of the accident and condition of equipment. It is important that these forms of evidence are taken as close in time to the accident as possible, and that nothing is moved or altered

- Witnesses who come on the scene shortly after the accident may also be valuable if they have additional information which backs up the eye witness, or in the event that no-one saw the accident happen

- Evidence as to the surrounding circumstances may also be important, eg. whether the injured party was drunk, what type of orders he had been given and whether he was supervised

- Speculation by witnesses as to the cause of an accident where this is not clear from the facts, may be prejudicial. A witness statement should record what was seen or heard. The witness should not give an opinion on the cause of the accident which he is not qualified to give. Equally, witnesses who just repeat what others have said happened (and not what they saw) is not useful. The exception being where the master is unable to interview the source of the information, or the source of that information has changed his story.

After any injury the ship operator / their insurers may request the attendance of lawyers and / or surveyor on board to interview the crew and any other witnesses and inspect the scene of the accident. There may also be attendance from a flag State Administration Investigator or Recognised Organisation (R/O). Maybe the port State Control or other local authority, such as the police, may board to conduct an investigation. It is important, therefore, for the master, immediately after the accident, to collect the basic factual information, names of the witnesses, photographs and details of the scene of the accident, as it may be some time before the lawyers/surveyors are able to attend. In the event of death or very serious injury, the master may find the local police or accident investigation body also attending to interview him and the crew. As with the accident report form, the master should keep his answers as factual as possible and avoid speculating on the possible cause of the accident.

In the event that the injury was caused by a failure of a part of the ship's equipment, the master should ensure that the damaged part is retained for future inspection. In certain jurisdictions, if owners are unable to produce the allegedly defective piece of equipment, there is a presumption that the equipment was damaged and owners will be put in a position of considerable disadvantage. If the item of ship's equipment is seriously damaged, the master should request owners to call in a surveyor to inspect the damaged part.

### e. Report

It is most likely that the Company will have a standard accident report form as part of the SMS documentation. This should be completed by the master or the safety officer as soon as possible after an accident following an investigation into the circumstances. This should include the full name and address of the injured party, as well as a space provided for the comments of the individual or any witnesses to the event.

The master's report should be headed as with the report form, "Confidential report prepared for the information of owners' solicitors and owners' P&I Club for use in litigation". Any basic report should include the following information in addition to a completed incident report form:

- Details of the circumstances surrounding the incident, eg. when and where the accident took place and what the third party was doing at the time

- The conditions at the time of the accident and whether or not they contributed to the accident, eg. wet/dry, dark/light, deck clean, weather and sea state

- Whether or not the injured party in any way contributed to the accident and whether any third party was involved

- The names and contact details of the witnesses to the accident, including other third parties and crew members. Briefly, what the witnesses saw and where they were positioned, unless the accident is serious and solicitors will be attending to take formal statements

- What the injured party said happened at the time. The nature of his injuries and whether he had any obvious pre-existing injury or bad health

- Whether the accident may be linked with a system on board for carrying out the particular job e.g. as part of the SMS, or any standing orders, and, if so, whether these were complied with. Whether there were any warning signs and whether these were complied with?

- The report should as far as possible be a factual record and not extend to speculation or personal opinions on what might have caused the accident. Remember all reports may be the subject of legal proceedings at a later date, often many years after a particular incident.

In the case of a third party reporting an injury to ship's personnel, his/her version of events should be recorded and their interpretation of how the accident was caused. At this point the master should be careful not to concur with any statement provided or give his opinion on what has been said. Details of where the accident occurred on board should be included in the report being as precise as possible, and if deemed appropriate, photographs to be taken of the site and of any ship's equipment involved. Any medication or treatment administered to the third party should be recorded, including when the medicine was given. Complaints of shipowners' negligence due to lack of medicine, professional assistance at the time of the illness/injury may be alleged at a later date.

## f. Case study

### Background to the incident

A 70,000 DWT bulk carrier was alongside discharging a grain cargo. The master and chief engineer had received a message from head office that an engineer superintendent and Classification Society surveyor would board at some time that day with the intention of undertaking an internal inspection of six of the top-side ballast wing tanks. The request was made to have the tanks opened and ready for inspection.

By 1500 hrs neither the master nor the chief engineer had heard anything from the superintendent and they therefore put a phone call through to the office to establish what time the visitors could be expected. The office advised that they should have been onboard by lunchtime.

On checking with the gangway watchman and duty deck officer it appeared that the superintendent and the surveyor had boarded at 1145 hrs — having confirmed their identity, had signed the visitors book and had been issued with a security badge. Because the superintendent was known to the gangway watchman he was allowed to enter the accommodation unescorted. Neither the gangway watchman nor the duty officer saw the visitors after that nor did they know what there intentions were.

A search was immediately instigated. The two men were spotted, apparently unconscious, at the bottom of the access ladder into Number 3 Port side Upper Wing tank. The emergency party was mustered and a rescue attempted wearing breathing apparatus. An ambulance was called but the two men were found to be dead. The local P&I Correspondents were contacted who, in turn, notified the harbour police.

## *Consideration of relevant evidence*

There was little by way of evidence to prove exactly what had happened.

The suits and overnight bags of the superintendent and surveyor were found in a spare cabin in the officers accommodation – this was a cabin the superintendent had used on previous visits to the ship.

Statements from the chief officer and bosun confirmed that the man hole covers of the particular top side tanks had been opened up at around 0900 hrs and the tanks were being ventilated. They were under the impression that they were on stand by waiting for the superintendent and surveyor to board when they would then implement the Permit to Work Procedure for entering an enclosed space. The crew had been briefed about what was happening and told not to enter any of the tanks.

In the meantime the chief officer had concentrated his attentions on the cargo operation and the bosun and crew were involved with some hatch cover maintenance. Neither the chief officer nor the bosun was aware that the visitors had boarded at 1145 hrs.

## *Outcome*

An autopsy was held locally and the cause of death was confirmed as 'asphyxiation'. The local police conducted an investigation helped by the master and ship's staff. The conclusion reached was that immediately after the superintendent and surveyor boarded they must have proceeded to the spare cabin and changed into their boiler suits. For reasons which will only ever be known to themselves, they then went on deck and into the top side tank to start their inspection — without making contact with the master, chief engineer or anyone else on board and without following the correct Permit to Work Procedure for Entry into an Enclosed Space. The superintendent was very familiar with the procedure since he had, on a number of previous occasions, conducted ISM Internal Audits on that ship.

Clearly, the procedures set out in the Safety Management Manual / SMS must be followed by everyone on board — whoever they are.

### Illness

Illnesses on board a ship can be just as serious, if not more so, than personal injuries. If the illness is infectious / contagious or is otherwise capable of being contracted by many people in a confined community then it could have very serious consequences affecting the safety of the ship and all on board. For example an outbreak of so-called Legionnaires Disease on board a ship with a full complement of crew of only 15 people could very easily mean that there are insufficient people unaffected who are capable of safely managing / navigating the ship. Similarly, an outbreak amongst passengers could be very difficult to contain.

The ship operator has a duty, as far as is reasonably practicable, to prevent situations developing on board which might lead to the spread of illness — e.g. taking care over general hygiene, keeping galleys and store rooms clean, ensuring food and drinking water are fresh and of a high standard etc.

Of course there are some illnesses which may occur in any community — whether on shore or on board a ship — which may be very difficult to avoid completely — such as a common cold.

## Illness — Crew

### a. Conceptual background

The most effective risk management tool which can be used to minimise the risk of illnesses amongst the crew is a thorough pre-employment medical examination. This will be a most worthwhile and, in the medium term, cost effective investment.

If a seafarer becomes ill whilst on board then the ship operator is likely to have an obligation, under the terms of employment, to pay for any medical treatment required, including hospitalisation, repatriation of the seafarer concerned, possibly sick pay and / or other compensation and the costs of sending out a replacement seafarer. A typical cost for a relatively minor illness will amount to a figure in the region of U.S.$20,000 — for a more serious illness the costs involved will be very much more.

### b. Potential exposure / problem

The ship operator will, in all probability, have insurance cover for such liabilities with its P&I Club. However, the claims record will be affected and many of the inconveniences suffered, including loss of time to the ship, will not be covered.

There may also be practical problems in actually maintaining safe operations on board if even a relatively small number of crew members become ill.

### c. ISM implications

Section 6.2 of the ISM Code draws specific attention to the requirement for the Company to employ medically fit seafarers:

6.2 The Company should ensure that each ship is manned with qualified, certificated and medically fit seafarers in accordance with national and international requirements.

The real implications as far as ISM is concerned is, probably, how safety, and indeed the ship, will be managed with a reduced workforce. With one person down with an illness then it may not be a serious problem; with four or six then the problem may start to become very serious. Amongst the objectives there is included, at Section 1.2.2.2, a requirement of the Company to '…establish safeguards against all identifiable risks…'

Section 1.2.3 requires the SMS to ensure compliance with mandatory rules and regulations etc. Most of the relevant requirements with regard to occupational health and safety will be found in various ILO Resolutions, Conventions and Recommendations for example C155 Occupational Safety and Health Convention, 1981 with P155 Protocol of 2002, C164 Health Protection and Medical Care (Seafarers) Convention, 1987 etc. — as implemented into the domestic legislation of the flag State.

Hours of rest / work may also need to be checked to ensure that there could be no link between the illness suffered and overwork or stress.

### d. Nature of evidence required

- Pre-employment medical certificate
- Vaccination certificates
- Extract from ships hospital / sick bay records
- Reports from doctors / clinics

### e. Report

The report should include the following details of the individual seafarer(s)

| |
|---|
| Full name |
| Home address |
| Nationality |
| Date of Birth |
| Sex |
| Passport or Seaman's book number |
| Details of illness |
| Description of symptoms |
| Person to whom was the Illness first reported |
| Treatment on board |
| Treatment ashore:<br>Doctor / Clinic<br>Medication |
| Number of days off work |

| |
|---|
| Final outcome of illness |
|   e.g. returned to work, |
|   hospitalized, |
|   repatriated |
| Capacity on board |
| Certificate of Competency/License: |
|   grade; |
|   date of issue; |
|   issuing country/authority; |
| other Certificates of Competency held |
| Date of joining vessel concerned |
| Total time in the service of the Company |
| Number of hours spent on duty on the day the illness first reported and the previous days |
| Number of hours sleep in the 96 hours prior to the illness being first reported |
| Any other factors, on board or personal, that may have affected sleep |
| Whether smoker, and if so, quantity |
| Normal alcohol habit |
| Alcohol consumption immediately prior to incident or in the previous 24 hours |
| Whether under prescribed medication |
| Any ingested non-prescribed drugs |
| Records of drug and alcohol tests |

## f. Case study

### *Background to the incident*

Whilst on passage from Europe to the Gulf of Mexico, the third engineer on board a chemical tanker started to complain of pains in his stomach and in his side. He was given some non-prescription indigestion medication by the chief officer from the ship's hospital. The pain increased over the next few days to a point where the man was clearly in agony. The master made a request for medical advice by radio.

The vessel diverted into a U.S. port where, after formalities, the man was taken to hospital in an ambulance. The ship departed later that day for its scheduled discharge port. News was received that evening from the agent in the port where the third engineer had been landed that one of his kidneys had failed and he was to undergo major surgery and would require hospitalisation for a number of months.

## Consideration of relevant evidence

The third engineer was 57 years of age and had been on board the ship for only three weeks. He had not previously sailed with the Company.

He had undergone a pre-employment medical a week before joining the ship. The medical examination did not reveal any particular problem. (on further investigation it was learned that the medical examination was superficial and the set fee charged by the clinic was just US $20 — a full and detailed medical examination in the same clinic was US $130.)

The report from the U.S. Hospital where the third engineer had been landed indicated that the problem with the kidney would have been developing over some period of time and should have been detectable for many months if a proper medical examination had been carried out.

## Outcome

The third engineer's second kidney was saved and he was eventually repatriated to his home in South East Asia after eight weeks in hospital.

The final hospital bill came to over $150,000, on top of which were the agents fees, repatriation costs and the original diversion expenses. The ship operator was able to recover from his P&I Club although the Club insisted that the Company adopts a more rigorous pre-employment medical screening of its seafarers for the future.

It was suspected, but could not be proved, that the third engineer was well aware of his medical condition before he signed on. It was probably part of a pre-conceived plan to have his failing kidney problem treated in a country where the health care facilities were going to be superior to those he could expect in a hospital in his home country. It was probably also part of his plan to have someone else pay for the expensive treatment.

## Illness — Passengers

### a. Conceptual background

Passengers on a cruise ship are, almost by definition, probably on holiday — for which they will have paid a lot of money and they will be there to enjoy themselves. Clearly the last thing they want to happen is to fall ill during their cruise. The ship operator has a responsibility to do all that is reasonably practicable to ensure that it provides a safe environment for the passengers — this will extend to making sure that the risk of contracting an illness whilst on board is reduced to a low level. Hygiene and general cleanliness will be of paramount importance. The galleys, store-rooms and fridges, water tanks, restaurants, cabins, toilet facilities, swimming pools etc. must all be cleaned to a very high level. The drinking water and food must all be fresh and of a high standard. The personal hygiene of the ships staff, particularly the catering / hotel staff, will have to be ensured.

## b. Potential exposure / problem

If a passenger does become ill during the voyage then this will surely disrupt their holiday. The extent to which it may disrupt the holiday will clearly depend upon the severity and type of illness. Whilst there is likely to be proper medical facilities and staff on board this may still be of little consolation to a passenger who is spending their holiday in bed suffering.

Accordingly, if the illness has been caused by some negligence on the part of the ship operator, and if the passenger can prove this, then the passenger is very likely to pursue a claim for damages against the Company

## c. ISM implications

Of course there is the general requirement to have systems in place to comply with various mandatory rules and regulations, under Section 1.2.3, relating to passenger vessels and to ensure that properly qualified and experienced staff are on board as required by Sections 5 and 6 of the Code.

The most likely ISM related implication of passenger illness is in the event that the illness is contagious / infectious and is quickly spreading around the passengers. In which case it may well warrant its own 'Emergency Preparedness' procedure under Section 8 of the ISM Code

## d. Nature of evidence required

- Vaccination certificates
- Extract from ships hospital / sick bay records
- Reports from doctors / clinics
- Independent witness reports / statements relating to the illness

## e. Report

The report should include the following details of the individual passenger(s)

| |
|---|
| Full name |
| Home address |
| Nationality |
| Date of Birth |
| Sex |
| Passport number |
| Cabin number |

| Details of any accompanying passengers |
|---|
| Details of illness |
| Description of symptoms |
| Person to whom was the Illness first reported |
| Treatment on board |
| Treatment ashore: <br> Doctor / Clinic <br> Medication |
| Number of days ill |
| Final outcome of illness <br> e.g. returned to normal activities, <br> hospitalized, <br> repatriated |
| Date and place of joining vessel / cruise |
| Date and place of leaving the vessel / cruise |
| Details of any known excursions ashore |
| Whether smoker, and if so, quantity |
| Normal alcohol habit |
| Alcohol consumption immediately prior to incident or in the previous 24 hours |
| Whether under prescribed medication |
| Any ingested non-prescribed drugs |
| Records of drug and alcohol tests |

Pt B3

P
E
O
P
L
E

## f. Case study

### *Background to the incident*

Mr and Mrs Smith, both in their late 60s, had booked a three week cruise which was to take them around a range of South East Asian ports. Mr and Mrs Smith had shared a dining table on board the ship with the second officer.

After five days on board the ship's doctor was called to the cabin of Mr and Mrs Smith and found them with severe stomach cramps, convulsive vomiting and diarrhoea. The doctor diagnosed food poisoning and prescribed medication. However, by the following morning the symptoms had not subsided and the doctor feared that dehydration was starting to occur. He was concerned about the general state of health of Mr and Mrs Smith and the decision was taken to send them ashore into a hospital where they would have better facilities to care for them.

Mr and Mrs Smith remained in hospital for three days. In the meantime the vessel had sailed. The local agent of the cruise Company arranged for Mr and Mrs Smith to fly home.

Upon their return home Mr Smith contacted a lawyer who subsequently sent in a letter to the cruise line head office advising them that Mr and Mrs Smith would be submitting a formal claim for substantial damages as a result of contracting food poisoning whilst on board their vessel.

### Consideration of relevant evidence

The ships doctor had properly documented his attendance, diagnosis and treatment of Mr and Mrs Smith. The ships doctor was able to confirm that there were no other cases of food poisoning reported on board the vessel at that time.

On the day Mr and Mrs Smith had become ill the ship had sailed from a port after an overnight stay. The second officer recalled bumping into Mr and Mrs Smith in a street market where they were ordering some seafood from a vending stall. The second officer also recalled warning Mr and Mrs Smith about buying food from street vendors. The second officer wrote down these recollections in a signed statement.

### Outcome

The signed statement of the second officer was sent to Mr and Mrs Smith, via their lawyer, who subsequently withdrew their claim.

## Illness — Third parties

### a. Conceptual background

Third parties on board a ship can be exposed to situations whereby they may become ill. For example a pilot or surveyor may be given a meal or a drink and may suffer the effects of food poisoning or similar, stevedores working in a cargo compartment may be affected by fumes from a leaking drum etc.

The ship operator has an obligation to exercise a duty of care towards third parties whilst they are on board its ship.

### b. Potential exposure / problem

If a third party contracts an illness whilst on board ship and can demonstrate that this was as a result of some negligence on the part of the ship operator then they may well have a claim against the ship operator.

### c. ISM implications

Of course there is the general requirement to have systems in place to comply with various mandatory rules and regulations, under Section 1.2.3. There may be local occupational health and safety regulations as well as the flag State legislation which may need to be complied with.

There will also be the general requirement to ensure that properly qualified and experienced staff are on board as required by Sections 5 and 6 of the Code.

### d. Nature of evidence required

- Extract from ships hospital / sick bay records
- Reports from doctors / clinics
- Independent witness reports / statements relating to the illness

### e. Report

The report should include the following details of the individual third party(s)

| |
|---|
| Full name |
| Home address |
| Nationality |
| Date of birth |
| Sex |
| Passport number |
| Capacity / reason for being on board |
| Details of illness |
| Description of symptoms |
| Person to whom was the illness first reported |
| Treatment on board |
| Treatment ashore:<br>Doctor / Clinic<br>Medication |
| Number of days ill |
| Final outcome of illness<br>e.g. returned to normal activities,<br>hospitalized,<br>repatriated |

| Date and place of joining vessel |
| --- |
| Date and place of leaving the vessel |
| Whether smoker, and if so, quantity |
| Normal alcohol habit |
| Alcohol consumption immediately prior to incident or in the previous 24 hours |
| Whether under prescribed medication |
| Any ingested non-prescribed drugs |
| Records of drug and alcohol tests |

## f. Case study

### *Background to the incident*

A 12,000 ton general cargo vessel was involved in a liner service from Canada to a number of Caribbean Islands. The cargoes included traditional general cargo of packaged and boxed goods along with some containerised cargo.

It was normal practice for the ship to provide fresh drinking water for the stevedore labour force at the Caribbean Islands.

Whilst discharging at one of the Islands many of the stevedores suddenly developed severe diarrhoea. The stevedore foreman lodged a formal complaint with the captain of the ship and the local Port Health Officer alleging that the drinking water was contaminated.

Delays occurred to the ship whilst the stevedores tidied themselves up and recovered sufficiently to return to discharging the cargo.

### *Consideration of relevant evidence*

Samples of the drinking water were analysed at a local laboratory and found to be pure.

On checking the cargo hold where the affected stevedores had been working a number of boxes were found to have been broached and the contents removed. From the discarded wrappers found in the adjacent area it became apparent that the content was laxative chocolate. It became apparent that the stevedores had eaten significant quantities of the chocolate not realising that it was laxative.

### *Outcome*

The circumstantial evidence was sufficient to satisfy the stevedore foreman and the port health authorities that the problems experienced by the stevedores were of their own making. A formal letter of protest was subsequently sent to the stevedore Company on account of the stevedores pilfering the cargo.

## Employment — Labour disputes and disciplinary procedures

### a. Conceptual background

The master in the course of his duties may be confronted by problems relating to the crew either in the form of collective trade disputes involving strike action or individual disciplinary offences. The legitimacy of such trade disputes and the recourse to disciplinary procedures open to the master is determined by the law of the flag State. These may be simple civil sanctions or full criminal proceedings. Although the discussion in this chapter of trade disputes on board a vessel and disciplinary procedures is limited to English law, the principles, especially in relation to the recording of evidence, will be of general application. In addition, this chapter discusses briefly the procedures to be followed by the master in the event of strike action by shore personnel and also industrial action by the International Transport Workers Federation (ITF). Finally, the chapter examines the problems which arise from the growing incidence of drug smuggling on board cargo vessels.

This introductory chapter on the conceptual background will be split into three topic areas:

- Trade disputes —

    - On board the vessel

    - ITF disputes

    - Strikes by shore personnel

- Disciplinary procedures

- Drug smuggling

### *Trade disputes*

Under English law, a trade dispute is a dispute between workers and their own employers which relates wholly or mainly to the conditions of employment, the engagement and non-engagement of workers, allocation of work and duties, discipline, and trade union matters. Industrial action is lawful only if the trade union has obtained the support of its members through a secret and properly conducted ballot.

#### *On board the vessel*

A seaman on a United Kingdom registered vessel may leave the ship in contemplation of furtherance of a trade dispute if he has given the master at least 48 hours' notice. This notice will be valid only if given when the vessel is within the United Kingdom and is securely moored to a safe berth. If the notice is valid, the seaman cannot be compelled to go to sea in the 48 hour period following the giving of the notice even if there are clauses in the crew agreement which prevent him from participating in trade disputes.

Any industrial action on board a United Kingdom ship when the ship is not safely moored in the United Kingdom is a criminal offence. The owners in such a situation may consider bringing criminal charges against the seamen participating in the action.

Whenever there is the likelihood of a trade dispute on board the vessel, the master should follow carefully all the procedures listed below. The master should ensure that:

- The seamen's accounts of wages are up-to-date and any payments which are due are made promptly.

- All necessary steps are taken to guarantee the safety of all persons on board the vessel and the medical staff are alerted.

- As soon as any industrial action is contemplated owners and their local agents are informed and kept closely advised of all developments.

- The ship and her equipment are kept in a seaworthy condition in order to allow the vessel to continue the voyage as soon after the resolution of the dispute as possible and all steps taken to maintain the vessel are fully and accurately recorded.

All work on board the vessel should be done in a discrete manner so as not to provoke any incidents with the seamen involved in the industrial action.

- The names of the seamen involved in any action are recorded in the official log book.

The record in the log book should set out the full factual details and record what is said, by whom and when. The master may also consider keeping his own separate record of the factual details surrounding the industrial action in his notebook. This record could then be made available to the owners if they wish to bring any claims against the striking seamen (although the owners are unlikely to pursue such claims). However, the master should note that if his notebook is used as evidence, the entire notebook must be made available to the opposing side. Therefore, it is important that such notebooks only contain facts and not opinions or other material which could prejudice owners (please refer to the introduction of this book). It should also be remembered that such note books should supplement any log book entries but it should never replace the formal entries in the log.

- In the event that picket lines are set up, the picketers are assured that any officers crossing the picket line are only doing so to reach their living quarters and are not attempting to break the strike.

- Before taking the vessel to sea, a full and properly trained and qualified crew are on board and all safety requirements are fulfilled.

Finally, in the interests of all the parties involved, the master should never participate in any strike of seamen or officers, or attempt to break the strike. If the master becomes implicated in the strike, the danger exists that local police, military, or Company agents will over rule his authority and displace the authority of the master.

## ITF disputes

Since 1972, the ITF has been active in organising boycotts and crew strikes against vessels flying "flags of convenience". The aim of the ITF is to enforce minimum ITF conditions on these vessels relating to wages and terms of employment.

An ITF boycott, or "blacking" as it is sometimes called, occurs when shore personnel, which could include stevedores, lock keepers, boatmen and line handlers, tug crews, and pilots, refuse to provide services to a particular vessel earmarked by the ITF. The shore personnel involved in the boycott usually will belong to an ITF affiliated trade union. The ITF action also may be supported by a crew strike on board.

In order to avoid boycotts against a vessel, many charterers now insist on the owners obtaining a "blue certificate" from the ITF which would exempt the vessel from any ITF action. The effect of the "blue certificate" is that crew agreements are governed by the terms of the current ITF Collective Agreement.

If a boycott is directed against a vessel, it is likely that ITF inspectors will attempt to persuade the master to enter into an ITF agreement. The master should immediately inform his owners and ask for full instructions or request owners to send a representative to deal with the demands. Subject to his owner's instructions on the point, the master may prefer not to sign any document until he has received specific instructions from his owners.

At all stages, the master should ensure that a full and accurate record of the events is made and that owners are kept fully informed. ITF boycotts are legal in only a few countries, but when they do arise the master can do very little else but sit out the boycott. A boycott carries less force and is pursued with less enthusiasm by both the strikers and the media if the master and officers act calmly and are not antagonistic.

## Strikes by shore personnel

In the event of strike action on shore, loading and discharging operations on the vessel are likely to be delayed. The wording of any charterparty under which the vessel is operating will determine whether the charterers or the owners will bear the responsibility for any losses incurred as a result of the delay.

As there are likely to be claims arising as a result of the strike with regard to the running of laytime, off-hire, or in the case of a perishable cargo, cargo damage, the master should contact the local P&I correspondent as soon as possible. If the vessel is carrying a perishable cargo, the claims may be potentially very large, and the P&I correspondent will assist the master to minimise the damage. The master may contact the P&I correspondent without any fear of escalating the action being taken on shore as the correspondent will not be a party to the dispute.

If a load or discharge port is named in the bill of lading or similar contract there is an absolute obligation on the master to take his ship to that port although it is strike bound. However, there is the possibility that the charterparty under which the ship is operating allows for the vessel to load or discharge at an alternative port. If the master is approaching a port which is strike bound, he should contact owners to discuss this possibility.

While a vessel is in a strike bound port, the master should ensure that the officers and crew do nothing that will aggravate the dispute. He also should ensure that all the facts relating to the strike are fully and accurately recorded in the log book. This record should include the amount of time lost and any additional expenses incurred by the vessel. In addition, the master should keep a scrapbook of local newspaper reports of the strike.

## Disciplinary procedures

Disciplinary procedures on board a United Kingdom vessel are governed by the Merchant Navy Code of Conduct. This code of conduct allows five sanctions of successively greater intensity which must be used for dealing with disciplinary problems. These sanctions are as follows:

• Informal warning

  This warning is given for first offences of a minor nature. It usually is given by an officer at an appropriate level lower than the master and is given immediately with no written record being kept of the incident.

• Formal warning

  This warning is given for more serious offences or for repetition of a minor offence. It is given by the head of department and is recorded in the Company files.

• Master's formal warning

  This warning is recorded in the official log book and follows on after the two previously mentioned sanctions, or alternatively it is given for a serious disciplinary offence.

• Master's written reprimand

  This is a last chance warning which is recorded in the official log book. A copy of the reprimand is also given to the offender.

• Dismissal

  This sanction may only be used for the most serious of offences.

Discipline on board a United Kingdom ship, in all cases, should be maintained according to this code of conduct (or any similar codes provided by other flag states). In addition, offences should be dealt with as soon as possible after the event. However, in the case of more serious offences which warrant formal treatment, the master should wait a few hours after the offence has been committed before disciplining the crew member in question. The master, thus, will have the opportunity to ascertain all the facts surrounding the incident before he interviews the crew member and he can conduct the interview in an orderly manner.

A disciplinary interview must be conducted in accordance with the rules of natural justice. Thus, the charge against the offender must be read out and both the offender and his accuser must be present throughout the interview. If there is more than one offender, the master should not take sides, but treat them impartially. The offender should be allowed to be represented by a friend, and any statements made by witnesses will be subject to cross examination. The decision will be made once the offender has been given the chance to make his statement. When a decision has been made, the master should ensure that all the relevant forms are prepared in the presence of the offender and that all concerned are informed of the decision.

The most common offence committed on board is absence without leave from the place of duty, often in conjunction with being drunk. If a crew member does come on duty under the influence of alcohol, he should be sent to his quarters for his own safety and the safety of others. The master should ensure that all witnesses make a written statement, testifying to the unsuitable condition of the crew member.

The master himself should deal with all cases of refusal to obey an order and all cases of fighting so he is aware of the underlying problems which led to the incident. He also should personally deal with crew members who go missing from the ship and later rejoin. All cases dealt with by the master should be recorded in the official log book. If the vessel incurs extra expenses in the form of hiring replacement labour as a result of the crew member's conduct, the master may make a suitable deduction from his wages. The master should ensure that a record is kept of all expenses incurred and deductions made.

The master, in the case of the most serious offences listed in the code of conduct, may dismiss the offender. The code of conduct provides that the master may summarily dismiss an offender without any prior warnings in certain circumstances. The master should only resort to summary dismissal in cases of gross misconduct. Most dismissals will be preceded by at least one recorded warning. In the majority of cases, the master will dismiss a crew member at the end of the voyage.

Whenever a crew member has been dismissed from the vessel, the master, in order to counter a possible unfair dismissal claim, should keep a full and accurate record of all warnings both formal and informal given to the crew member over as long a period as possible and a detailed account of the reasons why he was dismissed. In addition, a detailed account should be kept of any expenses deducted from the crew member's wages in order to cover repatriation costs. This account as well as the crew member's account of wages should be entered in the log book.

If a crew member has committed a very serious offence, as defined in the appropriate code of conduct, or the criminal code, dismissal alone may not be sufficient. The master, in this case, instead of imposing his usual sanctions, should instead refer the offending crew member to the Discipline Organisation ashore. He should collect and document as much evidence as possible to accompany his report. The report and enclosures must then be sent to the appropriate shore discipline organisation and a copy sent to the owners. Another copy must be given to the crew member in question, and a fourth copy placed in the ship's files. A shore based tribunal will conduct an inquiry and decide whether to dismiss the crew member from the merchant marine.

If the crew member has committed a criminal offence or an offence under the Merchant Shipping Acts, the master and owners may decide to refer the case to the authorities. The master should ensure that all witnesses make written statements, and a complete account of the incident is entered in the log book with the statements annexed to the log. The entire file must be sent to the owners so they may present the case to the authorities.

## Drug smuggling — United States' policy

Drug smuggling on merchant ships has been on the increase during the last two decades or so. Although smuggling occurs in most parts of the world, the largest markets are North America and Western Europe. In some countries such as Malaysia and Thailand, the death penalty may be imposed on offenders. If drugs are found on a merchant vessel, the ship will be subject to heavy fines, and in some cases, confiscation.

In 1986, the United States adopted a zero tolerance policy towards the carriage of illicit drugs on merchant ships which has placed a heavy financial burden on shipowners and their P&I Clubs. Although confiscation of the vessel and fines for criminal offences are outside the traditional cover provided by P&I insurance, the Clubs generally are prepared to cover owners in cases where there has been no complicity by the owners or their employees.

Drug smugglers have found it increasingly easier to smuggle drugs in merchant ships with little cost to themselves, rather than to use the former methods of speed boats and aeroplanes. In 1986, only 1.7% of the marijuana smuggled into the United States came from merchant ships. By 1988, the amount of marijuana smuggled into the United States in merchant ships had increased to 37.9%. The United States customs in one instance seized as much as 12,000 pounds of cocaine with a street value of almost $100,000,000. The problem has affected all carriers and even the largest and most respectable carriers have found themselves the innocent victims of smugglers.

Under United States law, if drugs are found on a merchant ship, owners will be subject to the penalties mentioned. Owners will be held liable even if the drugs are concealed in a sealed container which, under normal circumstances, would not be opened prior to loading, unless they can show that all possible precautions were taken to prevent smuggling.

The United States customs believes that shipping lines must improve their security to ensure that they are not being used as the unwitting agents of drug smugglers and has been pressing shipping lines to impose strict security measures during loading. In recent years, a total of 256 carriers to the United States have signed a Carriers Initiative Agreement with the authorities under which the carriers undertake to co-operate with customs and to take "the utmost care" to prevent their vessels from being used by smugglers. Under the agreement, shipowners have agreed that the ship's officers will regularly search for narcotics, seal specific compartments on the vessel, provide advance copies of manifests, and assist customs and inform them of any suspicious activity[2].

The master should ensure that anything done in connection with the agreement is fully and accurately entered in the log book. masters and ship's officers should also be aware of the International Chamber of Shipping guidelines on the recognition and detection of drugs.

### a. Potential exposure / problem

This subsection has addressed a range of potential employment related issues which could affect and interfere with a ship owners commercial operations. The potential exposure and the ensuing problems have been explored within the conceptual background discussions in the section above. It should always be kept firmly in mind that that the categories of incidents addressed in this section must be handled both with considerable tact and diplomacy on the one hand and, on the other hand in a thoroughly methodical, systematic and objective manner.

### b. ISM implications

The types of employment related incidents which are the subject of this section can have a major impact upon safety, and possibly security, related issues. Clearly the safety of the people on board, the ship itself, the cargo and the environment must tack precedence over commercial aspects. The rules and regulations governing employment related matters on board ship will have taken that general principle very much into account. Accordingly it can be anticipated that various sections of the ISM Code will need to be considered when dealing with employment related problems and in collecting relevant evidence and preparing reports.

A copy of the text of Resolution A.741(18) as amended by MSC.104(73), the International Management Code for the Safe Operation of Ships and for Pollution Prevention (International Safety Management (ISM) Code, appears in Part C 1 towards the rear of this book.

---

[2]     The Carriage of Illegal Drugs by Sea, B.A.H. Parritt, The Nautical Institute, 1998.

The ISM Code is about having a management system in place to take care of safety and environmental protection aspects — as such there will be many sections relevant to employment related issues. However, we will focus on some of the more obvious / relevant sections:

Preamble     Paragraph 6

6.   The cornerstone of good safety management is commitment from the top. In matters of safety and pollution prevention it is the commitment, competence, attitudes and motivation of individuals at all levels that determine the end result.

Good leadership is crucial throughout the Company not only in the management of safety but in the management of the Company generally and personnel specifically. With good leadership and management there will be a reduced risk of encountering the types of problems identified within this section.

Section 1.2

1.2.2 Safety management objectives of the Company should, inter alia

.1   provide for safe practices in ship operation and a safe working environment;

.2   establish safeguards against all identified risks; and

.3   continuously improve safety management skills of personnel ashore and aboard ships, including preparing for emergencies related both to safety and environmental protection.

The possibility of scenarios similar to those identified in the conceptual background section above can be anticipated as possibilities such that proactive steps could be taken to ensure that their likelihood is reduced to a minimum and thus prevent them ever becoming an issue.

1.2.3 The safety management system should ensure:

.1   compliance with mandatory rules and regulations; and

.2   that applicable codes, guidelines and standards recommended by the Organization, Administrations, classification societies and maritime industry organizations are taken into account.

The Company should ensure that those involved are fully aware of the relevant laws, rules and regulations relating to employment terms, disciplinary procedures and drug smuggling and that the SMS will adequately ensure that those rules and regulations are complied with.

Section 3     Company responsibility and authority

3.2   The Company should define and document the responsibility, authority and interrelation of all personnel who manage, perform and verify work relating to and affecting safety and pollution prevention.

Clearly defined job roles and where each individual fits into the organisation can help considerably in reducing the risk of disagreements and disputes arising between employers and employees.

Section 5    Master's responsibility and authority

The master, along with his officers and petty officers, will be the one directly involved in ensuring that the Company policy, as well as the law, is complied with relating to labour disputes, disciplinary procedures and drug smuggling. The authority of the master must be clear and unambiguous.

Section 6    Resources and personnel

There is considerable responsibility put upon the Company under Section 6 to not only ensure that it recruits the proper people but also ensure that the seafarers it employs are adequately trained and familiarised such that they can undertake their tasks on board in a safe and efficient manner. By paying careful attention to their various obligations under Section 6 the Company should ensure that their exposure to the types of problems identified in this section dealing with Employment problems should be reduced to a minimum. Of course personnel related issues will, invariably, also involve the active participation of the employee – who must also accept responsibility for his or own actions and obligations.

Section 7    Development of plans for shipboard operations

It can be anticipated that clearly laid out procedures will be in place relating to the behaviour and conduct of the crew and the consequences of not complying with that code of conduct — of course this must be in line with the law of the flag state administration and any national or other agreement applicable to the seafarers contract of employment.

It is very likely that there will be a section relating to drug smuggling, and the consequences, set out in the Company 'Drug and Alcohol' policy which will be found within the SMM.

Section 8    Emergency preparedness

The relevance of this section will clearly depend upon the circumstances in which the employment related incident occurred.

Section 9    Reports and analysis of non-conformities, accidents and hazardous occurrences

Employment problems, particularly relating to disciplinary procedures may very well impact upon safety on board. If that is the case then they may very well fall within the types of incidents anticipated by Section 9 of the Code. Records of the activities anticipated by Section 9 may well be examined to confirm that learning opportunities were being taken as part of the SMS. Similarly minutes of on board safety committee meetings may be examined to determine the level of involvement and commitment to safety management on board.

Section 12    Company verification, review and evaluation

There is a very clear obligation on the Company to ensure that the SMS is working properly on board its vessels. If a serious incident has arisen related to the types of problems identified in the section on employment related issues, then it can be anticipated that the active monitoring by the Company will be looked at very closely by way of audit trails. The Company may need to demonstrate that they were checking and satisfied themselves that the correct procedures were being followed and the law was being complied with.

Certification and verification

As a matter of course the validity of the SMC and DOC will be checked.

## c. Nature of evidence required

Within the general discussion where the conceptual background was being considered above, various items of evidence was identified in respect of the different categories of issues addressed. Summaries of those are set out below.

### *Labour disputes*

- Relevant extract from the SMM

- Crew contract and any other related contractual terms

- Official notice of intention with regard to withdrawing labour / striking

- Risk assessment relating to situation on board if labour is withdrawn

- Record of seaman's accounts / wages

- Official log book

- Deck log book

- Any other factual records relating to the dispute and the activities of individuals

- Copies of correspondence and records of telephone and other discussions related to the dispute

- Crew list

- Details of any individuals representing particular Union or other similar organisations who attended on board or attempted to board the vessel

- Statement of facts

- Master's report

- 'Blue Certificate' – if ITF related

- Relevant charterparty – particularly if strike by shore labour involved.

## Disciplinary procedures

- Relevant extract from the SMM

- Crew contract and any other related contractual terms

- Details of relevant and applicable Code of Conduct governing disciplinary procedures on board that particular ship with that particular crew

- Official log book

- Records of any steps taken under the relevant disciplinary procedures code

- Supporting evidence, e.g. witness statements, photographs etc. relating to or illustrating the offence(s) for which the disciplinary action has been taken

- Copies of the individual seamen's identification documents and other papers

- Master's report.


## Drug smuggling

- Relevant extracts from the Ship Security Plan (where allowable)

- Relevant extract from the SMM and / or the Company 'Drug and Alcohol' policy

- Records of any relevant training and familiarisation provided to the crew relating to drug smuggling and the consequences

- Details of any anti drug smuggling initiatives or steps taken on board prior to the incident — including participation in the US Sea Carriers Initiative

- Details and records of any searches undertaken on board prior to the incident

- Witness statements

- Details of what was found, by whom, where it was found, when it was found

- Official log book

- Deck log book

- Details of previous ports visited

- Details of individuals who might have boarded the ship in previous ports

- Statement of facts

- Copies of relevant correspondence and notes of telephone and other conversations

- If specific crew members identified as being implicated in the smuggling — details of their recruitment and background and the checks carried out by the Company prior to employing them

- Master's report

- Charterparty and bills of lading if drugs found in the cargo.

## d. Report

The master's report should be a factual and objective account of what happened — and should include:

- Background to the search

- What drugs were found

- Who found them

- Where they were found

- When they were found

- Details of any crew members implicated or suspected of being implicated

- Details of further investigations and / or inquiry undertaken by shore authorities

- Actions taken by the shore authorities

- Follow up actions taken on board

## Stowaways

Historically, stowaways have caused considerable difficulties both to the master and ship operator, particularly in areas of Africa and South and Central America where the problem is widespread. Additionally, there has been a significant rise in the number of cases where stowaways have boarded ships, seeking to flee countries which are in civil conflict, and also where it is the case that work is not available. These days the stowaway problem is very much part of the bigger 'security' problem facing shipboard management.

It is particularly important when considering the suggestions in this section that you do so in conjunction with your Ship Security Plan under the International Ship and Port Security (ISPS) Code requirements and / or any related procedures you may have as part of the SMS under the ISM system. Remember the ship's systems and plans must take priority and the suggestions set out in this section, and the book generally, are intended to complement and not replace the ships systems and plans[34].

## a. Conceptual background

### Procedures to prevent stowaways boarding a vessel

As a part of the ISPS procedures, the master should ensure that whilst the vessel is in port, a constant gangway watch is maintained and careful control established over who comes on board the ship. This may be done by utilising the services of

---

[3] *Stowaways by Sea*, B.A.H. Parritt, 3rd edition, The Nautical Institute, 2001

[4] *Maritime Security*, S. Jones, The Nautical Institute, 2006.

crew, which although incurring the additional cost of overtime pay, will save the additional expense of instructing a private security guard to carry out watch duty.

A very useful checklist of action to be taken to prevent stowaways is reproduced in the section dealing with 'The Nature of Evidence Required' below (this is reproduced with the kind permission of the North of England P&I Association).

Prior to leaving the berth a thorough and systematic search of the entire ship should take place. This should include (depending upon the type of ship):

* The accommodation

* The engine room

* The decks (including the monkey island)

* The cargo compartments

* Unlocked store rooms

* Mast houses

* Enclosed spaces, eg forepeak, chain locker, steering gear compartment, etc.

* The lifeboats

* Any other spaces where people may hide.

Stowaway search checklists should be used wherever possible to confirm that each space has been searched, by whom and this should be dated and timed. An entry should be made in the log book confirming that the stowaway search was carried out and the results of the search.

Extra diligence will need to be taken in areas of the world where the problem of stowaways is most prevalent.

### Procedures once stowaways have been discovered

If stowaways are discovered onboard the vessel, the master should immediately inform the ship operator's agents at the next port of call, and ship operator who will generally inform their P&I Club, who will in turn, contact the local club correspondents for assistance. The stowaway(s) should be searched for any documentation (e.g. seaman's book, passport etc.) and a further search for any documents should be made on the vessel. Should any form of identity card be found, the repatriation process will be made much easier. If no documents are found, it is possible that the stowaways may be on board for a lengthy period of time whilst negotiations take place between the P&I correspondents, the local immigration authorities and the consul, or embassy of the alleged country of the stowaways.

If documents are not found, the stowaway should be questioned to try and discover relevant information.

### *Treatment of stowaways whilst onboard*

Stowaways should be guarded as closely as possible while the vessel is in port to prevent them from jumping ship which may render the ship operator liable to pay heavy fines as a result of allowing "illegal immigrants" into a country. Moreover, if the stowaways are recaptured, the ship operator will also be held liable for all future expenses inclusive of guard costs.

It is not unknown for masters to put stowaways to work onboard a vessel whilst a voyage is in process. Whilst some may find this an acceptable course of action to take, it is not one which would be recommended especially in cases where a significant number of stowaways are found onboard.

In cases as above, contact with the crew should be kept to a minimum as this may cause unrest. The stowaways should be placed in secure quarters, guarded if possible and provided with adequate food and water to remain healthy.

### b. Potential exposure / problem

Stowaways have always created problems for those on board the ship and for the ship operators. However, post ISPS they can pose very serious problems because their very presence would suggest a breach or failure of the Ship Security System — they may cause additional delays when entering subsequent ports whilst further security checks are carried out.

In addition to the inconvenience and the potential security threat, the presence of stowaways on board can lead to the following exposures / problems:

- There may not be sufficient life saving appliances on board.

- The use of crew members' time guarding / feeding / exercising the stowaways

- The provision of food, water, clothes etc.

- The use of and potential damage to the accommodation on board

- The effect on moral on board.

- The risk of potential violence from the stowaways against the crew

- The potential health risk — the stowaways may be carrying contagious diseases and / or may not be vaccinated against certain diseases

- The ship may be fined in certain countries if there are stowaways on board — this likelihood is significantly increased if they have not been declared to the immigration authorities

- The local immigration / security authorities may insist that shore side security guards must be placed on board to guard the stowaways whilst in port or they may insist that the stowaways be landed and placed into secure custody ashore until the ship sails — in either case considerable expenses will be incurred

- The stowaways may escape which will almost certainly incur very serious problems / fines against the ship and probably delays to the ship sailing

- The costs, in time and money, of establishing the true identity / nationality can be considerable

- The subsequent repatriation, if such can be achieved at all, will be expensive. Although in contravention of international agreements there are fewer and fewer countries who are prepared to recognise their obligations and responsibilities with regard to trying to assist with stowaways — i.e. preventing them getting on board ships as well as helping with repatriation — thus the problem invariably remains with the ship operator and the ship's crew

However difficult or inconvenient it might be to maintain tight security to prevent stowaways getting on board in the first place and to conduct thorough searches before sailing – it is infinitely less of a problem than dealing with the problem of allowing stowaways to sail with the vessel.

### c. ISM implications

The ISM implications may depend upon the threat posed by the stowaways. The following non-exhaustive list attempts to identify some of the more obvious potential implications and, consequently, suggest areas of the SMS which will come under close scrutiny:

Section 1.2.2.2    (establish safeguards against all identified risks)

This would probably link up with the emergency preparedness under Section 8.

Section 6    Resources and personnel

The crew should have been adequately trained / familiarised with the security plan to deal with the prevention of stowaways boarding , or dealing with them should they be discovered on board.

Section 7    Development of plans for shipboard operations

Clearly the navigation of the vessel and watchkeeping are likely to be affected and thus the enhanced requirements which may need to be introduced whilst in high risk areas.

Section 8    Emergency preparedness

Stowaways could pose a serious security risk and may fall within the category of 'potential emergency situations' anticipated in Section 8 although, as mentioned earlier, such a scenario may fall under the procedures of the ISPS Code. The results of related emergency drills and exercises may be inspected.

Section 9    Reports and analysis of non-conformities, accidents and hazardous occurrences

Records of the activities anticipated by Section 9 may well be examined to confirm that learning opportunities were being taken as part of the SMS. Similarly minutes of on board safety committee meetings may be examined to determine the level of involvement and commitment to safety management on board.

Section 11    Documentation

If there appear to have been problems with compliance with the SMS or ship security plan then it is likely that a closer look will be made at the documented procedures themselves. If these are voluminous, irrelevant or otherwise inadequate then the Company is likely to come under severe criticism.

Section 12    Company verification, review and evaluation

There is a very clear obligation on the Company to ensure that the SMS is working properly on board its vessels. If a serious incident has arisen, as in this case with stowaways having gained access to the ship, then it can be anticipated that the active monitoring by the Company will be looked at very closely by way of audit trails.

### Certification and verification

As a matter of course the validity of the SMC and DOC will be checked.

Thanks are due to the North of England P&I Association for permission to reproduce the checklists following.

## *Nature of evidence required*

Checklist – Action to be taken to prevent stowaways

---

**CHECKLIST – Action to be taken to prevent stowaways**

This checklist should be used in conjunction with the ship operator's procedures for the prevention of stowaways, including those within the Safety Management System required by the ISM Code, and the North of England Stowaway Search Checklist cards.

### General

1. Access to the ship restricted to the gangway only ............................................... [ ]

2. Security personnel from a reputable shore Company employed if necessary ........ [ ]

### Gangway

3. Full-time gangway watch kept.............................................................................. [ ]

4. All embarkation and disembarkation movements tallied ...................................... [ ]

5. Pass system in operation for visitors .................................................................. [ ]

6. Pass system in operation for stevedores .............................................................. [ ]

### Deck

7. Full-time watch kept at loading arms, ro-ro ramps and other potential

 access points ...................................................................................................... [ ]

8. Roving deck patrol............................................................................................. [ ]

9. Decks and potential access points well illuminated .............................................. [ ]

10. Mooring lines fitted with rat guards .................................................................. [ ]

11. Covers fitted and locked over hawse pipes ........................................................ [ ]

12. Pilot ladders and other ladders turned inboard ................................................. [ ]

13. Accommodation entrances locked and sealed where safe to do so ....................... [ ]

14. Engine room entrances locked and sealed where safe to do so ............................. [ ]

15. Store room entrances locked and sealed where safe to do so .............................. [ ]

16. Internal cabins, storerooms and other spaces locked ......................................... [ ]

### Cargo Spaces

17. Cargo space accesses locked and sealed where safe to do so................................ [ ]

18. Hatch covers closed when cargo work has stopped, or been completed,

 and when safe to do so ....................................................................................... [ ]

19. Pontoon type hatch covers that have been landed ashore inspected

 before being replaced on the ship........................................................................ [ ]

20. Warning notices posted about fumigation of cargo spaces .................................... [ ]

---

21. Audible warning given before fumigation of cargo spaces .................................... [ ]

**Containers and ro-ro trailers**

22. Seals checked prior to loading to ensure they are intact ........................................ [ ]

23. Empty units inspected and sealed prior to loading ................................................ [ ]

24. Open-sided and / or open topped units inspected prior to loading...................... [ ]

**Stowaway search**

25. Simultaneous stowaway search of the accommodation, engine room,

    cargo spaces and main deck carried out immediately prior to sailing ................... [ ]

26. Second stowaway search carried out after sailing .................................................. [ ]

27. Details and results of the searches recorded in the log book................................. [ ]

Checklist – Action to be taken if stowaways are found

**CHECKLIST – Action to be taken if stowaways are found**

This checklist should be used in conjunction with the ship operator's procedures, including those contained in the ISM Code Safety Management System and the Ship Security Plan.

**Search**

1. Area in vicinity of where the stowaways are discovered -

    search for other stowaways ..................................................................................... [ ]

2. Area in vicinity of where the stowaways are discovered –

    search for papers and personal belongings.............................................................. [ ]

3. Stowaways searched for papers and personal belongings ....................................... [ ]

**Security**

4. Objects that could be used as weapons confiscated................................................. [ ]

5. Larger groups of stowaways separated into smaller groups..................................... [ ]

6. Appropriate measures taken to ensure security of the stowaways by locking

    them in a suitable cabin or storeroom..................................................................... [ ]

7. Guard(s) posted....................................................................................................... [ ]

**Health & welfare**

8. General health check of stowaways carried out....................................................... [ ]

9. Expert medical advice sought if necessary.............................................................. [ ]

10. Stowaways provided with food and water ............................................................ [ ]

11. Stowaways provided with clothing and bedding ................................................... [ ]

## Repatriation arrangements

12. Stowaways landed before ship leaves the embarkation port or harbour waters

    (see important note 1 below)............................................................................... [ ]

13. Ship operator notified...................................................................................... [ ]

14. P&I Club notified ........................................................................................... [ ]

15. Stowaway questionnaire completed for each stowaway (see instructions below) ... [ ]

16. Statement for the appropriate authorities prepared containing

    all relevant information ................................................................................... [ ]

17. Relevant details notified to the authorities at the port of embarkation.................. [ ]

18. Relevant details notified to the authorities at the flag State ................................... [ ]

## Important notes

1. Except in an emergency, do not depart from the planned voyage to seek disembarkation of a stowaway unless advice has been sought from the ship operators.

2. Stowaways should not be put to work.

3. Keep contact between stowaways and crew members to a minimum.

## Instructions for completing stowaway questionnaire

1. Keep original laminated questionnaire in a file and photocopy as required.

2. Do not write on the original.

3. Arrange for the stowaways to complete the questionnaire in the appropriate language themselves, using black ink or black ball pen.

4. Take four passport type photographs of the stowaways and attach one to the questionnaire in the space provided.

5. Send a copy of the completed questionnaire for each stowaway to the P&I Club.

Questionnaire – Stowaway / Person Rescued at Sea (English)

---

**Questionnaire – Stowaways / Person Rescued at Sea – English**

This form can be used to record details of stowaways or persons in distress rescued at sea.

| | |
|---|---|
| Attach photograph of stowaway here | 9. Full Name.................................................<br>10. Place of birth ..........................................<br>11. Date of birth ................ 12. Nationality ..............<br>13. Religion ...................... 14. Gender .....................<br>15. Language(s) spoken ................................<br>15. Home address............................................<br>.................................................................. |
| Signature<br>............................ | 17. Father's name ...........................................<br>18. Father's birth place ....................................<br>19. Mother's name ..........................................<br>20. Mother's birth place ..................................<br>21. Parents address ........................................<br>.................................................................. |
| Description<br>1. Age<br>.............................. | |
| 2. Height<br>.............................. | 22. Marital status ..........................................<br>23. Name of spouse ........................................ |
| 3. Weight<br>.............................. | 24. Nationality of spouse ................................<br>25. Spouse's address ......................................<br>.................................................................. |
| 4. Complexion<br>.............................. | 26. Occupation ............................................. |
| 5. Hair<br>.............................. | 27. Employer's name ......................................<br>28. Employer's address .................................. |
| 6. Eyes<br>.............................. | ..................................................................<br>29. Date and time found .................................. |
| 7. Form of face<br>.............................. | 30. Place of hiding ........................................<br>31. Port of boarding ......................................<br>32. Date and time of boarding ......................... |
| 8. Marks / characteristics<br>..............................<br>..............................<br>..............................<br>..............................<br>.............................. | 33. Method of boarding ..................................<br>34. Reasons for boarding ................................<br>35. Type of ID - Passport [ ] ID Card [ ]<br>       Seaman's Card [ ] Other [ ]<br>36. Number ...................................................<br>37. Place of issue ..........................................<br>38. Date of issue ................ Date of expiry ........... |

Other information (Previous record, possessions, contacts in other parts of the world)

---

Pt B3

P
E
O
P
L
E

Records should be kept, and log entries made, of the following:

- What food, water and clothing provided to the stowaways.

- Any medical treatment given to the stowaways.

- Where the stowaways are being kept and the security arrangements in place.

- Any additional security arrangements put in place, eg employment of shore security guards.

## d. Report

A report with as much of the following information as possible should be sent as quickly as possible to the ship operators and/or the P&I Club, correspondents, agents. Ideally the information as required in the checklists set out above should be included but, as a minimum, should include the following:

- Last port visited

- Date and time of sailing from last port

- Does the vessel have cargo on board?

- How many stowaways have been found?

- When and where were the stowaways found?

- Do the stowaways have travel documents?

- Is communication possible with stowaways?

- State of health of stowaways

- Where have stowaways been placed?

- Do the stowaways pose any particular threat to the safety of the crew or vessel?

- Are the stowaways co-operative?

For each stowaway the following information should be provided (where possible):

- Full name

- Sex

- Date of birth

- Place of birth

- Name of both parents

- Home address

- Nationality

Once this information is received then the shipowners, P&I Clubs, correspondents, etc. will liaise regarding further action to be taken regarding repatriation.

Once in port, the owner's agents, together with the P&I correspondents, will arrange for a full and formal interview and for photographs to be taken of the stowaways. It is possible that stowaways will have to remain on board if there is either insufficient time to arrange for repatriation or if a local authority refuses to assist or to become involved.

### Diversion expenses

If it is decided to divert the vessel to land the stowaways, the shipowner may recover the expenses of doing so from its P&I Club. To do so, however, the owner will need to submit certain information from the vessel. Accordingly an additional report will be required from the master, which should include the following:

- Position of vessel when diversion commenced

- Date/time when diversion commenced

- Distance steamed and time taken to reach part of disembarkation of stowaways

- Details of port expenses

- Statement of facts

- Distance steamed and time taken to reach original course line

- Position, date and time diversion completed

- Details of fuel used during diversion

- Details of seamen's wages, stores and provisions used during the diversion

It should be remembered however, that if the vessel has cargo on board then such a diversion would probably constitute a deviation. As such there may be a breach of the Contract of Carriage such that if the cargo was lost or damaged during the deviation, then the ship operator may not be in a position to rely upon the exceptions and defences of, for example, the Hague Rules. The ship operator may also prejudice his P&I cover. Whether or not the deviation would be considered reasonable and justifiable will be determined from the factual circumstances of the case. Such a deviation should not therefore take place without clear instructions from the ship operator.

### e. Case study

#### Background to the incident

A 6,600 gt purpose built heavy lift ship carried a full project cargo from Northern Europe to a West African port. The cargo was to be utilised as part of an inland oil and gas drilling and exploration project. A return cargo was to be loaded at the same terminal consisting of damaged or otherwise discarded items of oil drilling equipment, some containerised, which was being returned to the European headquarters for repair or scrapping / disposal.

There seemed to be no identifiable security arrangements within the port area. The ship did have a Ship Security Plan in place. Gangway security was established but the gunwale of the ship was on the same level as the quayside such that people from ashore could just step across the gap and didn't use the gangway. The crew of nine, including master, used their best endeavours to control access but eventually conceded defeat.

On completion of loading the master solicited the help of the terminal managers and stevedore foremen to help him and the crew conduct a thorough stowaway search. During a search which lasted two hours they found seven stowaways who were subsequently removed ashore. The ship sailed and after dropping the pilot the master dropped anchor and had the crew conduct a second stowaway search.

No more stowaways were found and the vessel commenced her voyage back to Northern Europe. However, one day later banging and shouting was heard from number two cargo hold and two young men / boys announced their presence. They did not have any identification documents on them and none was found subsequently. They did not speak a language which was understood by the master or any of the other officers and crew. The stowaways were uncooperative although they were not violent.

The master sought instructions from the ship operator and it was decided to continue towards the discharge port and try and repatriate the stowaways from Northern Europe.

On arrival at the discharge port the vessel was boarded by port State Control Inspectors who cited various alleged violations under the ISPS Code and delayed the entry of the ship for six days whilst they searched the ship and conducted a full scale security investigation.

Armed security guards were placed on board through discharge to stand guard over the stowaways until the ship sailed. The ship owners were presented with a bill for US$10,000 in respect of this 'security service'. The local immigration authorities refused to consider the possibility of repatriation through their country.

The true identity of the stowaways, and even confirmation of their nationality, could not be established and, consequently, no country visited by the ship would assist with attempts to repatriate them. The ship continued to face serious problems with alleged violations of security and ISPS Code wherever she went causing delays and consequential losses.

## Relevant evidence

Evidence was required for two main reasons:

1. To demonstrate to PSC and Port Security Officers that the ship had done their best to control access to the ship and maintain a proper ship security system,

2. To persuade the P&I Club to reimburse the ship owner for all the various costs and expenses involved in keeping the stowaways on board and, eventually, repatriating them.

Evidence obtained from the ship included:

- Extracts from ships log books

- Relevant extracts from ship security plan (where allowable)

- Checklist or other record to show what steps were taken to prevent stowaways boarding

- Record of stowaway searches

- Master's report covering the searches and the discovery of the stowaways

- Checklist or other record to show what action was taken once stowaways were found

- Completed stowaway questionnaire or other records of attempted interviews with the stowaways

- Photographs, fingerprints and details of any distinguishing marks

- Record of any medical treatment given to the stowaways

- Record of food, water and clothing given to the stowaways

- Details of accommodation provided to the stowaways (photographs would be useful)

- Record of physical exercise provided to the stowaways

- (if appropriate) details of any diversion expenses

In addition, the following evidence was subsequently collected:

- Photographs and any other useful information could be sent to organisations who specialise in stowaway repatriation – their extensive experience and local knowledge may allow them, from examining photographs, to identify which tribe or country the individual may belong. They may even recognise the individual as being a 'career' stowaway

- Receipts, invoices, bills etc for all incidental expenses involved in having the stowaways on board — including repatriation

*Outcome*

Eventually, by a stroke of luck and quick thinking by a visiting P&I Surveyor a breakthrough was made. The surveyor was on board to inspect some damaged cargo and had his camera with him to record the damage. As he was returning to the accommodation, to see the master, he came across the two stowaways who were being walked around the deck by two crew members as part of their daily exercise. The surveyor said 'Hi' to the stowaways and gestured towards his camera seeking their approval for him to take their photograph. This seemed to be received with some amusement and interest and the stowaways posed with big smiles whilst their photographs were taken. Then one of the young men spoke in broken English and asked the surveyor if he would send a copy of the photograph to his parents — the surveyor agreed and gave the stowaway a pen and some paper on which he wrote down his fathers name and full address. That was all that was needed to process the paperwork to arrange for travel documents which would allow for his repatriation. The other stowaway quickly volunteered his details when he understood that he would be left alone on board.

## Refugees

In certain parts of the world, the master may encounter refugees in distress on the high seas. The United Nations High Commission for Refugees (UNHCR) may be in a position to assist the master and owners in the event refugees are taken on board the vessel to save their lives.

This chapter outlines the recommendations of the UNHCR contained in a booklet entitled "Guidelines for the disembarkation of Refugees".

In particular, this chapter examines the following:

- Procedures in the event refugees are safely embarked on the vessel

- Sequence of events

## Procedure

If the vessel on the high seas has taken on board refugees, the master should immediately prepare a communication for owners and owners' agents at the next scheduled port containing the following information:

- Name of rescuing ship

- Flag and port of registry

- Name and address of managing owners

- Owners' agent at next scheduled port

- Estimated date and time of arrival at next scheduled port

- Estimated date and time of departure from next scheduled port

- Exact number of refugees on board

- Date, time, and exact location of rescue

- Details of events leading up to rescue

- State of health of refugees and details of any urgent medical assistance required

- A list of the refugees citing their full names, family groups, dates of birth, nationality, and sex

### Sequence of events

Once the master's message is received by the owners, the following sequence of events should begin and hopefully lead to the swift disembarkation of the refugees with the assistance of the UNHCR and the authorities involved:

- UNHCR and other authorities involved are informed of the refugee problem

- UNHCR and the flag state arrange for resettlement of the refugees

- Vessel arrives in the next scheduled port

- UNHCR issues guarantee of resettlement to local authorities

- UNHCR and local authorities board vessel to interview refugees

- Refugees disembark under care of UNHCR and cease to be the responsibility of the owners

- Refugees examined by local health authorities and await resettlement arrangements

If it is decided to divert the vessel to land the refugees, the shipowner may recover the expenses of doing so from its P&I Club. To do so, however, the owner will need to submit certain information from the vessel. Accordingly an additional report will be required from the master, which should include the following:

- Position of vessel when diversion commenced

- Date/time when diversion commenced

- Distance steamed and time taken to reach part of disembarkation of stowaways

- Details of port expenses

- Statement of facts

- Distance steamed and time taken to reach original course line

- Position, date and time diversion completed

- Details of fuel used during diversion

- Details of seamen's wages, stores and provisions used during the diversion.

It should be remembered however, that if the vessel has cargo on board then such a diversion would probably constitute a deviation. As such there may be a breach of the Contract of Carriage such that if the cargo was lost or damaged during the deviation, then the ship operator may not be in a position to rely upon the exceptions and defences of, for example, the Hague Rules. The ship operator may also prejudice its P&I cover. Whether or not the deviation would be considered reasonable and justifiable will be determined from the factual circumstances of the case.

Except in cases of extreme urgency, such a diversion should not therefore take place without clear instructions from the ship operator.

The claim for diversion expenses must be supported by as much documentation as possible. The master will be required to provide statements giving details of time and fuel used during any deviation and provide copies of all messages sent and received.

The master also should make available a copy of the official log book entry covering the rescue. If possible, the master should provide photographic evidence of the refugees.

## Case study

### *Background to the incident*

Whilst on passage to its discharge port on the European side of the Mediterranean Sea — the bridge look out reported what appeared to be a small boat and someone on board waving. It was July, late afternoon but still good daylight and the weather was good with a slight sea and light winds. The chief officer, who was the officer of the watch at the time, altered course to take a closer look. It quickly became apparent that there were many people, of African type origin, on board this small boat although very few were showing any sign of active movement. The master was called and general emergency stations were sounded.

The chief officer, with some crew members launched a life boat and went across to the boat in distress. They were horrified by what they found. There was a total of about thirty men, women and children in the boat — most of them either not conscious or barely conscious. No-one spoke a language which was understood by the chief officer of the crew members. Attempts were made to take the boat in tow but the boat started to break up and so the occupants of the boat were transferred into the lifeboat — except six bodies which were clearly dead and which had started to decay. The boat subsequently sank with the six bodies on board.

The lifeboat was recovered on board the vessel and first aid, water, food and clothing were given to the people who had been saved from the boat. The master sent word ahead to the agents, and the ship owners, as to what had happened and to advise that they had 24 refugees on board in need of medical assistance.

The ship arrived at its destination twenty hours later. The vessel was immediately boarded by immigration officers and police who arrested the master and chief officer on a charge of alleged smuggling of illegal immigrants. The master and chief officer were escorted off the ship and detained in a prison cell ashore.

A police guard was placed on board the ship although no medical aid was allowed aboard. The officers remaining on board managed to contact the ship owners who alerted the local P&I Club correspondent to the situation. Through the intervention of the Club Correspondent a medical team was allowed on board and the refugees were taken ashore to hospital facilities.

A lawyer was appointed by the Club Correspondent to facilitate the release of the master and chief officer. By this time the local newspapers, radio and television were carrying stories about how this ship had been caught trying to smuggle in illegal immigrants.

Whilst the P&I Correspondent was on board it came to light that the cook on board had filmed the whole rescue operation on his video camera.

### Relevant evidence

Evidence obtained from the ship included:

- Original working chart

- Original deck log book, which included an itinerary of where the vessel had been for the last three months

- Original official log book

- Engine room log book

- Radio log and copies of email exchanges which had taken place relating to the rescue

- Statements from all the remaining individual officers and crew who remained on board as to what actually happened

- The cook's video film

In addition, the following evidence was subsequently collected:

- Statements from the master and chief officer

- A statement from one of the survivors / refugees which had been taken in hospital via an interpreter

### Outcome

The European country in question had, allegedly, been encountering a growing problem of illegal immigrants finding their way onto the shores of that country and had decided to implement very strict controls and punish severely anyone caught helping illegal immigrants. Their enthusiasm would appear to have got the better of them and was verging on paranoia.

It took four days before a hearing could be arranged with a judge and then only after diplomatic intervention at a high level by the government of the ships flag and the national governments of the master and chief officer — although the local media had already tried and condemned the ship without hearing any of their version of events.

When the video film was shown to the judge it was clear beyond any shadow of a doubt that the people on board the ship were not smugglers of illegal immigrants but rather heroes who had gallantly rescued and saved the lives of 24 human beings — who were now being treated as criminals in a supposed civilised country.

The master and chief officer were released with charges dropped — but without even an apology. The ship was also released and allowed to sail.

It is not known what happened at the diplomatic level but neither the seafarers nor the ship operators ever received an apology or offer of compensation. However, following discussions between the owners, master, officers and crew as well as relevant trade associations and unions that it was decided not to pursue the matter further.

If it had not been for the cook taking the initiative to film the rescue and producing that incontrovertible evidence about what actually happened then the heroes who were doing what every good and professional mariner would do under the circumstances, and doing what they are legally obliged to do, may very well have been wrongly convicted as criminals and spent maybe a long time in a jail in a country which no doubt thinks of itself as democratic, civilised and just.

If any mariners finds themselves in a similar situation they must have no doubts about their humanitarian, professional and legal obligations and must render assistance to people in distress at sea. However, they should ensure that photographic and video evidence is produced to record the rescue events.

### Piracy

Acts of piracy and armed robbery against ships continue to be of considerable concern to the shipping industry as well as flag State and coastal State Administrations. Counter piracy procedures will almost certainly be contained within the Ship Security Plan as prepared in compliance with the International Ship and Port Facility Security Code.

It is not the intention in this book to try and describe the problem in detail nor to address issues of preparing for such attacks or dealing with the attacks themselves – these issues will be dealt with in some detail in the Ship Security Plan and / or in various publications including:

- IMO MSC/Circ.623/Rev.3 – Piracy and Armed Robbery against Ships — Guidance to shipowners and ship operators, shipmasters and crews on preventing and suppressing acts of piracy and armed robbery against ships

- U.K. Marine Guidance Note 241 — Measures to Counter Piracy, Armed Robbery and Acts of Violence against Merchant Shipping

- BIMCO Publication 'The Shipmaster's Security Manual'

- ICS / ISF 'Pirates and Armed Robbers — A Master's Guide

- IMB Special Report on Piracy and Armed Robbery

- Maritime Security — The Nautical Institute, 2006.

### a. Conceptual background

MSC/Circ.623/Rev.3 provides much detailed advice and recommendations about the steps which can be taken to anticipate and prepare for possible attacks by pirates and armed robbers as well as suggestions and guidelines on what to do if attacked. As explained above, it is not the intention here to repeat those guidelines except to draw attention to the recommendation to have a formal ship security plan. Clearly these guidelines predated the 9/11 attacks on the World Trade Centre in New York and the subsequent development of the International Ship & Port Facility Security Code (the ISPS Code). It is likely that such a procedure covering pirate / armed robbery attacks would be included within the ISPS Code procedures although it may still exist within the general ISM procedures. In any event it is felt appropriate, within the context of this book, dealing specifically with the collection of evidence and the preparation of reports to consider briefly the ship security plan guidelines set out in MSC/Circ.623.

### *The pre-piracy/armed robbery phase — ship security plan*

All ships expected to operate in waters where attacks occur should have a ship security plan which pertains to piracy and armed robbery against ships. The ship security plan should be prepared having regard to the risks that may be faced, the crew members available, their capability and training, the ability to establish secure areas on board ship and the surveillance and detection equipment that has been provided.

The plan should, *inter alia*, cover:

1  The need for enhanced surveillance and the use of lighting, surveillance and detection equipment;

2  Crew responses, if a potential attack is detected or an attack is underway;

3  The radio alarm procedures to be followed; and

4  The reports to be made after an attack or an attempted attack.

Ship security plans should ensure that masters and crews are made fully aware of the risks involved during attacks by pirates or armed robbers. In particular, they should address the dangers that may arise if a crew adopts an aggressive response to an attack. Early detection of a possible attack is the most effective deterrent. Aggressive responses, once an attack is underway and, in particular, once the attackers have boarded the ship, could significantly increase the risk to the ship and those on board.

### b. Potential exposure / problem

Clearly the initial concern is with the safety and welfare of those on board the ship. Secondly, the safety of the ship, the environment, the cargo on board and other property. Insurance claims relating to attacks from pirates and armed robbers are likely to fall under the H&M Policy although certain aspects may fall under P&I. Damage and loss could include:

- Personal injuries / death
- Damage to ship
- Loss of ships equipment / stores / cash
- Loss of crew / passengers personal effects
- Loss / damage to cargo
- Pollution
- Damage to third party property

There could be other losses and kinds of damage depending upon the nature of the particular attack and the developments following the incident e.g. the ship may strand or collide with another ship.

### c. ISM implications

The ISM implications may depend upon how the attack happened and the responses by those on board to the attack — as well as the subsequent developments following the attack.. The following, non-exhaustive, list attempts to address some of the more obvious potential implications and, consequently, suggest areas of the SMS which will come under close scrutiny:

Section 1.2.2.2   (establish safeguards against all identified risks)

This would probably link up with the emergency preparedness under Section 8.

Section 6     Resources and personnel

The crew should have been adequately trained / familiarised with the security plan and their actions should an attack be threatened or occur.

Section 7      Development of plans for shipboard operations

Clearly the navigation of the vessel and watchkeeping are likely to be affected and thus the enhanced requirements which may need to be introduced whilst transitting particular geographical areas may need to be mentioned or cross referenced.

Section 8      Emergency preparedness

A pirate attack would, most certainly, fall within the category of 'potential emergency situations' anticipated in Section 8 although, as mentioned earlier, such a scenario may fall under the procedures of the ISPS Code. The results of related emergency drills and exercises may be inspected.

Section 9      Reports and analysis of non-conformities, accidents and hazardous occurrences

Records of the activities anticipated by Section 9 may well be examined to confirm that learning opportunities were being taken as part of the SMS. Similarly minutes of on board safety committee meetings may be examined to determine the level of involvement and commitment to safety management on board.

Section 11     Documentation

If there appear to have been problems with compliance with the SMS or ship security plan then it is likely that a closer look will be made at the documented procedures themselves. If these are voluminous, irrelevant or otherwise inadequate then the Company is likely to come under severe criticism.

Section 12     Company verification, review and evaluation

There is a very clear obligation on the Company to ensure that the SMS is working properly on board its vessels. If a serious incident has arisen, as in this case with a pirate attack, then it can be anticipated that the active monitoring by the Company will be looked at very closely by way of audit trails.

Certification and verification

As a matter of course the validity of the SMC and DOC will be checked.


**d. Nature of evidence required**

There will be evidence required on at least two different, but related levels:

1  Evidence relating to the attack itself — suggestions are contained in the extract from MSC/Circ.623 set out below — this will be useful to those involved in the investigation as well as insurers

2  Evidence that the ship operator had done all that it reasonably could to avoid or minimise the risk of the attack — e.g. by following its own ship security plan — this may be required by the insurers to satisfy themselves that reasonable care had been taken.

(From MSC/Circ.623/Rev.3)

Any CCTV or other recording of the incident should be secured. If practicable, areas that have been damaged or turned over should be secured and remain untouched by crew members pending possible forensic examination by the security forces of a coastal State. Crew members who came into contact with the attackers should be asked to prepare an individual report on their experience noting, in particular, any distinguishing features which could help subsequent identification of the attackers. A full inventory, including a description of any personal possessions or equipment taken, with serial numbers when known, should also be prepared.

### e. Report

(From MSC/Circ.623/Rev.3)

Immediately after securing the safety of the ship and crew a post attack report (Follow-up report, as shown in ships' message formats in form A below) should be made to the relevant RCC and, through them, to the security forces of the coastal State concerned. As well as information on the identity and location of the ship, any injuries to crew members or damage to the ship should be reported as should the direction in which the attackers departed together with brief details of their numbers and, if possible, a description of their craft. If the crew have apprehended an attacker, that should also be reported in this report.

If an attack has resulted in the death of, or serious injury to, any person on board the ship or serious damage to the ship itself, an immediate report should also be sent to the ship's maritime Administration. In any event a report of an attack is vital if follow-up action is to be taken by the ship's maritime Administration.

MSC/Circ.623/Rev.3 Form A

SHIPS' MESSAGE FORMATS

---

**Report 1 - Initial message - Piracy/armed robbery attack alert**

1. Ship's name and, callsign, IMO number, INMARSAT IDs (plus ocean region code) and MMSI

   MAYDAY/DISTRESS ALERT (see note)

   URGENCY SIGNAL

   PIRACY/ARMED ROBBERY ATTACK

2. Ship's position (and time of position UTC)

   Latitude Longitude

---

Course Speed KTS

3 . Nature of event

**Note:** It is expected that this message will be a Distress Message because the ship or persons will be in grave or imminent danger when under attack. Where this is not the case, the word MAYDAY/DISTRESS ALERT is to be omitted.

Use of distress priority (3) in the INMARSAT system will not require MAYDAY/DISTRESS ALERT to be included.

---

## Report 2 - Follow-up report - Piracy/armed robbery attack alert

1. Ship's name and callsign, IMO number

2. Reference initial PIRACY/ARMED ROBBERY ALERT

3. Position of incident

Latitude Longitude

Name of the area

4. Details of incident, e.g.:

While sailing, at anchor or at berth?

Method of attack

Description/number of suspect craft

Number and brief description of pirates/robbers

What kind of weapons did the pirates/robbers carry ?

Any other information (e.g. language spoken)

Injuries to crew and passengers

Damage to ship (Which part of the ship was attacked?)

Brief details of stolen property/cargo

Action taken by the master and crew

Was incident reported to the coastal authority and to whom?

Action taken by the Coastal State

5. Last observed movements of pirate/suspect craft, e.g.:

Date/time/course/position/speed

6. Assistance required

7. Preferred communications with reporting ship, e.g.:

Appropriate Coast Radio Station

HF/MF/VHF

INMARSAT IDs (plus ocean region code)

MMSI

8. Date/time of report (UTC)

As soon as possible after the incident, a fuller report should be transmitted to the authorities of the coastal State in whose waters the attack occurred or, if on the high seas, to the authorities of the nearest coastal State. Due and serious consideration should be given to complying with any request made by the competent authorities of the coastal State to allow officers of the security forces to board the ship, take statements from crew members and undertake forensic and other investigations. Copies of any CCTV recordings, photographs, etc. should be provided if they are available.

Ships should take the necessary precautions, and implement the necessary procedures to ensure rapid reporting of any case of attack or attempted attack to the authorities in the relevant coastal States to enhance the possibility of security forces apprehending the attackers.

Any report transmitted to a coastal State should also be transmitted to the ship's maritime Administration at the earliest opportunity. A complete report of the incident, including details of any follow-up action that was taken or difficulties that may have been experienced, should eventually be submitted to the ship's maritime Administration. The report received by maritime Administrations may be used in any diplomatic approaches made by the flag State to the Government of the coastal State in which the incident occurred. This will also provide the basis for the report to IMO.

The format required for reports to IMO through maritime Administrations or international organizations is set out below in Form B. Indeed, at present the lack of adequate and accurate reporting of attacks is directly affecting the ability to secure governmental and international action. Reports may also contribute to future refining and updating any advice that might be issued to ships.

MSC/Circ.623/Rev.3 Form B

## FORMAT FOR REPORTING TO IMO THROUGH MARITIME ADMINISTRATIONS OR INTERNATIONAL ORGANIZATIONS

1  Ship's name and IMO number

2  Type of ship

   Flag

   Gross tonnage

3  Date and time

4  Latitude Longitude

   Name of the area**

   While sailing, at anchor or at berth?

5  Method of attack

   Description/number of suspect craft

   Number and brief description of pirates/robbers

   What kind of weapons did the pirates/robbers carry ?

   Any other information (e.g. language spoken)

6  Injuries to crew and passengers

   Damage to ship (Which part of the ship was attacked?)

   Brief details of stolen property/cargo

7  Action taken by the master and crew

8  Was incident reported to the coastal authority and to whom?

9  Reporting State or international organization

10 Action taken by the Coastal State

**Conclusion**

It will be apparent, with people related incidents, that evidence is required to establish the facts related to a case, not only to establish actual liability but to enable the master and the Company to demonstrate good practice and refute unwarranted allegations which are either put forward fraudulently or by shore administrations motivated by political considerations.

# ENVIRONMENT RELATED INCIDENTS

## General introduction

POLLUTION INCIDENTS ON THE SCALE of the *Exxon Valdez*, the *Haven*, *Sea Empress*, *Erika* and *Prestige* are rare. However, the resulting devastation to the environment and marine life has had such a far-reaching effect on international opinion that most countries will now deal severely with vessels which discharge even small quantities of pollutant within their territorial waters. It should be noted that pollution incidents may not necessarily be limited to discharges of oil as cargo or bunkers. Pollution may also emanate from non-tank vessels whether from cargo, bunkers, hazardous or noxious substances, garbage, sewage, ballast water or smoke emissions.

IMO Resolution A.849(20) — 'Code for the Investigation of Marine Casualties and Incidents' categorises 'severe pollution' as a 'very serious casualty' and 'pollution (regardless of quantity)' as a 'serious casualty'. As such any pollution is likely to be the subject of a flag State investigation and / or by some other 'substantially interested state.

There are three main causes of pollution:

- Collision, fire, explosion, grounding or similar type of incident

- Intentional discharge of oil, cargo residue, garbage or other waste from the vessel; for example, the pumping of bilges, or deballasting of cargo tanks

- Accidental pollution while transferring fuel, cargo, garbage or other waste to or from the vessel.

The main international Convention relating to the prevention of pollution is MARPOL 73/78 which includes six detailed annexes. Almost all maritime nations have ratified parts but not necessarily the whole of MARPOL 73/78 and its Annexes and have incorporated the Convention into their domestic legislation. Details of the six Annexes and their current status are set out below:

Annex I     – Regulations for the Prevention of Pollution by Oil

         Entered into force 2 October 1983

         Latest amendments entered into force 1 September 2002

Annex II     – Regulations for the Control of Pollution by Noxious Liquid Substances in bulk

         Entered into force 6 April 1987

         Latest amendments entered into force 1 January 2001

Annex III    – Regulations for the Prevention of Pollution by Harmful Substances Carried by Sea in Packaged Form

Entered into force 1 July 1992

Latest amendment entered into force 1 January 2002

Annex IV  –  Regulations for the Prevention of Pollution by Sewage from Ships

Not yet in force

Annex V  –  Regulations for the Prevention of Pollution by Garbage from Ships

Entered into force 31 December 1988

Latest amendment entered into force 1 March 2002

Annex VI  –  Regulations for the Prevention of Air Pollution from Ships

Not yet in force

Whilst some of the Annexes may be awaiting sufficient numbers of contracting States to ratify them — it should be noted that many countries have already introduced their own domestic legislation. Clearly this legislation will be enforced against ships in their own territorial waters. The safest advice therefore is to work on the assumption that the relevant Annexes will apply and prevent pollution accordingly — also collect the relevant evidence.

Vessels which pollute the environment will almost certainly pay for the consequences — whether or not the master or crew were in any way to blame; this is often referred to as "strict liability" or "the polluter pays" principle. However, in instances where strict liability applies, it still remains possible for the ship operator to recover from other parties who are at fault in causing the incident; for example, from the owners of another vessel involved in a collision.

One may question therefore what purpose is served in collecting evidence if the ship operator is going to be liable in any event? Firstly, quantum can always be challenged — but to do so the ship operator must have good and reliable evidence. Secondly, in many jurisdictions, if it can be established that the pollution was not caused by the deliberate fault or carelessness of the vessel and that all reasonable precautions were taken to minimise or prevent the pollution, fines or other penalties may be reduced or waived.

However, the extent to which other parties to the incident may be pursued and successful recoveries made, or establishing that reasonable steps were taken to minimise or prevent the pollution will depend upon the evidence which can be gathered at the time of the incident and immediately thereafter. It will be necessary, and appropriate, to examine the procedures contained within the Safety Management System (SMS) which should have been in place to prevent such an occurrence. This would not be just in respect of the time immediately prior to the incident but would extend backwards maybe two years or more. From there it will be necessary to produce evidence to prove that those procedures were being followed in practice but, in spite of that, something had still gone wrong — maybe someone had made an unintended mistake — and the pollution resulted.

It is perhaps worth noting the content of Article 12 of **MARPOL** 73/78 which relates to:

*Casualties to ships*

*(1) Each Administration undertakes to conduct an investigation of any casualty occurring to any of its ships subject to the provisions of the regulations if such casualty has produced a major deleterious effect on the marine environment.*

*(2) Each Party to the Convention undertakes to supply the Organisation with information concerning the findings of such investigation, when it judges that such information may assist in determining what changes in the present Convention might be desirable.*

It can be anticipated therefore that, following a pollution incident, inquiries will take place possibly by both the local port State Authority and from the flag State Administration. The ability to readily produce good quality evidence during these investigations should help considerably to mitigate any penalty which may be anticipated against the vessel and individuals.

Useful guidance is provided in IMO Resolution A.849(20) — (see Part C 2 to this book) which has specific relevance to evidence collection and which may apply to any pollution incident.

Firstly, some general issues set out in its Appendix — Section 2.5:

* *Type of pollutant*
* *UN number / IMO hazard class (if applicable)*
* *Type of packing (if applicable)*
* *Quantity on board*
* *Quantity lost*
* *Method of stowage and securing*
* *Where stowed and quantities in each compartment / container*
* *Tanks / spaces breached*
* *Tanks / spaces liable to be breached*
* *Action taken to prevent further loss*
* *Action taken to mitigate pollution*
* *Dispersant / neutraliser used, if any*
* *Restricting boom used, if any*

Secondly, probably most pollution incidents will have a 'human factor' involvement. It will be important therefore to obtain relevant information about individuals who may have been directly involved. Suggested details are set out in Section 1.4 of the Appendix to the Resolution.

- *Full name*
- *Age*
- *Details of injury*
- *Description of accident*
- *Person supervising activity*
- *First aid or other action on board*
- *Capacity on board*
- *Certificate of Competency/Licence:*
    - *grade;*
    - *date of issue;*
    - *issuing country/authority;*
    - *other Certificates of Competency held*
- *Time spent on vessel concerned*
- *Experience on similar vessels*
- *Experience on other types of vessels*
- *Experience in current capacity*
- *Experience in other ranks*
- *Number of hours spent on duty on that day and the previous days*
- *Number of hours sleep in the 96 hours prior to the incident*
- *Any other factors, on board or personal, that may have affected sleep*
- *Whether smoker, and if so, quantity*
- *Normal alcohol habit*
- *Alcohol consumption immediately prior to incident or in the previous 24 hours*
- *Whether under prescribed medication*
- *Any ingested non-prescribed drugs*
- *Records of drug and alcohol tests*

A worrying phenomena has been developing from the late 1990s and into the 21st century of arresting and incarcerating the master and sometimes officers and crews of vessels following a pollution incident. Whilst pollution incidents may be considered criminal acts in many jurisdictions — the legality of imprisoning foreign masters and seafarers in the manner which has occurred and basically holding them for ransom is questionable.

In some instances, for example where additional pipework has been installed to by-pass the oily water separator, then those involved must be prepared to face the consequences of their irresponsible behaviour. However, if a pollution occurs as a result of a simple mistake, accident or some other unintended event then it really is questionable as to what is to be achieved by severely punishing those involved — whether that be by way of heavy fines or prison sentences. In those circumstances it is infinitely more important to understand exactly what went wrong, why it went wrong and why the management systems did not prevent the accident happening. From that position it will then be possible to learn important lessons such that corrective action can be introduced to ensure that the accident will not be repeated. The only way we will get into a fully informed position to learn the lessons will be if those involved feel sufficiently comfortable to disclose all details and relevant evidence without the fear that they will go directly to jail or be the recipients of very hefty fines.

What is important for masters, mariners and indeed ship operators to understand is that the prosecutions may be directed at them personally. Their defences will be based upon the contemporaneous evidence which will be produced on board and which will be the subject of this chapter. In this regard it is important to remember that the best evidence which can be produced will not be limited to the events immediately surrounding the particular pollution incident but, rather, will be a record of the daily working life of the ship going back maybe two or three years — particularly the smooth running and continual improvement of the Safety Management System. The records should show that there were good procedures in place and that those procedures were being diligently followed. This can include the identifying and reporting of accidents, hazardous occurrences and non-conformities but of course the evidence must also show what corrective action was taken.

### Oil pollution

The review of oil pollution requirements will be split between cargo related (which can also be applied to some aspects of engine room operations) and bunker related. There will be at least three main Conventions or Liability regimes to keep in mind — MARPOL 73/78 — Annex I, the United States Oil Pollution Act of 1990 — OPA'90 and the new European Union Legislation — commonly referred to as ERIKA 3 — although the actual collection of evidence will be very similar whichever legal regime applies.

### A. MARPOL 73/78

All vessels except oil tankers of less than 150 gt and non-tank vessels of less than 400 gt must comply with the International Convention for the Prevention of Pollution from Ships (the "Convention") and the Protocol known as MARPOL 73/78 made pursuant to the convention, when trading in countries which are parties to the Convention. In outline, the Convention lays down requirements relating to:

- The discharge of oil or oily water mixture in parts per million of oil with reference to the distance travelled during discharge

- Segregated ballast systems in oil tankers — IGS and COW

- Adequate reception facilities in ports for oil residues from ships

- The keeping of proper records with regard to oil transfers and tank cleaning

- Mandatory reporting requirements

## B. OPA 90

All vessels which handle, store or transport oil in bulk as cargo, or cargo residue, operating in the navigable waters of the United States must carry a response plan which meet the requirements of the Vessel Response Plan (VRP) regulations and has been approved by the United States Coast Guard. It is important that masters are familiar with the VRP, particularly the reporting procedures as a failure to comply with the reporting procedures will have serious consequences upon the shipowner's right to rely upon defences under OPA 90.

## C. ERIKA 3

Following a number of years when some very worrying proposals with regard to pollution legislation were being considered by the European Commission — some common sense prevailed and it was agreed in the so-called 'ERIKA 3' initiative that any major proposals would be channelled through IMO and dealt with at an international level rather than at a European level. However, it can be anticipated that Countries within the EU will punish polluters very severely — including prison sentences.

### Oil pollution — cargo related

### a. Conceptual background

Procedures relating to oil transfers during cargo operations should form part of every vessels' standing instructions and should be found with the documentation supporting the ISM Safety Management System — including relevant checklists. These procedures should include the name of a supervising officer who is in charge of transfer operations, and an outline of pipe-lines and valve operations. The procedures should also emphasise the necessity of cementing scuppers and save-all plugs in drip trays and the checking of moorings. They should also contain an outline of clean-up operations.

Owners, together with the master, should ensure that the system of safe operation is not only in place on paper but also fully implemented and operated in practice to minimise the risk of oil spills during cargo operations. Such a system should include the following practices:

- Oil spill drills of the same type as boat drills, fire drills and emergency tank drills. All crew must be carefully trained in the use and application of appropriate dispersants/neutralising agents but it should be clearly pointed out that in any event, such dispersants/neutralising agents should not be used without the prior consent of the master who in turn must check with the appropriate local authority that such use is permissible

- Careful disposal of ballast water which may have been contaminated with oil whether the vessel is at sea or within port limits

- Frequent inspections of the equipment used in cargo operations, the times and results of which are noted in the appropriate log book. Oil spills have often occurred as a result of leaking ships' side valves and manifold connections, tank overflows, and hose fractures caused by excessive pressurisation or the closure of valves against the liquid flow

- A regular watch system for checking rates and ullages during loading/discharging and bunkering operations should be laid down. This demarcation should include shore staff as well as the ship's officers and crew

- A system of record keeping of all cargo, bunkering and tank cleaning operations

- An agreed rate of loading the cargo should be established. Close communications should be established between the vessel and the shore facilities through which the shore should be kept closely informed of any fluctuations

- There should be an established procedure for the careful transfer of oil on board during the voyage. In fact, this type of transfer should be treated in the same regard as loading/discharging operation

- Careful transfer of bunkers and/or ballast (if applicable) whilst in port in order to counteract any list caused by cargo

- The retention of records of oil presently on board the vessel. These records should be kept on the bridge together with the fire envelope and should include such details as the product trade name, the wax content, specific gravity, viscosity, distillation characteristics, etc. in order to assist in the containment or dispersal of the pollutant in the event of a spill, and

- Compliance with the local loading/discharging procedures

## b. Potential exposure / problem

In the event of an oil pollution incident, however minor, it is important for masters to follow carefully, the instructions contained in the SHIPBOARD OIL POLLUTION EMERGENCY PLAN (SOPEP). The SOPEP has been drafted to comply with the provisions of MARPOL 73/78 and although this International Convention does not apply worldwide, it is nevertheless an extremely useful guide to follow when the vessel is involved in a pollution incident. Under the provisions of MARPOL 73/78, every oil tanker of 150 gt and above, and every vessel other than an oil tanker of 400 gt and above, must carry an approved SOPEP before the vessel may enter the port of a country that has ratified the MARPOL convention.

Similarly, vessels required to carry a VESSEL RESPONSE PLAN (VRP) in order to comply with the provisions of the US Oil Pollution Act, 1990, MUST ensure that the reporting of incidents is in strict accordance with the approved vessel response plan on board. It is advisable, that the relevant section of the plan relating to the particular port of call is clearly marked, prior to port entry, in order that it can be referred to quickly in an emergency.

In addition to following the requirements of the VRP and/or the SOPEP, the master must consult the local P&I Club representative. The representative will advise on the steps which should be taken to inform the local authorities and will make arrangements for legal representation and attendance of surveyors if necessary. The representative will also assist the master in dealing with the local authorities.

It is imperative that the master and crew co-operate fully with the authorities and SHOW CONCERN, regardless of the extent of the pollution. If the authorities request permission to board the vessel, the master should attempt to obtain the advice of a legal representative, via the local P&I representative, before granting permission. In some cases the authorities may have the right, or be able to obtain a court order, or similar compulsory order, to be given access to the vessel. It is therefore important not to be obstructive. At the same time it is important to ensure that the authorities' actions are within the powers granted to them and this can be ascertained by reference to a local legal representative. If this is not possible, and the authorities insist on boarding the vessel, the master should allow them supervised access to the vessel. However, if access to the vessel is provided to the authorities, the master should make a note of the time and date, their names, the government department which they represent, and a note of their activities while on board. If the authorities wish to conduct interviews or take statements from the master or crew, it is important that such interviews are conducted in the presence of a local P&I Club or legal representative. In any event, the master should ascertain whether the master and crew have the right to be legally represented before such interviews or statements are taken.

The master should also ensure that steps are taken to prevent further pollution, and if possible to contain, clean-up and/or remove the pollutant from the area of pollution. Therefore, immediate action is essential. Steps to prevent further pollution may include cleaning up the pollutant on deck and transfer of pollutant into available tanks or spaces. The P&I Club representative will be able to assist the master in deciding what action is suitable and necessary.

It is of considerable assistance to shore personnel involved in the clean-up operation following a liquid cargo spill or bunker spill, that the master obtain calculations of the relative quantities of the potential pollutant on board, in the pipeline and in the shore tank. These quantities will also be of importance in avoiding a costly overestimation of the spill.

Finally, the use of certain dispersants/neutralising agents may be prohibited in certain parts of the world, it is important therefore that the master should ensure that before any dispersants/neutralising agents are used, local authorisation is obtained.

### c. ISM implications

The ISM implications will clearly depend very much upon the primary and any underlying causes which led to the pollution. The following, non-exhaustive, list attempts to address some of the more obvious potential implications and, consequently, suggest areas of the SMS which will come under close scrutiny:

Section 1.2.3.1    (compliance with mandatory rules and regulations)

Obviously MARPOL 73/78, or similar, would fall under this Section — but also such regulations as the STCW Convention and Code. Hours of rest / work of the individual(s) involved would be examined as well as the management system which was in place to ensure that Section A-VIII/1 of STCW Code was being complied with.

Section 6    Resources and personnel

In the vast majority of pollution cases one or more individuals did, or did not, do something which ultimately contributed to the pollution — often referred to as 'human error'. It may have been the duty deck or engineer officer. Under Section 6 there is a very clear obligation upon the Company to engage only qualified, skilled and suitably experienced personnel. It can therefore be anticipated that a potential claimant or investigator will look very carefully not only at the qualifications and alleged experience of the individual but may also require to examine the Company selection and recruiting procedures and to follow an audit trail to demonstrate that these procedures were indeed followed when recruiting the particular individual who is the focus of attention.

It may also be necessary to produce evidence to show that suitable and adequate familiarisation and training was provided to the individual — e.g. in the cargo loading operations etc. Relevant sections of STCW would also need to be considered.

Section 7    Development of plans for shipboard operations

Clearly loading and discharging of cargo would be included as one of the 'key shipboard operations' anticipated by Section 7. As such it should be expected that there are clear Company procedures set out in a Procedures Manual. Those procedures will be examined very carefully, not only in light of the pollution incident itself but also during other periods of the ship's life. This would be done by following audit trails.

Section 8    Emergency preparedness

An oil spill incident would, most certainly, fall within the category of 'potential emergency situations' anticipated in Section 8. The response of the master and those on board, following the pollution event, will be examined against the written procedures. No doubt records of simulated drills involving oil spill type incidents will also be examined.

Section 9    Reports and analysis of non-conformities, accidents and hazardous occurrences

Records of the activities anticipated by Section 9 may well be examined to confirm that learning opportunities were being taken as part of the SMS. Similarly minutes of on board safety committee meetings may be examined to determine the level of involvement and commitment to safety management on board.

Section 10    Maintenance of the ship and equipment

To what extent this may be relevant will obviously be determined by reference to the cause of the oil spill. If the failure of a piece of equipment was involved then the procedures and records will be examined very carefully.

Section 11    Documentation

If there appear to have been problems with compliance with the SMS then it is likely that a closer look will be made at the documented procedures themselves. If these are voluminous, irrelevant or otherwise inadequate then the Company is likely to come under severe criticism.

Section 12    Company verification, review and evaluation

There is a very clear obligation on the Company to ensure that the SMS is working properly on board its vessels. If a serious incident has arisen, as in this case with an oil spill, then it can be anticipated that the active monitoring by the Company will be looked at very closely by way of audit trails.

Certification and verification

As a matter of course the validity of the SMC and DOC will be checked.

### d. Nature of evidence required

The evidence produced from the ship should, hopefully, show that the vessel did have good procedures in place and provide confirmation that those procedures were being correctly followed. The evidence should also show that the ship, and office staff, responded to the spill effectively and in accordance with the contingency plan. Samples of the pollutant and an estimation of the quantity involved will also be crucial. The non-exhaustive list below will provide an indication of the type of information and documentation which is likely to be required:

- International Oil Pollution Prevention (IOPP) Certificate
- Relevant extracts from the SMS Manuals — including checklists

- Working Log Books

- Samples of the pollutant which has been spilled

- Video film and /or still photographs of the extent of the spill (if possible)

- Accounts of the events from all the members of crew involved in the incident

- The official log book in which the master should have recorded all the relevant facts, not opinions or conjecture

- All relevant telexes, cables and other communications/correspondence

- The cargo loading/discharging plan

- Tank and pipe line diagrams including sounding pipe and ullage plug diagrams

- Owner'/charterers' instructions

- Refinery or shore installation instructions or, where applicable, a copy of the bunker supplier's instructions or delivery note containing an agreed loading rate

- The Vessel Response Plan (VRP) and Shipboard Oil Pollution Emergency Plan (SOPEP)

- The vessel's OIL RECORD BOOK, (see note at end of list) which should always be kept up-to-date

- Records of Statutory Surveys

- Records of Internal Audits

- Records of External Audits — including any port State Control Inspections

As a matter of routine, regardless of whether or not there has been a pollution incident, the deck log book should always record:

- The use of such equipment as scupper plugs and drip trays

- The procedures that are followed during the transfer of potential pollutants within the vessel

- The carrying out of oil spill drills and other related exercises, and

- Evidence of any pollution incident, which has been witnessed by the shipboard staff (whether or not own vessel is involved).

The Oil Record Book is a particularly important piece of evidence which will be examined very closely following any pollution, or alleged pollution, by oil. The requirements for completing and maintaining the Oil Record Book are set out in Regulation 20 of the MARPOL 73/78 Convention — and it is thought useful here to repeat some of the key requirements:

When should the entries be made in the Oil Record Book?

*The Oil Record Book shall be completed on each occasion, on a tank-by-tank basis if appropriate, whenever any of the following operations take place in the ship:*

*(a) for machinery space operations (all ships)*

  *(i)    ballasting or cleaning of fuel tanks;*

  *(ii)   discharge of dirty ballast or cleaning water from tanks referred to under (i) of the subparagraph;*

  *(iii)  disposal of oily residues (sludge);*

  *(iv)   discharge overboard or disposal otherwise of bilge water which has accumulated in machinery spaces;*

*(b) for cargo / ballast operations (oil tankers)*

  *(i)    loading of oil cargo;*

  *(ii)   internal transfer of oil cargo during the voyage;*

  *(iii)  unloading of oil cargo;*

  *(iv)   ballasting of cargo tanks and dedicated clean ballast tanks;*

  *(v)    cleaning of cargo tanks including crude oil washing;*

  *(vi)   discharge of ballast except from segregated ballast tanks;*

  *(vii)  discharge of water from slop tanks;*

  *(viii) closing of all applicable valves or similar devices after slop tank discharge operations;*

  *(ix)   closing of valves necessary for isolation of dedicated clean ballast tanks from cargo and stripping lines after slop tank discharge operations;*

  *(x)    disposal of residues.*

Specific details of items to be recorded can be found in Appendix III of MARPOL Annex I.

It is very important that the Oil Record Book is kept constantly up to date with relevant entries. Obviously, it goes without saying, that the entries in the Oil Record Book must be correct and accurate. If it is ever shown, or even suspected, that the Oil Record Book contains inaccurate or wrong information then this can cause considerable problems for the ship operator as well as the personnel on board the ship.

### e. Report

In order to defend, or at least mitigate, claims of pollution and to prevent further incidents, owners and their insurers will require a detailed account of how the incident occurred, steps taken to prevent the incident and the efforts made to minimise damage. Such an account should be supported by the items of evidence highlighted above, and the master should ensure that such information and documents are retained and available. This report should include the following:

- Extracts from Log books, cargo work books, rough note books etc. in which the following information should be recorded:

  - Date, time and place / geographical position where the pollution incident occurred

  - The weather conditions and the state of the tide at the time of the pollution incident

  - Operations being carried out at the time of the spill and the grades/types of pollutant involved. If the pollution incident is caused by broken equipment on board the vessel, the broken parts should be preserved

  - The quantity of pollutant which went overboard and the quantity spilled on deck

  - The extent of pollution, the area covered by the spill and whether it has or may effect other property or vessels

  - Details of the actions taken on board the vessel and on shore to contain and clean-up the pollutant

  - The equipment used to contain and clean-up the pollutant including the type, industrial name and quantity of the oil dispersant or any other chemical used. An inventory of the cleaning materials, dispersants and absorbent material on board the vessel should always be kept

  - Actions taken to report the pollution incident, not only to the vessel owners, but also to the statutory authority. Careful records should also be kept in the vessel's radio log of all WT, RT, VHF and Satcom exchanges, and

  - The identity of any vessels in the vicinity when the pollution incident occurred

### f. Case study

### CASE STUDY — 1

***Background to the incident***

A 36,887 dwt, 2,394 TEU container ship, operated by one of the world's leading container ship operators, was boarded by a US Coast Guard inspection team. During their inspection they found a three-piece bypass pipe which had apparently been manufactured on board the ship to attach to the oily water separator.

It was subsequently established that a quantity of 40 tonnes or 10,640 gallons of sludge had been discharged during a five-month period.

### Consideration of relevant evidence

Log books and the Oil Record Book were examined and it was established that entries had been falsified claiming the use of the oily water separator and omitting reference to dumping overboard using bypass equipment. It was further established that the ships engineers concealed an 'alarm' printout from the ship's computer and a log containing actual tank volumes to cover up the falsifications.

### Outcome

The ship operating Company eventually admitted that it had directed its staff to lie to the US Coast Guard, '...denying knowledge about the existence and use of the bypass equipment; concealing evidence and concealing oil pollution...'

The ship operator was fined US$10,000,000 (ten million US Dollars) and was obliged to pay a further $500,000 in community service. The chief engineer faced a maximum sentence of 40 years imprisonment and the second engineer a maximum sentence of five years and a fine of $250,000.

There has been some criticism that some prosecuting authorities are becoming over-zealous with regard to oily water separators and the alleged illegal dumping of oil sludge or residues. Clearly the solution is not to become involved in such practices but, just as importantly, maintain accurate records in the Oil Record Book, Log Books and computer printouts etc. and never try to falsify or hide records. There is a very good chance that the truth will be established — and the punishments are likely to be very severe.

## CASE STUDY — 2

### Background to the incident

A ULCC built in 1977 and without fully segregated ballast, was loading in an Arabian Gulf port. As required by local regulations, the vessel was loading and discharging simultaneously. The ballast consisted of clean sea water loaded into cargo tanks, which was segregated from the incoming oil by at least two valve separation. However, cargo lines containing oil passed through the tanks containing water.

Despite MARPOL recommendations, no ballast reception facilities existed at this port, and all ballast was discharged to the sea.

When the ballast tanks were getting close to empty, a sheen of oil was seen on the surface of the sea. This rapidly worsened, and deballasting was stopped.

### Consideration of relevant evidence

At the time of the pollution incident, it was impossible to ascertain the cause of the pollution. Six weeks later, after discharging in the US Gulf, it was possible to enter the tanks for an inspection.

It was found that a hole had developed in one of the lines loading oil, allowing oil to contaminate the ballast. This line had been pressure tested during the previous ballast voyage, and found to be tight. Unfortunately, due to the age of the vessel, this kind of material failure is always going to be a risk.

This type of incident is quite prevalent, and can take place even on the most modern of tankers. It is one in which evidence in mitigation is very difficult to obtain at the time of the incident and invariably is blamed on the ship's staff. Evidence of mechanical or material failure obtained after the event, (in many cases weeks later), is usually too late, as all blame, fines, etc. are usually already apportioned.

### Outcome
The vessel ultimately had to sail with over 5,000 m³ of water on board, and was fined $25,000 plus clean-up costs.

## CASE STUDY - 3

### Background to the incident
A VLCC scheduled for dry-docking was carrying out a transfer of slops and a final wash of the last slop tank, immediately prior to docking. This was taking place off Port Limits near Singapore. The VLCC took all usual precautions prior to a transfer of oil, as per ISGOTT recommendations. In addition, the carrying capacity of the slop barge was obtained, in writing, and a suitable entry made in the log book.

During the transfer, the slop barge overflowed one of its tanks, and because there were no scupper plugs in (the slop barge), there was an escape of oily water to the sea. A passing patrol vessel observed the pollution, and both vessels were initially charged with causing a pollution.

### Consideration of relevant evidence
Photographs were taken from the VLCC, which clearly showed the slop barge's tank overflowing, and the fact that none of its scupper plugs were in.

### Outcome
On the basis of this conclusive evidence, the VLCC was absolved of all blame and the charges dropped.

Pt B<br>E<br>N<br>V<br>I<br>R<br>O<br>N<br>M<br>E<br>N<br>T

### Oil pollution — bunker related
To a very large degree, the advice with regard to collecting evidence following a bunker spill will be very similar to that given above in respect of a spill during the loading, discharging or carrying of oil cargo.

## a. Conceptual background

Procedures relating to bunker transfers should form part of every vessels' standing instructions and should be found within the documents supporting the Safety Management System — including relevant checklists. Such procedures should also be followed during bunkering operations which are common to not only oil/product tankers, but also to all types of vessel. These procedures should include the name of a supervising officer who is in charge of transfer operations, and an outline of pipe-lines and valve operations. The procedures should also emphasise the necessity of cementing scuppers and save-all plugs in drip trays and the checking of moorings. They should also contain an outline of clean-up operations.

Owners, together with the master, should ensure that a system of safe operation is installed on board the vessel to minimise the risk of bunker spills. Such a system should include the following practices:

- Bunker spill drills of the same type as boat drills, fire drills and emergency tank drills. All crew must be carefully trained in the use and application of appropriate dispersants/neutralising agents but it should be clearly pointed out that in any event, such dispersants/neutralising agents should not be used without the prior consent of the master who in turn must check with the appropriate local authority that such use is permissible

- Frequent inspections of the equipment used in bunkering operations, the times and results of which are noted in the appropriate log book. Oil spills have often occurred as a result of leaking ships' side valves and manifold connections, tank overflows, and hose fractures caused by excessive pressurisation or the closure of valves against the liquid flow

- A regular watch system for checking rates and ullages during loading/discharging and bunkering operations should be laid down. This demarcation should include shore staff as well as the ship's officers and crew

- A system of record keeping of all bunkering operations

- An agreed rate of loading of bunkers. Close communications should be established between the vessel and the shore facilities or bunkering barge through which the shore or barge should be kept closely informed of any fluctuations

- There should be an established procedure for the careful transfer of bunkers on board during the voyage. In fact, this type of transfer should be treated in the same regard as the bunkering operation itself

- Careful transfer of bunkers whilst in port in order to counteract any list caused by cargo.

- The retention of records of bunkers presently on board the vessel

- Compliance with the local bunkering procedures.

## b. Potential exposure / problem

In the event of an oil pollution incident, however minor, it is important for masters to follow carefully, the instructions contained in the SHIPBOARD OIL POLLUTION EMERGENCY PLAN (SOPEP). The SOPEP has been drafted to comply with the provisions of MARPOL 73/78 and although this International Convention does not apply worldwide, it is nevertheless an extremely useful guide to follow when the vessel is involved in a pollution incident. Under the provisions of MARPOL 73/78, every oil tanker of 150 gt and above, and every vessel other than an oil tanker of 400 gt and above, must carry an approved SOPEP before the vessel may enter the port of a country that has ratified the MARPOL convention.

Similarly, vessels required to carry a VESSEL RESPONSE PLAN (VRP) in order to comply with the provisions of the US Oil Pollution Act, 1990, MUST ensure that the reporting of incidents is in strict accordance with the approved vessel response plan on board. It is advisable, that the relevant section of the plan relating to the particular port of call is clearly marked, prior to port entry, in order that it can be referred to quickly in an emergency.

In addition to following the requirements of the VRP and/or the SOPEP, the master must consult the local P&I Club representative. The representative will advise on the steps which should be taken to inform the local authorities and will make arrangements for legal representation and attendance of surveyors if necessary. The representative will also assist the master in dealing with the local authorities.

It is imperative that the master and crew co-operate fully with the authorities and SHOW CONCERN regardless of the extent of the pollution. If the authorities request permission to board the vessel, the master should attempt to obtain the advice of a legal representative, via the local P&I representative, before granting permission. In some cases the authorities may have the right, or be able to obtain a court order, or similar compulsory order, to be given access to the vessel. It is therefore important not to be obstructive. At the same time it is important to ensure that the authorities' actions are within the powers granted to them and this can be ascertained by reference to a local legal representative. If this is not possible, and the authorities insist on boarding the vessel, the master should allow them supervised access to the vessel. However, if access to the vessel is provided to the authorities, the master should make a note of the time and date, their names, the government department which they represent, and a note of their activities while on board. If the authorities wish to conduct interviews or take statements from the master or crew, it is important that such interviews are conducted in the presence of a local P&I Club or legal representative. In any event, the master should ascertain whether the master and crew have the right to be legally represented before such interviews or statements are taken.

The master should also ensure that steps are taken to prevent further pollution, and if possible to contain, clean-up and / or remove the pollutant from the area of pollution. Therefore, immediate action is essential. Steps to prevent further pollution may include cleaning up the pollutant on deck and transfer of pollutant into available tanks or spaces. The P&I Club representative will be able to assist the master on deciding what action is suitable and necessary.

It is of considerable assistance to shore personnel involved in the clean-up operation following a bunker spill that the master obtain calculations of the relative quantities of the potential pollutant on board, in the pipeline and in the shore tank or bunker barge (as applicable). These quantities will also be of importance in avoiding a costly overestimation of the spill.

Finally, the use of certain dispersants/neutralising agents may be prohibited in certain parts of the world, it is very important therefore that the master should ensure that before any dispersants/neutralising agents are used, local authorisation is obtained.

### c. ISM implications

The ISM implications will clearly depend very much upon the primary and any underlying causes which led to the bunker spill. The following, non-exhaustive, list attempts to address some of the more obvious potential implications and, consequently, suggest areas of the SMS which will come under close scrutiny:

Section 1.2.3.1    (compliance with mandatory rules and regulations)

Obviously MARPOL 73/78, or similar, would fall under this Section — but also such regulations as the STCW Convention and Code. Hours of rest / work of the individual(s) involved would be examined as well as the management system which was in place to ensure that Section A-VIII/1 of STCW Code was being complied with.

Section 6    Resources and personnel

In the vast majority of bunker spill incidents, one or more individuals did, or did not, do something which ultimately contributed to the pollution — often referred to as a 'human error'. It may have been the duty deck or engineer officer. Under Section 6 there is a very clear obligation upon the Company to engage only qualified, skilled and suitably experienced personnel. It can therefore be anticipated that a potential claimant or investigator will look very carefully not only at the qualifications and alleged experience of the individual but may also require to examine the Company selection and recruiting procedures and to follow an audit trail to demonstrate that these procedures were indeed followed when recruiting the particular individual who is the focus of attention.

It may also be necessary to produce evidence to show that suitable and adequate familiarisation and training was provided to the individual — e.g. in bunkering operations etc. Relevant sections of STCW would also need to be considered.

Section 7    Development of plans for shipboard operations

Clearly taking on bunkers would be included as one of the 'key shipboard operations' anticipated by Section 7. As such it should be expected that there are clear Company procedures set out in a Procedures Manual. Those procedures will be examined very carefully, not only in light of the pollution incident itself but also during other periods of the ships life. This would be done by following audit trails.

Section 8    Emergency preparedness

A bunker spill incident would, most certainly, fall within the category of 'potential emergency situations' anticipated in Section 8. The response of the master and those on board, following the pollution event, will be examined against the written procedures. No doubt records of simulated drills involving bunker spill type incidents will also be examined.

Section 9    Reports and analysis of non-conformities, accidents and hazardous occurrences

Records of the activities anticipated by Section 9 may well be examined to confirm that learning opportunities were being taken as part of the SMS. Similarly minutes of on board safety committee meetings may be examined to determine the level of involvement and commitment to safety management on board.

Section 10    Maintenance of the ship and equipment

To what extent this may be relevant will obviously be determined by reference to the cause of the bunker spill. If the failure of a piece of equipment was involved then the procedures and records will be examined very carefully.

Section 11    Documentation

If there appear to have been problems with compliance with the SMS then it is likely that a closer look will be made at the documented procedures themselves. If these are voluminous, irrelevant or otherwise inadequate then the Company is likely to come under severe criticism.

Section 12    Company verification, review and evaluation

There is a very clear obligation on the Company to ensure that the SMS is working properly on board its vessels. If a serious incident has arisen, as in this case with a bunker spill, then it can be anticipated that the active monitoring by the Company will be looked at very closely by way of audit trails.

Certification and verification

As a matter of course the validity of the SMC and DOC will be checked.

**d. Nature of evidence required**

The evidence produced from the ship should, hopefully, show that the vessel did have good procedures in place and provide confirmation that those procedures were being correctly followed. The evidence should also show that the ship, and office staff, responded to the spill effectively and in accordance with the contingency plan. Samples of the bunker fuel and an estimation of the quantity involved will also be crucial. The non-exhaustive list below will provide an indication of the type of information and documentation which is likely to be required:

- International Oil Pollution Prevention (IOPP) Certificate
- Relevant extracts from the SMS Manuals — including checklists
- Working Log Books
- Samples of the bunker fuel which has been spilled
- Video film and/or still photographs of the extent of the spill (if possible)
- Accounts of the events from all the members of crew involved in the incident
- The official log book in which the master should have recorded all the relevant facts, not opinions or conjecture
- All relevant telexes, cables and other communications/correspondence
- The bunkering plan
- Tank and pipe line diagrams including sounding pipe and ullage plug diagrams
- Owner'/charterers' instructions
- A copy of the bunker supplier's instructions or delivery note containing an agreed loading rate
- The Vessel Response Plan (VRP) and Ship Board Oil Pollution Emergency Plan (SOPEP)
- The vessel's OIL RECORD BOOK, which should always be kept up-to-date.

As a matter of routine, regardless of whether or not there has been a pollution incident, the deck log book should always record:

- The use of such equipment as scupper plugs and drip trays
- The procedures that are followed during the transfer of potential pollutants within the vessel
- The carrying out of oil spill drills and other related exercises, and
- Evidence of any pollution incident, which has been witnessed by the shipboard staff (whether or not own vessel is involved).
- Records of Statutory Surveys
- Records of Internal Audits
- Records of External Audits — including any port State Control Inspections

Engine room log books should, as a matter of routine, record the following:

- Bunkering procedures

- The members of the crew in charge of bunkering operations

- Methods of effecting emergency stops for bunkering operations

- The times and results of inspections of equipment used in cargo and bunkering operations, and

- A record of the ullages taken during bunkering operations.

## e. Report

In order to defend, or at least mitigate, claims of pollution and to prevent further incidents, owners and their insurers will require a detailed account of how the incident occurred, steps taken to prevent the incident and the efforts made to minimise damage. Such an account should be supported by the items of evidence above, and the master should ensure that such information and documents are retained and available. This report should include the following:

- Information extracted from Log books, cargo work books, rough note books etc. in which the following information should be recorded:

  - Date, time and place / geographical location where the pollution incident occurred

  - The weather conditions and the state of the tide at the time of the pollution incident

  - Operations being carried out at the time of the spill and the grades/types of pollutant involved. If the pollution incident is caused by broken equipment on board the vessel, the broken parts should be preserved

  - The quantity of pollutant which went overboard and the quantity spilled on deck

  - The extent of pollution, the area covered by the spill and whether it has or may effect other property or vessels

  - Details of the actions taken on board the vessel and on shore to contain and clean-up the pollutant

  - The equipment used to contain and clean-up the pollutant including the type, industrial name and quantity of the oil dispersant or any other chemical used. An inventory of the cleaning materials, dispersants and absorbent material on board the vessel should always be kept

  - Actions taken to report the pollution incident, not only to the vessel owners, but also to the statutory authority. Careful records should also be kept in the vessel's radio log of all WT, RT, VHF and Satcom exchanges, and

  - The identity of any vessels in the vicinity when the pollution incident occurred.

## f. Case study

### Background to the incident

A 35,000 gt bulk carrier was taking on board a full stem of heavy fuel and diesel oil bunkers at the commencement of a long term time charter. A well tested set of bunker procedures were in place as part of the Company SMS. The officers and crew were well trained, experienced and were fully familiar with the relevant procedures. The chief engineer was personally in charge of the bunkering operation and was assisted by the third engineer officer and an engine room crew member. The second mate was the duty deck officer.

A pre-bunkering meeting had taken place with the relevant ship staff and a representative from the bunker Company. A plan was drawn up and approved. The deck was properly prepared with scupper plugs in place and clean up equipment readily available. Relevant pipe-work and tanks were checked and confirmed to be in order. Communication systems were checked and found working satisfactorily. Checklists were used throughout to confirm that the correct procedures were being followed.

The bunkering operation was proceeding smoothly and the quantity of F.O. being loaded into Number 3 double bottom bunker tank was being monitored carefully. As the tank started to approach a full status the chief engineer instructed the third engineer to start opening up Number 4 double bottom bunker tank and stand by to close Number 3. These operations had to be undertaken in the engine room. On his way down to the bottom plates the third engineer slipped and was temporarily knocked unconscious. When he recovered consciousness he immediately called the chief on his Walkie-Talkie to tell him what had happened but at that time fuel oil started to flow out of the Number 3 DB sounding and air pipes. By the time the chief realised what had happened and communicated to the shore bunker station to stop pumping — a substantial quantity of fuel oil had leaked onto the deck and had started overflowing over the side.

### Consideration of relevant evidence

The bunkering procedures were examined and found to be adequate for most anticipated situations. The Company was able to demonstrate that not only were the correct procures carefully followed on this particular occasion but also on all previous occasions since the procedures were introduced five years earlier.

Through witness testimony the facts of what happened to the third engineer were accepted as an explanation.

An investigation was conducted by the Company very soon after the incident and a number of amendments to the existing procedures were identified and implemented to prevent, or at least reduce to an absolute minimum, a recurrence of such an incident by building in additional safety checks. These changes were disseminated around the fleet within two weeks of the incident occurring.

The clean up costs and damage claims amounted in total to slightly over US$220,000. This was promptly paid by the ship operator / their P&I Club.

Having considered the evidence, the local prosecuting authority decided that it would not impose a punitive fine but rather issued a two year probation notice on the ship operating Company.

## Pollution — noxious liquid substances

Within this section we will consider possible pollution incidents resulting from a spill or discharge of noxious liquid substances in bulk as described in MARPOL 73/78 ANNEX II.

### a. Conceptual background

Procedures relating to loading, handling or discharging noxious liquid substances should form part of every vessels' standing instructions and should be found within the documents supporting the Safety Management System — including relevant checklists. These procedures should include the name of a supervising officer who is in charge of cargo operations, and an outline of pipe-lines and valve operations — where appropriate. The procedures should also emphasise the necessity of cementing scuppers and save-all plugs in drip trays and the checking of moorings. They should also contain an outline of clean-up operations.

Owners, together with the master, should ensure that a system of safe operation is installed on board the vessel to minimise the risk of cargo spills. Such a system should include the following practices:

- Emergency drills involving a spill of a noxious substance should take place in a similar way to boat drills and, fire drills. All crew must be carefully trained in the use and application of appropriate dispersants/neutralising agents but it should be clearly pointed out that in any event, such dispersants/neutralising agents should not be used without the prior consent of the master who in turn must check with the appropriate local authority that such use is permissible

- Frequent inspections of the equipment used in cargo operations, the times and results of which are noted in the appropriate log book.

- A regular watch system for checking rates and ullages during loading/discharging of liquid noxious substances. This demarcation should include shore staff as well as the ship's officers and crew

- A system of record keeping of all cargo operations

- An agreed rate of loading of liquid cargo. Close communications should be established between the vessel and the shore facilities through which the shore can be kept closely informed of any problems

- There should be an established procedure for the careful transfer of cargo on board during the voyage. In fact, this type of transfer should be treated in the same regard as the loading operation itself

- Careful transfer of cargo whilst in port in order to counteract any list caused by cargo

- The retention of records of cargo presently on board the vessel

- Compliance with the local cargo operations procedures.


## b. Potential exposure / problem

In the event of a cargo pollution incident, however minor, it is important for masters to follow carefully, the instructions contained in the Emergency Response Plan — which would be contained within the Safety Management Manual — or similar.

In addition to following the requirements of the Shipboard Marine Pollution Emergency Plan for Noxious Liquid Substances, as required under Regulation 16 of Annex II, the master must consult the local P&I Club representative. The representative will advise on the steps which should be taken to inform the local authorities and will make arrangements for legal representation and attendance of surveyors if necessary. The representative will also assist the master in dealing with the local authorities.

It is very important that the master and crew co-operate fully with the authorities and SHOW CONCERN regardless of the extent of any possible pollution. If the authorities request permission to board the vessel, the master should attempt to obtain the advice of a legal representative, via the local P&I representative, before granting permission. In some cases the authorities may have the right, or be able to obtain a court order, or similar compulsory order, to be given access to the vessel. It is therefore important not to be obstructive. At the same time it is important to ensure that the authorities' actions are within the powers granted to them and this can be ascertained by reference to a local legal representative. If this is not possible, and the authorities insist on boarding the vessel, the master should allow them supervised access to the vessel. However, if access to the vessel is provided to the authorities, the master should make a note of the time and date, their names, the government department which they represent, and a note of their activities while on board. If the authorities wish to conduct interviews or take statements from the master or crew, it is important that such interviews are conducted in the presence of a local P&I Club or legal representative. In any event, the master should ascertain whether the master and crew have the right to be legally represented before such interviews or statements are taken.

The master should also ensure that steps are taken to prevent further pollution, and if possible to contain, clean-up and/or remove the pollutant from the area of pollution. Therefore, immediate action is essential. Steps to prevent further pollution may include cleaning up the pollutant on deck and transfer of pollutant into available tanks or spaces. The P&I Club representative will be able to assist the master on deciding what action is suitable and necessary. It is of considerable assistance to shore personnel involved in the clean-up operation following a liquid cargo spill, that the master obtain calculations of the relative quantities of the potential pollutant on board, in the pipeline and in the shore tank or container. These quantities will also be of importance in avoiding a costly overestimation of the spill.

Finally, the use of certain dispersants/neutralising agents may be prohibited in certain parts of the world, it is important therefore that the master should ensure that before any dispersants/neutralising agents are used, local authorisation is obtained.

## c. ISM implications

The ISM implications will clearly depend very much upon the primary and any underlying causes which led to the pollution. The following, non-exhaustive, list attempts to address some of the more obvious potential implications and, consequently, suggest areas of the SMS which will come under close scrutiny:

Section 1.2.3.1    (compliance with mandatory rules and regulations)

Obviously MARPOL 73/78, Annexes II and III, or similar, would fall under this Section — but also such regulations as the STCW Convention and Code. Hours of rest / work of the individual(s) involved would be examined as well as the management system which was in place to ensure that Section A-VIII/1 of STCW Code was being complied with.

Section 6    Resources and personnel

In the vast majority of pollution cases one or more individuals did, or did not, do something which ultimately contributed to the pollution — often referred to a 'human error'. It may have been the duty deck officer. Under Section 6 there is a very clear obligation upon the Company to engage only qualified, skilled and suitably experienced personnel. It can therefore be anticipated that a potential claimant or investigator will look very carefully not only at the qualifications and alleged experience of the individual but may also require to examine the Company selection and recruiting procedures and to follow an audit trail to demonstrate that these procedures were indeed followed when recruiting the particular individual who is the focus of attention.

It may also be necessary to produce evidence to show that suitable and adequate familiarisation and training was provided to the individual — e.g. in the cargo loading operations etc. Relevant sections of STCW would also need to be considered.

Section 7    Development of plans for shipboard operations

Clearly loading and discharging of cargo, particularly dangerous cargo, would be included as one of the 'key shipboard operations' anticipated by Section 7. As such it should be expected that there are clear Company procedures set out in a Procedures Manual. Those procedures will be examined very carefully, not only in light of the pollution incident itself but also during other periods of the ships life. This would be done by following audit trails.

Section 8        Emergency preparedness

A spill or pollution from noxious liquid cargo would, most certainly, fall within the category of 'potential emergency situations' anticipated in Section 8. The response of the master and those on board, following the pollution event, will be examined against the written procedures. No doubt records of simulated drills involving such type of incident will also be examined.

Section 9        Reports and analysis of non-conformities, accidents and hazardous occurrences

Records of the activities anticipated by Section 9 may well be examined to confirm that learning opportunities were being taken as part of the SMS. Similarly minutes of on board safety committee meetings may be examined to determine the level of involvement and commitment to safety management on board.

Section 10       Maintenance of the ship and equipment

To what extent this may be relevant will obviously be determined by reference to the cause of the cargo spill or pollution. If the failure of a piece of equipment was involved then the procedures and records will be examined very carefully.

Section 11       Documentation

If there appear to have been problems with compliance with the SMS then it is likely that a closer look will be made at the documented procedures themselves. If these are voluminous, irrelevant or otherwise inadequate then the Company is likely to come under severe criticism.

Section 12       Company verification, review and evaluation

There is a very clear obligation on the Company to ensure that the SMS is working properly on board its vessels. If a serious incident has arisen, as in this case with a spill of Noxious cargo, then it can be anticipated that the active monitoring by the Company will be looked at very closely by way of audit trails.

Certification and verification

As a matter of course the validity of the SMC and DOC will be checked.

### d. Nature of evidence required

The evidence produced from the ship should, hopefully, show that the vessel did have good procedures in place and provide confirmation that those procedures were being correctly followed. The evidence should also show that the ship, and office staff, responded to the pollution incident effectively and in accordance with the contingency plan. Samples of the pollutant and an estimation of the quantity involved will also be very important. The non-exhaustive list below will provide an indication of the type of information and documentation which is likely to be required:

- International Pollution Prevention Certificate for the Carriage of Noxious Liquid Substances in Bulk

- Relevant extracts from the SMS Manuals — including checklists

- Working Log Books

- Samples of the noxious liquid substance — if safe to take samples

- Video film and/or still photographs of the extent of the spill (if possible)

- Accounts of the events from all the members of crew involved in the incident

- The official log book in which the master should have recorded all the relevant facts, not opinions or conjecture

- All relevant telexes, cables and other communications/correspondence

- The cargo loading/discharging plan

- Dangerous cargo manifest

- Tank and pipe line diagrams including sounding pipe and ullage plug diagrams

- Owner'/charterers' or shippers instructions

- Refinery or shore installation terminal instructions containing an agreed loading rate

- The Emergency Response Plan

- The vessel's CARGO RECORD BOOK, (see note at end of list) which should always be kept up-to-date.

- Records of Statutory Surveys

- Records of Internal Audits

- Records of External Audits — including any port State Control Inspections

As a matter of routine, regardless of whether or not there has been a pollution incident, the deck log book should always record:

- The use of such equipment as scupper plugs and drip trays

- The procedures that are followed during the transfer of potential pollutants within the vessel

- The carrying out of noxious substance spill drills and other related exercises, and

- Evidence of any pollution incident, which has been witnessed by the shipboard staff (whether or not own vessel is involved).

Regulation 9 of Annex II of MARPOL 73/78 sets out details of when the Cargo Record Book is to be maintained:

*The Cargo Record Book shall be completed, on a tank-to-tank basis, whenever any of the following operations with respect to noxious liquid substance take place in the ship:*

(i)    *loading of cargo;*

(ii)   *internal transfer of cargo;*

(iii)  *unloading of cargo;*

(iv)  *cleaning of cargo tanks;*

(v)   *ballasting of cargo tanks;*

(vi)  *discharge of ballast from cargo tanks;*

(vii) *disposal of residues to reception facilities;*

(viii) *discharge into the sea or removal by ventilation of residues in accordance with regulation 5 of this Annex.*

It is important to remember that the Cargo Record Book forms part of the ships Official Log Book and must be kept permanently up to date. This is a very important piece of documentary evidence and will certainly be examined very closely in the event of a spill or alleged discharge.

### e. Report

In order to defend, or at least mitigate, claims of pollution and to prevent further incidents, owners and their insurers will require a detailed account of how the incident occurred, steps taken to prevent the incident and the efforts made to minimise damage. Such an account should be supported by the items of evidence above, and the master should ensure that such information and documents are retained and available. This report should include the following:

- Referring to Log Books, cargo work books, rough note books etc. in which the following information should be recorded:

    - Date, time and place / geographical location where the pollution incident occurred

    - The weather conditions and the state of the tide at the time of the pollution incident

    - Operations being carried out at the time of the spill and the grades/types of pollutant involved. If the pollution incident is caused by broken equipment on board the vessel, the broken parts should be preserved

- The quantity of pollutant which went overboard and the quantity spilled on deck

- The extent of pollution, the area covered by the spill and whether it has or may effect other property or vessels

- Details of the actions taken on board the vessel and on shore to contain and clean-up the pollutant

- The equipment used to contain and clean-up the pollutant including the type, industrial name and quantity of the oil dispersant or any other chemical used. An inventory of the cleaning materials, dispersants and absorbent material on board the vessel should always be kept

- Actions taken to report the pollution incident, not only to the vessel owners, but also to the statutory authority. Careful records should also be kept in the vessel's radio log of all WT, RT, VHF and Satcom exchanges, and

- The identity of any vessels in the vicinity when the pollution incident occurred.

## f. Case study

### Background to the incident

A 6,000 gt chemical tanker was fully loaded with a cargo of acid which was being transported between two countries in Northern Europe. The total voyage, including loading, sea passage and discharge lasted a little over 72 hours.

Whilst on passage to the discharge port, at approximately 0400 hrs. the vessel ran onto rocks close offshore. The hull was seriously broached and almost all the acid cargo was lost into the sea.

An investigation subsequently revealed that the second mate, who had been alone on the bridge, had fallen asleep.

### Consideration of relevant evidence

The investigation focused initially on the passage plan and navigation / bridge procedures. The passage plan appeared to be in order and the written procedures with regard to navigation and bridge management were reasonable.

However, it became apparent that the procedures were not being followed on board the ship and evidence could not be produced to show that they had ever been followed.

The investigation turned to explore manning levels, hours of work and hours of rest — not only of the second mate but also of the master and other officers and crew. Whilst the records indicated that the mandatory minimum hours of rest were being taken by those on board — it was possible to demonstrate from other contemporaneous evidence that excessive hours were being worked and that the records had been falsified.

### *Outcome*

It was concluded that the second mate was suffering from extreme tiredness and fatigue due to working excessive hours. He was not in a suitable condition to be in charge of a bridge watch. Contrary to procedures the second mate had stood part of the watch alone — the lookout having been dispatched to undertake other duties.

Financial compensation had to be paid to local fishermen as well as local authorities and various tourist related claimants who had suffered losses directly as a result of the incident.

The ship operator was fined £250,000. The master and the second mate subsequently had their Certificates of Competency suspended.

## Other pollution incidents

The review of collecting evidence following a pollution incident with regard to oil cargo, bunkers or liquid noxious cargo, as set out above, should provide a good general set of guidelines addressing the issues involved, the collection of evidence and the preparation of a report. It is not intended therefore to repeat those detailed guidelines for each of the remaining categories of pollutants, according to the MARPOL 73/78 Annexes, but rather highlight some specific issues to take into account for each and to direct the reader to one of the above sections for general guidance.

The remaining four pollutant categories are:

- Harmful Substances Carried by Sea in Packaged Form

- Sewage

- Garbage

- Air Pollution

We will address each of these in turn.

### • Harmful substances carried by sea in packaged form

Harmful substances are dealt with under MARPOL 73/78 Annex III and are those substances which are identified as marine pollutants in the International Maritime Dangerous Goods Code (IMDG Code). These are frequently carried in freight containers but not always so.

On the packaging, and in the relevant paperwork, the nature of the goods should be accurately described and / or its relevant **IMDG** Number along with the correct labelling according to the **IMDG** Category. If the substance poses a potential pollution risk then an additional 'Marine Pollutant' label should also be attached — see a selection of the **IMDG** Labels below — including the marine pollutant label.

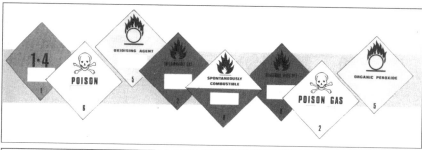

the provisions of IMDG Code, Annex I.

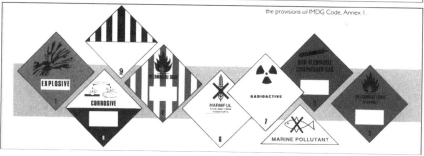

A dangerous cargo manifest should be prepared listing the hazardous cargoes along with relevant details.

The IMDG Code will prescribe where such cargo can and cannot be stowed and their stowage position should be shown on the stowage plan and in the accompanying paperwork.

There should be procedures in place to check the labelling of the cargo coming on board and to ensure that it is loaded and stowed in accordance with the IMDG Code.

From an evidence collection perspective it is important that copies of all the relevant paperwork — dangerous cargo manifests, stowage plans etc are retained.

One of the most common events which occur and which leads to pollution or possible pollution from 'harmful substances in packaged form' is the loss of deck containers overboard from container ships in heavy weather. Accordingly, the evidence collection should also include full details of the lashing and securing system in operation – and remember to include photographs. If there are items of equipment which have failed — e.g. lashing bars, securing chains, twist-locks, etc. then these must be retained for expert inspection — possibly by a metallurgist. Full and accurate details of the heavy weather encountered will also be required. This will include weather forecasts as well as contemporaneous records of what weather was actually experienced on location — although remember not to be tempted to exaggerate — there are many independent means of checking what the weather conditions actually were at any given location at any particular time. If the vessel was 'weather routed' by a professional weather routing organisation then copies of relevant correspondence should also be included.

## • Sewage

The requirements with regard to the application of sewage pollution prevention and control are set out in MARPOL 73/78 Annex IV. If the particular ship is obliged to comply with those regulations then it will have been subjected to survey and should be issued with an International Sewage Pollution Prevention Certificate (1973). Copies of those surveys and the Certificate should be included in the evidence produced.

Depending upon the arrangements which have been approved on board the specific ship — it is very likely that the sewage will have to be treated on board and can only be discharged in specific areas. It will be a good practice, and will provide good evidence, if there is a system in place to record when the treatment plant is operated and when and where any discharges take place. If an accidental discharge does occur in a prohibited area then full and relevant details should be recorded.

## • Garbage

The risk of pollution may also arise from the uncontrolled, unauthorised and indiscriminate dumping of garbage. Whilst many of the practices designed to minimise oil pollution as listed in the previous section can also be practically applied to the control of shipboard garbage, additional steps could include:

- The appointment of a supervising crew member designated to be in charge of the collection, containment, segregation and disposal of garbage.

- Proper procedures should be established for the removal of garbage from the various shipboard departments to a centralised containment area.

- Careful records should be maintained of the quantities and types of garbage retained on board and accumulated from time to time.

- There should be clear instructions as to when, where and how the different types of garbage may be properly disposed. The supervising crew members in charge of garbage must be fully conversant with the MARPOL regulations — specifically Annex V.

- Careful records should be maintained of the garbage disposed to shore and/or incinerated. Receipts and invoices should be retained where possible.

There must be a garbage management plan established and a Garbage Record Book maintained. These will be examined very carefully in the event of an alleged pollution by garbage. The following would represent the minimum entries which would need to be made in the Garbage Record Book:

a) when garbage is discharged into the sea

b) when garbage is discharged to reception facilities

c) when garbage is incinerated

d) accidental or other exceptional discharges of garbage.

The relevant entries should include, for example, date and time of the occurrence, geographical position of the ship at the time of the occurrence, the category and amount of garbage involved and a signature of a responsible officer in charge.

Receipts should be obtained for any garbage discharged to reception facilities ashore.

Where, when and if garbage can be discharged are set out in detail in Annex V of MARPOL which must be consulted and fully understood by those on board.


### • Air pollution

Annex VI of MARPOL sets out details of the requirements with regard to air pollution from ships. If Annex VI, or similar apply, either through flag State legislation or local port State regulations, the emissions from the ship will need to be very carefully monitored and controlled.

Where applicable, ships will have been surveyed to verify compliance with the requirements and will have been issued with an International Air Pollution Prevention Certificate. The reports of the survey and the certificate should be included in with the other documentary evidence in the event of an alleged air pollution incident.

In the event of an alleged incident, it is very likely that attention will be drawn to the emission monitoring and control devices. It is important that accurate records are maintained of the maintenance and any calibration of such equipment.


### b. Case study

#### *Background to the incident*
*(taken from a media release issued by the Australian Maritime Safety Authority [AMSA] on 4 May 2005)*

Fines totalling $97,500 were handed down today in the Sydney Magistrates Court against the owners of a Hong Kong registered chemical tanker for garbage pollution in waters off New South Wales.

### Consideration of relevant evidence

A member of the public found a large plastic bag bearing an Australian Quarantine Inspection Service seal floating in Hastings River in January 2003.

It was one of four bags used by AQIS officers to seal meat products found aboard the chemical tanker during an inspection in December 2002.

Each bag was sealed with a numbered plastic tie, which was used by officers from the Australian Maritime Safety Authority, assisted by AQIS, to identify the vessel.

### Outcome

The owners pleaded guilty to the offences under the Commonwealth Protection of the Sea (Prevention of Pollution from Ships) Act 1983. The maximum fine for these offences is $110,000 for the ship owner and $22,000 for the ship's master

## Postscript

Of course, there are other types of pollution which may occur during a marine adventure and which may result in civil or indeed criminal actions against the ship and individuals on board — for example ballast water may be considered a pollutant and noise from a ship may, in some countries be considered a pollutant. If the advice given above is understood and applied in practice it should put the master, crew and ship operator in a good position to mitigate the effects and potential consequences.

Remember, it is vitally important to ensure that there is in place a good management system, which is properly documented and accurate records maintained of the actual operation of those procedures. However, if an accident does occur and there is a pollution incident then emergency contingency plans should be in place to respond quickly and effectively to deal with the problem — this will be as a result of appropriate training, drills and exercises.

The level of punishment handed out to the ship operator and individuals following a pollution incident will be proportional to how much effort had been put in to setting up and operating the SMS. If those involved had been trying their very best and can prove that from the documentary records — but still an accident happened — then their punishment should be minimal. It is much more important to understand what went wrong and to implement corrective action to prevent a recurrence in the future. However, if only lip service has been paid to SMS implementation or if supporting records cannot be produced then the Company, and individuals involved can expect little sympathy from the courts or enforcement agencies and must expect to face the consequences.

# COMMERCIAL/OPERATIONAL RELATED INCIDENTS

## General introduction

Tʜɪѕ ᴄʜᴀᴘᴛᴇʀ ᴀᴅᴅʀᴇѕѕᴇѕ ᴀ ɴᴜᴍʙᴇʀ ᴏꜰ ᴄᴏᴍᴍᴇʀᴄɪᴀʟ and operational incidents which can prove very costly for a ship operator — particularly if the correct evidence is not available to pursue or defend claims. Because of the nature of the claims and disputes anticipated in this chapter the relevance of the ISM Code is less than in early chapters but, nevertheless, does still have some relevance

## Under-performance and over-consumption

### a. Conceptual background

Time charterparties usually describe a vessel as being capable of steaming fully laden, under good weather conditions, at about "x" knots on a consumption of about "y" tonnes of fuel oil and "z" tonnes of diesel oil. At the commencement of the charterparty the owners are required to ensure that the vessel is capable of performing in accordance with this description. Furthermore, commonly throughout the period of the charterparty the vessel will be required to maintain the warranted level of performance.

### b. Potential exposure / problem

#### Speed and consumption of fuel

Claims by time charterers for alleged under-performance of a vessel are commonly brought at the conclusion of a charterparty period. Under-performance claims in respect of speed usually go hand in hand with claims for "over-consumption of fuel". Defence of such claims requires accurate and comprehensive data to be collected by the vessel. This evidence must be detailed and comprehensive and the responsibility for collecting such evidence falls largely to the master, chief engineer and their officers.

#### Speed

The first point of reference for the determination of a vessel's performance should be the charterparty. The charterparty will often provide a detailed method of assessment of a vessel's performance. Where no specific method of assessment is given in the charterparty a vessel's performance is assessed in good weather conditions (commonly Beaufort force 4 or less — unless otherwise described in the charterparty). The vessel's performance in good weather periods should be calculated. The good weather speed is then simply extrapolated and applied to the whole duration of the charterparty, when compared with the warranted charterparty speed, any time lost (or saved) can be determined.

Whilst the vessel's deck log book will often contain most of the basic details required in order to perform the necessary calculations, further information may be of considerable assistance. Details of any factors reducing the vessel's performance should be noted (either in the deck log or movement book, including engine room log book and chief engineer's log/fuel extracts). For example, alterations of course for traffic avoidance purposes, periods of slow steaming, stoppages, engine/machinery breakdown, adverse tidal streams and currents experienced should all be noted.

Accurate details of the weather conditions experienced should be noted in the vessel's deck log book. In addition independent verification of the weather conditions can be of assistance in avoiding disputes as to the extent of any "good weather periods", in this regard copies of all weather reports received by the vessel should be retained.

### Consumption of fuel

In addition to the weather records contained within the deck log books and independent weather forecasts etc. details of the fuel consumed by the vessel whilst on passage should be retained. In addition careful records of all periods when the vessel is instructed to proceed at an economical speed or when the vessel is navigating in congested waters and using diesel oil should be made.

It is of vital importance that an accurate record of fuel consumption is maintained, both for main engines, boilers and auxiliaries. On watchkeeping vessels the fuel flow meter readings should be recorded on a watch by watch basis, whilst on UMS ships this should be recorded at least daily, usually at noon. When changing over fuel, if applicable, for manoeuvring all flow meter readings should be updated.

### c. ISM implications

The direct implications of ISM to these types of 'commercial disputes' may not be particularly obvious. However, it is the documentation which is being continuously created within a good and efficient shipboard management system — such as Log Books and other contemporaneous records which will prove crucial in providing the evidence needed by the ship operator if they are to succeed with their claim or otherwise adequately defend themselves against allegations from their charterers.

### d. Nature of evidence required

The following items are essential in collecting sufficient evidence to properly defend a speed/consumption claim.

Whenever possible this information must be collected contemporaneously and recorded on a daily basis.

- Direction of wind and sea
- Beaufort wind force
- Swell
- Direction of swell
- Height and length of waves
- Propeller rpm
- Noon position
- Observed speed — if an accurate position fixing device is fitted
- Log speed
- Air and sea temperature
- Barometric pressure
- Vessel's course
- Fuel flow meter readings
- Fuel tank soundings
- Periods when vessel full away on passage
- Periods when manoeuvring - when change over fuels if applicable
- Periods of increase fuel consumption:
    - Air conditioning
    - High electrical load
    - Tank cleaning
    - Incinerators, etc.
- Alterations of course
- Reduction in speed:
    - Charterer's instruction — slow steaming
    - Owner's instruction
    - Weather conditions
    - Machinery factors/failure, etc.
    - Change of ballast
- Prevailing currents
- Deck log books

THE MARINER'S ROLE IN COLLECTING EVIDENCE  265

- Engine log books

- Oil record books - purification, transfer etc.

- Fuel loading, handling, consumption records (C/E Extracts)


## e. Report

In addition to the range of documentary evidence and records referred to above — it may also be necessary and appropriate for the master and / or chief engineer to prepare a written report explaining in more detail particular circumstances which may have a direct bearing on the alleged under-performance / over-consumption claim. For example if a particular ocean route was taken, which may not have been the most direct route or the route recommended by a weather routing service, then it would be useful for the master to explain his decision / choice.


## f. Case study

### Background to the incident

A relatively small bulk carrier was time chartered on the basis that she would be '...capable of steaming, fully laden, under good weather conditions about 14 knots on a consumption of about 20 metric tonnes of best grade fuel oil...'

During the six month charter period the ship averaged 13.7 knots on an average consumption of 20.5 metric tonnes. The charterers claimed that the vessel had failed to meet the charterparty performance specification in respect of both speed and consumption.

### Consideration of relevant evidence

Evidence from the vessel's Log Books confirmed that for much of the six month period the ship had been operating in weather conditions slightly in excess of Force 4 — although not in particularly heavy weather. It was also possible to establish, and confirm, that the vessel was regularly sailing against adverse currents.

The charterers contended that there was nothing at all unusual about the weather the vessel had been experiencing nor the currents.

### Outcome

The dispute was referred to arbitration. The arbitrators agreed that there had not been any particularly bad adverse weather or currents but, bearing in mind that the charterparty used the word 'about' then the speed and consumption achieved was within reasonable levels of tolerance in the circumstances. Charterers claim consequently failed.

# Bunker quality

## a. Conceptual background

In recent years there has been a general deterioration in the quality of fuel supplied for bunkers. Sub-standard fuel is one major cause of loss of speed and over-consumption of fuel and may also have a detrimental effect on the vessel's machinery. The master should take care to ensure that the bunkers supplied match the specifications required by the vessel.

If poor quality fuel has been supplied, the master should follow the correct procedures, which are listed below, in order to minimise damage. In case the fuel does cause engine damage and any subsequent expense and loss of time, it is important that the master records all the relevant information listed below in order to establish the cause of the damage, particular attention being given to the retention and preservation of samples. Finally, in addition to thorough reporting procedures, the master should promptly report the matter to owners.

## b. Potential exposure / problem

The danger is that bunker suppliers, who may be acting on behalf of time charterers, may supply bunkers which are not of a suitable specification for the particular machinery on board. This may be done accidentally or, as has been known to happen, the ship is deliberately supplied with bunkers which contain 'slops' or other contaminants.

At one end of the scale the ensuing problem may be limited to discharging again the unsuitable bunkers and possibly cleaning tanks — but at the other end of the scale the problem could be very much worse. If unsuitable bunkers are used this may cause very serious damage to the engine and other machinery and may even lead to explosions and fires which, in turn, could lead to injuries to personnel.

## c. ISM implications

Whilst the essence of bunker quality disputes tends to be 'commercial' — there are elements of the ISM Code and the management of safety which do have a bearing. Specifically under Section 7 of the ISM Code there should be correct procedures in place for safe bunkering operations. Also, under Section 10 — specifically Section 10.3 which requires the Company to '…establish procedures in its SMS to identify equipment and technical systems the sudden operational failure of which may result in hazardous situations…'

The section further provides that: 'The safety management system should provide for specific measures aimed at promoting the reliability of such equipment and systems…' It is suggested that bunker quality sampling procedures should be included here.

Pt B5
COMMERCIAL

### d. Nature of evidence required

The nature of the evidence which will need to be collected will depend upon the problem which subsequently develops. This could range from the severe inconvenience of having an unsuitable stem of bunkers on board to the much more serious situation of having used unsuitable bunkers which had been supplied and which resulted in actual damage to the main engine and possibly other crucial items of the ships machinery. Much of the evidence will be created as a natural consequence of following correct procedures, maintaining records and of having followed those procedures. An outline of the key procedures are set out below but again it is important for each ship to follow its own Company SMS or other procedures.

### *Procedure at commencement of bunkering — all of which should be suitably documented or recorded:*

- The chief engineer should be responsible for supervising bunkering and should liaise closely with the officer of the watch. Company bunkering procedures should be strictly adhered to and all safety and anti-pollution measures must be fully considered.

- The flash point, viscosity and other characteristics of fuel supplied should be checked to ensure that the fuel is suitable for the vessel for on board combustion. Particular care should be taken, with the use of very heavy fuel oils, to ensure the vessel's fuel heating capacity is sufficient to enable efficient combustion of any bunkers loaded.

    If the fuel fails to confirm with the specifications required by the vessel, the master should notify in writing the bunker supplier and charterers' port agents (sample letters which should be sent to bunker supplier and charterers' port agents are provided at pages 271 to 274).

- The chief engineer, barge master/shoreman should check the security of the hose couplings on the bunker barge and on the receiving vessel, take appropriate anti-pollution precautions and should agree start up, topping off and bunkering rates. A clear system of communications must be established between barge/shore and ship. Emergency shut down signals must be confirmed.

    Failure to observe these precautions may lead to oil pollution and result in heavy fines and possibly even the arrest of the vessel.

- Sound all tanks on board the vessel and the bunker barge, where the supply is by barge and where this is possible, before taking bunkers and on completion of bunkering and record all soundings. Where bunkers are loaded from shore, whenever possible, shore readings should be confirmed including flow meter readings and tank sounds.

- New bunkers should be segregated from old bunkers on board. If bunkers are mixed, a mixed sample of the old and new fuels must be tested for compatibility. An additional sample should be retained on board the vessel.

- New bunkers should be tested regularly for the presence of water after loading. To do so it should be ensured that the vessel is well provided with a good quality water finding preparation. The on board treatment of fuel oil is vital, particularly centrifuging. The results should then be checked against engine manufacturer's specifications.

- Normal representative samples taken, for example, by continuous drip during bunkering, which should be marked and sealed, should be taken at the vessel's manifold and the master should request in writing the supplier or charterers' port agents to attend during sampling (the sample letter is provided in Sample Letter 3 — see page 273). Only special sample containers should be used and it must be ensured that these are scrupulously clean before use.

  If the suppliers or port agents fail to attend, the master must make a protest in writing (a sample letter is provided in Sample Letter 4 (see page 274).

  One sample should be sent for analysis immediately. If possible the bunkers should not be used until the results are available.

  The use of reputable fuel analysis laboratories is strongly recommended, some major analysis programmes can supply very prompt results. It may also be appropriate to consider appointing a duly qualified independent surveyor to carry out or oversee the taking of bunker samples.

- Often the ship will be presented with samples by the supplier. If possible, try to attend that sampling and record the details of where and when it was carried out, by whom, by what method, and who was in attendance.

### *Procedure if it is suspected that sub-standard bunkers have been placed on board:*

- Records must be kept of which tanks the bunkers were placed on delivery and whether or not there was oil in the tanks prior to delivery and if so, full details must be given, including the specification of those bunkers, where and when they were supplied, how much and by whom

- The location of the tank in which the suspect bunkers had been kept must be recorded and full details of all movements of bunkers between tanks must be noted

- Details of ullages must be noted and copies of bunker receipts for the new bunkers must be preserved together with copies of bunker receipts for the most recent previous bunkerings

- All notes of protest and the engine and deck logs must be preserved

- At least one sealed sample taken during bunkering must be retained and samples from previous bunkers kept safe on board until specific instructions received from owners to dispose of the samples

- A note must be kept of the following:

  - The chief engineer and other crew members involved in the bunkering operation

  - The names of those present at the time the bunker samples were taken

  - The crew members involved in correcting any problems associated with sub-standard bunkers

- Owners must be notified promptly.

### *Procedures if sub-standard bunkers are used and damage results:*

- In addition to the information referred to above, the master should also keep records of the following:

  - When was fuel first burned

  - What were the immediate manifestations of the problem

  - What action was taken to reduce the problem

  - Was the action effective

  - When were repairs carried out and under whose supervision

  - What parts were overhauled or renewed

  - When was contaminated fuel last burnt

  - Disposition of contaminated fuel

  - Performance of engine once the vessel had ceased to burn contaminated fuel

  - Any additives that may have been used in the fuel, the quantities used, how and when they were added and into which tanks

    - How the particular batch of fuel in question was treated on board prior to use, for example how separators and filters were used

- If available, all contemporaneous reports of repairs from owners, charterers, engine manufacturers and underwriters' surveyors should be kept

- Any damaged machinery parts should be kept for future inspection

- Photographs should be taken of damaged parts when discovered.

### e. Report

A report may be required from the master and / or the chief engineer to expand upon the documentary evidence and records highlighted above. This will particularly be the case if the supply of unsuitable bunkers has led to substantial

## SAMPLE LETTER 1

**Notification by master to charterers' port agents and bunker supplier that supplied fuel does not conform with specifications required by the vessel**

FROM:

COMPANY:

TO:                                          DATE:

                                             TIME:

                                             AT:

**Re: MV**

**Bunkers loaded at**

I hereby give you notice that an analysis carried out on this vessel of a representative sample of the bunkers supplied by you indicates the deficiencies listed below. The fuel is therefore outside the specification of fuel suitable to the vessel's engines and auxiliary machinery and has been submitted for further analysis.

Deficiencies were noted in:

1    Density            [ ]

2    Viscosity          [ ]

3    Pour point         [ ]

4    Water content      [ ]

5    Salt water         [ ]

6    Compatibility      [ ]

7    Catalytic fines    [ ]

Owners await charterers' instructions and until these are received, the vessel cannot proceed. In the meantime, the vessel's engineering staff will use their best endeavours to protect the vessel's engines (including the slowing and stopping of the ship's machinery when necessary). Owners hold charterers fully responsible for any damage, delays, poor performance, over-consumption or any other loss or expense arising as a direct or indirect consequence of your failure to supply suitable fuel.

Yours faithfully

Master

Make and model of sampling equipment:

Make and model of main engine:

# SAMPLE LETTER 2

## Notification by master to charterers' port agents and bunker supplier that fuel supplied does not conform with specification required by the vessel and is unusable

FROM:

COMPANY:

TO:                                          DATE:

                                             TIME:

                                             AT:


**Re: MV**

**Bunkers loaded at**


I hereby give you notice that a shipboard analysis of a representative sample of the bunkers supplied by you to the vessel indicates that the fuel is wholly unsuitable for use in the vessel's machinery.

In the circumstances, I cannot jeopardise the safety of the vessel, crew, or cargo by accepting or using the bunkers supplied without first receiving express instructions to do so from you and owners.

In the meantime, owners hold charterers wholly responsible for all damages and delays and other loss and expense arising as a direct or indirect consequence from your failure to supply suitable fuel.


Yours faithfully



Master



Make and model of sampling equipment:

Make and model of main engine:

## SAMPLE LETTER 3

### Request from master to charterers' port agents and bunker supplier to attend during representative sampling

FROM:

COMPANY:

TO:                                                DATE:

                                                   TIME:

                                                   AT:


**Re: MV**

**Samples of bunkers**


[In accordance with charterparty conditions] I hereby request you to ensure that representative samples of the bunkers to be supplied to the vessel will be taken and sealed in the presence of competent and authorised representatives of charterers and the vessel, such samples to be taken during bunkering at the vessel's manifold. The vessel will require two samples.

It will be of assistance to you to know that the vessel has facility for drawing continuous samples at the manifold. If no joint samples are taken during bunkering by a satisfactory alternative system, only those samples drawn at the manifold by the vessel's representatives will be regarded as representative samples.

I shall be grateful if you will advise me as soon as possible what arrangements have been made by you or the bunker supplier in respect of bunkering and sampling.


Yours faithfully


Master


Vessel's authorised personnel:

Make and model of sampling equipment:

Make and model of main engine:

**Protest by master for failure of charterers' port agents or bunker supplier to attend during representative sampling**

FROM:

COMPANY:

TO:                                                      DATE:

TIME:

AT:

**Re: MV**

**Samples of bunkers**

I hereby make a formal protest that you and the bunker supplier have failed to participate in the proper obtaining and sealing during bunkering time of representative samples of the bunkers supplied to the vessel.

In particular:

> No samples have been drawn by you and supplied          [ ]
>
> Ready sealed samples have been supplied                [ ]
>
> Samples were drawn in a method which is unsatisfactory
>
> and susceptible to gross error                         [ ]

I hereby give you notice that the vessel has taken her own samples during the bunkering operation [which were sealed in the presence of charterers or bunker supplier's representative] [in the absence of a response to my invitation to attend joint sampling] and only these samples will be regarded as representative. Two sealed samples drawn by the vessel are available to you on request.

Yours faithfully

Master

Make and model of sampling equipment:

Make and model of main engine:

delays in prosecuting the voyage and / or in serious damage having been caused to the main engine or other items of equipment. The list of suggested evidence above should provide a good guidance as to the sort of information which should be included in such a report.

## f. Case study

### Background to the incident

A 15,000 gt general cargo ship entered into a new one year time charter. At the commencement of the charter she had on board 500 metric tonnes of bunker fuel oil from a previous employment. The new time charterers arranged to put on board, at the first load port, a further 1,000 metric tonnes of bunker fuel. Sealed samples of the bunkers supplied were provided by the bunker supplier.

Two days after sailing from the load port the main engine had to be stopped as a result of excessively high temperatures and pressures being experienced. The engine could not be restarted and the vessel was eventually towed back to the original load port for investigation and repair.

It subsequently transpired that the fuel which had been used in the main engine was seriously contaminated and had caused considerable damage to the main engine. The entire cargo had to be transhipped onto another carrying vessel.

The ship operator claimed against the time charterers for damage to the main engine as well as substantial damages through loss of earnings — alleging that the bunkers supplied were contaminated or otherwise unsuitable and not according to the required specification of the charterparty.

The time charterers alleged that they had supplied bunkers in accordance with the charterparty specs but the bunkers must have been contaminated by the fuel which was already on board.

### Consideration of relevant evidence

The sealed sample of fuel oil supplied by the bunker suppler was analysed and complied with the charterparty specification. It was not known exactly when this sample was bottled or sealed except that the supplier insisted that it was drawn from the shore tank immediately prior to loading on board the ship. The chief engineer had signed a receipt for the sample.

The ship did not draw its own sample of bunker fuel at the time of loading and there were no efforts made to have any samples analysed.

Records were available from the ship indicating which double bottom tanks were used to receive the bunkers but at least two of these double bottom tanks did contain some remnants of previous bunkers.

### Outcome

Whilst it was strongly argued by the ship operator that there was absolutely nothing wrong with the bunkers which were already on board — and which had been used during the previous voyage — and consequently it must be the case that contaminated bunkers had been supplied — the ship operators were unable to produce overwhelming evidence to support such an assertion. Accordingly their claim in respect of the damage to the main engine failed. Charterers maintained their off hire position and successfully claimed costs and damages in respect of having to tranship the cargo.

It is almost certainly the case that if the ship operators had followed correct procedures and collected contemporaneous evidence at the time of taking the stem then the outcome would have been very different.

### Unsafe ports and berths

#### a. Conceptual background

Charterparties often provide that a port or berth is "safe". This means the charterers must nominate a port which at the relevant time the particular ship may approach, use, and depart from without — in the absence of some abnormal occurrence — being exposed to danger which cannot be avoided by good seamanship and navigation.

#### b. Potential exposure / problem

The potential exposure to claims and other problems can best be understood by analysing the relevant charterers obligations.

#### Time charters

Where time charters have the option to nominate a safe port within a specified range, the obligation to nominate a safe port arises at the time when the order is given, so they must nominate a port which is then expected to be safe for the ship to approach, use, and leave. If the port later becomes unsafe, charterers must issue new orders — if necessary to proceed to another port. However, this obligation does not arise in a case where the port later becomes unsafe due to an unexpected and abnormal danger which the charterers were unaware.

If charterers nominate a port which, in the master's opinion is unsafe, he should immediately contact his owners explaining in detail the reasons for his opinion and request further instructions. If the master reasonably obeys the charterer's orders to proceed to the port and the ship becomes damaged as a result, charterers will be liable; he must, however, act reasonably. If, for example, the weather deteriorates and the ship faces ranging damage if she stays on the berth the master should depart from the berth if he can do so safely; if he remains on the berth the damage arising will not automatically fall on the charterers even though the berth is an unsafe one.

It is important the master considers carefully voyage orders given by the charterers before proceeding to a port and follows closely any instructions given by the charterers.

### *Voyage charters*

Voyage charterers must nominate, from the range of ports specified within the charterparty, a safe port. However, it is uncertain whether the secondary obligation to issue new orders for another safe port arises in the case of voyage charters. Where a port is specifically named in a voyage charter it is up to the owners to establish that the port is safe before fixing, unless the charterers have stated that it is safe.

### *Oil charters*

Oil charters often provide that the charterers only have to exercise due diligence to select a safe port. The charterers' obligations are clearly more limited in this case.

## Elements of safety

### *Port must be safe to approach and leave*

Charterers must nominate a port which the ship can both safely approach and depart from. If the berth is upriver the river passage must be safe. Although charterers are not under an obligation to ensure that the most direct route or any particular route to or from the port (or berth) is safe, they must ensure that the voyage they order is one that an ordinarily prudent and skilful master can make safely.

### *The particular ship*

The port must be safe for the particular ship at the relevant time. The fact that ships of a different size or characteristics or differently laden, could have safely used the port is irrelevant. A port will be unsafe if the ship cannot approach it without dismantling part of her structure, or if the ship has to discharge part of her cargo into lighters if her draft is too great for the port. However, "safe" does not mean "without delay". So a bar harbour will not be unsafe simply because a ship cannot use it without delay at all times and tides.

### *Port must be safe to use*

The location, layout and other physical characteristics of a nominated port must be safe for the ship. A structured and integrated arrangement of "port systems" as required by the ship should be provided by a port, ie:

- Available port information, charting, etc.

- Navigation aids, lights, buoys, etc.

- Pilotage service

- Tugs

- Berth protection, fendering

- Mooring facilities

- Weather service

- Communications.

A port will not be unsafe because the vessel has to leave in certain weather conditions, provided the onset of these conditions are predictable and the master has been given adequate warning to leave or been made aware that he should keep watch for local warnings. The port must also have an adequate system to warn of approaching danger and an adequate weather forecasting system, a sufficient number of pilots and tugs available, and an adequate system for ensuring that there is always sea room and room to manoeuvre.

### Good navigation and seamanship

A port will not be unsafe if any dangers inherent in it may be avoided by good navigation and seamanship. The master is under a duty to take whatever reasonable steps are necessary to avoid or reduce these dangers.

If, for example, the weather deteriorates and the ship faces ranging damage if she stays on the berth the master should depart from the berth if he can do so safely; if he remains on the berth the damage arising will not automatically fall on the charterers even though the berth is an unsafe one.

However, if the dangers may be overcome only by exercising extraordinary standards of navigation and seamanship, the port will be considered unsafe.

The shipowner is usually responsible for the pilot's errors or omissions in navigation and shiphandling; and also for the utilisation and disposition of port tugs provided under a standard towage contract. The owners can only avoid this responsibility if they can show the pilotage or tug "system" at the port to be defective as a whole; so that pilots are, for example, habitually ill-trained, incompetent or drunk, or are provided with inadequate hydrographic or other information to do a competent job and advise the master accurately on port matters.

VTS (Vessel Traffic Service) information should never be regarded as pilotage information or advice; the law concerning pilotage is unambiguous inasmuch as the conning of the vessel may only be undertaken from the wheelhouse or within the vicinity of the ship.

### Abnormal occurrences

A port will not be unsafe in the legal sense if the damage to the vessel occurred as a result of an abnormal occurrence, ie one not characteristic of the port. Abnormal occurrences are typically unexpected wars and ships stranding in the channel — not occurrences which arise out of the operation of the port systems.

### c. ISM implications

The ISM implications will clearly depend very much upon the primary and any underlying causes which led to the unsafe berth or port claim / dispute — but such incidents are likely to involve aspects of the navigation of the vessel. Accordingly, aspects of the ISM Code will be relevant. The following, non-exhaustive, list attempts to address some of the more obvious potential implications and, consequently, suggest areas of the SMS which will come under close scrutiny:

Section 1.2.3.1    (compliance with mandatory rules and regulations)

Regulations such as the STCW Convention and Code may need to be considered. Levels of competency may very well appear as having been causative of the incident. Also, hours of rest / work of the individual(s) involved could be examined as well as the management system which was in place to ensure that Section A-VIII/1 of STCW Code was being complied with.

Section 6    Resources and personnel

In many unsafe berth or ports incidents one or more individuals on board may be accused of doing or not doing something which ultimately contributed to the incident — often referred to a 'human error'. It may have been the master and / or the officer of the watch (OOW) or pilot. Under Section 6 there is a very clear obligation upon the Company to engage only qualified, skilled and suitably experienced personnel. It can therefore be anticipated that a potential claimant or investigator will look very carefully not only at the qualifications and alleged experience of the individual but may also require to examine the Company selection and recruiting procedures and to follow an audit trail to demonstrate that these procedures were indeed followed when recruiting the particular individual who is the focus of attention. Bridge team and crew resource management may also be an issue to be investigated. Passage /voyage planning and master / pilot relationship are other areas which may be relevant.

It may also be necessary to produce evidence that suitable and adequate familiarisation and training was provided to the individual — e.g. in the operation of the radar etc. Relevant sections of STCW would also need to be considered.

Section 7    Development of plans for shipboard operations

Clearly the navigation of the vessel (which would include navigating in and out of the alleged unsafe port) would be included as one of the 'key shipboard operations' anticipated by Section 7. As such it should be expected that there are clear Company procedures set out in a Procedures Manual. Those procedures will be examined very carefully, not only in light of the incident itself but also during other periods of the ships life. This would be done by following audit trails.

Section 8        Emergency preparedness

The type of incident anticipated within an unsafe berth / port scenario may very well fall within the category of 'potential emergency situations' anticipated in Section 8. The response of the master and those on board, following such an incident will be examined against the written procedures. No doubt records of simulated drills involving contact type incidents will also be examined.

Section 9        Reports and analysis of non-conformities, accidents and hazardous occurrences

Records of the activities anticipated by Section 9 may well be examined to confirm that learning opportunities were being taken as part of the SMS. Similarly minutes of on board safety committee meetings may be examined to determine the level of involvement and commitment to safety management on board.

Section 10      Maintenance of the ship and equipment

To what extent this may be relevant will obviously be determined by reference to the cause of the incident. It may include damage to the ship itself but also items of equipment such as mooring ropes and winches. If the failure of a piece of equipment was involved then the procedures and records will be examined very carefully.

Section 11      Documentation

If there appear to have been problems with compliance with the SMS then it is likely that a closer look will be made at the documented procedures themselves. If these are voluminous, irrelevant or otherwise inadequate then the Company is likely to come under severe criticism.

Section 12      Company verification, review and evaluation

There is a very clear obligation on the Company to ensure that the SMS is working properly on board its vessels. If a serious incident has arisen then it can be anticipated that the active monitoring by the Company will be looked at very closely by way of audit trails.

Certification and verification

As a matter of course the validity of the SMC and DOC will be checked.

## d. Nature of evidence required

### Evidence required from the mariner

When an accident involving an unsafe berth or port occurs, the information required to bring a claim against charterers may concern not only the facts of the incident, but relate back to matters as early as the port at which the voyage planning commenced.

To ensure that all relevant information required is available, the master/mariner should consult the following checklists and maintain and retain relevant records.

### Port CCTV and VHF recordings

It is worth bearing in mind that a great many ports employ Closed Circuit Television (CCTV) and Very High Frequency Radio (VHF) recording facilities themselves, especially for critical areas of navigation (such as areas of restricted manoeuvrability, passage through lock systems, etc.) it is therefore important that the master strives to obtain the fullest details for preparation of the vessel's defence or claim.

### The approach voyage

Charterers' safe port promise also applies to any necessary route to or from the port, eg via a river. Details of up-to-date information supplied to river pilots by the pilotage or port authority should be requested and any refusal or inability on the part of the pilot to share such information should be noted in the deck log book.

### General

- Complete record of communications dealing with the voyage and voyage orders

- Charts, plans of port, berth or anchorage

- General arrangement plans, mooring arrangement plan and other relevant ship's plans

- Deck, engine, radio logs, bell book, chief officer's cargo book

- Sketch of berth facilities

- Miscellaneous published information concerning port

- Note of protest

- Detailed records of all services supplied by third parties

- Printed record information, course recorder, engine movement, echo sounder, etc.

- A record of when bridge and engine clocks were synchronised

- All charts in use at the time of the incident (no alteration should be made) together with all rough notes and calculations from the chart table, including passage planning documentation

- All communications with third parties together with any hand-written notes of oral/VHF communications

- Third parties should be requested to issue reports of services provided to be verified by the master.


## *Pilotage*

If an accident occurs whilst the ship is under pilotage or awaiting a pilot for sailing, details should be sought concerning the following points, where appropriate:

- Names of pilots on duty

- Berthing procedures

- Call-out procedures

- Date of last hydrographic survey

- Names of other vessels in port and where berthed, together with traffic movements

- Name of person advising pilot of ship's details and record of details given.


## *Tugs*

- Tugs owners / authority / tugs names

- Number of units available

- Horsepower / bollard pull / propulsion

- Where stationed

- Call-out procedure

- Communication facilities / radio watch

- Duty roster / crew lists

- Operational limits.


## *Moorings*

*On-board:*

- Sketch of mooring arrangements identifying station, material, size and security system

- Anti-chafe measures

- Mooring rope / wire details — invoices, test certificates, repairs, when first used

- Retain failed / damaged equipment as evidence

- Storage details
- Winch details
- Mooring watch details
- Damaged / parted rope / wire, where parted and how secured
- Number of lines onboard
- Mooring advice from pilot, berthing master, port authority, etc.
- Photographs, samples.

*Ashore:*
- Bollards — type, distance apart, etc.
- Mooring line lead
- Mooring gangs
- Mooring arrangements approval by port authority / terminal operator.

## The berth
- Design / construction details
- Fender type — sketch or photograph
- Sketch or photograph of fender positions along ship's length
- Condition of fenders at time of berthing
- Advice from agent, pilot, port authority
- Communication with agent, etc. about missing or defective fenders
- Fender arrangements at adjacent berths — condition, disposition, etc.
- Ship's fenders
- Constraints at berth — water depth, position of other vessels, turning area, etc.

## Weather services
*In port:*

Details of the following should be obtained:
- Port information booklet
- Port weather service
- Local radio
- Warnings provided by port authority to vessels and/or agents

- Any specific advice on arrival about local weather characteristics

- Storm signal — where sited?

- Record of all weather forecasts and weather fax charts.


*On board:*

- ALRS Volume 3 — Radio Weather Services (or similar publication)

- NP283a — Weather Reporting and Forecast Areas (or similar publication)

- Weather facsimile — working? performance? stations used?

- Radio officer's watch keeping schedule

- Radio log

- Log book or other record of weather, swell, barometric pressure, etc.

- Communications with port authority, agents, pilotage authority, other vessels, etc.

- Weather charts and messages received

- Anemometer - where sited?


### Photographic evidence

The importance of contemporaneous photographic evidence cannot be over-emphasised. In order to assist the successful prosecution of an unsafe port claim, the officer should consider it part of his duties to arrange for a crew member to photograph the following during the approach stage and after coming alongside, as may be appropriate:

- Sea conditions at anchorage

- Strong currents in rivers, ice, and other hazards

- The berths fenders and condition of concrete apron

- Approaches to locks, condition of fendering for entry and within, if appropriate

- Condition of locks and evidence of any previous damage

- Mooring arrangements

- Areas of berth particularly exposed to swell

- Other vessels affected by adverse conditions

- Any lack of room to manoeuvre in port

- Fender arrangements at adjacent berths (for comparative purposes)

- Any damage to the ship or port installations.

## e. Report

Incidents such as those involved in unsafe berths and ports can be difficult and hard to fight. The evidence from the vessel will be absolutely crucial and it is quite likely that a full and detailed report from the master will be needed to explain exactly what happened. The required evidence suggested above will provide a good idea of the areas which the master will need to cover in his report, depending upon the actual set of circumstances which have led to the dispute. Independent evidence which can collaborate and verify the masters own account of the unsafe nature of the berth or port would be of considerable value.

## f. Case studies

### Background to the incident (Number 1)

The vessel involved in this incident was a 120,000 dwt bulk carrier which had been time chartered for a period of 11 to 13 months, charterer's option. The charterparty was on the New York Produce Exchange Form with the vessel to be employed carrying lawful merchandise between safe ports within institute warranty limits. The charterparty contained an arbitration clause whereby all disputes between owners and charterers were to be resolved by arbitration in London. In accordance with the terms of the charterparty, the charterers ordered the vessel to load a cargo of coal in Queensland for discharge at a nominated port in Japan.

The vessel arrived at the named port in December and commenced discharge on arrival. Weather conditions deteriorated, and northerly winds caused the vessel to range against the quay on a heavy swell. The stress generated on the fenders by the vessel's movement resulted in the disintegration and failure of one fender unit, which caused the fracture of the vessel's shell plating in a number of places. Further damage was then caused by contact with the unprotected section of wharf under continued pressure from the wind and swell.

As a consequence of this accident, owners incurred substantial off-hire and repair costs. Owners commenced arbitration proceedings in London to recover the loss from the charterer.

### Consideration of relevant evidence

Owners claimed that the nominated port was unsafe for the following reasons:

- There was no protection from northerly winds in the port.

- There was no system in operation at the port to provide protection at the berth or to enable the vessel to leave the berth quickly if weather conditions demanded such action.

- There was no satisfactory system in operation at the port for providing warnings about deteriorating weather conditions.

- The fenders on the wharf were inadequate for vessels of the size scheduled to use the facility. Additionally, the fenders were not properly equipped in that the chains required to limit the upward and downward movement of the fenders were missing on some units.

- The berth was not provided with a system of mooring points which allowed balanced and effective use of mooring ropes and wires. This unbalanced mooring system resulted in bits being placed at other than optimum angles which exacerbated the movement of the vessel against the quay when under the influence of a strong northerly wind.

### Outcome

The arbitrators found that the charterer's were in breach of their contractual obligation to nominate a safe port for the following reasons:

- The berth was over-exposed to the elements. The breakwater afforded little protection in the wind and swell conditions present at the time of the casualty.

- No tugs were immediately available.

- The construction of the berth was such that the facilities to moor did not enable the vessel to have a symmetrical mooring layout. The berth had been lengthened to accommodate two vessels, and as a result, the stern of the vessel overhung the end of the berth. There were no mooring posts on the berth for stern lines except a distant post on the shore. Therefore, the stern lines were some three times the length of the head lines. In bad weather conditions, the movement of the vessel caused excessive pressure on one fender as a result of which it collapsed into the water. Further movement brought the vessel into contact with the exposed concrete causing severe shell damage.

- The fender which collapsed may not have been sufficiently strong.

The arbitrators rejected the charterer's arguments that the weather was exceptionally severe. They found that although weather conditions were unusual, they were not abnormally so. The arbitrators further rejected the charterer's arguments that the master had been negligent in the mooring of the vessel and the lines had become slack. They held that the master had acted in accordance with the standards of prudent seamanship.

### Background to the incident (Number 2)

This case history, also involving a bulk carrier, emphasises not only the obligations of the charterers, but also the duty of those onboard to exercise reasonable care.

The bulk carrier was lying alongside in a port subject, on occasion, to heavy swell conditions and the likelihood of ranging at the berth.

The port "system" did not provide for warning moored vessels of the onset of deteriorating weather conditions or the likelihood of a dangerous swell in the inner harbour. There was no system which could forewarn the master of the possible need to vacate the berth, and no information was passed to the vessel by either the port authority or ship's agents.

The sequence of events was as follows:

| 1000 | Wind suddenly increased, RSBE, mooring lines continuously tended and further moorings set out |
| 1030 | Westerly wind blowing strong, both anchors dropped, ballast tanks filled, parted aft breast-line immediately replaced |
| 1100 | Westerly wind still blowing strong, heavy northerly swell entering inner harbour causing ship to range alongside quay, vessel rolling heavily, additional fendering placed but crushed due to ship's movement |
| 1120 | Gale force wind, rain and hail, forward and after ropes continually parting but immediately replaced, vessel's violent movement alongside quay causing hull damage on contact with quay, main engines used to assist in easing vessel's fore and aft motion |
| 1230 | Continuation of same weather conditions and vessel's heavy ranging against quay, request made through pilot station for tugs assistance to hold and secure vessel |
| 1240 | Contact established with pilot station |
| 1310-1316 | Two tugs in attendance assisting vessel, but vessel continuing to strike quay |
| 1330 | Master requested agent (via landline telephone) for vessel to be shifted to another safer berth as present discharge berth totally unsafe |
| 1400 | Tugs depart, weather improves slightly allowing a visual inspection of considerable impact damage |
| 1500 | Agent onboard and, following discussion and contact with port authority, permission granted to shift. Harbour radio indicated weather forecast to deteriorate after nightfall |
| 1600 | Pilot onboard, three tugs in attendance, commenced singling-up |
| 1830 | Vessel secured to different berth. |

The charterers alleged the master was negligent in not leaving the berth as soon as the weather deteriorated, that is about 1000, rather than awaiting assistance from pilot and tugs. The master's evidence indicated that by 1030 if he remained alongside, his vessel would suffer hull damage, indeed, he was inclined to this view as early as 1000.

### Consideration of relevant evidence

Expert opinion suggested that if it was bad enough to drop both anchors then it was bad enough to vacate the berth.

### Outcome

The arbitrators took the view that the master should not have left the berth immediately as to have done so without tug and pilot assistance would have placed the vessel in further danger. However, he should have decided to leave the berth at 1030 and ordered tugs and pilot then. He did not do this and therefore failed to exercise reasonable care and skill at that time.

Since the significant damage commenced at 1100, the arbitrators judged the charterers liable for damage between 1100 and 1130, and the shipowner liable for damage thereafter because of the master's actions.

The claim was apportioned in such a manner that owners had to pay 85% damage cost repairs, and charterers 15%.

# PART C
# CODES AND REPORTS

## CONTENTS

All IMO and MAIB sources gratefully acknowledged

# PART C 1

# THE ISM CODE

## Preamble

1    The purpose of this Code is to provide an international standard for the safe management and operation of ships and for pollution prevention.

2    The Assembly adopted resolution A.443(XI), by which it invited all Governments to take the necessary steps to safeguard the shipmaster in the proper discharge of his responsibilities with regard to maritime safety and the protection of the marine environment.

3    The Assembly also adopted resolution A.680(17), by which it further recognized the need for appropriate organization of management to enable it to respond to the need of those on board ships to achieve and maintain high standards of safety and environmental protection.

4    Recognizing that no two shipping companies or shipowners are the same, and that ships operate under a wide range of different conditions, the Code is based on general principles and objectives.

5    The Code is expressed in broad terms so that it can have a widespread application. Clearly, different levels of management, whether shore-based or at sea, will require varying levels of knowledge and awareness of the items outlined.

6    The cornerstone of good safety management is commitment from the top. In matters of safety and pollution prevention it is the commitment, competence, attitudes and motivation of individuals at all levels that determines the end result.

## PART A - IMPLEMENTATION

1 GENERAL

1.1 Definitions

The following definitions apply to parts A and B of this Code.

1.1.1 "International Safety Management (ISM) Code" means the International Management Code for the Safe Operation of Ships and for Pollution Prevention as adopted by the Assembly, as may be amended by the Organization.

1.1.2 "Company" means the owner of the ship or any other organization or person such as the manager, or the bareboat charterer, who has assumed the responsibility for operation of the ship from the shipowner and who, on assuming such responsibility, has agreed to take over all duties and responsibility imposed by the Code.

1.1.3 "Administration" means the Government of the State whose flag the ship is entitled to fly.

1.1.4 "Safety management system" means a structured and documented system enabling Company personnel to implement effectively the Company safety and environmental protection policy.

1.1.5 "Document of Compliance" means a document issued to a Company which complies with the requirements of this Code.

1.1.6 "Safety Management Certificate" means a document issued to a ship which signifies that the Company and its shipboard management operate in accordance with the approved safety management system.

1.1.7 "Objective evidence" means quantitative or qualitative information, records or statements of fact pertaining to safety or to the existence and implementation of a safety management system element, which is based on observation, measurement or test and which can be verified.

1.1.8 "Observation" means a statement of fact made during a safety management audit and substantiated by objective evidence.

1.1.9 "Non-conformity" means an observed situation where objective evidence indicates the non-fulfilment of a specified requirement.

1.1.10 "Major non-conformity" means an identifiable deviation that poses a serious threat to the safety of personnel or the ship or a serious risk to the environment that requires immediate corrective action and includes the lack of effective and systematic implementation of a requirement of this Code.

1.1.11 "Anniversary date" means the day and month of each year that corresponds to the date of expiry of the relevant document or certificate.

1.1.12 "Convention" means the International Convention for the Safety of Life at Sea, 1974, as amended.

1.2 Objectives

1.2.1 The objectives of the Code are to ensure safety at sea, prevention of human injury or loss of life, and avoidance of damage to the environment, in particular to the marine environment and to property.

1.2.2 Safety management objectives of the Company should, inter alia:

.1 provide for safe practices in ship operation and a safe working environment;

.2 establish safeguards against all identified risks; and

.3 continuously improve safety management skills of personnel ashore and aboard ships, including preparing for emergencies related both to safety and environmental protection.

1.2.3 The safety management system should ensure:

.1 compliance with mandatory rules and regulations; and

.2 that applicable codes, guidelines and standards recommended by the Organization, Administrations, classification societies and maritime industry organizations are taken into account.

1.3 Application

The requirements of this Code may be applied to all ships.

1.4 Functional requirements for a safety management system

Every Company should develop, implement and maintain a safety management system which includes the following functional requirements:

.1 a safety and environmental-protection policy;

.2 instructions and procedures to ensure safe operation of ships and protection of the environment in compliance with relevant international and flag State legislation;

.3 defined levels of authority and lines of communication between, and amongst, shore and shipboard personnel;

.4 procedures for reporting accidents and non-conformities with the provisions of this Code;

.5 procedures to prepare for and respond to emergency situations; and

.6 procedures for internal audits and management reviews.

## 2 SAFETY AND ENVIRONMENTAL-PROTECTION POLICY

2.1 The Company should establish a safety and environmental-protection policy which describes how the objectives given in paragraph 1.2 will be achieved.

2.2 The Company should ensure that the policy is implemented and maintained at all levels of the organization, both ship-based and shore-based.

## 3 COMPANY RESPONSIBILITIES AND AUTHORITY

3.1 If the entity who is responsible for the operation of the ship is other than the owner, the owner must report the full name and details of such entity to the Administration.

3.2 The Company should define and document the responsibility, authority and interrelation of all personnel who manage, perform and verify work relating to and affecting safety and pollution prevention.

3.3 The Company is responsible for ensuring that adequate resources and shore-based support are provided to enable the designated person or persons to carry out their functions.

## 4 DESIGNATED PERSON(S)

To ensure the safe operation of each ship and to provide a link between the Company and those on board, every Company, as appropriate, should designate a person or persons ashore having direct access to the highest level of management. The responsibility and authority of the designated person or persons should include monitoring the safety and pollution-prevention aspects of the operation of each ship and ensuring that adequate resources and shore-based support are applied, as required.

## 5 MASTER'S RESPONSIBILITY AND AUTHORITY

5.1 The Company should clearly define and document the master's responsibility with regard to:

.1 implementing the safety and environmental-protection policy of the Company;

.2 motivating the crew in the observation of that policy;

.3 issuing appropriate orders and instructions in a clear and simple manner;

.4 verifying that specified requirements are observed; and

.5 reviewing the safety management system and reporting its deficiencies to the shore-based management.

5.2 The Company should ensure that the safety management system operating on board the ship contains a clear statement emphasizing the master's authority. The Company should establish in the safety management system that the master has the overriding authority and the responsibility to make decisions with respect to safety and pollution prevention and to request the Company's assistance as may be necessary.

## 6 RESOURCES AND PERSONNEL

6.1 The Company should ensure that the master is:

.1 properly qualified for command;

.2 fully conversant with the Company's safety management system; and

.3 given the necessary support so that the master's duties can be safely performed.

6.2 The Company should ensure that each ship is manned with qualified, certificated and medically fit seafarers in accordance with national and international requirements.

6.3 The Company should establish procedures to ensure that new personnel and personnel transferred to new assignments related to safety and protection of the environment are given proper familiarization with their duties. Instructions which are essential to be provided prior to sailing should be identified, documented and given.

6.4 The Company should ensure that all personnel involved in the Company's safety management system have an adequate understanding of relevant rules, regulations, codes and guidelines.

6.5 The Company should establish and maintain procedures for identifying any training which may be required in support of the safety management system and ensure that such training is provided for all personnel concerned.

6.6 The Company should establish procedures by which the ship's personnel receive relevant information on the safety management system in a working language or languages understood by them.

6.7 The Company should ensure that the ship's personnel are able to communicate effectively in the execution of their duties related to the safety management system.

## 7 DEVELOPMENT OF PLANS FOR SHIPBOARD OPERATIONS

The Company should establish procedures for the preparation of plans and instructions, including checklists as appropriate, for key shipboard operations concerning the safety of the ship and the prevention of pollution. The various tasks involved should be defined and assigned to qualified personnel.

# 8 EMERGENCY PREPAREDNESS

8.1 The Company should establish procedures to identify, describe and respond to potential emergency shipboard situations.

8.2 The Company should establish programmes for drills and exercises to prepare for emergency actions.

8.3 The safety management system should provide for measures ensuring that the Company's organization can respond at any time to hazards, accidents and emergency situations involving its ships.

# 9 REPORTS AND ANALYSIS OF NON-CONFORMITIES, ACCIDENTS AND HAZARDOUS OCCURRENCES

9.1 The safety management system should include procedures ensuring that non-conformities, accidents and hazardous situations are reported to the Company, investigated and analysed with the objective of improving safety and pollution prevention.

9.2 The Company should establish procedures for the implementation of corrective action.

# 10 MAINTENANCE OF THE SHIP AND EQUIPMENT

10.1 The Company should establish procedures to ensure that the ship is maintained in conformity with the provisions of the relevant rules and regulations and with any additional requirements which may be established by the Company.

10.2 In meeting these requirements the Company should ensure that:

.1 inspections are held at appropriate intervals;

.2 any non-conformity is reported, with its possible cause, if known;

.3 appropriate corrective action is taken; and

.4 records of these activities are maintained.

10.3 The Company should establish procedures in its safety management system to identify equipment and technical systems the sudden operational failure of which may result in hazardous situations. The safety management system should provide for specific measures aimed at promoting the reliability of such equipment or systems. These measures should include the regular testing of stand-by arrangements and equipment or technical systems that are not in continuous use.

10.4 The inspections mentioned in 10.2 as well as the measures referred to in 10.3 should be integrated into the ship's operational maintenance routine.

# 11 DOCUMENTATION

11.1 The Company should establish and maintain procedures to control all documents and data which are relevant to the safety management system.

11.2 The Company should ensure that:

.1 valid documents are available at all relevant locations;

.2 changes to documents are reviewed and approved by authorized personnel; and

.3 obsolete documents are promptly removed.

11.3 The documents used to describe and implement the safety management system may be referred to as the Safety Management Manual. Documentation should be kept in a form that the Company considers most effective. Each ship should carry on board all documentation relevant to that ship.

## 12 COMPANY VERIFICATION, REVIEW AND EVALUATION

12.1 The Company should carry out internal safety audits to verify whether safety and pollution-prevention activities comply with the safety management system.

12.2 The Company should periodically evaluate the efficiency of and, when needed, review the safety management system in accordance with procedures established by the Company.

12.3 The audits and possible corrective actions should be carried out in accordance with documented procedures.

12.4 Personnel carrying out audits should be independent of the areas being audited unless this is impracticable due to the size and the nature of the Company.

12.5 The results of the audits and reviews should be brought to the attention of all personnel having responsibility in the area involved.

12.6 The management personnel responsible for the area involved should take timely corrective action on deficiencies found.

## PART B - CERTIFICATION AND VERIFICATION

## 13 CERTIFICATION AND PERIODICAL VERIFICATION

13.1 The ship should be operated by a Company which has been issued with a Document of Compliance or with an Interim Document of Compliance in accordance with paragraph 14.1, relevant to that ship.

13.2 The Document of Compliance should be issued by the Administration, by an organization recognized by the Administration or, at the request of the Administration, by another Contracting Government to the Convention to any Company complying with the requirements of this Code for a period specified by the Administration which should not exceed five years. Such a document should be accepted as evidence that the Company is capable of complying with the requirements of this Code.

13.3 The Document of Compliance is only valid for the ship types explicitly indicated in the document. Such indication should be based on the types of ships on which the initial verification was based. Other ship types should only be added after verification of the Company's capability to comply with the requirements of this Code applicable to such ship types. In this context, ship types are those referred to in regulation IX/1 of the Convention.

13.4 The validity of a Document of Compliance should be subject to annual verification by the Administration or by an organization recognized by the Administration or, at the request of the Administration, by another Contracting Government within three months before or after the anniversary date.

13.5 The Document of Compliance should be withdrawn by the Administration or, at its request, by the Contracting Government which issued the Document when the annual verification required in paragraph 13.4 is not requested or if there is evidence of major non-conformities with this Code.

13.5.1 All associated Safety Management Certificates and/or Interim Safety Management Certificates should also be withdrawn if the Document of Compliance is withdrawn.

13.6 A copy of the Document of Compliance should be placed on board in order that the master of the ship, if so requested, may produce it for verification by the Administration or by an organization recognized by the Administration or for the purposes of the control referred to in regulation IX/6.2 of the Convention. The copy of the Document is not required to be authenticated or certified.

13.7 The Safety Management Certificate should be issued to a ship for a period which should not exceed five years by the Administration or an organization recognized by the Administration or, at the request of the Administration, by another Contracting Government. The Safety Management Certificate should be issued after verifying that the Company and its shipboard management operate in accordance with the approved safety management system. Such a Certificate should be accepted as evidence that the ship is complying with the requirements of this Code.

13.8 The validity of the Safety Management Certificate should be subject to at least one intermediate verification by the Administration or an organization recognized by the Administration or, at the request of the Administration, by another Contracting Government. If only one intermediate verification is to be carried out and the period of validity of the Safety Management Certificate is five years, it should take place between the second and third anniversary dates of the Safety Management Certificate.

13.9 In addition to the requirements of paragraph 13.5.1, the Safety Management Certificate should be withdrawn by the Administration or, at the request of the Administration, by the Contracting Government which has issued it when the intermediate verification required in paragraph 13.8 is not requested or if there is evidence of major non-conformity with this Code.

13.10 ,Notwithstanding the requirements of paragraphs 13.2 and 13.7, when the renewal verification is completed within three months before the expiry date of the existing Document of Compliance or Safety Management Certificate, the new Document of Compliance or the new Safety Management Certificate should be valid from the date of completion of the renewal verification for a period not exceeding five years from the date of expiry of the existing Document of Compliance or Safety Management Certificate.

13.11 ,When the renewal verification is completed more than three months before the expiry date of the existing Document of Compliance or Safety Management Certificate, the new Document of Compliance or the new Safety Management Certificate should be valid from the date of completion of the renewal verification for a period not exceeding five years from the date of completion of the renewal verification."

14 INTERIM CERTIFICATION

14.1 An Interim Document of Compliance may be issued to facilitate initial implementation of this Code when:

.1 a Company is newly established; or

.2 new ship types are to be added to an existing Document of Compliance, following verification that the Company has a safety management system that meets the objectives of paragraph 1.2.3 of this Code, provided the Company demonstrates plans to implement a safety management system meeting the full requirements of this Code within the period of validity of the Interim Document of Compliance. Such an Interim Document of Compliance should be issued for a period not exceeding 12 months by the Administration or by an organization recognized by the Administration or, at the request of the Administration, by another Contracting Government. A copy of the Interim Document of Compliance should be placed on board in order that the master of the ship, if so requested, may produce it for verification by the Administration or by an organization recognized by the Administration or for the purposes of the control referred to in regulation IX/6.2 of the Convention. The copy of the Document is not required to be authenticated or certified.

14.2 An Interim Safety Management Certificate may be issued:

.1 to new ships on delivery;

.2 when a Company takes on responsibility for the operation of a ship which is new to the Company; or

.3 when a ship changes flag.

Such an Interim Safety Management Certificate should be issued for a period not exceeding 6 months by the Administration or an organization recognized by the Administration or, at the request of the Administration, by another Contracting Government.

14.3 An Administration or, at the request of the Administration, another Contracting Government may, in special cases, extend the validity of an Interim Safety Management Certificate for a further period which should not exceed 6 months from the date of expiry.

14.4 An Interim Safety Management Certificate may be issued following verification that:

.1 the Document of Compliance, or the Interim Document of Compliance, is relevant to the ship concerned;

.2 the safety management system provided by the Company for the ship concerned includes key elements of this Code and has been assessed during the audit for issuance of the Document of Compliance or demonstrated for issuance of the Interim Document of Compliance;

.3 the Company has planned the audit of the ship within three months;

.4 the master and officers are familiar with the safety management system and the planned arrangements for its implementation;

.5 instructions, which have been identified as being essential, are provided prior to sailing; and

.6 relevant information on the safety management system has been given in a working language or languages understood by the ship's personnel.

## 15 VERIFICATION

15.1 All verifications required by the provisions of this Code should be carried out in accordance with procedures acceptable to the Administration, taking into account the guidelines developed by the Organization.

## 16 FORMS OF CERTIFICATES

16.1 The Document of Compliance, the Safety Management Certificate, the Interim Document of Compliance and the Interim Safety Management Certificate should be drawn up in a form corresponding to the models given in the appendix to this Code. If the language used is neither English nor French, the text should include a translation into one of these languages.

16.2 In addition to the requirements of paragraph 13.3, the ship types indicated on the Document of Compliance and the Interim Document of Compliance may be endorsed to reflect any limitations in the operations of the ships described in the safety management system.

# PART C 2

INTERNATIONAL MARITIME ORGANIZATION

*E*

ASSEMBLY
20th session
Agenda item 11

A 20/Res.849
1 December 1997
Original: ENGLISH

## RESOLUTION A.849(20)

**adopted on 27 November 1997**

### CODE FOR THE INVESTIGATION OF MARINE CASUALTIES AND INCIDENTS

THE ASSEMBLY,

RECALLING article 15(j) of the Convention on the International Maritime Organization concerning the functions of the Assembly in relation to regulations and guidelines concerning maritime safety and the prevention and control of marine pollution from ships,

NOTING with concern that, despite the best endeavours of the Organization, casualties and incidents resulting in loss of life, loss of ships and pollution of the marine environment continue to occur,

NOTING ALSO that the safety of seafarers and passengers and the protection of the marine environment can be enhanced by timely and accurate reports identifying the circumstances and causes of marine casualties and incidents,

NOTING FURTHER the rights and obligations of coastal and flag States under the provisions of articles 2 and 94 of the United Nations Convention on the Law of the Sea (UNCLOS),

NOTING IN ADDITION the responsibilities of flag States under the provisions of the International Convention for the Safety of Life at Sea, 1974 (regulation I/21), the International Convention on Load Lines, 1966 (article 23) and the International Convention for the Prevention of Pollution from Ships, 1973 (article 12), to conduct casualty investigations and to supply the Organization with relevant findings,

CONSIDERING the need to ensure that flag States are required, under the aforementioned conventions, to investigate all cases of serious and very serious casualties,

ACKNOWLEDGING that the investigation and proper analysis of marine casualties and incidents can lead to greater awareness of casualty causation and result in remedial measures, including better training, for the purpose of enhancing safety of life at sea and protection of the marine environment,

RECOGNIZING the need for a code to provide, as far as national laws allow, a standard approach to marine casualty and incident investigation with the sole purpose of correctly identifying the causes and underlying causes of casualties and incidents,

RECOGNIZING ALSO the international nature of shipping and the need for co-operation between Governments having a substantial interest in a marine casualty or incident for the purpose of determining the circumstances and causes thereof,

HAVING CONSIDERED the recommendations made by the Maritime Safety Committee at its sixty-eighth session and by the Marine Environment Protection Committee at its fortieth session:

1. ADOPTS the Code for the Investigation of Marine Casualties and Incidents set out in the Annex to the present resolution;

2. INVITES all Governments concerned to take appropriate measures to give effect to the Code as soon as possible;

3. REQUESTS flag States to conduct an investigation into all very serious and serious marine casualties and to supply the Organization with all relevant findings;

4. REVOKES resolutions A.173(ES.IV), A.440 (XI) and A.637(16).

# CODE FOR THE INVESTIGATION OF MARINE CASUALTIES AND INCIDENTS

## 1 Introduction

1.1      This Code recognizes that under IMO conventions each flag State has a duty to conduct an investigation into any casualty occurring to any of its ships when it judges that such an investigation may assist in determining what changes in the present regulations may be desirable or if such a casualty has produced a major deleterious effect upon the environment. The Code also takes into account that under the provisions of UNCLOS article 94, a flag State shall cause an inquiry to be held, by or before a suitably qualified person or persons into certain casualties or incidents of navigation on the high seas. However, the Code also recognises that where a casualty occurs within the territorial sea or internal waters of a State, that State has a right, under UNCLOS article 2, to investigate the cause of any such casualty which might pose a risk to life or to the environment, involve the coastal State's search and rescue authorities, or otherwise affect the coastal State.

1.2      The aim of this Code is to promote a common approach to the safety investigation of marine casualties and incidents, and also to promote co-operation between States in identifying the contributing factors leading to marine casualties. The result of this common approach and co-operation will be to aid remedial action and to enhance the safety of seafarers and passengers and the protection of the marine environment. In achieving these aims, this Code recognizes the need for mutual respect for national rules and practices and puts particular emphasis upon co-operation.

1.3      By introducing a common approach to marine casualty investigations and the reporting on such casualties, the international maritime community may be better informed about the factors which lead up to and cause, or contribute to, marine casualties. This may be facilitated by:

.1      Clearly defining the purpose of marine casualty investigation and the guiding principles for its conduct.

.2 Defining a framework for consultation and co-operation between substantially interested States.

.3 Recognizing that the free flow of information will be promoted if individuals who are attempting to assist the investigation may be offered a degree of immunity, both from self-incrimination and from any ensuing risk to their livelihood.

.4 Establishing a common format for reports to facilitate publication and sharing of the lessons to be learned.

1.4 It is not the purpose of the Code to preclude any other form of investigation, whether for civil, criminal, administrative, or any other form of action, but to create a marine casualty investigation process the aim of which is to establish the circumstances relevant to the casualty, to establish the causal factors, to publicise the causes of the casualty and to make appropriate safety recommendations. Ideally, marine casualty investigation should be separate from, and independent of, any other form of investigation.

## 2 Objective

The objective of any marine casualty investigation is to prevent similar casualties in the future. Investigations identify the circumstances of the casualty under investigation and establish the causes and contributing factors, by gathering and analysing information and drawing conclusions. Ideally, it is not the purpose of such investigations to determine liability, or apportion blame. However, the investigating authority should not refrain from fully reporting the causes because fault or liability may be inferred from the findings.

## 3 Application

This Code applies, as far as national laws allow, to the investigation of marine casualties or incidents where either one or more interested States have a substantial interest in a marine casualty involving a ship under their jurisdiction.

## 4 Definitions

For the purpose of this Code:

4.1 *Marine casualty* means an event that has resulted in any of the following:

.1 the death of, or serious injury to, a person that is caused by, or in connection with, the operations of a ship; or

.2 the loss of a person from a ship that is caused by, or in connection with, the operations of a ship; or

.3 the loss, presumed loss or abandonment of a ship; or

.4 material damage to a ship; or

.5 the stranding or disabling of a ship, or the involvement of a ship in a collision; or

.6 material damage being caused by, or in connection with, the operation of a ship; or

.7    damage to the environment brought about by the damage of a ship or ships being caused by, or in connection with, the operations of a ship or ships.

4.2    *Very serious casualty* means a casualty to a ship which involves the total loss of the ship, loss of life or severe pollution.

4.3    *Serious casualty* means a casualty which does not qualify as a very serious casualty and which involves:

    .1    a fire, explosion, grounding, contact, heavy weather damage, ice damage, hull cracking or suspected hull defect, etc., resulting in;

    .2    structural damage rendering the ship unseaworthy, such as penetration of the hull underwater, immobilization of main engines, extensive accommodation damage etc.; or

    .3    pollution (regardless of quantity); and/or

    .4    a breakdown necessitating towage or shore assistance.

4.4    *Marine incident* means an occurrence or event being caused by, or in connection with, the operations of a ship by which the ship or any person is imperilled, or as a result of which serious damage to the ship or structure or the environment might be caused.

4.5    *Causes* means actions, omissions, events, existing or pre-existing conditions or a combination thereof, which led to the casualty or incident.

4.6    *Marine casualty or incident safety investigation* means a process held either in public or in camera conducted for the purpose of casualty prevention which includes the gathering and analysis of information, the drawing of conclusions, including the identification of the circumstances and the determination of causes and contributing factors and, when appropriate, the making of safety recommendations.

4.7    *Marine casualty investigator* means a person or persons qualified and appointed to investigate a casualty, or incident, under procedures laid down in national legislation for the furtherance of marine safety and protection of the marine environment.

4.8    *Serious injury* means an injury which is sustained by a person in a casualty resulting in incapacitation for more than 72 hours commencing within seven days from the date of injury.

4.9    *Ship* means any kind of vessel which is used in navigation by water.

4.10    *Lead investigating State* means the State that takes responsibility for the conduct of the investigation as mutually agreed between the substantially interested States.

4.11    *Substantially interested State* means a State:

    .1    which is the flag State of a ship that is the subject of an investigation; or

    .2    in whose internal waters or territorial sea a marine casualty has occurred; or

    .3    where a marine casualty caused, or threatened, serious harm to the environment of that State, or within those areas over which the State is entitled to exercise jurisdiction as recognised under international law; or

    .4    where the consequences of a marine casualty caused, or threatened, serious harm to that State or to artificial islands, installations, or structures over which it is entitled to exercise jurisdiction; or

.5 where, as a result of a casualty, nationals of that State lost their lives or received serious injuries; or

.6 that has at its disposal important information that may be of use to the investigation; or

.7 that for some other reason establishes an interest that is considered significant by the lead investigating State.

## 5 Conduct of marine casualty investigations

5.1 Where an investigation is to be conducted, the following should be taken into consideration:

.1 Thorough and unbiased marine casualty investigations are the most effective way of establishing the circumstances and causes of a casualty.

.2 Only through co-operation between States with a substantial interest can a full analysis be made of a marine casualty.

.3 Marine casualty investigations should be given the same priority as criminal or other investigations held to determine responsibility or blame.

.4 Marine casualty investigators should have ready access to relevant safety information including survey records held by the flag State, the owners, and classification societies. Access to information should not be barred by reason of competing investigations.

.5 Effective use should be made of all recorded data, including Voyage Data Recorders (VDR), if fitted, in the investigation of a marine casualty or marine incident wherever it occurred. The State conducting the investigation should arrange for the read-out of the VDR.

.6 Marine casualty investigators should be afforded access to Government surveyors, coastguard officers, vessel traffic service operators, pilots or other marine personnel of the respective States.

.7 The investigation should take into account any recommendations or instruments published by IMO or ILO, in particular those relating to the human factor, and any other recommendations or instruments adopted by other relevant international organizations.

.8 Reports of investigations are most effective when released to the shipping industry and public.

5.2 In accordance with 9, other substantially interested States should be invited to be represented during any such investigation and should be admitted as a party in the proceedings and have equal standing, rights and access to evidence as the State conducting the investigation.

5.3 Recognizing that any vessel involved in a casualty may continue in service and that a ship should not be delayed more than is absolutely necessary, the State conducting the investigation should start the investigation as soon as practicable, without delaying the ship unreasonably. Other substantially interested States may, by mutual agreement, join the investigation either immediately or at a later stage.

# 6 Responsibility for investigating casualties and incidents

6.1     Flag States are encouraged to ensure that investigations are carried out into all casualties occurring to its ships. All cases of serious and very serious casualties should be investigated.

6.2     Where a marine casualty or incident occurs within the territorial sea of a State, the flag and coastal States recognizing the obligations of that State to its citizens and the legal status of the territorial sea under the provisions of UNCLOS and also recognising the duties placed on a flag State, the flag and coastal States should co-operate to the maximum extent possible, and mutually agree which State should take the role of lead investigating State.

6.3     Where a marine casualty or incident occurs on the high seas, a flag State should carry out an investigation into a casualty to, or on, any of its ships. If that casualty is a collision involving a ship of another flag State, then the States should consult with each other and agree which will be the lead investigating State and determine the best means of co-operation under this Code. In line with 9.1, if another State is a substantially interested State by virtue of the nationality of the ship's crew, passengers or other persons, or the location of the casualty, that State or States should be invited to take part in the investigation.

6.4     By fully participating in an investigation conducted by another substantially interested State, the flag State shall be considered as fulfilling its obligations under UNCLOS article 94, section 7.

6.5     An investigation should be started as soon as practicable after the casualty occurs. Substantially interested States should, by mutual agreement, be allowed to join an investigation conducted by another substantially interested State at any stage of the investigation.

# 7 Responsibilities of the lead investigating State

The lead investigating State should be responsible for:

.1     developing a common strategy for investigating the casualty in liaison with substantially interested States;

.2     providing the investigator in charge and co-ordinating the investigation;

.3     establishing the investigation parameters based on the laws of the investigating State and ensuring that the investigation respects those laws;

.4     being the custodian of records of interviews and other evidence gathered by the investigation;

.5     preparing the report of the investigation, and obtaining and reflecting the views of the substantially interested States;

.6     co-ordinating, when applicable, with other agencies conducting other investigations;

.7     providing reasonable logistical support; and for

.8     liaison with agencies, organizations and individuals not part of the investigating team.

## 8 Consultation

8.1        Notwithstanding the obligation placed on the master or owners of a ship to inform its flag State authority of any casualty occurring to the ship, where a casualty or incident occurs in the internal waters or territorial sea of another State, the coastal State should notify, with a minimum of delay, the flag State or States of the circumstances and what, if any, action is proposed by the coastal State.

8.2        Following a casualty, the investigating State should inform the other substantially interested States, either through the Consular Office in that State or by contacting the relevant authorities listed in MSC/Circ.781/ MEPC.6/Circ.2. That State and the other substantially interested States should consult, at the earliest opportunity, on the conduct of the investigation and to determine details of co-operation.

8.3        Nothing should prejudice the right of any State to conduct its own separate investigation into a marine casualty occurring within its jurisdiction according to its own legislation. Ideally, if more than one State desires to conduct an investigation of its own, the procedures recommended by this Code should be followed, and those States should co-ordinate the timing of such investigations to avoid conflicting demands upon witnesses and access to evidence.

## 9 Co-operation

9.1        Where two or more States have agreed to co-operate and have agreed the procedures for a marine casualty investigation, the State conducting the investigation should invite representatives of other substantially interested States to take part in the investigation and, consistent with the purpose of this Code, allow such representatives to:

.1      question witnesses;

.2      view and examine evidence and take copies of documentation;

.3      produce witnesses or other evidence;

.4      make submissions in respect of the evidence, comment on and have their views properly reflected in the final report; and

.5      be provided with transcripts, statements and the final report relating to the investigation.

9.2        States are encouraged to provide for maximum participation in the investigation by all States with a substantial interest in the marine casualty.

9.3        The flag State of a ship involved in a marine casualty should help to facilitate the availability of the crew to the investigation and encourage the crew to co-operate with the State conducting the investigation.

## 10 Disclosure of records

10.1      The State conducting the investigation of a casualty or incident, wherever it has occurred, should not make the following records, obtained during the conduct of the investigation, available for purposes other than casualty investigation, unless the appropriate authority for the administration of justice in that State determines that their disclosure outweighs any possible adverse domestic and international impact on that or any future investigation, and the State providing the information authorizes its release:

.1     all statements taken from persons by the investigating authorities in the course of the investigation;

.2     all communications between persons having been involved in the operation of the ship;

.3     medical or private information regarding persons involved in the casualty or incident;

.4     opinions expressed during the conduct of the investigation.

10.2     These records should be included in the final report, or its appendices, only when pertinent to the analysis of the casualty or incident. Parts of the record not pertinent, and not included in the final report, should not be disclosed.

## 11 Personnel and material resources

Governments should take all necessary steps to ensure that they have available sufficient means and suitably qualified personnel and material resources to enable them to undertake casualty investigations.

## 12 Issue of marine casualty reports and submission to IMO

12.1     The lead investigating State should send a copy of the draft of the final report to all substantially interested States, inviting their significant and substantiated comments on the report as soon as possible. If the lead investigating State receives comments within thirty days, or within some mutually agreed period, it should either amend the draft final report to include the substance of the comments, or append the comments to the final report. If the lead investigating State receives no comments after the mutually agreed period has expired, it should send the final report to the Organization in accordance with applicable requirements and cause the report to be published.

12.2     By fully participating in an investigation conducted by another substantially interested State that will be reporting to IMO, the flag State shall be considered as fulfilling its obligations under IMO conventions.

12.3     Reports, or relevant parts of reports, into the circumstances and causes of a marine casualty should be completed as quickly as practicable, and be made available to the public and the shipping industry in order to enhance safety of life at sea and protection of the marine environment through improved awareness of the factors which combine to cause marine casualties.

12.4     Where a substantially interested State disagrees with whole or part of the report referred to in 12.1 above, it may submit its own report to the Organization.

12.5     The investigating State, upon determining that urgent safety action is needed, may initiate interim recommendations to the appropriate authority.

## 13 Re-opening of investigations

When new evidence relating to any casualty is presented, it should be fully assessed and referred to other substantially interested States for appropriate input. In the case of new evidence which may materially alter the determination of the circumstances under which the marine casualty occurred, and may materially alter the findings in relation to its cause or any consequential recommendations, States should reconsider their findings.

## 14 Contents of reports

14.1    To facilitate the flow of information from casualty investigations, each report should conform to the basic format outlined in 14.2 below.

14.2    Reports should include, wherever possible:

.1    a summary outlining the basic facts of the casualty and stating whether any deaths, injuries or pollution occurred as a result;

.2    the identity of the flag State, owners, managers, Company and classification society;

.3    details of the dimensions and engines of any ship involved, together with a description of the crew, work routine and other relevant matters, such as time served on the ship;

.4    a narrative detailing the circumstances of the casualty;

.5    analysis and comment which should enable the report to reach logical conclusions, or findings, establishing all the factors that contributed to the casualty;

.6    a section, or sections, analysing and commenting on the causal elements, including both mechanical and human factors, meeting the requirements of the IMO casualty data base; and

.7    where appropriate, recommendations with a view to preventing similar casualties.

## 15 Contact between Administrations

To facilitate implementation of this Code, States should inform the Organization of the responsible authorities within their Governments that may be contacted regarding cooperation in casualty investigations.

## Appendix

## Guidelines to assist investigators in the implementation of the Code

## Introduction

The contents of this section should be treated as guidelines to assist investigators co-operating in an investigation. Investigators should bear in mind the information required under the IMO marine casualties and incidents reporting system.

In following this Code, participating investigators must be guided by the requirements of the legal system of the State in which the investigation is being conducted. In particular, co-operating investigators must be guided by the requirements of national law over issues such as:

- providing formal notification of an investigation to interested parties;
- boarding ships and securing documents;
- arranging interviews with witnesses;
- the presence of legal advisers or other third parties during an interview.

## 1. Information generally required in all cases

### 1.1 Particulars of the ship

Name, IMO number, nationality, port of registry, call sign

Name and address of owners and operators, if applicable, also, if an overseas ship, of agents

Type of ship

Name and address of charterer, and type of charter

Deadweight, net and gross tonnages, and principal dimensions

Means of propulsion; particulars of engines

When, where and by whom built

Any relevant structural peculiarities

Amount of fuel carried, and position of fuel tanks

Radio (type, make)

Radar (number, type, make)

Gyro compass (make, model)

Automatic pilot (make, model)

Electronic positioning equipment (make, model) (GPS, Decca, etc.)

Life saving equipment (dates of survey/expiry)

### 1.2 Documents to be produced

*(Note: Any documents that may have relevance to the investigation should be produced. Where possible original documents should be retained, otherwise authenticated and dated photocopies should be taken in accordance with 9.1.2 of the Code. A number of these documents will contain details sought under 1.1 of these Guidelines.)*

Ship's register

Current statutory certificates

ISM Code certification

Classification society or survey authority certificates

Official log book

Crew list

Crew qualifications (see also 1.4 of these Guidelines)

Deck log book

Port log, log abstract and cargo log book

Engine movement book

Engine-room log book

Data logger print-out

Course recorder chart

Echo sounder chart

Oil record book

Soundings book

Night order book

Master's/Chief Engineer's Standing Orders

Company Standing Orders/ Operations Manual

Company Safety Manual

Compass error book or records

Radar log book

Planned maintenance schedules

Repair requisition records

Articles of Agreement

Bar records - daily purchases - voyage receipts, etc.

Records of drug and alcohol tests

Passenger list

Radio log

Ship Reporting records

Voyage Plan

Charts and record of chart corrections

Equipment/machinery manufacturer's operational/ maintenance manuals

Any other documentation relevant to the inquiry

## 1.3 Particulars of voyage

Port at which voyage commenced and port at which it was to have ended, with dates

Details of cargo

Last port and date of departure

Draughts (forward, aft and midships) and any list

Port bound for at time of occurrence

Any incident during the voyage that may have a material bearing on the incident, or unusual occurrence, whether or not it appears to be relevant to the incident

Plan view of ship's layout including cargo spaces, slop tanks, bunker/fuel lube oil tanks (diagrams from

IOPP Certificate)

Details of cargo, bunkers, fresh water and ballast and consumption

## 1.4 Particulars of personnel involved in incident

Full name

Age

Details of injury

Description of accident

Person supervising activity

First aid or other action on board

Capacity on board

Certificate of Competency/ Licence:

   grade;

   date of issue;

   issuing country/authority;

other Certificates of Competency held

Time spent on vessel concerned

Experience on similar vessels

Experience on other types of vessels

Experience in current capacity

Experience in other ranks

Number of hours spent on duty on that day and the previous days

Number of hours sleep in the 96 hours prior to the incident

Any other factors, on board or personal, that may have affected sleep

Whether smoker, and if so, quantity

Normal alcohol habit

Alcohol consumption immediately prior to incident or in the previous 24 hours

Whether under prescribed medication

Any ingested non-prescribed drugs

Records of drug and alcohol tests

## 1.5 Particulars of sea state, weather and tide

Direction and force of wind

Direction and state of sea and swell

Atmospheric conditions and visibility

State and height of tide

Direction and strength of tidal and other currents, bearing in mind local conditions

## 1.6 Particulars of the incident

Type of incident

Date, time and place of incident

Details of incident and of the events leading up to it and following it

Details of the performance of relevant equipment with special regard to any malfunction

Persons on bridge

Persons in engine-room

Whereabouts of the master and chief engineer

Mode of steering (auto or manual)

Extracts from all relevant ship and, if applicable, shore documents including details of entries in official, bridge, scrap/rough and engine-room log books, data log printout, computer printouts, course and engine speed recorder, radar log, etc.

Details of communications made between vessel and radio stations, SAR centres and control centres, etc., with transcript of tape recordings where available

Details of any injuries/fatalities

Voyage data recorder information (if fitted) for analysis

## 1.7 Assistance after the incident

If assistance was summoned, what form and by what means

If assistance was offered or given, by whom and of what nature, and whether it was effective and competent

If assistance was offered and refused, the reason for refusal

## 1.8 Authentication of documents

The master should be asked to authenticate all documents and to sign all copies taken of documents as being true copies, also to authenticate relevant dates and times

## 1.9 Engine-room orders

In all cases where a collision or a stranding is the subject of an investigation, and the movements of the engine are involved, the master or officer on watch and other persons in a position to speak with knowledge are to be asked whether the orders to the engine-room were promptly carried out. If there is any doubt on the matter, the investigator shall refer to it in his report.

## 1.10 External sources of information

Investigators should consider independent corroborating information from external sources such as radar or voice recordings from vessel traffic systems, shore radar and radio surveillance systems, marine rescue co-ordination centres, coroners and medical records.

## 2. Additional information required in specific cases

## 2.1 Fire/Explosion

*(Investigators should bear in mind the IMO Fire Casualty Record.)*

How was the ship alerted to the fire?

How was the individual alerted to the fire?

Where did it start?

How did it start (if known)?

What was the immediate action taken?

Condition of fire-fighting equipment, supported by dates of survey/examination

Extinguishers available:

Type available in the vicinity; Types available on the ship; Types used

Hoses available/used

Pumps available/used

Was water immediately available?

Were air vents closed off to the space?

What was the nature of the material on fire and surrounding the fire?

Fire retardant specification of bulkheads surrounding the fire

Restrictions caused by (a) smoke, (b) heat, (c) fumes

Freedom of access

Access availability for fire fighting equipment

Preparedness of crew — frequency, duration, content and locations of fire musters and drills

Response by land-based fire-fighting brigades

## 2.2 Collision

*(Investigators should bear in mind the IMO Damage Cards and intact stability reporting format.)*

### General

Local or other special rules for navigation

Obstructions, if any, to manoeuvring, e.g. by a third vessel, shallow or narrow waters, beacon, buoy, etc.

Circumstances affecting visibility and audibility, e.g. state of the sun, dazzle of shore lights, strength of wind, ship-board noise and whether any door or window could obstruct look-out and/or audibility

Geographical plot

Possibilities of interaction

Name, IMO number, nationality and other details of other vessel

### For each ship:

Time, position, course and speed (and method by which established), when presence of other ship first became known

Details of all subsequent alterations of course and speed up to collision by own ship

Bearing, distance and heading of other ship, if sighted visually, time of sighting, and subsequent alterations

Bearing and distance of other ship, if observed by radar, timing of observations and subsequent alterations of bearing

If other ship was plotted and by what method (auto-plot, reflection plotter, etc.), and copy of plot, if available

Check performance of equipment

Course recorder

Lights/day signals carried and operated in ship, and those seen in other ship

Sound signals, including fog signals, made by ship and when, and those heard from other ship and when

If a listening watch was kept on VHF radio channel 16, or other frequency, and any messages sent, received or overheard

Number of radars carried on ship, number operational at time of casualty, together with ranges used on each radar

Whether steering by hand or automatic

Check that steering was operating correctly

Details of look-out

The parts of each ship which first came into contact and the angle between ships at that time

Nature and extent of damage

Compliance with statutory requirement to give name and nationality to other ship and to stand by after collision

## 2.3 Grounding

Details of voyage plan, or evidence of voyage planning

Last accurate position and how obtained

Subsequent opportunities for fixing position or position lines, by celestial or terrestrial observations,

GPS, radio, radar or otherwise, or by lines of soundings and, if not taken, why not

Chart datum comparison to WGS datum

Subsequent weather and tidal or other currents experienced

Effect on compass of any magnetic cargo, electrical disturbance or local attraction

Radar/s in use, respective ranges used, and evidence of radar performance monitoring and logging

Charts, sailing directions and relevant notices to mariners held, if corrected to date, and if any warnings they contain had been observed

Depth sounding taken, when and by what means

Tank soundings taken, when and by what means

Draught of ship before grounding and how determined

Position of grounding and how determined

Cause and nature of any engine or steering failure before the grounding

Readiness of anchors, their use and effectiveness

Nature and extent of damage

Action taken, and movements of ship, after grounding

(Note: information as in cases of foundering may also be required)

## 2.4 Foundering

*(Investigators should bear in mind the IMO damage cards and intact stability reporting format.)*

Draught and freeboard on leaving last port and changes consequent upon consumption of stores and fuel

Freeboard appropriate to zone and date

Loading procedures, hull stresses

Particulars of any alterations to hull or equipment, since survey, and by whom such alterations sanctioned

Condition of ship, possible effects on seaworthiness

Stability data and when determined

Factors affecting stability, e.g. structural alterations, nature, weight, distribution and shift of any cargo and ballast, free surface in tanks or of loose water in ship

Subdivision by watertight bulkheads

Position of, and watertight integrity of, hatches, scuttles, ports and other openings

Number and capacity of pumps and their effectiveness; the position of suctions

Cause and nature of water first entering ship

Other circumstances leading up to foundering

Measures taken to prevent foundering

Position where ship foundered and how established

Life-saving appliances provided and used, and any difficulties experienced in their use

## 2.5 Pollution resulting from an incident

*(Investigators should bear in mind IMO reporting of incidental spillages of liquids, 50 tonnes or more, and reporting of information from investigation of incidents involving dangerous goods or marine pollutants in packaged form.)*

Type of pollutant.

UN number/IMO hazard class (if applicable).

Type of packaging (if applicable).

Quantity on board.

Quantity lost.

Method of stowage and securing.

Where stowed and quantities in each compartment/container.

Tanks/spaces breached.

Tanks/spaces liable to be breached.

Action taken to prevent further loss.

Action taken to mitigate pollution.

Dispersant/neutraliser used, if any.

Restricting boom used, if any.

## 3. Securing of physical evidence

3.1     Occasions may arise where physical evidence may be available and which will require scientific examination. Some examples are oil, paint/scale, pieces of equipment and machinery, pieces of structure.

3.2     Before removal, such evidence should first be photographed 'in situ'. The sample should then be photographed on a clear background before being placed in an appropriate clean container(s), glass bottle, plastic bag, tin container, etc. The container should be sealed and clearly labelled, showing contents, name of vessel, location from which the evidence was taken, the date and the name of the investigator. For items of equipment and machinery, copies of the relevant certificates should be obtained.

3.3     Where paint samples are being taken for identification purposes in collision cases, a sample of paint from the ship's paint drum should also be obtained if possible.

3.4     Advice should be sought on the correct container to use. For example, plastic bags are suitable for paint samples, but are not suitable in investigations of fires where materials may need to be tested for accelerant, in which case sealable tin cans are preferred.

## 4. Voyage data recorders

Where information from a voyage data recorder (VDR) is available, in the event that the State conducting the investigation into a casualty or serious incident does not have appropriate facilities for readout of the VDR, it should seek and use the facilities of another State, giving consideration to the following:

.1     the capabilities of the readout facility;

.2     the timeliness of the availability of the facility; and

.3     the location of the readout facility.

## 5. Other sources of information

Investigators should bear in mind that other Government agencies, such as customs, quarantine and State Authorities, may have useful information relating to crew lists, the general condition of the ship, stores lists (including alcohol on board), ship certificates, etc. Port authorities and independent surveyors may also hold information of use to an investigation.

# HUMAN ACTIVITY DATA FORM

| Investigation | : | Rank | : |
| Name | : | Training/Courses | : |
| Qualifications | : | | |
| Address | : | Facsimile | : |
| Phone | : | | |
| Managers | : | Facsimile | : |
| Phone | : | Place joined | : |
| Joined ship | : | | |
| Travel time | : | | |

## TABLE OF PREVIOUS 96 HOURS ACTIVITY (D-X day of Casualty)

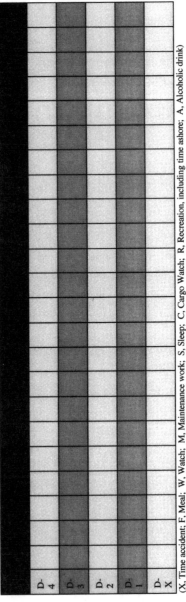

(X, Time accident; F, Meal; W, Watch; M, Maintenance work; S, Sleep; C, Cargo Watch; R, Recreation, including time ashore; A, Alcoholic drink)

Health :
Personal Issues :

# PART C 3

INTERNATIONAL MARITIME ORGANIZATION

IMO

*E*

ASSEMBLY
21st session
Agenda item 5

A 21/Res.884
4 February 2000
Original: ENGLISH

**RESOLUTION A.884(21)**
**adopted on 25 November 1999**

**AMENDMENTS TO THE CODE FOR THE INVESTIGATION OF MARINE**
**CASUALTIES AND INCIDENTS (RESOLUTION A.849(20))**

THE ASSEMBLY,

RECALLING Article 15(j) of the Convention on the International Maritime Organization concerning the functions of the Assembly in relation to regulations and guidelines concerning maritime safety and the prevention and control of marine pollution from ships,

RECALLING ALSO resolution A.849(20) by which it adopted the Code for the Investigation of Marine Casualties and Incidents,

CONSIDERING that practical advice for the systematic investigation of human factors in marine casualties and incidents will assist an effective analysis and promote the identification and implementation of preventive action,

RECOGNIZING the need for development and use, as appropriate, of practical guidelines for the investigation of human factors in marine casualties and incidents,

HAVING CONSIDERED the recommendations made by the Maritime Safety Committee at its seventy-first session and by the Marine Environment Protection Committee at its forty-third session,

1. ADOPTS amendments to the Code for the Investigation of Marine Casualties and Incidents incorporating the Guidelines for the Investigation of Human Factors in Marine Casualties and Incidents, as set out in the Annex to the present resolution;

2. INVITES Governments to implement the Guidelines as soon as practicable, as far as national law allows, with a view to improving the quality and completeness of casualty investigations and reports;

3. REQUESTS the Maritime Safety Committee and the Marine Environment Protection Committee to keep the Guidelines under review and to amend them as necessary.

## Resolution A.884 (21)

## AMENDMENTS TO THE CODE FOR THE INVESTIGATION OF MARINE CASUALTIES AND INCIDENTS (RESOLUTION A.849(20))

1   The existing appendix is renumbered as appendix 1.

2   A new appendix 2 is added as follows:

## GUIDELINES FOR THE INVESTIGATION OF HUMAN FACTORS IN MARINE CASUALTIES AND INCIDENTS

### CONTENTS

3   Reporting procedures

4   Qualifications and training of investigators

## APPENDICES

## 1 INTRODUCTION — PURPOSE OF THE GUIDELINES

1.1      The purpose of these Guidelines is to provide practical advice for the systematic investigation of human factors in marine casualties and incidents and to allow the development of effective analysis and preventive action. The long-term intent is to prevent similar casualties and incidents in the future[i].

1.2      Ships operate in a highly dynamic environment; frequently the people on board follow a set routine of shift work disrupted by arrival at, working in, and sailing from port. This is an existence which involves living in the place of work for prolonged periods, creating a unique form of working life which almost certainly increases the risk of human error.

1.3      Historically, the international maritime community has approached maritime safety from a predominantly technical perspective. The conventional wisdom has been to apply engineering and technological solutions to promote safety and to minimize the consequences of marine casualties and incidents. Accordingly, safety standards have primarily addressed ship design and equipment requirements. Despite these technical innovations, significant marine casualties and incidents have continued to occur.

1.4      Analyses of marine casualties and incidents that have occurred over the past 30 years have prompted the international maritime community, and the various safety regimes concerned, to evolve from an approach which focuses on technical requirements for ship design and equipment to one which seeks to recognize and more fully address the role of human factors in maritime safety within the entire marine industry. These general analyses have indicated that given the involvement of the human in all aspects of marine endeavours, including design, manufacture, management, operations and maintenance, almost all marine casualties and incidents involve human factors.

1.5      One way the maritime community has sought to address the contribution of the human factor to marine casualties and incidents has been to emphasize the proper training and certification of ships' crews. It has become increasingly clear, however, that training is only one aspect of the human factor. There are other factors which contribute to marine casualties and incidents which must be understood, investigated and addressed. The following are examples of these factors relevant to

---

[i]    For the purpose of these Guidelines, the term "marine casualties and incidents" includes occupational accidents resulting in loss of life or serious personal injury.

the maritime industry: communication, competence, culture, experience, fatigue, health, situational awareness, stress and working conditions.

1.6    Human factors which contribute to marine casualties and incidents may be broadly defined as the acts or omissions, intentional or otherwise, which adversely affect the proper functioning of a particular system, or the successful performance of a particular task. Understanding human factors thus requires a study and analysis of the design of the equipment, the interaction of the human operator with the equipment, and the procedures followed by crew and management.

1.7    It has been recognized that there is a critical need for guidance for accident investigators which will help them to identify specific human factors which have contributed to marine casualties and incidents. There is also a need to provide practical information on techniques and procedures for the systematic collection and analysis of information on human factors during investigations. These Guidelines seek to fulfil those needs. They include a list of topics which should be considered by investigators, and procedures for recording and reporting the results.

1.8    These Guidelines should result in an increased awareness by all involved in the marine industry of the role human factors play in marine casualties and incidents. This awareness should lead to proactive measures by the maritime community which in turn should result in the saving of lives, ships, cargo and the protection of the marine environment, improvements to the lives of marine personnel, and more efficient and safer shipping operations.

1.9    These Guidelines apply, as far as national laws allow, to the investigation of marine casualties or incidents in which either one or more States have a substantial interest because the casualty or incident involves a ship under or within their jurisdiction.

## 2 INVESTIGATION PROCEDURES AND TECHNIQUES

### 2.1 A systematic approach

2.1.1    The following is a process that provides a step-by-step systematic approach for use in the investigation of human factors. The process is an integration and adaptation of a number of established human factor frameworks. The process can be applied to any type of marine casualty or incident and consists of the following steps:

.1    collect occurrence data;

.2    determine occurrence sequence;

.3    identify unsafe acts or decisions and unsafe conditions, and then for each unsafe act or decision,

.4    identify the error type or violation;

.5    identify underlying factors; and

.6    identify potential safety problems and develop safety actions.

This process is detailed in appendix 1.

2.1.2    A systematic approach to step 1 is crucial to ensure that critical information is not overlooked or lost and that a comprehensive analysis can be made.

2.1.3    Step 2 involves organizing the data collected in step 1 to develop a sequence of events and circumstances.

2.1.4    In step 3, the information gathered and organized is used to initiate the identification of occurrence causal factors, i.e., unsafe acts, decisions or conditions. Once an unsafe act, decision or condition has been identified, the next stage is to determine the genesis of that particular act, decision or condition.

2.1.5    Step 4 is initiated in order to specify the type of error or violation involved in each identified unsafe act or decision.

2.1.6    In step 5, the focus is on uncovering the underlying factors behind the unsafe act, decision or condition. Fundamental to the process is the notion that for each underlying factor there may be one or more associated unsafe acts, decisions or conditions. The re-examination of each step of the process may show where further investigation is necessary.

2.1.7    Finally, step 6 requires the identification of potential safety problems and the proposing of safety action based on the identified underlying factors.

## 2.2 General consideration

An occurrence may result in serious injury, illness, damage or environmental impact and sometimes all four. The purpose of a marine casualty or occurrence safety investigation is to prevent recurrence of similar occurrences by identifying and recommending remedial action. All minor occurrences of high potential in terms of credible result should be subjected to a full investigation. Studies have shown that occurrences can have many causal factors and that underlying causes often exist remote from the incident site. Proper identification of such causes requires timely and methodical investigation, going far beyond the immediate evidence and looking for underlying conditions which may cause other future occurrences. Occurrence investigation should therefore be seen as a means of identifying not only immediate causes, but also failures in the total management of the operation from policy through to implementation. For this reason investigations should be broad enough to meet these overriding criteria.

### 2.2.1 Timing of the investigation

An investigation should be carried out as soon as possible after an occurrence. The quality of evidence, particularly that relying on the accuracy of human recollection, can deteriorate rapidly with time, and delayed investigations are usually not as conclusive as those performed promptly. A prompt investigation is also a good demonstration of commitment by all those concerned.

### 2.2.2 The occurrence site

Where possible, the site of the occurrence should be left unchanged until the investigation team has inspected it. Where this is not possible, for instance because of the need to make essential and immediate repairs following serious structural damage, the scene should be documented by photographs, audio visual recordings, sketches or any other relevant means available with the object of preserving vital evidence and possibly recreating the circumstances at a later date. Of particular importance is the recording of the position of individuals at the site, the condition and position of equipment, supervisory instructions, work permits and recording charts. Damage or failed components should be kept in a secure location to await the arrival of the investigation team, who may require detailed scientific examination of certain key objects. Such key objects should be carefully marked.

### 2.2.3 Witness information

Once the situation in the immediate aftermath of an occurrence has been stabilised and the threat to people, plant and the environment has been removed, everyone involved should commit their recollections to paper to assist in preserving their memory of events. In the event that local authorities take over responsibility for the investigation, the organisation/Company involved should nominate a focal point to liaise with the authorities and to assist them in assembling the information they require. Where necessary, legal assistance should be provided.

### 2.2.4 Background information

Appropriate background information should be obtained before visiting the occurrence location. Such information might include, but is not necessarily limited to:

- procedures for the type of operation involved;
- records of instructions / briefings given on the particular job being investigated;
- location plans;
- command structure and persons involved;
- messages, directions, etc., given from base/headquarters concerning the work;
- ship particulars and plans; and
- any other relevant information that may enable the investigator to understand the context of the incident.

### 2.2.5 The investigation sequence

2.2.5.1 The method for fact-finding while conducting an investigation includes, but is not necessarily limited to, the following activities:

- inspecting the location;
- gathering or recording physical evidence;
- interviewing witnesses taking into account cultural and language differences (on-site and external);
- reviewing of documents, procedures and records;
- conducting specialised studies (as required);
- identifying conflicts in evidence;
- identifying missing information; and
- recording additional factors and possible underlying causes.

2.2.5.2 Following the fact-finding a typical marine casualty or incident investigation includes analysis of the facts, conclusions and safety recommendations.

## 2.2.6 Fact-finding

2.2.6.1  The objective of this stage of the investigation is to collect as many facts as possible which may help understanding of the incident and the events surrounding it. The scope of any investigation can be divided into five areas:

- people;
- environment;
- equipment;
- procedures; and
- organization.

2.2.6.2  Conditions, actions or omissions for each of these may be identified, which could be factors contributing to the incident or to subsequent injury, damage or loss.

2.2.6.3  During the initial stages of every investigation, investigators should aim to gather and record all the facts which may be of interest in determining causes. Investigators should be aware of the danger of reaching conclusions too early, thereby failing to keep an open mind and to consider the full range of possibilities. With this in mind, it is recommended that the fact-finding stage of the investigation process itself be kept separate from the complete analysis of the collected evidence leading to conclusions and recommendations, and that a structured methodology be adopted to ensure the effectiveness of that analysis. The analysis may well help to identify missing pieces of evidence, or different lines of enquiry that may otherwise have gone undetected.

2.2.6.4  Investigation checklists can be very useful in the early stages to keep the full range of enquiry in mind, but they cannot cover all possible aspects of an investigation, neither can they follow all individual leads back to basic causal factors. When checklists are used, their limitations should be clearly understood.

2.2.6.5  The initial stages of an investigation normally focus on conditions and activities close to the incident and only primary causes, also called "active failures", are usually identified at this stage. However, conditions or circumstances underlying these causes, also called "latent failures", should also be investigated.

2.2.6.6  A factor to consider during an investigation is recent change. In many cases it has been found that some change occurred prior to an occurrence which, combining with other causal factors already present, served to initiate the occurrence. Changes in personnel, organisation, procedures, processes, and equipment should be investigated, particularly the hand-over of control and instructions, and the communication of information about the change to those who needed to know.

2.2.6.7  The effect of work cycles and work-related stress could have an impact on an individual's performance prior to an occurrence. The impact of social and domestic pressures (so-called error-enforcing conditions) related to an individual's behaviour should not be overlooked.

2.2.6.8  Information should be verified wherever possible. Statements made by different witnesses may conflict and further supporting evidence may be needed. To ensure that all the facts are uncovered, the broad questions of "who?, what?, when?, where?, why?, and how?" should be asked.

## 2.2.7 Conducting interviews

2.2.7.1  An interview should start with the introduction of the interviewing party, the purpose of the investigation and of the interview, and the possible future use to be made of the knowledge and material obtained during the interview. Investigators should be guided by the requirements of national law regarding the presence of legal advisers or other third parties during an interview.

2.2.7.2  People should be interviewed singly and be asked to go step-by-step through the events surrounding the occurrence, describing both their own actions and the actions of others. The interviewer should take into account the culture and language of the interviewee.

2.2.7.3  Notwithstanding any previously made written statements, the value of a witness's statement can be greatly influenced by the style of the interviewer, whose main task is to listen to the witness's story and not to influence him/her.

2.2.7.4  If the investigation is a team effort, great care should be taken not to make a witness feel intimidated by too many interviewers. Experience has shown that interviews can be effectively conducted by two interviewers and if appropriate, the witness could be accompanied by an independent "friend".

2.2.7.5  It should be remembered that an investigation team is often seen as having a prosecuting role, and there may be reluctance to talk freely if interviewees think they may incriminate themselves or their colleagues. An investigator is not in the position to give immunity in return for evidence, but should try to convince interviewees of the purpose of the investigation and of the need for frankness.

2.2.7.6  In addition to requiring both patience and understanding, successful interviewing requires the existence of a "no-blame" atmosphere in which the witness can be made to feel comfortable and is encouraged to tell the truth. It is not the role of the interviewer, or indeed the investigation team, to apportion blame. Their role is to establish the facts and to establish why the occurrence happened.

2.2.7.7  At the end of an interview the discussion should be summarised to make sure that no misunderstandings exist. A written record may be made of the interview and this may be discussed with the witness to clarify any anomalies. Subject to any national law, it may be possible to provide the interviewee with a copy of the written record.

## 2.2.8 Selection of interviewees

Established marine casualty and incident investigation procedures should be taken into account when determining whom to interview following a marine casualty. Safety concerns should be paramount in the scheduling of interviews.

The aim should always be to get the investigation team to the site of the occurrence as soon as possible and to interview those most closely involved, which in the marine sense will always be the ship first. When that is not possible due to external factors such as the geographical location of the occurrence or political considerations, it may be possible to nominate a local representative to carry out an interim investigation. From an investigation management point of view, it should be possible to start the process by carrying out at least some interviews of individuals ashore.

It may not be possible to speak directly with port or pilotage authorities in some parts of the world. Where that is so, every effort should be made to obtain at least a transcript of the pilot's statement if one is involved. In the event of a collision in enclosed waters, evidence from the operators of shore-based electronic surveillance equipment can be particularly useful. There are no "hard and fast" rules for selecting whom to interview, and the following is offered as an example only:

### 2.2.8.1 On site (those nearest the incident)

Generally it is beneficial to begin the interview process with the ship management team, including the master and chief engineer, who typically can provide an overview of the occurrence.

- First-hand witnesses present at the occurrence site at the time of the occurrence itself, regardless of rank/position in the organization.
- First-hand witnesses present at the occurrence site at the time of the occurrence itself, but from outside the organization, for instance berthing or mooring assistants, or visiting personnel such as agents or contractors.
- First-hand witnesses present at the time of the occurrence but not at the occurrence location itself, for instance ship's staff on the bridge of a ship witnessing a mooring occurrence on the main deck below.
- First-hand witnesses present at the time of the occurrence but not at the occurrence location itself and from outside the organization, for instance a pilot on the bridge witnessing a mooring occurrence on the main deck below.
- Those not involved with the occurrence itself but involved in the immediate aftermath of an occurrence, for instance those engaged in damage control, shipboard fire- fighting or first-aid medical treatment.
- Tug, mooring boat or pilot cutter crews.
- Search and rescue personnel including helicopter crews.
- Shore-based fire-fighters.
- Jetty/terminal staff.
- Other vessels in the immediate vicinity.
- Operators of Vessel Traffic Services (VTS) or monitoring systems.

### 2.2.8.2 Remote from occurrence site

- Designated person under the ISM Code.
- Ship operators ashore.
- Technical superintendents ashore.
- Company general managers ashore.
- Specialists/consultants (relevant to the occurrence).
- Port State inspectors.
- Flag State inspectors.
- Regulatory authorities.
- Representatives of classification societies.
- Safety committee members including crew representatives.
- Designers, shipbuilders, manufacturers and repairers.

### 2.3 Topics to be covered by the investigator[ii]

    The diagram shows a number of factors that have a direct or indirect impact on human behaviour and the potential to perform tasks. The headings in the diagram are expanded below:

### 2.3.1 People factors

- ability, skills, knowledge (outcome of training and experience)
- personality (mental condition, emotional state)
- physical condition (medical fitness, drugs and alcohol, fatigue)
- activities prior to accident/occurrence
- assigned duties at time of accident/occurrence
- actual behaviour at time of accident/occurrence
- attitude

### 2.3.2 Organization on board

- division of tasks and responsibilities
- composition of the crew (nationality/competence)
- manning level
- workload/complexity of tasks
- working hours/rest hours
- procedures and standing orders
- communication (internal and external)
- on-board management and supervision
- organization of on-board training and drills
- teamwork, including resource management
- planning (voyages, cargo, maintenance)

### 2.3.3 Working and living conditions

- level of automation
- ergonomic design of working, living and recreation areas and equipment
- adequacy of living conditions
- opportunities for recreation
- adequacy of food
- level of ship motion, vibrations, heat and noise

### 2.3.4 Ship factors

- design

---

[ii] Appendix 2 provides appropriate areas of inquiry and Appendix 3 provides definitions of common human element terms.

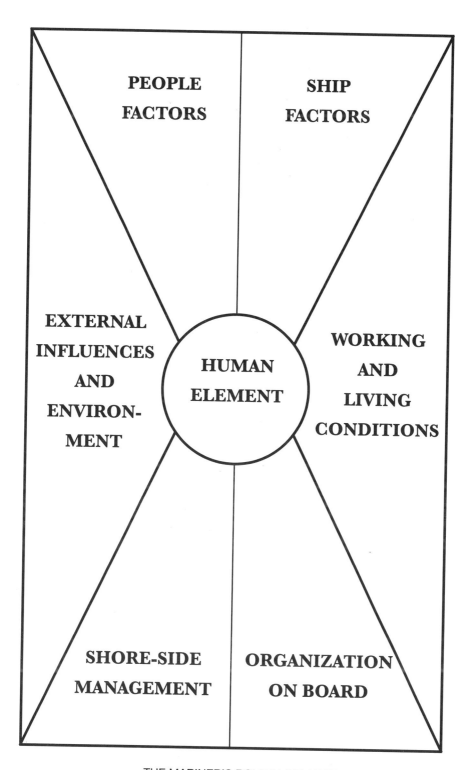

PEOPLE FACTORS

SHIP FACTORS

EXTERNAL INFLUENCES AND ENVIRON- MENT

HUMAN ELEMENT

WORKING AND LIVING CONDITIONS

SHORE-SIDE MANAGEMENT

ORGANIZATION ON BOARD

- state of maintenance
- equipment (availability, reliability)
- cargo characteristics, including securing, handling and care
- certificates

### 2.3.5 Shore-side management

- policy on recruitment
- safety policy and philosophy (culture, attitude and trust)
- management commitment to safety
- scheduling of leave periods
- general management policy
- port scheduling
- contractual and/or industrial arrangements and agreements
- assignment of duties
- ship-shore communication

### 2.3.6 External influences and environment

- weather and sea conditions
- port and transit conditions (VTS, pilots, etc)
- traffic density
- ice conditions
- organizations representing shipowners and seafarers
- regulations, surveys and inspections (international, national, port, classification societies, etc.)

### 2.4 Analysis

Once facts are collected, they need to be analysed to help establish the sequence of events in the occurrence, and to draw conclusions about safety deficiencies uncovered by the investigation. Analysis is a disciplined activity that employs logic and reasoning to build a bridge between the factual information and the conclusions.

The first step in analysis is to review the factual information to clarify what is relevant and what is not, and to ensure the information is complete. This process can give guidance to the investigator as to what additional investigation needs to be carried out.

In normal investigation practice, gaps in information that cannot be resolved are usually filled in by logical extrapolation and reasonable assumptions. Such extrapolation and assumptions should be identified and a statement of the measure of certainty provided.

Despite best efforts, analysis may not lead to firm conclusions. In these cases, the more likely hypotheses should be presented.

## 2.4.1 Fact-finding and analysis

After fact-finding and analysis it should be possible to give a description of the occurrence, its background, the time it took place, and the events leading to it. The description should include such factual items as:

- the weather conditions;
- the operation(s) involved;
- the equipment in use, its capabilities, performance and any failures;
- the location of key personnel and their actions immediately before the incident;
- the pertinent regulations and instructions;
- uncontrolled hazards;
- changes of staff, procedures, equipment or processes that could have contributed to the occurrence;
- what safeguards were or were not in place to prevent the incident;
- response to the occurrence (first-aid, shut-down, fire-fighting, evacuation, search and rescue);
- medical treatment actions taken to mitigate the effects of the occurrence and the condition of injured parties, particularly if disabling injuries or death ensued;
- damage control including salvage;
- inventory of all consequences of the occurrence (injury, loss, damage or environmental damage); and
- general ship's condition.

It should also be possible to identify active and underlying factors such as:

- operational deviations;
- design aspects of hull structural failure;
- defects in resources and equipment;
- inappropriate use of resources and equipment;
- relevant personnel skill levels and their application;
- physiological factors (e.g. fatigue, stress, alcohol, illegal drugs, prescription medicine);
- why safeguards in place were inadequate or failed;
- role of safety programmes;
- problems relating to the effectiveness of regulations and instructions;
- management issues; and
- communication issues.

## 2.5 Safety action

2.5.1    The ultimate goal of a marine safety investigation is to advance maritime safety and protection of the marine environment. In the context of these Guidelines, this goal is achieved by identifying safety deficiencies through a systematic investigation of marine casualties and incidents, and then recommending or effecting change in the maritime system to correct these deficiencies.

2.5.2    In a report that clearly lays out the facts relevant to the occurrence, and then logically analyses those facts to draw reasoned conclusions including those relating to human factors, the required safety action may appear self-evident to the reader.

2.5.3    Recommended safety action in whatever form should clearly identify what needs to be done, who or what organization is responsible for effecting change, and, where possible, the urgency for completion of the change.

## 3 REPORTING PROCEDURES

3.1    To facilitate the flow of information from casualty investigations, each report should conform to a basic format as outlined in section 14 of this resolution.

3.2    Reports should be made to IMO in accordance with established procedures[iii].

3.3    Persons and/or organizations with a vested interest in a report should be given the opportunity to comment on the report or relevant parts thereof before it is finalized.

3.4    The final report should be distributed to relevant parties involved and should preferably be made public.

## 4 QUALIFICATIONS AND TRAINING OF INVESTIGATORS

4.1    A variety of contributory factors can play a significant part in the events preceding a marine casualty or incident. The question of who should be charged with the responsibility for investigating and analysing human factors therefore becomes important. The skilled marine casualty and incident investigator generally is the person best suited to conduct all but the most specialized aspects of human factor investigation.

4.2    An investigator should have appropriate experience and formal training in marine casualty investigation. The formal training should include specific training in the identification of human factors in marine casualties and incidents.

4.3    In some cases, a human factors specialist may be of significant value in the investigation.

---

[iii]    Refer to MSC/Circ.827-MEPC/Circ.333 of 9 December 1997 on reports on marine casualties and incidents.

## Appendix 1 to Resolution A.884(21)

## THE IMO/ILO PROCESS FOR INVESTIGATING HUMAN FACTORS

The following is a process that provides a step-by-step systematic approach for use in the investigation of human factors. The process is an integration and adaptation of a number of human factor frameworks — SHEL (Hawkins, 1987) and Reason's (1990) Accident Causation and generic error-modelling system (GEMS) frameworks, as well as Rasmussen's Taxonomy of Error (1987).

The process can be applied to both types of occurrences, i.e., accidents and incidents. The process consists of the following steps:

.1    collect occurrence data;

.2    determine occurrence sequence;

.3    identify unsafe acts/decisions and unsafe conditions; and then for each unsafe act/decision,

.4    identify the error type or violation;

.5    identify underlying factors; and

.6    identify potential safety problems and develop safety actions.

Steps 3 to 5 are useful to the investigation because they facilitate the identification of latent unsafe conditions. Step 6, the identification of potential safety problems, is based extensively on what factors were identified as underlying factors. At times, an unsafe condition may be a result of a natural occurrence; in that case, the investigator may jump from step 3 to step 6. At other times, an unsafe act or decision may result from an unsafe condition which itself was established by a fallible decision; in such a case, the investigator should proceed through steps 3 to 6.

## Step 1 — Collect occurrence data

The first step in the human factors investigation process is the collection of work-related information regarding the personnel, tasks, equipment, and environmental conditions involved in the occurrence. A systematic approach to this step is crucial to ensure that a comprehensive analysis is possible and that the logistical requirements of collecting, organizing and maintaining a relevant occurrence related database are met.

For complex systems, where there are numerous interactions between the component elements, there is constant danger that critical information will be overlooked or lost during an investigation.

Use of the SHEL model as an organizational tool for the investigator's workplace data collection helps avoid downstream problems because:

.1    it takes into consideration all the important work system elements;

.2    it promotes the consideration of the interrelationships between these work system elements; and

.3    it focuses on the factors which influence human performance by relating all peripheral elements to the central liveware element.

PART C 3

The process initially attempts to answer the more simplistic questions of "what, who, and when" and then moves to the more complicated questions of "how and why". The resulting data becomes, for the most part, a collection of events and circumstances comprised of acts and conditions. Some of these will be of interest as unsafe acts and unsafe conditions.

There are four components to the SHEL model:

**Liveware - L , Hardware - H , Software - S , Environment - E.**

The SHEL Model is commonly depicted graphically to display not only the four components but also the relationships, or interfaces, between the liveware and all the other components. Figure 1 attempts to portray the fact that the match or mismatch of the interfaces is just as important as the characteristics of the blocks themselves. A mismatch can be a source of human error and identification of a mismatch may be the identification of a safety deficiency in the system. Figure 2 also depicts how this model can be applied to a complex system where multiple liveware, hardware, software and environmental elements exist.

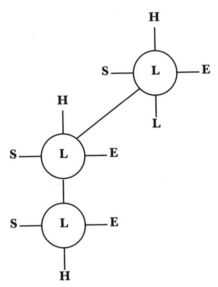

*Figure 1. (Adapted from Hawkins, 1987) SHEL Model*

### Liveware (central component)
The most valuable and flexible component in the system is the human element, the liveware, placed at the centre of the model. Each person brings his or her own capabilities and limitations, be they physical, physiological, psychological, or psychosocial. This component can be applied to any person involved with the operation or in support of the operation. The person under consideration interacts directly with each one of the four other elements. Each person and each interaction, or interface, constitute potential areas of human performance investigation.

### Liveware (peripheral)
The peripheral liveware refers to the system's human-human interactions, including such factors as management, supervision, crew interactions and communications.

## Hardware

Hardware refers to the equipment part of a transportation system. It includes the design of work stations, displays, controls, seats, etc.

## Software

Software is the non-physical part of the system including organizational policies, procedures, manuals, checklist layout, charts, maps, advisories and, increasingly, computer programs.

## Environment

Environment includes the internal and external climate, temperature, visibility, vibration, noise and other factors which constitute the conditions within which people are working. Sometimes the broad political and economic constraints under which the system operates are included in this element. The regulatory climate is a part of the environment inasmuch as it affects communications, decision-making, control, and co-ordination.

## Step 2 — Determine occurrence sequence

As the investigator moves to addressing questions of "how and why", there is a need to link the data identified in the first step of the process. Reason's (1990) model of accident causation, utilizing a production framework, can be used by an investigator as a guide to developing an occurrence sequence. Reason's model facilitates further organization of the work system data collected using the SHEL model, and an improved understanding of the influence of that data on human performance. The occurrence sequence is developed by arranging the information regarding occurrence events and circumstances around one of five production elements, i.e., *decision makers, line management, preconditions, productive activities, and defence.*

The production elements themselves are basically aligned in a temporal context. This temporal aspect is an important organizing factor since the events and circumstances that can lead to an accident or incident are not necessarily proximate in time, nor in location, to the site of occurrence. By establishing a sequential ordering of the data, Reason's (1990) concept of *active* versus *latent* factors is introduced.

Active factors are the final events or circumstances which led to an occurrence. Their effect is often immediate because they occur either directly in the system's defence (e.g., disabled warning system) or the site of the productive activities (i.e., the integrated activities of the work system's *liveware, software* and *hardware* elements), which would indirectly result in the breaching of the system's defence (e.g., use of the wrong procedure).

*Underlying factors* may reside at both the personal and the organizational levels; they may be present in the conditions that exist within a given work system (referring to the preconditions element in the model). Examples of *underlying factors* include inadequate regulations, inadequate procedures, insufficient training, high workload and undue time pressure.

In practice, steps 1 and 2 may not be mutually exclusive. As the investigator begins the data collection step, it would be only natural that an attempt be made to place the information, albeit often fragmentary in the preliminary stages of an investigation, into the context of an occurrence sequence. To facilitate this concurrent activity, the SHEL and Reason models can be combined as illustrated in figure 2 (overleaf).

PART

C

3

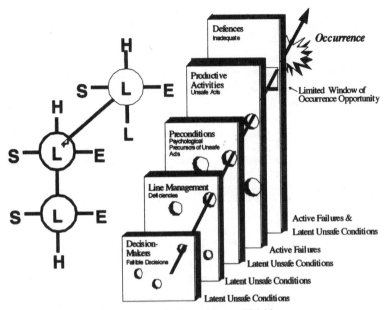

*Figure 2. SHEL and Reason Hybrid*

*The data collected during an investigation (i.e. events and circumstances) can be organized, using multiple components of the modified SHEL model, into a framework surrounding an occurrence template (in this case the occurrence scenario), based upon the Reason model. Causal factors, i.e. the unsafe acts/decisions and conditions, are thereby identified.*

### Steps 3 to 5 — An overview

Steps 3 to 5 are based upon the GEMS framework. The framework provides "pathways" that lead from the identification of the unsafe act/decision (Step 3) to the identification of what was erroneous about the action or decision (Step 4) and finally to its placement within a behavioural context (i.e., a failure mode within a given level of performance in Step 5). The GEMS framework illustrated in figure 3 is particularly useful in exploring hypothetical reconstructions of the occurrence.

### Step 3 — Identify unsafe acts/decisions and conditions

In step 3 of the process, the information gathered and organized using the SHEL and Reason frameworks is used to initiate identification of causal factors, i.e., unsafe acts/decisions and conditions. An unsafe act is defined as an error or violation that is committed in the presence of a hazard or potential unsafe condition. Decisions where there are no apparent resultant actions but which have a negative impact on safety should also be considered as unsafe acts. An unsafe condition or hazard, as noted above, is an event or circumstance that has the potential to result in a mishap. There may be several acts, decisions and/or conditions which are potential unsafe candidates, thus necessitating iterative assessments of the occurrence facts. The SHEL and Reason hybrid tool (refer to figure 2) can provide a useful base for conducting such iterative assessments.

Once an unsafe act, decision or condition has been identified, the next stage is to determine the genesis of that particular act or condition. Further investigation and/or analysis may reveal other unsafe acts/decisions or conditions antecedent to the causal factor that was initially identified.

As noted earlier, several unsafe acts and decisions may be identified throughout steps 1 and 2 of the process. The last unsafe act precipitating the occurrence often provides a convenient starting point for reconstruction of the occurrence. This last act or decision differs from the others in that it can be viewed as the definitive action or decision which led to the occurrence, i.e., the last act or decision that made the accident or incident inevitable — **the primary cause of the initial event**. Although it is usually an active failure, the last unsafe act or decision can be embedded in a latent unsafe condition, such as a flawed design decision which led to a system failure.

## Step 4 — Identify error or violation type

This portion of the process is initiated for each unsafe act/decision by posing the simple question "What is erroneous or wrong about the action or decision that eventually made it unsafe?".

The identification of the type of error or violation involves two sub-steps (see figure 3):

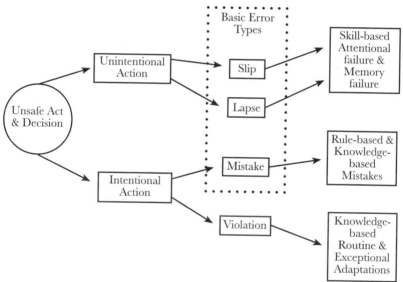

*Figure 3. The GEMS Framework (Adapted from Reason, 1990)*

*The GEMS framework facilitates the linkage of an error/violation to an individual's level of performance at the time the failure occurred.*

### 1) Unintentional or intentional action

First it is necessary to determine whether the error or violation was an unintentional or intentional action. "Did the person intend the action?" If the answer to that question is no, then it is an unintentional action. Unintentional actions are actions that do not go as planned; these are errors in execution.

If the answer to the question "Did the person intend the action?" is yes, then the action is intentional. Intentional actions are actions that are carried out as planned but the actions are inappropriate; these are errors in planning.

THE MARINER'S ROLE IN COLLECTING EVIDENCE 335

## 2) Error type or violation

The second sub-step is the selection of the error type or violation that best describes the failure, keeping in mind the decision regarding intentionality. There are four potential error/violation categories, i.e., *slip, lapse, mistake and violation*. A *slip* is an unintentional action where the failure involves attention. These are errors in execution. A *lapse* is an unintentional action where the failure involves memory. These are also errors in execution. A *mistake* is an intentional action, but there is no deliberate decision to act against a rule or plan. These are errors in planning. A *violation* is a planning failure where a deliberate decision to act against a rule or plan has been made. Routine violations occur everyday as people regularly modify or do not strictly comply with work procedures, often because of poorly designed or defined work practices. In contrast, an exceptional violation tends to be a one-time breach of a work practice, such as where safety regulations are deliberately ignored to carry out a task. Even so, the intention was not to commit a malevolent act but just to get the job done.

## Step 5 — Identify underlying factors

The designation of separate activities implied by steps 4 and 5 may be somewhat arbitrary in terms of what actually occurs when an investigator attempts to reveal the relationship between the occurrence errors/violations and the behaviour that lead to them. In simplest terms, behaviour consists of a decision and an action or movement. In step 3, the action or decision (i.e., unsafe act or decision) was identified. In step 4, what was erroneous regarding that action or decision was revealed. In step 5, the focus is on uncovering the underlying causes behind the act or decision of an individual or group. To do so it is important to determine whether there were any factors in the work system that may have facilitated the expression of the given failure mode (and hence the error/violation and the unsafe act). These factors have been termed underlying factors. They can be found by examining the work system information collected and organized using the SHEL or Reason frameworks in steps 1 and 2. The re-examination of these data emphasizes the iterative nature of this investigative process in that it may even be deemed necessary to conduct further investigations into the occurrence.

## Step 6 — Identify potential safety problems and develop safety actions

The identification of potential safety problems is based extensively on what factors were identified as underlying factors. Once again this underscores the importance of the application of a systematic approach to steps 1 and 2 of the process, which lays the foundation for the subsequent analysis steps. Where appropriate, potential safety problems can be further analysed to identify the associated risk to the system and to develop safety actions.

## References

Edwards, E (1972). Man and machine: Systems for safety. In *Proceedings of the BALPA Technical Symposium*, London.

Hawkins, F.H. (1987). *Human factors in flight*. Aldershot, UK: Gower Technical Press.

Nagel, D.C. (1988). Human error in aviation operations. In E.L. Weiner and D.C. Nagel (Eds.), *Human factors in aviation* (pp. 263-303). San Diego, CA: Academic Press.

Norman, D.A. (1981). Categorization of action slips, *Psychological Review*, 88 (1), 1-15.

Norman, D.A. (1988). *The psychology of everyday things*. New York: Basic Books.

Rasmussen, J. (1987). The definition of human error and a taxonomy for technical system design. In J. Rasmussen, K. Duncan, and J. Leplat (Eds.), *New technology and human error*. Toronto: John Wiley & Sons.

Reason, J. (1990). *Human error*. New York: Cambridge University Press.

## Appendix 2 to Resolution A.884(21)

## AREAS OF HUMAN FACTORS INQUIRY

The following questions are designed to aid the investigator while investigating for human factors. Skilful questioning can help the investigator eliminate irrelevant lines of inquiry and focus on areas of greater potential significance.

The order and manner in which the questions are asked will depend on who is being interviewed and on his or her willingness and ability to describe personal behaviour and personal impressions. It may be necessary to verify, cross-check or augment information received from one person by interviewing others on the same points.

These areas of inquiry can be used in planning interviews. The following questions are not meant to be exhaustive, or be used as a checklist, and some may not be relevant in the investigation of a particular accident. As new human factors issues emerge, new areas of inquiry will need to be explored by investigators.

## SHIPBOARD ISSUES

### 1 Safety policy

.1 Does the Company have a written safety policy?

.2 Is there a designated person to deal with shipboard safety matters in the Company?

.3 When did a Company representative last visit the ship, or when were you last in contact with the Company?

.4 When were you last given safety training? What was the training and how was it provided?

.5 When was the last emergency drill (e.g., fire, abandon ship, man overboard, pollution response, etc) and what did you do during the drill?

.6 Was appropriate personal protective equipment provided and did you use it?

.7 Are you aware of any personal accidents which occurred on board in the period prior to the accident?

### 2 Activities prior to incident

.1 (If the ship was leaving port at the time of the accident) In general, how did you spend your time while the ship was in port?

.2 (If the ship was approaching port or at sea at the time of the accident) How long has the ship been on passage since its last port or terminal operation?

.3    What were you doing immediately prior to coming on watch or reporting for duty, and for how long? Recreational activity? Physical exercise? Sleeping? Reading? Watching television? Eating? Paperwork? Travelling to vessel?

.4    Specifically what were you doing approximately 4 h ....., 1 h ....., 30 min ..... before the accident?

.5    What evolution was the ship involved in when the accident occurred? What was your role during that evolution?

.6    Immediately prior to the accident, what were you thinking about?

.7    At any time before the accident, did you have any indication that anyone was tired or unable to perform their duty?

## 3 Duties at the time of accident

.1    Where were you on the ship when the accident occurred?

.2    What specific job or duty were you assigned at the time? By whom? Did you understand your assignment? Did you receive any conflicting orders?

.3    How often have you performed this job in the past (on the specific ship involved in the accident)?

## 4 Actual behaviour at time of accident

.1    Precisely where were you located at the time of the accident?

.2    What specific task were you performing at the time of the accident?

.3    Had you at any time since reporting for duty found that you could not concentrate (focus your attention/keep your mind) on a task you were trying to perform?

## 5 Training/education/certification/professional experience

.1    How long have you been assigned to this ship? Have you requested that your assignment be lengthened or shortened?

.2    How long have you filled your crew position? What other crew positions have you held on this ship?

.3    How long have you held the certificate indicating your qualifications?

.4    Before being assigned to this ship, did you work on other ships? If so, what crew positions have you held?

.5    What is the longest time you have been to sea in a single voyage? How long have you been at sea on this passage? What was your longest single passage?

## 6 Physical condition

.1    Were you feeling ill or sick at any time in the 24 hours immediately before the accident? If so, what symptoms did you have? Did you have a fever, vomit, feel dizzy, other? Also, did you tell anyone? What do you believe the cause was?

.2    When was the last meal you had prior the accident? What did you eat? Was it adequate?

.3    Do you exercise regularly while on board? When did you last exercise (before the accident)? How long was the session?

# 7 Psychological, emotional, mental condition and employment conditions

.1    When was the last time you felt cheerful or elated on board the ship, and what were the circumstances that generated this emotion?

.2    When was the last time you were sad or depressed or dejected, on board the ship? Why? Did you talk about it with anyone else?

.3    Have you had to make any difficult personal decisions recently? Have you had any financial or family worries on your mind recently?

.4    Have you been criticized for how you are doing your work lately? By whom? Was it justified?

.5    What was the most stressful situation you had to deal with on the voyage (prior to the accident)? When did the situation occur? How was it resolved?

.6    What are the contractual arrangements for all crew members?

.7    Have there been any complaints or industrial action in the last (12) months?

# 8 Workload/complexity of tasks

.1    What is the shipboard organization?

.2    Is the shipboard organization effective?

.3    What is your position in the shipboard organization (i.e., who do you work for, report to or assign duties to)?

.4    What is the nature of your work? Sedentary? Physically demanding?

.5    Was anyone involved in the accident impaired due to heavy workload?

# 9 Work-period/rest-period/recreation pattern

.1    What is your normal duty schedule?

.2    Are you a day worker or a watchkeeper?

.3    What was your duty schedule on the day before the accident and during the week before the accident?

.4    Were you on overtime at the time of the accident?

.5    How long had you been on duty, or awake performing other work, at the time of the accident?

.6    When was your last period of sleep? How long did it last? How often did you awaken during your last sleep period? Did you awaken refreshed? If not, what would have made your sleep period more restful?

.7    How do you normally spend your off-duty time while on board? Play cards? Read? Listen to music? Watch television? Other?

.8    When was your last extended period of off duty time when your were able to rest?

## 10 Relationship with other crew members and superiors/subordinates

.1   Who among the crew would you consider to be a friend?

.2   Do you find any members of the crew unpleasant to be with?

.3   Do you have difficulty talking with any of the crew members because of language barriers?

.4   Have any new crew members recently joined the ship? Have you had a chance to get acquainted with them?

.5   Did you have any argument recently with another crew member?

.6   In an emergency, would you trust your fellow crew members to come to your assistance?

.7   Has another crew member ever offered to take your place on watch or perform a duty for you to let you get some extra rest?

.8   What was the subject of your last conversation with another crew member before reporting for duty (when the accident occurred)?

.9   Have you talked with any other crew members since the accident? If so, what was the subject of your conversation? Have you talked with anyone else about the accident prior to being interviewed?

## 11 Living conditions and shipboard environment

.1   Do you consider your personal area on board the ship to be comfortable? If not, how would you like it to be improved?

.2   Prior to the accident, did you have any difficulty resting as a result of severe weather, noise levels, heat/cold, ship's motion, etc.?

## 12 Manning levels

Is the manning level sufficient in your opinion for the operation of the ship?

## 13 Master's standing orders

.1   Are there written standing orders to the whole crew complement from the master?

.2   Did the master/chief engineer provide written or verbal standing orders to the watchkeeping personnel?

.3   Were the orders in conflict with the Company safety policy?

## 14 Level of automation/reliability of equipment

.1   In your opinion, was the system reliable?

.2   Were there earlier failures in the system?

.3   Were the failures repaired by the crew or shore-based workers?

## 15 Ship design, motion/cargo characteristics

Did you observe anything out of the ordinary on this passage concerning ship design or motion or cargo characteristics?

## SHORE-SIDE MANAGEMENT ISSUES

### 16  Scheduling of work and rest periods

What is the Company's work schedule and relief policy?

### 17  Manning level

How is the manning level determined for your fleet?

### 18  Watchkeeping practices

.1    Do you require the master to stand watch?

.2    Do you leave the watchkeeping practices to the discretion of the master?

### 19  Assignment of duties

Do you leave this matter to the master?

### 20  Shore-ship-shore support and communications

How do you support the ship's master?

### 21  Management policies

Does the Company have a written safety policy?

### 22  Voyage planning and port call schedules

How does the master plan the voyages?

### 23  Recreational facilities

Are welfare/recreational services and facilities provided on board?

### 24  Contractual and/or industrial arrangements and agreements

.1    What are the contractual agreements for all crew members?

.2    Have there been any complaints or industrial action in the last (12) months?

### 25  National/international requirements

Are the management and master complying with the requirements and recommendations of the applicable international conventions and flag State regulations?

PART C 3

## Appendix 3 to Resolution A.884(21)

## DEFINITIONS — COMMON HUMAN ELEMENT TERMS

| | |
|---|---|
| Human error: | A departure from acceptable or desirable practice on the part of an individual or group of individuals that can result in unacceptable or undesirable results. |

**Diminished human performance:**

| | |
|---|---|
| Emotional: | A physiological state of agitation or disturbance which can affect an individual's normal ability to perform required tasks. |
| Panic: | A sudden overpowering fear that reduces the ability to perform required tasks. |
| Anxiety: | A state of uneasiness and distress about future uncertainties which may reduce the ability to focus properly on a required task. |
| Personal problem: | A problem which preoccupies the emotions and reduces the ability to perform required tasks. Examples include physical disabilities, death or illness in the family, marital and other relationship problems, health concerns, financial problems, anger, or poor interactions with shipmates. |
| Mental impairment: | Diminished mental ability that can reduce or impede an individual's normal ability to perform the mental part of required tasks. |
| Alcohol use: | Consumption of alcoholic beverages which diminishes an individual's abilities to perform required tasks. Examples include drinking on or too close to duty, which can impede an individual's abilities; drunkenness on duty; drinking off duty, which results in poor performance while on duty; and excessive drinking over a longer period of time, which results in a permanent decrease in mental abilities. |
| Drug use: | Use of a medicine or narcotic which affects an individual's abilities to perform required tasks. There are many different effects on mental and physical capabilities that can result from the use of legal and illegal drugs, including extreme drowsiness, a false sense of competence, and hallucinations. The mental abilities of the user may also be distracted by the constant need to obtain more drugs. In addition, individuals may not be aware of the side-effects of legal drugs and may take them while on duty or forget to report taking them. |
| Inattention: | The loss of attention, notice or regard; neglect. Examples include failing to monitor displays; not maintaining a proper lookout; forgetting to perform an assigned duty. Inattention may also be the result of other causes such as a personal problem, fatigue, drugs, boredom, or hearing problems. |

| | |
|---|---|
| Injury: | Physical damage to the body which causes a decrease in mental or physical abilities. Examples include a head injury, other injuries such as a smashed finger, or a severe burn, where pain causes distraction and a loss of mental ability. |
| Mental illness: | Psychotic or erratic behaviour; depression; hallucinations; other forms of abnormal behaviour which are unexplainable. |
| Physical illness: | Sickness which produces a decrease in mental or physical abilities, but not generally considered as mental illness. Examples include: general disability accompanying colds and flu; hallucinations due to high fever; migraine headaches; seasickness and even severe indigestion and exposure to toxic substances. |
| Diminished motivation: | Lack of will or desire to perform well, resulting in a decrease of an individual's normal performance of required tasks. |
| Deliberate misaction: | Purposely taking an incorrect action or purposely failing to take the correct action. Examples include dereliction of duty; refusal to obey commands; sabotage, theft or ignoring procedures. |
| Fatigue: | A reduction in physical and/or mental capability as the result of physical, mental or emotional exertion, which may impair nearly all physical abilities including: strength; speed; reaction time; co-ordination; decision making, or balance. |
| Low morale: | A problem with individual or group motivation as shown by reduced willingness, confidence or discipline to perform assigned tasks. Examples/causes may include interpersonal conflict amongst the crew, officers with poor interpersonal skills, lack of a strong corporate or shipboard safety culture; excessively long tours of duty. |
| Lack of self-discipline: | Inadequate ability of an individual to control personal conduct. Examples include loss of temper or unprofessional behaviour. |
| Visual problem: | A reduced visual acuity due to a specific physical disability. Causes may include eye injury causing total or partial blindness; not wearing prescribed glasses or contacts; inability to adequately adapt to darkness. |
| Excessive workload: | Diminished physical or mental capability as the result of the sum total of all the mental and physical tasks a human must perform within a prescribed time resulting in a diminished job performance. |

**Marine environment:**

| | |
|---|---|
| Hazardous natural | A situation in which the natural environment causes required tasks to become more difficult than usual. Examples include storms; high waves; shallow water; severe shoaling; strong currents or tides; ice, rocks, submerged wrecks, severe eddies, ship traffic, wind; fog; mist; rain; snow; sleet; haze; dust; airborne debris. |

P
A
R
T

C

3

| Poor human factors design: | Poor design of the ship, its subsystems, its environmental controls, engineering or its human-machine interfaces, which results in an increased difficulty to perform shipboard tasks. Examples of poor human factors engineering design include inadequate lighting; excessive noise; excessive vibration; inadequate heating, cooling, or ventilation systems; hazardous deck stair, ladder, bulkhead, or work surfaces; inadequate provision for foul weather or degraded mode operations; inadequate restraints, guards, or hand-holds; poor work station orientation in regard to ship dynamics; poor hull seakeeping characteristics; controls which allow accidental actuation; illegible or ambiguous control markings; illegible or ambiguous displays or display labels; poor layout, sizing, and colouring of controls and displays; inadequate design for operational or maintenance access; inadequate design for safety. |
|---|---|
| Poor operations: | A situation in which individuals or groups of individuals degrade the shipboard environment making the performance of some required tasks more difficult. Examples include ship manoeuvres (e.g. increased speed, change in course, erratic manoeuvres) impact on ship dynamics, causing balance and restraint difficulties when personnel performing one task interfere with those performing another; or where storage of cargo impedes access or transit. |
| Poor maintenance: | Failure to keep any part of the ship or its equipment in the condition in which it was designed to function within a designated lifetime or operational period, thus degrading the shipboard environment and making the performance of some required tasks more difficult. Examples of poor maintenance impacting on required tasks: inadequate replacement parts and tools to perform proper maintenance, resulting from a lack of commitment from management. |

**Marine environment:**

| Inadequate technical knowledge | Not having, due to inadequate experience and/or training, the general knowledge which is required for the individual's job on board. Examples include navigation, seamanship, propulsion systems, cargo handling, communications, and weather. |
|---|---|
| Inadequate situational communication/ awareness | Not knowing, due to inadequate experience, lack of communication, co-ordination and/or training, the current status of the ship, its systems, or its environment. Examples include lack of knowledge of location, heading or speed and lack of knowledge of status of ongoing maintenance on board. |

| Lack of communication or coordination | Not making use of all available information sources to determine current status. This may be the result of a lack of initiative on the part of the individual or a lack of initiative and/or co-operation on the part of others. Examples of poor communication/co-ordination include: poor communication between bridge officers, poor communication with pilots, and poor deck-to-engine-room co-ordination |
|---|---|
| Inadequate knowledge of ship operations: | Lack of knowledge resulting from inadequate experience, ignorance of regulations, inadequate knowledge of procedures, inadequate training, and/or unawareness of role/task/responsibility. Examples of areas where an individual might lack knowledge: navigation, seamanship, propulsion systems, cargo handling, communications, and weather. |
| Inadequate knowledge of regulations/standards: | Lack of knowledge or understanding of required regulations due to inadequate experience and/or training. Examples of possible regulations; company policies and standards, national and international regulations, maritime regulations of other port States, local jurisdiction regulations, shipboard regulations, cautionary notices, chart notations, or labelling. |
| Inadequate knowledge of ship procedures: | Not knowing due to inadequate experience and/or training the shipboard and company policies requiring adequate knowledge of your own ship's operation. Examples include emergency procedures, maintenance procedures, administrative procedures, and safety system procedures. |
| Unaware of role/task responsibility: | Inadequate knowledge of the specific job required of an individual. Examples include a lack of understanding of command responsibilities, communications responsibilities, safety responsibilities, maintenance responsibilities and emergency responsibilities. |
| Inadequate language skills: | A lack of the basic language skills necessary to communicate and perform duties as required. This includes total or partial inability to speak, read or comprehend the primary language and/or other required language sufficiently to understand shipboard commands, instructions, procedures, labels, warnings and regulations. |

**Management:**

| Failure to maintain discipline: | Failing to ensure that personnel submit to authority, regulations and procedures. Examples include: tolerating unqualified or inept personnel, not enforcing regulations and procedures, tolerating insubordination. |
|---|---|
| Failure of command: | Mistakes in giving commands. Examples of faulty command include: proper command not given, proper command not given at the appropriate time or out of sequence with other commands, incorrect commands, conflicting commands. |

| | |
|---|---|
| Inadequate supervision: | Inadequate oversight of activities of personnel under an individual's supervision. Examples of faulty supervision include: not checking to see that a job was performed in a timely and correct manner, not providing proper resources to deal with problems brought to the attention of supervising individual, unequal treatment of personnel. |
| Inadequate coordination or communication: | Failure to communicate and co-ordinate to address issues, problems and tasks both aboard ship and ashore. Examples include: poor communication between bridge officers, poor communication with pilots, poor communication with home office, poor deck-to-engine-room co-ordination. |
| Inadequate management of physical resources: | Poor management of physical resources, namely the tools, equipment, supplies, facilities, food, water, fuel, etc., needed to perform tasks. Examples of faulty management of physical resources include: absence of physical resources, shortage of physical resources, inappropriate physical resources, physical resources stored improperly, physical resources difficult to obtain when needed. |
| Inadequate manning: | Failing to ensure that all required tasks aboard ship can be properly performed and that there are adequate personnel of the proper skill level, physical and mental ability, experience, certification, and inclination to properly perform those tasks. |
| Inadequate manpower available: | Not assigning, or not ensuring the availability of, adequate personnel with appropriate skill levels to a ship, or to a specific task aboard the ship, to ensure safe and efficient operation. |
| Poor job design: | Specifying job or task requirements which are unreasonable, inefficient, impossible, excessive, or impractical. Examples include: excessive watch duration or frequency, requiring a single person to monitor simultaneously displays that are spastically separated, requiring exposure to hazardous materials without proper protective gear. |
| Poor regulations, policies, procedures or practices: | Any problem with standards, regulations, policies, procedures or practices. For example: standards, regulations, policies, procedures, or practices may be conflicting, inaccurate, inadequate, lacking in sufficient detail, or outdated. |
| Misapplication of good regulations, policies, procedures or practices: | The application of standards, regulations, policies, procedures or practices at an incorrect time or in an inappropriate circumstance. |

PART C 3

**Mental action:**

| | |
|---|---|
| Lack of situational awareness | An incorrect understanding of the current situation which can lead to a faulty hypothesis regarding a future situation, or an understanding which is based upon incorrect beliefs, leading to compounded errors that can substantially increase the risk to the ship. Examples include arriving at a hypothesis without confirmation of which direction an oncoming ship will steer, incorrect interpretation of alarms on board ship (e.g. seawater contamination of a fuel system during high seas). |
| Lack of perception: | When an individual does not properly understand that a problem or situation exists. Examples include misreading a dial, mishearing a command, misunderstanding a garbled radio message, thinking you smell engine oil when it's actually crude, not noticing a list to starboard, overestimating the distance to the dock. |
| Incorrect recognition: | The misdiagnosis of a particular situation or problem once it has been perceived. While it may be perceived that a problem or situation exists, the identification is incorrect. Examples include misdiagnosis of a sounded alarm that sounds similar to other alarms on board ship, incorrect recognition of a visual display alarm on the bridge. |
| Incorrect identification: | The incorrect identification of a problem or hazard once it has been recognized that a problem or hazard exists. The alarms on a display panel may have identified a particular hazard to the ship (e.g. low fuel oil pressure), but the individual may have misinterpreted the alarm and identified the problem incorrectly. |

## Appendix 4 to Resolution A.884(21)

## SELECTED BIBLIOGRAPHY OF UNCLOS/ILO/IMO REQUIREMENTS AND RECOMMENDATIONS RELATED TO INVESTIGATION OF HUMAN FACTORS IN MARINE CASUALTIES AND INCIDENTS

## UNITED NATIONS CONVENTION ON THE LAW OF THE SEA

Article 94, Duties of the flag State, provides, in paragraph 7:

> *Each State shall cause an inquiry to be held by or before a suitably qualified person or persons into every marine casualty or incident of navigation on the high seas involving a ship flying its flag and causing loss of life or serious injury to nationals of another State or serious damage to ships or installations of another State or to the marine environment. The flag State and the other State shall co-operate in the conduct of any inquiry held by that other State into any such marine casualty or incident of navigation.*

### ILO (INTERNATIONAL LABOUR ORGANIZATION) CONVENTIONS AND RECOMMENDATIONS

#### Merchant Shipping (Minimum Standards) Convention, 1976 (No. 147)

**Article 2** provides:

> *Each Member which ratifies this Conventions undertakes" ..... "(g) to hold an official inquiry into any serious marine casualty involving ships registered in its territory, particularly those involving injury and/or loss of life, the final report of such inquiry normally to be made public."*

#### Prevention of Accidents (Seafarers) Convention, 1970 (No. 134)

**Article 2** provides:

> 1. *The competent authority in each maritime country shall take the necessary measures to ensure that occupational accidents are adequately reported and investigated, and comprehensive statistics of such accidents kept and analysed.*
>
> 2. *All occupational accidents shall be reported and statistics shall not be limited to fatalities or to accidents involving the ship.*
>
> 3. *The statistics shall record the numbers, nature, causes and effects of occupational accidents, with a clear indication of the department on board ship - for instance, deck, engine or catering - and of the area - for instance, at sea or in port - where the accident occurred.*
>
> 4. *The competent authority shall undertake an investigation into the causes and circumstances of occupational accidents resulting in loss of life or serious personal injury, and such other accidents as may be specified in national laws or regulations.*

**Article 3** provides:

> *In order to provide a sound basis for the prevention of accidents which are due to particular hazards of maritime employment, research shall be undertaken into general trends and into such hazards as are brought out by statistics.*

**Article 9** provides, in paragraph 2:

*All appropriate and practical measures shall also be taken to bring to the attention of seafarers information concerning particular hazards, for instance by means of official notices containing relevant instructions.*

## Prevention of Accidents (Seafarers) Recommendation, 1970 (No. 142)

**Paragraph 3** provides:

*Subjects to be investigated in pursuance of Article 3 of the Prevention of Accidents (Seafarers) Convention, 1970, might include -*

(a) *working environment, such as working surfaces, layout of machinery and means of access and lighting, and methods of work;*

(b) *incidence of accidents in different age groups;*

(c) *special physiological or psychological problems created by the shipboard environment;*

(d) *problems arising from physical stress on board ship, in particular as a consequence of increased workload;*

(e) *problems arising from and effects of technical developments and their influence on the composition of crews;*

(f) *problems arising from any human failures such as carelessness.*

## Dissemination of information to shipowner and seafarers

In addition to the provisions referred to above, Convention No. 134 also includes provisions concerning the responsibility of the competent authority to disseminate information gained from accident investigations and research and to bring it to the attention of shipowners and seafarers. The competent authority also has the responsibility to promote and ensure the training of seafarers in the prevention of accidents and in to take measures for their health and protection. Recommendation No. 142 provides further guidance on these subjects.

## IMO (INTERNATIONAL MARITIME ORGANIZATION) CONVENTIONS

## International Convention for the Safety of Life at Sea (SOLAS), 1974, as amended

**Regulation I/21**, *Casualties*, provides:

*(a) Each Administration undertakes to conduct an investigation of any casualty occurring to any of its ships subject to the provisions of the present Convention when it judges that such an investigation may assist in determining what changes in the present regulations might be desirable[iv].*

---

[iv]  Refer to the following resolutions adopted by the Organization: A.203(VII) - Recommendation on the conclusion of agreements and arrangements between States on the question of access and employment of foreign seaborne salvage equipment in territorial waters

| | |
|---|---|
| A.322(IX) | The conduct of investigation into casualties |
| A.442(XI) | Personnel and material resource needs of Administrations for the investigation of casualties and contravention of conventions |

Refer also to:

| | |
|---|---|
| MSC/Circ.70/Rev.1 | Questionnaire on the maritime distress system |
| MSC/Circ.224 | Submission of damage cards and intact stability casualty records |

*(b) Each Contracting Government undertakes to supply the Organization with pertinent information concerning the findings of such investigations. No reports or recommendations of the Organization based upon such information shall disclose the identity or nationality of the ships concerned or in any manner fix or imply responsibility upon any ship or person.*

## International Convention on Load Lines, 1966

Article 23, Casualties, provides:

*(1) Each Administration undertakes to conduct an investigation of any casualty occurring to ships for which it is responsible and which are subject to the provisions of the present Convention when it judges that such an investigation may assist in determining what changes in the Convention might be desirable.*

*(2) Each Contracting Government undertakes to supply the Organization with the pertinent information concerning the findings of such investigations. No reports or recommendations of the Organization based upon such information shall disclose the identity or nationality of the ships concerned or in any manner fix or imply responsibility upon any ship or person.*

## International Convention for the Prevention of Pollution from Ships, 1973, as modified by the Protocol of 1978 relating thereto (MARPOL 73/78)

**Article 8**, *Reports on incidents involving harmful substances*, provides:

*(1) A report of an incident shall be made without delay to the fullest extent possible in accordance with the provisions of Protocol I to the present Convention.*

*(2) Each Party to the Convention shall:*

.1 *make all arrangements necessary for an appropriate officer or agency to receive and process all reports on incidents; and*

.2 *notify the Organization with complete details of such arrangements for circulation to other Parties and Member States of the Organization.*

*(3) Whenever a Party receives a report under the provisions of the present article, that Party shall relay the report without delay to:*

.1 *the Administration of the ship involved; and*

.2 *any other State which may be affected.*

*(4) Each Party to the Convention undertakes to issue instructions to its maritime inspection vessels and aircraft and to other appropriate services, to report to its authorities any incident referred to in Protocol I to the present Convention. That Party shall, if it considers it appropriate, report accordingly to the Organization and to any other Party concerned.*

**Article 12**, *Casualties to ships*, provides:

*(1) Each Administration undertakes to conduct an investigation of any casualty occurring to any of its ships subject to the provisions of the Regulations if such a casualty has produced a major deleterious effect upon the marine environment.*

| | |
|---|---|
| MSC/Circ.388 | Fire casualty records |
| MSC/Circ.433 | Reports on investigations into serious casualties |
| MSC/Circ.539/Add.2 | Reports on casualty statistics concerning fishing vessels and fishermen at sea |
| MSC/Circ.559 | Guidelines to ensure the reporting to the Organization of incidents involving dangerous goods and marine pollutants in packaged form on board ships and in port areas |
| | MSC/Circ.621 Guidelines for the investigation of accidents where fatigue may have been a contributing factor |

*(2) Each Party to the Convention undertakes to supply the Organization with information concerning the findings of such investigation, when it judges that such information may assist in determining what changes in the present Convention might be desirable.*

## IMO ASSEMBLY RESOLUTIONS

### Assembly resolution A.849(20) - Code for the Investigation of Marine Casualties and Incidents

ADOPTS the Code for the Investigation of Marine Casualties and Incidents;

INVITES all Governments concerned to take appropriate measures to give effect to the annexed Code as soon as possible;

REQUESTS flag States to conduct an investigation into all very serious and serious marine casualties and to report all relevant findings to the Organization;

REVOKES resolutions A.173(ES.IV), A.440(XI) and A.637(16).

### Assembly resolution A.850(20) - Human element vision, principles and goals for the Organization

ADOPTS the human element vision, principles and goals for the Organization;

INVITES Governments to bring this resolution to the attention of their representatives who attend meetings of the Organization for appropriate action, and to encourage those responsible for the operation and design of ships to take the relevant principles into account when making design and operational decisions;

REQUESTS the Maritime Safety Committee and the Marine Environment Protection Committee to consider proposals for new or revised instruments of procedures relating to safety of life at sea or protection of the marine environment taking into account the annexed human element vision, principles and goals;

REQUESTS ALSO the Maritime Safety Committee and the Marine Environment Protection Committee to keep the annexed vision, principles and goals under review and take action as appropriate.

## IMO MARITIME SAFETY COMMITTEE CIRCULARS

### MSC/Circ.621 - Guidelines for the investigation of accidents where fatigue may have been a contributing factor

MSC/Circ.621, prepared by a Joint ILO/IMO Group of experts on fatigue, which finished its work in March 1993, provides guidance to those involved in determining whether, and to what extent, fatigue may have contributed to a maritime casualty or accident. The Guidelines cover such topics as investigator qualifications and training, criteria for selecting whom to interview and the sequence of interviews, and topics to be covered by the investigator. The Guidelines include forms for recording information for analysis at the national and international level.

**MSC/Circ.827 - MEPC/Circ.333 - Harmonized reporting procedures - Reports required under SOLAS 74 regulation I/21 and MARPOL 73/78 articles 8 and 12**

## IMO CODE

### Code for the Investigation of Marine Casualties and Incidents (resolution A.849(20))

The Code aims to promote a common approach to the safety investigation of marine casualties and incidents and also to promote co-operation between States in identifying the contributing factors leading to marine casualties. It provides that the result of a common approach and co-operation will be to aid remedial action and to enhance the safety of seafarers and passengers, and the protection of the marine environment. In achieving these aims, the Code recognises the need for mutual respect for national rules and practices and puts particular emphasis upon co-operation.

The Code further provides that the objective of any marine casualty investigation is to prevent such casualties in the future. Investigations identify the circumstances of the casualty under investigation and establish the causes and contributing factors, by gathering and analysing information and drawing conclusions. Ideally, it is not the purpose of such investigations to determine liability, or apportion blame. However, the Investigating Authority should not refrain from fully reporting the causes because fault or liability may be inferred from the findings.

The Code covers such topics as conduct of marine casualty investigations, responsibility to investigate casualties and incidents, responsibilities of the lead investigating State, consultation, co-operation (among States), disclosure of records, personnel and material resources, the issue and submission to IMO of marine casualty reports, the re-opening of investigations, contents of reports and contact between Administrations."

P
A
R
T

C

3

# PART C 4

INTERNATIONAL MARITIME ORGANIZATION
4 ALBERT EMBANKMENT
LONDON SE1 7SR

Telephone: 020-7735 7611
Fax:        020-7587 3210
Telex:      23588 IMOLDN G

IMO

*E*

MSC/Circ.953
MEPC/Circ.372
14 December 2000

Ref. T1/2.02
    T5/1.11(c)

## REPORTS ON MARINE CASUALTIES AND INCIDENTS

### Revised harmonized reporting procedures - Reports required under SOLAS regulation I/21 and MARPOL 73/78 articles 8 and 12

1       The Maritime Safety Committee, at its sixty-eighth session (28 May to 6 June 1997) and the Marine Environment Protection Committee, at its fortieth session (18 to 25 September 1997) approved an MSC/MEPC circular (MSC/Circ.827 - MEPC/Circ.333) on Reports on marine casualties and incidents - Harmonized reporting procedures, amalgamating and harmonizing the procedures for reporting casualties to the Organization contained in existing MSC and MEPC circulars.

2       The Maritime Safety Committee, at its seventy-second session (17 May to 26 May 2000) and the Marine Environment Protection Committee, at its forty-fourth and forty-fifth sessions (6 to 8, 10 and 13 March 2000 and 2 to 6 October 2000 respectively) approved amendments to MSC/Circ.827 - MEPC/Circ.333.

3       Under SOLAS regulation I/21 and MARPOL 73/78 articles 8 and 12, each Administration undertakes to conduct an investigation into any casualty occurring to ships under its flag subject to those conventions and to supply the Organization with pertinent information concerning the findings of such investigations.

4       The reporting formats contained in the annexes to this circular replace the reporting forms contained in MSC 59/33, Annex 3 regarding Damage cards, MSC/Circ.224 regarding Intact stability casualty records, , MSC/Circ.388 on Fire casualty records, MSC/Circ.433 on Reports on investigations into serious casualties, MSC/Circ.559 on Incidents involving dangerous goods or marine pollutants in packaged form, MSC/Circ.621 on Guidelines for the investigation of accidents where fatigue may have been a contributing factor and COM/Circ.70/Rev.1 Questionnaire on the maritime distress system. The reporting format on Incidental spillages of harmful substances of 50 tonnes or more has been added, as such reports are considered necessary when investigating a casualty or an incident (MARPOL 73/78, articles 8 and 12); however, this does not replace the one-line entry report required by the annual mandatory report under MARPOL 73/78, article 11 (MEPC/Circ.318, Part 1).

5       For the purpose of reporting information to the Organization, ship casualties are classified as "very serious casualties", "serious casualties", "less serious casualties" and "marine incidents". Administrations are requested to submit data for all "very serious casualties" and "serious casualties"*.

Where there are important lessons to be learned from "serious casualties", "less serious casualties" and "marine incidents", full investigation reports should be submitted along with the additional information indicated in annex 3.

---

* "Very serious casualties" are casualties to ships which involve total loss of the ship, loss of life, or severe pollution, the definition of which, as agreed by the Marine Environment Protection Committee at its thirty-seventh session (MEPC 37/22, paragraph 5.8), is as follows:

"Severe pollution" is a case of pollution which, as evaluated by the coastal State(s) affected or the flag State, as appropriate, produces a major deleterious effect upon the environment, or which would have produced such an effect without preventive action.

"Serious casualties" are casualties to ships which do not qualify as "very serious casualties" and which involve a fire, explosion, collision, grounding, contact, heavy weather damage, ice damage, hull cracking, or suspected hull defect, etc., resulting in:

- immobilization of main engines, extensive accommodation damage, severe structural damage, such as penetration of the hull under water, etc., rendering the ship unfit to proceed[i], or

- pollution (regardless of quantity); and/or

- a breakdown necessitating towage or shore assistance.

"Less serious casualties" are casualties to ships which do not qualify as "very serious casualties" or "serious casualties" and for the purpose of recording useful information also include "marine incidents" which themselves include "hazardous incidents" and "near misses".

6    Administrations are urged to submit data as indicated below.

Information to be submitted per casualty class

| Information to be sent in accordance with the type of casualty | Very serious casualties | Serious casualties | Less serious casualties | Marine incidents |
|---|---|---|---|---|
| Annex 1 of the attached reporting format | To be provided within 6 months after the casualty in all cases | To be provided within 6 months after the casualty in all cases | May be provided if there are important lessons to be learned | May be provided if there are important lessons to be learned |

---

i    The ship is in a condition which does not correspond substantially with the applicable conventions, presenting a danger to the ship and the persons on board or an unreasonable threat of harm to the marine environment.

| Annexes 2 and 3 of the attached reported format, as well as other relevant annexes | To be provided at the end of the investigation in all cases | To be provided at the end of the investigation in all cases | May be provided if there are important lessons to be learned | May be provided if there are important lessons to be learned |
|---|---|---|---|---|
| Full investigation report | To be provided at the end of the investigation in all cases | May be provided if there are important lessons to be learned | May be provided if there are important lessons to be learned | May be provided if there are important lessons to be learned |

### Very serious casualty

preliminary information as indicated in **Annex 1**[ii]

information as indicated in **Annexes 2 and 3, as well as other relevant annexes**

a full investigation report in all cases

### Serious casualty

preliminary information as indicated in **Annex 1**[ii]

information as indicated in **Annexes 2 and 3, as well as other relevant annexes**

a full investigation report only in cases of important lessons to be learnt regarding IMO regulations

### Less serious casualty and marine incident

information as indicated in **Annexes 1, 2 and 3, as well as other relevant annexes**, only in cases of important lessons to be learnt regarding IMO regulations

a full investigation report only in cases of important lessons to be learnt regarding IMO regulations

### Information to be submitted for casualties/incidents as indicated below.

Information from casualties involving dangerous goods on marine

pollutants in packaged form on board ships and in port areas.          → **Annex 4**

Damage cards and intact stability records          → **Annex 5**

Fire casualty record          → **Annex 6**

Global Maritime Distress and Safety System (GMDSS)          → **Annex 7**

Fatigue as a contributory cause to maritime accidents

---

[ii]     To be submitted within six months of the casualty date unless complete information is submitted within this time limit.

- Fatigue factors data compilation sheet → **Annex 8**

Incidental spillage of liquids of 50 tonnes or more → **Annex 9**

7        Member Governments are invited to give effect to the Code for the Investigation of Marine Casualties and Incidents, as amended, (resolutions A.849(20) and A.884(21)) when conducting investigations into marine casualties and incidents.

8        Member Governments are requested to use the present circular when reporting on marine casualties and incidents.

9        The present circular supersedes MSC/Circ.827 - MEPC/Circ.333.

## List of Annexes

ANNEX 1:   SHIP IDENTIFICATION AND PARTICULARS

Indicates the information to be submitted in all casualty reports.

ANNEX 2:   DATA FOR VERY SERIOUS AND SERIOUS CASUALTIES

Indicates information to be supplied on "very serious" and "serious" casualties.

ANNEX 3:   SUPPLEMENTARY INFORMATION ON VERY SERIOUS CASUALTIES AND SERIOUS CASUALTIES

Additional information required for "very serious casualties" and "serious" casualties.

ANNEX 4:   INFORMATION FROM CASUALTIES INVOLVING DANGEROUS GOODS OR MARINE POLLUTANTS IN PACKAGED FORM ON BOARD SHIPS AND IN PORT AREAS

This form may be applicable for marine casualties as defined as well as marine incidents.

ANNEX 5:   DAMAGE CARDS AND INTACT STABILITY CASUALTY RECORDS

This form may apply to "very serious" and "serious" casualties.

ANNEX 6:   FIRE CASUALTY RECORD

This form may apply to "very serious" and "serious" casualties.

ANNEX 7:   QUESTIONNAIRE RELATED TO THE GLOBAL MARITIME DISTRESS AND SAFETY SYSTEM

This form may apply to "very serious" and "serious" casualties.

ANNEX 8:   FATIGUE AS A CONTRIBUTORY CAUSE TO MARITIME ACCIDENTS - FATIGUE FACTORS DATA COMPILATION SHEET

This form will apply where fatigue is deemed to be a contributory factor in the casualty.

ANNEX 9:   INCIDENTAL SPILLAGE OF HARMFUL SUBSTANCES OF 50 TONNES OR MORE

This form relates to incidents involving harmful substances. The report is considered necessary when investigating a casualty or an incident (MARPOL 73/78, articles 8 and 12), however this does not replace the one-line entry report required by the annual mandatory report under MARPOL 73/78, article 11 (MEPC/Circ.318, Part 1).

# ANNEX 1

## IMO MARINE CASUALTY AND INCIDENT REPORT

## SHIP IDENTIFICATION AND PARTICULARS

Administrations are urged to supply the ship identification information listed in this annex for all marine casualty reports submitted to the Organization.

## SHIP PARTICULARS

**1. IMO Number:**

**2. Name of Ship:**

**3. Flag State:**

**4. Type of Ship**

| | | |
|---|---|---|
| .1 | Liquefied Gas Tanker | ❐ |
| .2 | Chemical Tanker | ❐ |
| .3 | Oil Tanker | ❐ |
| .4 | Other Liquids (non-flammable) Tanker | ❐ |
| .5 | Bulk Dry (general, ore) Carrier | ❐ |
| .6 | Bulk Dry! Oil Carrier | ❐ |
| .7 | Self-Discharging Bulk Dry Carrier | ❐ |
| .8 | Other Bulk Dry (cement, woodchips, urea and other specialized) Carrier | ❐ |
| .9 | General Cargo Ship | ❐ |
| .10 | Passenger! General Cargo Ship | ❐ |
| .11 | Container Ship | ❐ |
| .12 | Refrigerated Cargo Ship | ❐ |
| .13 | Ro-Ro Cargo Ship | ❐ |
| .14 | Passenger! Ro-Ro Cargo Ship | ❐ |
| .15 | Passenger Ship | ❐ |
| .16 | High Speed Craft | ❐ |
| .17 | Other Dry Cargo (livestock, barge, heavy cargo, etc.) Carrier | ❐ |
| .18 | Fish Catching Vessel | ❐ |
| .19 | Fish Factory Ship I Fish Carrier | ❐ |

.20  Offshore Supply Ship ..................................................................... ☐

.21  Other Offshore Ship ...................................................................... ☐

.22  Research Ship ................................................................................ ☐

.23  Towing / Pushing Tug ................................................................... ☐

.24  Dredger .......................................................................................... ☐

.25  Other Activities Ship ..................................................................... ☐

.26  Non-Propelled Ships ...................................................................... ☐

.27  Other Ships Structures ................................................................... ☐

5.  **Gross Tonnage:**

6.  **Length overall:**

7.  **Classification Society**

8.  **Registered Shipowner:**

9.  **Ship Manager/Operator:**

10. **Previous names:**

11. **Previous Flag:**

12. **Previous Class Society:**

13. **Date of contract/keel laid/delivery:**

14. **Date of major conversion:**

15. **Deadweight:**

16. **Hull material**

.1  steel ............................................................................................... ☐

.2  light alloy ....................................................................................... ☐

.3  ferrocement ................................................................................... ☐

.4  wood .............................................................................................. ☐

.5  GRP ............................................................................................... ☐

.6  composite materials ....................................................................... ☐

17. **Hull construction**

.1  single hull ...................................................................................... ☐

.2  double hull ..................................................................................... ☐

.3  double bottom ................................................................................ ☐

.4  double sides ................................................................................... ☐

.5  mid deck ........................................................................................ ☐

.6  other .............................................................................................. ☐

18. **Building yard:**

**19.Hull number:**

**20.Date of total loss/constructive total loss/scrapping:**

**21.Number of crew:**

**22.Number of passengers:**


## PRELIMINARY CASUALTY DATA

**1. Date and time (local onboard):**

**2. Position/ location:**

**3. Initial event[iii]**

- ❏     collision
- ❏     stranding! grounding
- ❏     contact
- ❏     fire or explosion
- ❏     hull failure! failure of watertight doors/ports, etc.
- ❏     machinery damage
- ❏     damages to ship or equipment
- ❏     capsizing! listing
- ❏     missing: assumed lost
- ❏     other

**4. Consequences**

- ❏     total loss of the ship
- ❏     ship rendered unfit to proceed[iv]
- ❏     ship remains fit to proceed[v]
- ❏     pollution
- ❏     loss of life
- ❏     serious injuries

**5. Summary of events**

P
A
R
T

C

4

---

[iii]   For an explanation of the terms below see annex 2.

[iv]   The ship is in a condition, which does not correspond substantially with the applicable conventions, presenting a danger to the ship and the persons on board or an unreasonable threat of harm to the marine environment.

[v]   The ship is in a condition, which corresponds substantially with the applicable conventions, presenting neither a danger to the ship and the persons on board nor an unreasonable threat of harm to the marine environment.

# ANNEX 2

## IMO MARINE CASUALTY AND INCIDENT REPORT

## DATA FOR VERY SERIOUS AND SERIOUS CASUALTIES

## CASUALTY DATA

1  **Date and local time of casualty: (24 hr clock) (YYMMDD)**

2  **Position of casualty (Latitude, Longitude):**

3  **Location of casualty:**

   3.1  At berth .............................................................................. ❒

   3.2  Anchorage .......................................................................... ❒

   3.3  Port ..................................................................................... ❒

   3.4  Port approach ................................................................... ❒

   3.5  Inland waters .................................................................... ❒

   3.6  Canal .................................................................................. ❒

   3.7  River ................................................................................... ❒

   3.8  Archipelagos ..................................................................... ❒

   3.9  Coastal waters (within 12 miles) .................................. ❒

   3.10 Open sea .......................................................................... ❒

4  **Pilot on board** ........................................................................ ❒

5  **Type of casualty (initial event):**

   5.1  Collision: striking or being struck by another ship (regardless of
whether under way, anchored or moored). ........................................... ❒

      5.1.1  IMO Number of other ship involved. (not coded)

      5.1.2  Name of other ship involved. (not coded)

   5.2  Stranding or grounding: being aground, or hitting/touching
shore or sea bottom or underwater objects (wrecks, etc.) ..................... ❒

   5.3  Contact: striking any fixed or floating object other than
those included in Nos. 1 or 2 ................................................................ ❒

   5.4  Fire or explosion ................................................................ ❒

   5.5  Hull failure or failure of watertight doors, ports, etc.:
not caused by Nos. 1 to 4. .................................................................... ❒

   5.6  Machinery damage: not caused by Nos. 1 to 5, and which
necessitated towage or shore assistance ............................................... ❒

   5.7  Damages to ship or equipment: not caused or covered by Nos. 1 to 6 ....... ❒

   5.8  Capsizing or listing: not caused by Nos. 1 to 7. ..................... ❒

P
A
R
T

C

4

5.9  Missing: assumed lost. ............................................................ ❏

5.10 Other: all casualties which are not covered by Nos. 1 to 9................... ❏

## 6 Type of subsequent events

6.1  Collision: striking or being struck by another ship (regardless of whether under way, anchored or moored). ......................................... ❏

6.1.1 IMO Number of other ship involved. (not coded)

6.1.2 Name of other ship involved. (not coded)

6.2  Stranding or grounding: being aground, or hitting/touching shore or sea bottom or underwater objects (wrecks, etc.). ............................ ❏

6.3  Contact: striking any fixed or floating object other than those included in Nos. 1 or 2. ....................................................................... ❏

6.4 Fire or explosion. ...................................................................... ❏

6.5 Hull failure or failure of watertight doors, ports, etc............................ ❏

6.6 Machinery damage which necessitated towage or shore assistance. ....... ❏

6.7 Damages to ship or equipment............................................................. ❏

6.8 Capsizing or listing. ................................................................... ❏

6.9 Missing: assumed lost. ............................................................... ❏

6.10 Other: all events which are not covered by Nos. 1 to 9. ...................... ❏

## 7 Consequences of the casualty

### 7.1  Consequences to the ship involved in the casualty:

7.1.1  Total loss

7.1.2  Ship rendered unfit to proceed[vi]

7.1.3  Ship remains fit to proceed[vii]

### 7.2  Consequences related to human beings:

7.2.1  Number of dead or missing crew                                      ———

7.2.2  Number of dead or missing passengers                          ———

7.2.3  Number of other dead or missing persons                      ———

7.2.4  Number of crew being seriously[viii] injured in the casualty                                                                              ———

7.2.5  Number of passengers being seriously[viii] injured in the casualty                                                                      ———

---

[vi]   The ship is in a condition, which does not correspond substantially with the applicable conventions, presenting a danger to the ship and the persons on board or an unreasonable threat of harm to the marine environment.

[vii]  The ship is in a condition, which corresponds substantially with the applicable conventions, presenting neither a danger to the ship and the persons on board nor an unreasonable threat of harm to the marine environment.

[viii] Incapacitated for 72 hours or more.

7.2.6 Number of other persons being seriously[viii] injured
in the casualty _____

## 7.3 Consequences to the environment (pollution):

### 7.3.1 Oil in bunkers

| 7.3.1.1 | Type of oil | Quantity spilled |
|---|---|---|
| ❏ Heavy fuel | | _____ |
| ❏ Diesel | | _____ |
| ❏ Lube oils | | _____ |
| ❏ Other | | _____ |

### 7.3.2 Oil cargo

| 7.3.2.1 | Type of oil (not coded) | Quantity spilled |
|---|---|---|
| ❏ Crude oil | | _____ |
| ❏ Persistent refined oil products | | _____ |
| ❏ Non-persistent refined oil products | | _____ |
| ❏ Other | | |

### 7.3.3 Chemicals in bulk

Category (Appendix I to Annex II of MARPOL 73/78)

| | Quantity in tons spilled |
|---|---|
| ❏ A | _____ |
| ❏ B | _____ |
| ❏ C | _____ |
| ❏ D | _____ |

### 7.3.4 Dangerous goods in packaged form

| Class (IMDG Code) | | Names | UN numbers | Quantity lost overboard |
|---|---|---|---|---|
| 1 | ❏ | ____ | _____ | _____ |
| 2 | ❏ | ____ | _____ | _____ |
| 3 | ❏ | ____ | _____ | _____ |
| 4.1 | ❏ | ____ | _____ | _____ |
| 4.2 | ❏ | ____ | _____ | _____ |
| 4.3 | ❏ | ____ | _____ | _____ |
| 5.1 | ❏ | ____ | _____ | _____ |
| 5.2 | ❏ | ____ | _____ | _____ |
| 6.1 | ❏ | ____ | _____ | _____ |
| 6.2 | ❏ | ____ | _____ | _____ |

| 7 | ☐ | — | — | | — |
| 8 | ☐ | — | — | | — |
| 9 | ☐ | — | — | | — |

## 8 Primary causes of the initial event

Coding principle:

a   The human element is a complex multi dimensional issue that affects maritime safety and marine environmental protection. It involves the entire spectrum of human activities performed by ships' crews, shore based management, regulatory bodies, classification societies, shipyards, legislators and other relevant parties

b   Effective remedial action following maritime casualties requires a sound understanding of the human element involvement in accident causation. This comes by the thorough investigation and systematic analysis of casualties for contributory factors and the causal chain of events.

8.1   Internal causes (related to the ship where the casualty occurred) .........☐

    8.1.1   Human violations or errors by the crew: ...................................☐

        .1   Human violations.......................................................☐

        .2   Human error................................................................☐

    8.1.2   Human violations or errors by the pilot...............................☐

        .1   Human violations.......................................................☐

        .2   Human error................................................................☐

    8.1.3 Structural failures of the ship.......................................................☐

    8.1.4   Technical failure of machinery/equipment including

        design errors..................................................................................☐

        .1   Failure of propulsion machinery..............................☐

        .2   Failure of essential auxiliary machinery ....................☐

        .3   Failure of steering gear ............................................☐

        .4   Failure of closing arrangements or seals ...................☐

        .5   Failure or inadequacy of navigational equipment.........☐

        .6   Failure of bilge pumping...........................................☐

        .7   Failure of electrical installation ...............................☐

        .8   Failure or inadequacy of communication equipment....☐

        .9   Failure or inadequacy of lifesaving appliances .............☐

        .10   Ship design errors (i.e. insufficient stability) ..................☐

        .11   Other........................................................................☐

    8.1.5 The ship's cargo ........................................................................☐

        .1   Cargo shifting.............................................................☐

        .2   Fire or explosion in cargo...........................................☐

## ANNEX 3

## IMO MARINE CASUALTY AND INCIDENT REPORT

## SUPPLEMENTARY INFORMATION ON VERY SERIOUS AND SERIOUS CASUALTIES

To assist completion of marine casualty analysis, in addition to the information in annexes 1 and 2, the following information is required:

**1.** **Principle findings and form of casualty investigation:**

**2.** **Action taken:**

**3.** **Findings affecting international regulations:**

**4.** **Assistance given (SAR operations):**

# ANNEX 4

## IMO MARINE CASUALTY AND INCIDENT REPORT

## INFORMATION FROM CASUALTIES INVOLVING DANGEROUS GOODS OR MARINE POLLUTANTS IN PACKAGED FORM ON BOARD SHIPS AND IN PORT AREAS

This report is a supplement to the report made by the master in accordance with guidelines and general principles adopted by the Organization by resolution A.648(16) in case of an incident involving dangerous goods and marine pollutants in packaged form on board ships and in port areas.

The information should be provided in case of:

- an accident with loss of life, injury or damage to ship or property; or

- an accident, where an unsafe situation, an emergency or loss has occurred involving dangerous goods in packaged form and marine pollutants.

The information should be provided by the Administration carrying out the investigation, if necessary in consultation with other parties involved (e.g. authorities of ports of loading, transit or discharge, etc.) and forwarded to the International Maritime Organization together with recommendations, if considered necessary, for rectifying any detected deficiencies.

The summary and recommendations of any subsequent investigations should also be reported to the Organization.

## INFORMATION FROM INVESTIGATION OF INCIDENTS INVOLVING DANGEROUS GOODS OR MARINE POLLUTANTS IN PACKAGED FORM

1. Cargo(es) Involved

    1.1 Name:    UN Number:    IMO Hazard Class[ix]:

    1.2 Name and address of manufacturer, or consignor, or consignee:

    1.3 Type of packaging/container:

    1.4 Quantity and condition of goods:

    1.5 Stowage/Securing arrangements:

2. Pollution - goods lost overboard (yes/no):

---

[ix]   Data should be provided only if not supplied otherwise.

If yes:

2.1 Quantity of goods lost:

2.2 Lost goods floated or sank:

2.3 Lost goods released from packaging (yes/no):

3. Brief account of the sequence of events[ix]:

4. Extent of damage[ix]:

5. Emergency response measures taken:

6. Comments on compliance with applicable convention/recommendation requirements:

7. Comments on effectiveness of applicable convention/recommendation requirements:

8. Measures/recommendations to prevent recurrence:

9. Further investigation (yes/no)[ix]:

# ANNEX 5

## IMO MARINE CASUALTY AND INCIDENT REPORT

## DAMAGE CARDS[x] AND INTACT STABILITY CASUALTY RECORDS

Statistics of damaged ships and of intact stability casualties are important to the work of the Organization in respect to improvement of subdivision and intact stability criteria in various conventions, codes, recommendations, and guidelines. Member Governments are invited to continue to submit to the Secretariat damage data and intact stability casualty data using the format in this annex.

## DAMAGE CARDS

### Damaged Ship

Length between perpendiculars* $L$ = _____

Moulded breadth* $B$ = _____  Moulded depth* $D$ = _____

Height of subdivision deck = _____

Draught before damage: amidships $d$ = _____ (or fore = ___ and aft = ___)

Struck/stricking _____

Bulkhead (or freeboard) deck

## Dimensions and location of damage (see sketch above)

| | |
|---|---|
| Distance from AP to centre of damage* | $X$ = _____ |
| Distance from baseline to the lower point of damage | $Z$ = _____ |
| Length of damage* | $1$ = _____    $1_1$ = _____ |
| Height of damage* | $h$ = _____    $h_1$ = _____ |
| Area = | |
| Penetration of damage* | $b$ = _____    $b_1$ = _____ |

(if damage extends above bulkhead (or freeboard) deck, additional dimensions should be given for the part located below this deck, these being marked with suffix "$_1$"

## Dimensions and location of bottom damage

Distance from AP to centre of damage* $X$ = _____

Distance from CL to centre of damage = _____ Port or starboard? _____

---

[x]  The Secretariat, while incorporating amendments to the cover and to annexes 1 and 2 of the present circular, also included the amendments to MSC!Circ.224, which were approved by the Maritime Safety Committee at its fifty-ninth session (MSC 59/33, annex 3).

Length of damage **l** = _____ Width of damage = _____ Area = _____

Depth of damage **d** = _____

**Second ship involved in collision** (to be completed in case of collision between two ships)

Length between perpendiculars * **L** =

Moulded breadth*         **B** = _____ Moulded depth* **D** = _____

Draught before damage: amidships **d** =_____ (or fore = ___ and aft = ___ )

Struck/stricking _____

## NOTES FOR DAMAGE CARD

1. Damage cards should be completed for decked, steel sea-going ships 25 m. in length and over, for all breaches of the hull causing flooding of any compartments (collision, stranding, etc.)

2. The term "damaged ship' refers to the ship for which this card is being completed.

3. A sketch showing location of damage and of main transverse bulkheads would be desirable.

4. Depth D should be measured to the bulkhead deck in passenger ships and to the freeboard deck in non-passenger ships (or to uppermost completed deck, if bulkhead or freeboard deck are not specified.

5. In case of collision with another ship, it is desirable to fill in damage cards for both ships.

6. All measurements should be given in metres.

7. Data marked with an asterisk (*) are the most important.

## Additional data to be supplied if available

1. Wind and sea (Beaufort scale) at time of casualty _____

2. Speed at time of impact, in knots:

   Damaged ship      $v_1$ _____

   Second ship       $v_2$ _____

3. Angle of encounter _____

4. Did the ship to which this card refers sink? _____

   *If not*, give draught after damage _____

   *If so*, indicate time taken to sink after collision _____

   and manner of sinking _____

5. Appropriation of breached compartment(s) (e.g. machinery room, cargo hold, etc.) _____

6. Type and quantity of cargo in damaged compartment, if any

   _____

7. Were there any special circumstances which influenced the results of damage (e.g. open watertight doors, manholes, sidescuttles, or pipes, fractures, etc.)?

_____

8. Position of watertight bulkheads in vicinity of damage (distance from AP to each of them) _____

9. Was a transverse subdivision bulkhead damaged? _____

10. Was the collision bulkhead damaged? _____

11. Number of compartments flooded _____

12. Was there a double bottom in the damaged area? _____

   *If so*, indicate whether the inner bottom was breached _____

13. Was there a separate penetration from the bulbous bow? _____

14. Any additional information considered useful (details of construction, etc.)

_____

15. Striking ship bow geometry   Xl = _____   X2 = _____   X3 = _____

                                                         Y1 = _____   Y2 = _____

## INTACT STABILITY CASUALTY RECORD

Length between perpendiculars* **Lpp** = _____

Breadth moulded* **B** = _____ Depth moulded* **D** = _____

Draught amidships to assigned loadline or subdivision line **d** _____

      (or forward _____ and aft _____ )

Service conditions (light or loaded, with approximate percentage of cargo, stores, fuel and passengers) _____

Type of cargo, if any _____ Disposition _____ stowage factor _____

Deck cargo, if any _____ type _____ quantity _____

Quantity of ballast water, if any _____

Sea and wind conditions at time of casualty:

        sea* _____ wind* (Beaufort scale) _____

PART
C
4

Wind velocity **u** _____ Wind pressure $\mathbf{P}_v$ _____

Wave length _____ Wave height $\mathbf{h}_w$ _____

Direction of wind relative to ships head _____ (degrees)

Direction of waves relative to ships head _____ (degrees)

Speed of ship at time of casualty **V** _____ knots

Name, length and height of enclosed superstructures and deck-houses above the deck to which **D** was measured _____

_____

Bilge keels: Width (°) _____ Longitudinal extent (°) _____

Depth of bar keel, if any (°) _____

Was water trapped on deck? _____ if so, indicate the extent _____

Were all vulnerable openings effectively closed at time of casualty? _____

Was icing a contributory factor to casualty? _____

Was the vessel under action of helm at time of casualty? _____

Were any special instructions relative to this ship in existence, concerning the maintenance of stability, e.g. filling tanks, etc.? _____

_____

Were any voyage limits and/or weather restrictions imposed for the vessel?

_____

Were any particular circumstances related to the casualty? _____

Give short description of casualty[xi] _____

_____

---

xi  Data should be provided only if not provided otherwise.

## NOTES FOR INTACT STABILITY CASUALTY RECORD

| | |
|---|---|
| 1. Casualty records to be completed for all sea-going passenger ships, sea-going cargo ships of 25 metres in length and over, and sea-going fishing vessels of 15 metres in length and over, in respect of both losses of ships and cases in which dangerous heeling occurred due to unsatisfactory intact stability, including those cases wher loss or heeling of the ship was due to shifting of cargo. | 2. Depth D should be measured to the bulkhead deck in passenger ships and to the freeboard deck in non-passenger ships (or to uppermost completed deck, if bulkhead or freeboard deck is not specified.)<br>3. The metric system should be used for all measurements.<br>4. Data marked with an asterisk (\*) are the most important.<br>5. The provision of data marked (o) is optional.<br>6. It is desirable to attach a sketch of statical stability curves, drawn for both the below loading conditions, using the following scales:<br>(i) 20mm for every 10° of inclination.<br>(ii) 10mm (or 20mm) for every 0.1 metre of righting lever. |

| General particulars | For ship in fully loaded homogeneous arrival condition (with 10% stores, fuel, etc.) | For ship in condition at time of loss |
|---|---|---|
| Draught (amidships)      **d** | | |
| Displacement*      $\Delta$ | | |
| Centre of gravity above moulded base line*   **KG** | | |
| Metacentric height (uncorrected)*   **GM** | | |
| Distance between the transverse metacentre and centre of buoyancy   **BM** | | |
| Reduction in GM due to any free surface of liquids* | | |
| Block coefficient of fineness of displacement*   $\delta$ | | |
| Coefficient of fineness of midship section   **ß** | | |
| Coefficient of fineness of waterplane   $\alpha$ | | |
| Height of centre of buoyancy above moulded base line  **KB** | | |
| Lateral area of ship's profile (including erections, etc.) exposed to wind   $A_v$ | | |
| Distance between centre of lateral area of ship's profile exposed to wind and corresponding waterline | | |
| Estimated rolling period (P-S-P) (in seconds) [o]   $T_r$ | | |
| Rated amplitude of roll (maximum)   $\emptyset_r$ | | |
| Angle of heel for immersion of uppermost continuous deck | | |
| Righting levers (**GZ**) based upon centre of gravity (**G**) corrected for any free surfaces, for the following angles of heel* | | |
| 0° | | |
| 10° | | |
| 20° | | |
| 30° | | |
| 40° | | |
| 50° | | |
| 60° | | |
| 70° | | |
| 80° | | |
| 90° | | |
| Maximum righting lever  $GZ_m$ | | |
| Angle of maximum stability  $\emptyset_m$ | | |
| Angle of vanishing stability  $\emptyset_v$ | | |

Lightship displacement $\Delta_0$ =      Centre of gravity above moulded base line $KG_o$ =

# ANNEX 6

# IMO MARINE CASUALTY AND INCIDENT REPORT

## FIRE CASUALTY RECORD

Administrations are urged to supply the additional information listed in this annex for all casualties involving vessel fires.

1. Were any voyage limits placed on the ship?2[xii]:

2. Propelling machinery (type, fuel, etc.):

3. Nature of cargo:

4. Location of ship[xiii]

    .1    Was the ship underway or in port?:

    .2    If in port, specify the condition (loading, unloading, under repair, or others):

5. Local conditions[xiii]

    .1    Time (daylight or darkness):

    .2    Wind force (Beaufort scale):

    .3    State of sea (and code used):

6. Part of ship where fire broke out[xii]:

7. Probable cause of fire[xii]:

8. Probable origin of flammable liquids, if applicable:

9. Description of damage[xii],[xiii]

10. No. of persons on board

    .1    Passengers:

    .2    Crew:

11. Structural fire protection (briefly describe fife resisting and fire retarding bulkheads, doors, decks, etc., through the whole of the area affected by fire):

12. Fire detection method at site of fife

    .1    Automatic:

    .2    Others[xii]:

13. Fixed fire-extinguishing installations

    .1    At site of fire:

    .2    Adjacent areas:

14. Ship's fire-extinguishing equipment used (foam, dry chemical, $CO_2$, water, steam. etc.)

    .1    Fixed[xii]:

xii  Data should be given as precisely as possible.
xiii  Data should be provided only if not provided otherwise.

PART C 4

.2 Portable[xii]:

15. Effectiveness of action taken by crew to extinguish fire:

16. Outside assistance given and equipment used (e.g. fife department, other ship, etc.)[xiii]:

17. Time taken to fight fire

.1 To control:

.2 To extinguish:

18. Observations[xiii]:

19. Classification (see classification scheme appended to this annex):

# APPENDIX A

## CLASSIFICATION SYSTEM FOR FIRE CASUALTY RECORDS

This classification system should be used when entering the "Classification" of fife casualty records (paragraph 19 of annex 6). For the purpose of correct usage of the classification system the Guidance for preparing the casualty classification is attached at appendix B. The numbering has been kept in consistence with the numbering in MSC/Circ. 388.

3   Service

   .1   International

   .2   Short international

   .3   Coastal sea trade

   .4   Inland waters

   .5   Not reported

4   Condition

   .1   Underway

   .2   In port — Loading

   .3   In port — Unloading

   .4   In port — Awaiting departure

   .5   In port — Other

   .6   Under repair

   .7   Others

   .8   Not reported

5   Time at which fire was discovered

   .1   Midnight to 0559

   .2   0600 to 1159

   .3   1200 to 1759

   .4   1800 to 2359

   .5   Not reported

6   Duration of fire

   .1   Extinguished within 1 minute

   .2   1 — 5 minutes

   .3   6 — 10 minutes

   .4   11 — 30 minutes

   .5   31 — 60 minutes

   .6   1 — 6 hours

   .7   More than 6 hours

   .8   Not reported

7   Position of outbreak

   .1   Accommodations

   .2   Cargo spaces

   .3   Machinery space of category A

   .4   Machinery space other than of category A

   .5   Galley

   .6   Cargo pump room

.7 Service space

.8 Other spaces

.9 Not reported

8 Combustibles involved

.1 Structural materials

.2 Furnishings and baggage

.3 Ship stores

.4 Dry cargo

.5 Liquid cargo

.6 Liquid fuel

.7 Lubricating oil

.8 Hydraulic oil

.9 Other flammable liquids

.10 Not reported

9 Origin of flammable liquid

.1 Burst piping

.2 Leaking valve

.3 Overflow from tank

.4 Leaking coupling or flanges

.5 Flexible hose

.6 Leaking gasket

.7 Oil soaked insulation material

.8 Others

.9 Not applicable

.10 Not reported

10 Source of ignition

.1 Cigarettes, matches, or similar smoking materials

.2 Open flames other than .1 and .8

.3 Static generation

.4 Electrical other than static charges

.5 Spontaneous combustion

.6 Collision

.7 Mechanical fault or breakdown

.8 Burning or welding

.9 Hot exhaust pipe or steam line

.10 Not on vessel concerned

.11 Other

.12 Not reported

11 Type of protection at space concerned

.1 Fire resisting division

.2 Fire mains and hydrants

.3 Inert gas system

.4 Fixed $CO_2$ system

.5 Halogenated hydrocarbon system

.6 Foam system

.7 Other fixed extinguishing system (e.g., automatic sprinkler or steam smothering)

.8 Other protection (portable and semi-portable extinguishers)

.9 Not reported

12 Means by which fire was detected

.1 Detection system installed and utilized

.2 Detection system installed, but fire detected by personnel

.3 No fire detection system installed, but fire detected by personnel

.4 Not reported

13 Fire-extinguishing effectiveness

.1 Fire-extinguishing equipment adequate

.2 Fire-extinguishing equipment not adequate

.3 Fire-extinguishing equipment improperly used

.4 Assistance from other ship required

.5 Assistance from shore fire brigade required

.6 Ship abandoned

.7 Not applicable

| .8 Not reported | .1 Construction |
|---|---|

14 Extent of damage

   .1   Slight damage

   .2   Extensive damage

   .3   Immobilization of ship due to serious damage

   .4   Total constructive loss

17 Observations pertaining to

.1 Construction

.2 Equipment

.3 Crew training

.4 Stowage requirements

.5 Housekeeping

.6 Improper maintenance

.7 Other

.8 None

## APPENDIX B

## GUIDANCE FOR PREPARING THE FIRE CASUALTY CLASSIFICATION

The following should be taken into account when preparing the casualty classification for the purpose of entering the fire casualty record. The numbering has been kept in consistence with MSC/Circ.388.

3   **Service**: There should be only one entry for each ship.

4   **Condition**: There should be only one entry for each ship. The entries "In port - Loading" and "In port - Unloading" apply only to the time during which transfer operations are taking place; any fire occurring while waiting to begin transfer operations should be entered as "In port - Other."

5   **Time at which fire was discovered**: There should be only one entry for each ship.

6   **Duration of fire**: There should be only one entry for each ship.

7   **Position of outbreak**: There should be only one entry for each ship. The definition of the spaces involved should be the same as those given in the latest version of the SOLAS Convention.

8   **Combustibles involved**: There may be more than one entry for each ship.

9   **Origin of flammable liquid**: There may be more than one entry for each ship.

10  **Source of ignition**: There may be more than one entry reported for each ship, especially if the damage was so severe that two or more likely sources can be identified.

11  **Type of protection at space concerned**: There will probably be more than one entry for each ship. Fixed systems should be entered only if they were in the space on fire; portable systems and those that use hoses should be entered if they can be brought to bear on the fire.

12  **Means by which the fire was detected**: There should be only one entry for each ship. The principle question is whether the fire detection system, if any, was the first to alert ship's personnel.

13  **Fire-extinguishing effectiveness**: There may be more than one entry for each ship. If the fire is extinguished without fire fighting, as with an explosion that "blows itself out," then enter "Not applicable."

14 **Extent of damage**: There may be more than one entry for each ship. The "Immobilization of ship due to serious damage" should also be entered when the propulsion system is shut down to aid in fire fighting.

15 **Observations**: There may be more than one entry for each ship. Favourable comments as well as unfavourable comments should be noted. This is the most important part of the casualty report and every effort should be made to record all observations to be made in paragraph 23 of the fire casualty record.

# ANNEX 7

## IMO MARINE CASUALTY AND INCIDENT REPORT

## QUESTIONNAIRE RELATED TO THE GLOBAL MARITIME DISTRESS AND SAFETY SYSTEM

1.   This questionnaire covers both the existing maritime communications system and the GMDSS and is intended for use during the latter's transition period (from 1 February 1992 to its full implementation on 1 February 1999).

2.   The purpose of this questionnaire is to enable the Sub-Committee on Radiocommunications and Search and Rescue to assess the effectiveness of the global maritime distress and safety system and to recommend improvements where necessary.

3.   Member Governments are urged to complete the questionnaire in respect of distress and safety incidents occurring to ships under their flag, adding any other information which, at their discretion, would provide lessons to be learned concerning the application of the global maritime distress and safety system.

4.   In addition, Member Governments are encouraged to pass any relevant information they may possess on casualties concerning foreign ships to the country in which such ships are registered.

   4.1   (a) GMDSS sea area or sea areas for which radio equipment was installed

   _____

   (b) Date and time of incident (UTC): _____

   4.2 Brief description of:

   (a) GMDSS sea area: _____

   (b) Weather conditions during SAR operations: _____

   _____

   4.3   Description of distress and safety radiocommunications, including particulars of the following items:

   (a) means of communication (radiotelegraphy, radiotelephony,

   INMARSAT SES, DSC, EPIRB) and frequencies used for:

   distress alert by ship: _____

   distress relay by RCC: _____

   SAR Coordinating communications:

(b) use of alarm signal: _____

(c) contents of distress message: _____

_____

(d) RCC(S), ships, coast station or coast earth stations which acknowledged distress message (state time and position):

_____

(e) language difficulties:

_____

4.4 If the ship was abandoned, description of distress radio communications and location signals from survival craft:

_____

4.5 If a satellite EPIRB or EPIRB was used for alerting and/or locating survivors, give details (frequency, type of activation, etc.) and which LUT/CES or coast station received the alerting signal:

_____

4.6 Description of on-scene radio communications, including surface/air communications:

_____

4.7 Any unusual, or additional, radiocommunication aspects, apparent shortcomings and/or lessons to be learned:

_____

## ANNEX 8

## IMO MARINE CASUALTY AND INCIDENT REPORT

## FATIGUE AS A CONTRIBUTORY FACTOR TO MARITIME ACCIDENTS
## FATIGUE FACTORS DATA COMPILATION SHEET

This compilation sheet should be completed and submitted with each maritime accident investigation report where fatigue has been identified as a contributory factor. The compilation sheet should indicate the cause of the identified fatigue. See MSC/Circ.621 for guidelines for the investigation of accidents where fatigue may have been a contributing factor.

**Fatigue identified in this accident was caused by** (Check all factors that apply):

1   **Management/regulatory factors**

   Contractual arrangement                               _____

   Work and rest period                                  _____

Manning level _____

Watchkeeping practice _____

Assignment of duties _____

Shore-ship-shore support and communication _____

Management policy _____

Voyage planning _____

Recreational facilities _____

2 **Ship factors**

Level of automation _____

Reliability of equipment _____

Motion characteristics _____

Vibration, heat and noise levels _____

Quality of working and living environment _____

Cargo characteristics/requirements _____

Ship design _____

3 **Crew factors**

Period on board _____

Experience/training _____

Crew composition, cohesiveness, and relationships _____

Crew competency and quality _____

Personal problems and condition _____

4 **External factors**

Weather _____

Port conditions _____

Ice conditions _____

Density of vessel traffic _____

# ANNEX 9

## IMO MARINE CASUALTY AND INCIDENT REPORT

## INCIDENTAL SPILLAGES OF HARMFUL SUBSTANCES OF 50 TONNES OR MORE

The following additional information should be submitted for each incident involving spillage of 50 tonnes or more of harmful substances. See annexes 1 and 2 of this circular for information to be submitted on vessel identification and casualty specifics. One copy of the report should be retained by the reporting State, one copy to be sent to the flag State, and one copy to be sent to the International Maritime Organization.

This reporting format on Incidental Spillages of Harmful Substances of 50 Tonnes or more has been added, as the report is considered necessary when investigating a casualty or an incident (MARPOL 73/78, articles 8 and 12), however this does not replace the one-line entry report required by the annual mandatory report under MARPOL 73/78, article 11 (MEPC/Circ.318, Part 1).

### Part 1

### To be completed by the reporting State

1. Was the date of the incident known or estimated? _____

2. Location of the incident (select one of the following):

    .1   in inland waters ................................................................................ ❐

    .2   in the territorial sea ........................................................................ ❐

    .3   within the exclusive economic zone .............................................. ❐

    .4   outside the exclusive economic zone in international waters ............... ❐

3. Reporting State: _____

    Report completed by: (Administration and address) _____

---

### Part 2

### Information to be supplied by the reporting State and/or the flag State

4. Action taken by reporting State:

    .1   Response to the spill:

        .1   no action ................................................................................. ❐

        .2   clean-up efforts ...................................................................... ❐

        .3   salvage efforts ........................................................................ ❐

        .4   other, i.e. ................................................................................ ❐

.2 Legal action:

    .1     no action .................................................................................. ❐

    .2     action to be taken by flag State ................................................ ❐

    .3     pending ...................................................................................... ❐

    .4     action taken by reporting State, i.e. ......................................... ❐

         _____

.3 Measures/recommendations to prevent recurrence:

         _____

.4 Additional information:

         _____

### Direct Natural Resource Damages

Loss of wildlife ........................................................................................ ❐

    Impact on birds .............................................................................. ❐

    Impact on marine mammals .......................................................... ❐

    Impact on fish................................................................................. ❐

    Impact on other marine life, including invertebrates .................... ❐

Loss of fisheries ...................................................................................... ❐

    Fin fish .......................................................................................... ❐

    Shellfish ......................................................................................... ❐

    Fish farming .................................................................................. ❐

Damage to marine environment .............................................................. ❐

Damage to shore environment................................................................. ❐

Habitat degradation ................................................................................ ❐

    Soft Habitats (salt marshes, mangroves, mudflats) ...................... ❐

    Shoreline (Beaches)........................................................................ ❐

    Rocky Coasts I Reefs, including coral ............................................ ❐

### Part 3

### To be completed by the flag State

5. Legal action taken by flag State

    .1    no action.......................................................................................... ❐

    .2    pending ........................................................................................... ❐

    .3    action taken, i.e. ............................................................................ ❐

         _____

         _____

# PART C 5

# MAIB — INCIDENT REPORT FORM

MARINE ACCIDENT INVESTIGATION BRANCH

## Incident Report Form

- The Merchant Shipping (Accident Reporting and Investigation) Regulations require Masters, Skippers and Owners to report accidents and dangerous occurrences. They are encouraged to report hazardous incidents as well. The terms are explained in the Regulations and in the Merchant Shipping Notice on accident reporting. Briefly, they include any accident leading to death or significant injury, or to loss or abandonment of the vessel or to her suffering material damage; any stranding, collision, fire, explosion or major breakdown; any incident causing harm to any person or the environment; and any incident which might have led to injury or which hazarded the ship.

- Please read the Merchant Shipping Notice for further details and advice, or telephone MAIB on 023 8039 5500.

- One form should be completed for each incident.

- Please return the completed form to: Marine Accident Investigation Branch
  First Floor, Carlton House,
  Carlton Place,
  Southampton, SO15 2DZ,
  United Kingdom

- Completing and signing this form does not constitute an admission of liability of any kind, either by the person making the report or any other person.

- Please complete the form clearly, using black or blue ink. Please ✔ the boxes.

## Section A

| | Day | Month | Year |
|---|---|---|---|
| Date of Incident | | | |

Time of Incident (state whether UTC (GMT) or local time): :

Name of vessel

Previous name (if changed in last 6 months)

Official Number or Fishing Number or (if non-UK) Call Sign

If fishing vessel please state type (eg stern trawler, crabber etc)

Name and address of owner or manager

Name and Port of Registry or Flag of any other vessel involved

Tel. No.

1

PART C 5

## Section B

Date and time of departure from last port

[  ] : [  ]

Voyage from and to:

From: [                    ]
To: [                    ]

Location of incident (eg latitude & longitude or name of port, or other geographical reference)

[                              ]

Weather and visibility at time of incident

[                              ]

Responsibility: was incident caused principally by persons on another vessel, or shoreside persons, or persons **not** sailing with your vessel?

Yes [  ]

No [  ]

Type of incident (please tick appropriate boxes)

Fatal injury [  ]          Non-fatal injury [  ]

Vessel lost or abandoned [  ]     Vessel damaged [  ]

Other accident or incident [  ]

## Section C - Details of person(s) killed or injured

(This section should be completed if any person has been killed or injured)

Place of incident (eg engine room; galley)

[                              ]

How many person(s) suffered an accident which resulted in death or injuries preventing the performance of the normal full range of duties for 3 days or more after the day of the incident?

[          ]

Please complete the questions in the table for each person.

| Position (eg rank; rating; passenger) | Age | Injured part of body | Kind of injury | * Hours worked before incident | * Duration of last off duty period | * Whether on duty |
|---|---|---|---|---|---|---|
| | | | | | | Yes [  ] No [  ] |
| | | | | | | Yes [  ] No [  ] |
| | | | | | | Yes [  ] No [  ] |
| | | | | | | Yes [  ] No [  ] |
| | | | | | | Yes [  ] No [  ] |
| | | | | | | Yes [  ] No [  ] |

* For operational staff only

If more than 6 persons suffered reportable accidents please continue on page 4.

2

PART C 5

## Section D

Please give a brief description of the sequence of events leading to the incident.

if necessary continue on page 4.

## Section E

1. Please state how you think the incident happened.

2. Has any action been recommended by you as a result and if so, what?

3. Has any action been taken and if so, what?

if necessary continue on page 4.

3

P
A
R
T

C

5

## Section F

Signed [                    ]

To be completed by the ship's
Safety Officer if applicable

Signed [                    ]

Name [                    ]

Master or
Owner's repre-
sentative [                    ]

Name [                    ]

Date [                    ]

Date [                    ]

## Section G          (if applicable)

If the incident involved a reportable personal accident or was a dangerous occurrence and there is an elected Safety Representative on board the vessel, he must be shown the completed report and allowed to write in this section any comments
which he may wish to make. If the injured persons are represented by different Safety Representatives, each may make
additional comments if desired in the space below but in any event, they should all sign the form.

Signed [                    ]

Safety Representative

Name [                    ]          Date [                    ]

This space may be used as an extension of Sections C, D, E and G. **Please state clearly which
sections are being expanded.**

If there is insufficient space in any part of this form for your answers or comments, please use a
plain sheet of paper as a continuation sheet and fasten it securely to this form. Please indicate in the
box below the number of sheets used.

Number of continuation sheets [          ]

4

PART C 5

# INDEX